AUSTRALIAN PIANO MUSIC
OF THE TWENTIETH CENTURY

**Recent Titles in
the Music Reference Collection**

Opera Singers in Recital, Concert, and Feature Film
Sharon G. Almquist, compiler

Appraisals of Original Wind Music: A Survey and Guide
David Lindsey Clark

Popular Singers of the Twentieth Century: A Bibliography of Biographical Materials
Robert H. Cowden

The Printed Elvis: The Complete Guide to Books about the King
Steven Opdyke

One Handed: A Guide to Piano Music for One Hand
Donald L. Patterson, compiler

Brainard's Biographies of American Musicians
E. Douglas Bomberger, editor

The Mozart–Da Ponte Operas: An Annotated Bibliography
Mary Du Mont

A Dictionary-Catalog of Modern British Composers
Alan Poulton

Songs of the Vietnam Conflict
James Perone

A Guide to Piano Music by Women Composers:
Volume I: Composers Born Before 1900
Pamela Youngdahl Dees

Music History During the Renaissance Period, 1520–1550: A Documented Chronology
Blanche Gangwere

Piano Music by Women Composers, Volume II: Composers Born After 1900
Pamela Youngdahl Dees

AUSTRALIAN PIANO MUSIC
OF THE TWENTIETH CENTURY

Larry Sitsky

Music Reference Collection, Number 87
Donald L. Hixon, Series Adviser

Westport, Connecticut
London

Library of Congress Cataloging-in-Publication Data

Sitsky, Larry.
  Australian piano music of the twentieth century / Larry Sitsky.
    p.   cm. —— (Music reference collection, ISSN 0736–7740 ; no. 87)
  Includes bibliographical references and index.
  ISBN 0–313–32286–4 (alk. paper)
    1. Piano music—Australia—20th century - History and criticism. I. Title. II. Series
ML742.A8S58   2005
786.2′0994′0904——dc22   2004043186

British Library Cataloguing in Publication Data is available.

Library of Congress Catalog Card Number: 2004043186
ISBN: 0–313–32286–4
ISSN: 0736–7740

First published in 2005

Praeger Publishers, 88 Post Road West, Westport, CT 06881
An imprint of Greenwood Publishing Group, Inc.
www.praeger.com

Printed in the United States of America

∞

Contents

Musical Examples ix

Acknowledgments 1

Preface 3

Part 1: The First Generation 6

**(i) Composers of Their Time: Early Modernists and
Neoclassicists** 6

Pianists: Hooper Brewster-Jones (1887–1949); Roy Agnew
(1891–1944); Margaret Sutherland (1897–1984); Raymond
Hanson (1913–1976); Dulcie Holland (1913–2000); Moneta
Eagles (1924–2003)

Non-Pianists: Fritz Bennicke Hart (1874–1949); Dorian Le
Gallienne (1915–1963)

(ii) Composers Looking Back: Late Romantics and the
Nineteenth-Century Legacy 55

Pianists: Ernest Hutcheson (1871–1956); Frederick Septimus
Kelly (1881–1916); Percy Grainger (1882–1961); Katherine
Parker (1886–1971); George Boyle (1886–1948); Arthur
Benjamin (1893–1960); Alex Burnard (1900–1971)

Mainly Miniaturists: Louis Lavater (1867–1953); Alfred Hill
(1870–1960); Frank Hutchens (1892–1965); Iris de Cairos-
Rego (1894–1987); Rex and George de Cairos-Rego; Lindley
Evans (1895–1982)

Non-Pianists: Ernest Wunderlich (1859–1945); G.W.L
Marshall-Hall (1862–1915); Arundel Orchard (1867–1961);
Adolphe Beutler (1882–1927); Edgar Bainton (1880–1956);
Esther Rofe (1904–2000); Horace Perkins (1901-1986)

Salon Music Composers: Marjorie Hesse (1911–1986); Una
Bourne (1882–1974); Henry Stewart (1885–1930); Frederick
Hall (1878–1956); Emanuel de Beaupuis (1860–1913)

(iii) The "Australian" Composers 97

Pianists: Mirrie Hill (1892–1986)

Non-Pianists: Henry Tate (1873–1926); Arthur S. Loam
(1896–?)

Part 2: The Second Generation 103

(i) Post-1945 Modernism Arrives in Australia 103

Pianists: Felix Werder (1922); Don Banks (1923–1980); Keith
Humble (1927–1995); Malcolm Williamson (1931–2003);
Richard Meale (1932); Donald Hollier (1934); Bozidar Kos
(1934); Nigel Butterley (1935)

Non-Pianists: Meta Overman (1907–1993); Peter Platt (1924–
2000); Harold Allen (1930–1983); Tristram Cary (1925); Peter
Tahourdin (1928); Lawrence Whiffin (1930); David
Lumsdaine (1931); Helen Gifford (1935); Derek Strahan
(1935); Jennifer Fowler (1939); Hellgart Mahler; John Exton
(1933); Stuart Davies-Slate; Stuart Hille.

(ii) Retrospective Composers 148

> **Pianists:** Miriam Hyde (1913); Eric Gross (1926); Mary
> Mageau (1934); Michael Bertram (1935); Richard Peter
> Maddox (1936)

> **Non-Pianists:** Lloyd Vick (1915); Noel Nickson (1919);
> Geoffrey Allen (1927); May Howlett (1931); Ralph
> Middenway (1932); David Morgan (1932); Colin Brumby
> (1933); Ann Carr-Boyd (1938); Sven Libaek (1938); Philip
> Bracanin (1942)

(iii) More "Australian" Composers: 166

> **Non-Pianists:** James Penberthy (1917–1999); Peter
> Sculthorpe (1929); Betty Beath (1932); Don Kay (1933)

(iv) Sitsky's Keyboard Music: *Si Yeoo Ki* 173
> Roger Woodward

Part 3: The Third Generation 216

(i) The Next Wave of Modernism 217

> **Pianists:** Ann Ghandar (1943); Gerald Glynn (1943); Graham
> Hair (1943); Roger Smalley (1943)

> **Non-Pianists:** Gillian Whitehead (1941); Ian Cugley (1945);
> Andrew Ford (1957); David Worrall (1954); Tim Dargaville
> (1962); John Polglase (1959)

> **More Modernists:** Beverley Lea; Michael Barkl; Michael
> Lonsdale; Andre Oosterbaan (1947); Stephen Benfall (1957);
> Raffaele Marcellino; Claudio Pompilli (1949); Jim Franklin
> (1959); Michael Whiticker (1954); Warren Burt (1949);
> Gordon Kerry (1961); Ross Hazeltine (1961); Julian Yu (1957)

(ii) Minimalism and Maximalism: 235

> **The Minimalists:** Robert Lloyd; Robert Davidson; Stephen
> Lalor; Mark Pollard; Nigel Sabin; Moya Henderson; Colin
> Spiers

The Maximalists: Chris Dench (1953); Michael Smetanin (1958); Gerard Brophy (1953); Riccardo Formosa (1954)

(iii) Pluralism: Popular Music/ Jazz/ Neotonality 241

Pianists: Simplicius Cheong (1942); Carl Vine (1954); Elena Kats-Chernin (1957); Mark Isaacs (1958)

Non-Pianists: Bruce Cale (1939); Martin Wesley-Smith (1945); Nigel Westlake (1958); Margaret Brandman (1951); Graeme Koehne (1956); David Joseph; Wendy Hiscocks (1963)

(iv) "Australian" Composers: The Next Generation 250

Non-Pianists: Moya Henderson (1941); Ross Edwards (1943); Robert Allworth (1943); Anne Boyd (1946); Colin Bright (1949); Andrew Schulz (1960)

(v) The Youngest Composers 254

Non-Pianists: Matthew Bienick (1976); Stephen Adams; Stephen Leek; Andrew Harrison; Elliott Gyger (1968); Robert Davidson (1965)

Pianist: Alistair Noble

Part 4: The Australian Piano Concerto 259

Conclusion.

The Anti-composer in Australian Society:
Kitsch Is Alive and Well 275

Bibliography 283

Appendix: Database of Piano Works Considered 293

Musical Examples

Part One:

H. Brewster-Jones.

Ex. 1.1	*Formula Series 1 - Prelude.* bars 1-5.	7
Ex. 2.1	*Formula Series 6 - Prelude.* bars 5-7.	7
Ex. 3.1	*Bronzewing's mating song.* bars 1-5.	10
Ex. 4.1	*Wattle Bird.* bars 1-6.	10
Ex. 5.1	*Song of the Yellow-Breasted Shrike Tit.* bars 1-4.	10
Ex. 6.1	*Pallid Cuckoo at Dawn.* Bars 1-4.	10
Ex. 7.1	*Golden Breasted Whistler.* bars 1-4.	11
Ex. 8.1	*Bronzewing and a Wet Dawn.* bars 1-7.	11
Ex. 9.1	*Calm after Rain.* bars 1-4.	11
Ex. 10.1	*Mopoke* bars 1-6.	11
Ex. 11.1	*Mysterious Mopoke* bars 1-4.	11
Ex. 12.1	*The Aimless Jockey takes his Horse Awalking.* bars 1-6.	12
Ex. 13.1	*The Trotting Pony.* bars 1-6.	13
Ex. 14.1	*A Horse with High Action.* bars 1-3.	13
Ex. 15.1	*A Pair of Horses.* bars 1-4.	13
Ex. 16.1	*Frog Etude.* bars 1-5.	14

Ex. 17.1   *Prelude - Poingnoi.* bars 1-3. 16
Ex. 18.1   *Prelude – to John Jeffreys.* bars 1-4. 16
Ex. 19.1   *Prelude – marked 'Largo'.* bars 1-4. 16
Ex. 20.1   *Le Soir.* bars 1-5. 17

R. Agnew.
Ex. 21.1   *Étude.* bars 1-3. 21
Ex. 22.1   *Toccata Tragica.* bars 1-3. 21
Ex. 23.1   *Sea-Surge.* bars 1-3. 21
Ex. 24.1   *Sonate Fantasie.* bars 20-22. 23
Ex. 25.1   *Sonate Fantasie.* bars 33-35. 23
Ex. 26.1   *Sonate Fantasie.* bars 53-55. 23
Ex. 27.1   *Sonata Fantasie.* bars 100-105. 24
Ex. 28.1   *Sonata Poème.* opening. 24
Ex. 29.1   *Sonata Poème.* bars 32-37. 25
Ex. 30.1   *Sonata Poème.* bars 41-45. 25
Ex. 31.1   *Sonata Ballade.* opening. 26
Ex. 32.1   *Sonata Ballade.* bars 29-32. 26
Ex. 33.1   *Sonata Legend.* opening. 27
Ex. 34.1   *Sonata 1929.* opening. 28
Ex. 35.1   *Sonata Symphonique.* opening. 29
Ex. 36.1   *The Wind.* bars 1-3. 29
Ex. 37.1   *Drifting Mists.* bars 1-3. 30
Ex. 38.1   *Exaltation..* bars 1-3. 30
Ex. 39.1   *Dance of the Wild Men.* ending. 30

M. Sutherland.
Ex. 40.1   *Sonatina.* bars 27-29 of III. 31
Ex. 41.1   *Sonatina.* bars 50-53 of I. 31
Ex. 42.1   *Sonatina.* bars 18-20 of III. 32
Ex. 43.1   *Two Choral Preludes.* bars 3-4 of I. 32
Ex. 44.1   *Six Profiles for Piano Solo.* bars 48-53 of III. 33
Ex. 45.1   *Six Profiles for Piano Solo.* bars 1-5 of IV. 33
Ex. 46.1   *Six Profiles for Piano Solo.* bars 39-41 of VI. 33
Ex. 47.1   *Chiaroscuro I.* bars 1-4. 34
Ex. 48.1   *Chiaroscuro II.* bars 1-4. 34
Ex. 49.1   *Extension.* bars 32-34. 34
Ex. 50.1   *Voices I.* bars 74-75. 35
Ex. 51.1   *Voices II.* bars 88-90. 35

R. Hanson.
Ex. 52.1   *Preludes Op.11.* bars 44-47 of II. 38
Ex. 53.1   *Preludes Op.11.* bars 5-7 of II. 38
Ex. 54.1   *Preludes Op.11.* bars 43-45 of IV. 38
Ex. 55.1   *Sonatina for Pianoforte Op. 24.* ending. 39
Ex. 56.1   *Piano Sonata Op. 12.* bars 1-3. 40

Ex. 57.1   *Piano Sonata Op. 12.* ending. 40

D. Holland.
Ex. 58.1   *The Lake.* bars 1-6. 42
Ex. 59.1   *Autumn Gold.* bars 25-28. 43
Ex. 60.1   *Dreamy John.* bars 1-7. 43
Ex. 61.1   *Prelude III.* bars 24-27. 44
Ex. 62.1   *Prelude I.* bars 29-38. 44
Ex. 63.1   *Asterisk.* bars 1-6. 45
Ex. 64.1   *At the Fountain.* bars 1-7. 45
Ex. 65.1   *Sonata.* bars 1-6 of I. 46
Ex. 66.1   *Sonata.* bars 192-7 of III. 46

M. Eagles.
Ex. 67.1   *Theme and Variations – Passacaglia.* bars 95-6. 47
Ex. 68.1   *Poetic Fragment.* bars 1-7. 47
Ex. 69.1   *Sonatina.* bars 1-5. 48
Ex. 70.1   *Quasi Minuet.* bars 1-5. 48
Ex. 71.1   *Toccatina.* bars 1-4. 49

D. Le Gallienne.
Ex. 72.1   *Three Piano Pieces.* bars 36-41 of I. 51
Ex. 73.1   *Three Piano Pieces.* bars 3-6 of II. 52
Ex. 74.1   *Sonata.* bars 1-5 of I. 53
Ex. 75.1   *Sonata.* bars 29-32 of I. 53
Ex. 76.1   *Sonata.* bars 189-92 of I. 53
Ex. 77.1   *Sonata.* bars 34-36 of II. 54
Ex. 78.1   *Sonata.* bars 23-25 of III. 54
Ex. 79.1   *Sonatina.* bars 1-6. 55
Ex. 80.1   *Sonatina.* bars 115-120. 55

E. Hutcheson.
Ex. 81.1   *Four Pieces for Pianoforte Op. 10,* bars 46-49 (III). ..57
Ex. 82.1   *E Flat Major Sonata,* bars 53-58 (II). 57

F. S. Kelly.
Ex. 83.1   *Waltz-Pageant.* bars 1-4 of V. 58
Ex. 84.1   *Scherzo-Etude.* Fugue Exposition, bars 1-17. 59
Ex. 85.1   *12 Studies for the Pianoforte, Op.9. Study no. 6,*
              bars 1-10. 60
Ex. 86.1   *12 Studies for the Pianoforte, Op.9. Study no. 7,*
              bars 1-8. 60
Ex. 87.1   *Twenty-four Monographs for Pianoforte Solo,*
              Op.11. No. 9, bars 1 -7. 61
Ex. 88.1   *Twenty-four Monographs for Pianoforte Solo,*
              Op.11. No. 16, bars 32-34. 61

Ex. 89.1   *Sonata in F minor for Pianoforte*,
             bars 1-6. 62

P. Grainger.
    Ex. 90.1   *Colonial Song*. bars 1-6. 64
    Ex. 91.1   *Irish Tune from County Derry*, bars 18-21. 64
    Ex. 92.1   *Lullaby* from *Tribute to Foster*, bars 1-5. 64

K. Parker.
    Ex. 93.1   *Down Longford Way*, bars 1-3. 66

G. Boyle.
    Ex. 94.1   *Habanera*, bars 1-7. 67
    Ex. 95.1   *Habanera*, bars 80-84. 67
    Ex. 96.1   *Gavotte and Musette*, bars 31-34. 68
    Ex. 97.1   *Five Piano Pieces*, bars 17-20. 68
    Ex. 98.1   *Five Piano Pieces*, bars 1-4 of III. 68
    Ex. 99.1   *Ballade*, bars 1-8. 69
    Ex. 100.1   *Sonata for Piano*, bars 1-8 of II. 69
    Ex. 101.1   *Sonata for Piano*, bars 54-57 of II. 69
    Ex. 102.1   *Sonata for Piano*, bars 36-37 of III. 70
    Ex. 103.1   *Sonata for Piano*, bars 125-128 of I. 70

A. Benjamin.
    Ex. 104.1   *Suite for Piano - Prelude*, bars 17-20. 71
    Ex. 105.1   *Suite for Piano - Toccata*, bars 16-18. 72
    Ex. 106.1   *Suite for Piano - Toccata*, bars 75-76. 72
    Ex. 107.1   *Pastorale, Arioso and Finale*, bars 31-36 of I. ... 72
    Ex. 108.1   *Pastorale, Arioso and Finale*, bars 86-89 of I. ... 73
    Ex. 109.1   *Pastorale, Arioso and Finale*, bars 29-30 of II. .. 73
    Ex. 110.1   *Pastorale, Arioso and Finale*, bars 8-11 of III. .. 73

A. Burnard.
    Ex. 111.1   *Three Experimental Preludes*, bars 55-57 of III. ... 75
    Ex. 112.1   *Farewell, my dearest Nancy*, bars 17-22. 75
    Ex. 113.1   *Fugue from Prelude and Fugue in D Major*.
                 bars 16-20. 76
    Ex. 114.1   *Brigg Fair*, bars 1-7. 77
    Ex. 115.1   *Fuga Elegiaca*, bars 1-14. 77
    Ex. 116.1   *Puck* from *Seven Piano Preludes*, bars 1-5. 78
    Ex. 117.1   *To Leone Stredwick* from *Seven Piano Preludes*,
                 bars 1-4. 78

L. Lavater.
    Ex. 118.1   *Valse Elégante*, bars 1-6. 79

A. Hill.

Ex. 119.1	*Adagio for an unwritten Sonata*, bars 1-7.	81
Ex. 120.1	*The Beating Heart*, bars 37-42.	82
Ex. 121.1	*Valse Triste*, bars 1-5.	82

F. Hutchens.

Ex. 122.1	*The Enchanted Isle*, bars 17-19.	84
Ex. 123.1	*Gavotte Brilliante*, bars 1-3.	85

E. Wunderlich.

Ex. 124.1	*Theme and Variations*, bars 37-40 of XX.	87
Ex. 125.1	*Theme and Variations, Third series.* bars 1-4 of VII.	88
Ex. 126.1	*Theme and Variations, Third series.* bars 1-4 of XV.	88
Ex. 127.1	*Twelve Small Pianoforte Pieces.* bars 1-12 of VI.	89

E. Rofe.

Ex. 128.1	*The Island.* bars 1-4.	93

H. Perkins.

Ex. 129.1	*Ballade.* bars 1-4.	94

M. Hill.

Ex. 130.1	*Brolga.* bars 5-10.	98
Ex. 131.1	*The Kunkarunkara Women.* bars 6-9.	98
Ex. 132.1	*Nalda of the Echo.* bars 44-48.	99
Ex. 133.1	*Rhapsody for Piano.* bars 29-31.	100
Ex. 134.1	*Aboriginal Song to the Whirlwind.* bars 1-4.	100

A. S. Loam.

Ex. 135.1	*Maranoa*, bars 13-16.	101

Part Two:

F. Werder.

Ex. 1.2	*Sonata No. 5.* bars 56-61.	105
Ex. 2.2	*Sonata No. 5.* bars 95-99.	105
Ex. 3.2	*Monograph.* bars 1-3.	106
Ex. 4.2	*Monograph.* bars 1-3 of III.	106

D. Banks.

Ex. 5.2	*Sonatina in C# Minor.* Bars 75-78.	107
Ex. 6.2	*Sonatina in C# Minor.* Bars 36-39 of II.	107

Ex. 7.2   *Sonatina in C# Minor*. Bars 87-89 of III. 108
Ex. 8.2   *Pezzo Dramatico*. opening. 108
Ex. 9.2   *Pezzo Dramatico*. bars 85-88. 109
Ex. 10.2   *Pezzo Dramatico*. bars 56-60. 109

K. Humble.
Ex. 11.2   *Sonata I*. opening. 111
Ex. 12.2   *Sonata II*. Bars 17-20. 112
Ex. 13.2   *Sonata II*. Bars 67-69. 112
Ex. 14.2   *Sonata III*. opening of *Epilogue*. 113
Ex. 15.2   *Sonata IV*. opening. 113

M. Williamson.
Ex. 16.2   *Sonata I*. bars 21-24 of III. 114
Ex. 17.2   *Sonata II*. bars 74-76 of I. 115
Ex. 18.2   *King's Cross*. opening. 115

R. Meale.
Ex. 19.2   *Sonatina Patetica*. bars 1-4. 116
Ex. 20.2   *Bagatelle No. 2*. opening. 117
Ex. 21.2   *Bagatelle No.3*. opening. 117

D. Hollier.
Ex. 22.2   *Sonnet No. 6*. opening. 119
Ex. 23.2   *Sonnet No.4*. opening. 119
Ex. 24.2   *Sonnet No.3*. opening of Quasi Chorale section. 123

B. Kos.
Ex. 25.2   *Reflections*. bars 3-4. 124
Ex. 26.2   *Reflections*. bars 19-21. 124
Ex. 27.2   *Kolo*. opening. 125
Ex. 28.2   *Piano Sonata*. bars 28-29. 126

N. Butterley.
Ex. 29.2   *Letter from Hardy's Bay*. end of section A. 128
Ex. 30.2   *Lawrence Hargrave Flying Alone*. bars 41-45. 129
Ex. 31.2   *Lawrence Hargrave Flying Alone*. bars 51-52. 129
Ex. 32.2   *Uttering Joyous Leaves*. bars 1-3. 130
Ex. 33.2   *Uttering Joyous Leaves*. bars 8-9. 130
Ex. 34.2   *Uttering Joyous Leaves*. bars 10-11. 130
Ex. 35.2   *Grevillea*. bars 1-4. 130

P. Platt.
Ex. 36.2   *A thoughtful piece for Eric*. bars 1-3. 132

P. Tahourdin.
Ex. 37.2   *Exposé*. bars 1-3. 135

L. Whiffin.
Ex. 38.2   *Prelude*. bars 32-33. 136
Ex. 39.2   *Mechanical Mirrors*. bars 323-325. 137

D. Lumsdaine.
Ex. 40.2   *Kelly Ground*. bars 12-15. 138
Ex. 41.2   *Ruhe sanfte, sanfte ruh*. circa bar 33. 139
Ex. 42.2   *Cambewarra*. circa bar 46. 139
Ex. 43.2   *Cambewarra*. circa bar 218. 140

H. Gifford.
Ex. 44.2   *Piano Sonata*. bars 86-91. 141
Ex. 45.2   *Piano Sonata*. ending. 141
Ex. 46.2   *Catalysis*. bars 46-47. 141
Ex. 47.2   *Cantillation*. bars 13-17. 142
Ex. 48.2   *The Spell*. bars 4-6. 142
Ex. 49.2   *Waltz*. bars 20-23. 142
Ex. 50.2   *Toccata Attacco*. bars 24-28. 143
Ex. 51.2   *Toccata Attacco*. bar 44. 143
Ex. 52.2   *As foretold to Khayyám*. bars 17-21. 144

J. Fowler.
Ex. 53.2   *Music for Piano – Ascending and Descending*.
            (unbarred) 146

M. Hyde.
Ex. 54.2   *Study for Left Hand Tenths*. bars 1-3. 150
Ex. 55.2   *The Fountain*. bars 1-3. 150
Ex. 56.2   *Rhapsody No. 2. A minor*. bars 1-3. 150
Ex. 57.2   *Valley of Rocks*. bars 1-5. 150
Ex. 58.2   *Humoresque*. bars 30-35. 151
Ex. 59.2   *Firewheel*. bars 53-54. 151

E. Gross.
Ex. 60.2   *Klavierstück III*. opening. 153

M. Bertram.
Ex. 61.2   *Fantasie-Sonata*. opening. 157

L. Vick.
Ex. 62.2   *Fantasia*. bars 40-42. 159
Ex. 63.2   *Fantasia*. ending. 159
Ex. 64.2   *Group of Three*. opening of *Canon*. 160

N. Nickson.
Ex. 65.2   *Sonatina.* opening. 160

G. Allen.
Ex. 66.2   *Piano Sonata no. 4.* bars 212-214. 161
Ex. 67.2   *Piano Sonata no. 7.* bars 13-16 of II. 162

J. Penberthy.
Ex. 68.2   *Clocks.* ending. 167
Ex. 69.2   *Sad Music for Thursday.* opening. 168

D. Kay.
Ex. 70.2   *Sonatina.* bars 186-188. 170
Ex. 71.2   *Dance Rituals.* bars 1-2. 170
Ex. 72.2   *Legend.* bars 1-4. 170
Ex. 73.2   *Sonata.* bars 1-4. 171

Sitsky's Keyboard Music:

Ex. 1:4   *Little Suite for Piano (IV): Two part invention
on a name.* explanatory note. 186
Ex. 2:4   *Sonatina Formalis.* explanatory note. 187
Ex. 3:4   *Fantasia No. 1 in memory of Egon Petri.* bar 37. 189
Ex. 4:4   *Fantasia No. 1 in memory of Egon Petri.* bar 38. 189
Ex. 5:4   *Fantasia No. 1 in memory of Egon Petri.* bar 3. 190
Ex. 6:4   *Petra.* bars 55-57. 194
Ex. 7:4   *Concerto for Piano and Orchestra.* opening. 196
Ex. 8:4   *Twelve Mystical Preludes (after the Nuctemeron of
Apollonius of Tyana).* opening of The Tenth Hour. 197
Ex. 9:4   *Twelve Mystical Preludes (after the Nuctemeron of
Apollonius of Tyana).* bars 10-11 of The Fifth Hour. 197
Ex. 10:4   *Twelve Mystical Preludes (after the Nuctemeron of
Apollonius of Tyana).* opening of The Eighth Hour. 198
Ex. 11:4   *Concerto for Piano and Orchestra.* Ending of
The Hermit. 198
Ex. 12:4   *Nocturne Canonique.* bars 9-12. 199
Ex. 13:4   *Sharagan: Fantasia No. 5.* top of page 7
(unbarred). 203
Ex. 14:4   *Si Yeoo Ki.* (unbarred). 204
Ex. 15:4   *Fantasy no.7 on a theme of Liszt.*
ossia at end of score. 205
Ex. 16:4   *Fantasy no.8 on D-B-A-S.* preface to score. 205
Ex. 17:4   *Fantasy no.8 on D-B-A-S.* bar 82. 206
Ex. 18:4   *Concerto for Piano and Orchestra.*
cadenza opening (XIII). 208

Ex. 19:4   *Concerto for Piano and Orchestra.*
                 from XV (unbarred)...209
Ex. 20:4   *Lotus (opening of Faust). bar 21.*......................212
Ex. 21:4   *Fantasy No. 11 "E". bars 52-57.*.......................212

Part Three:

A. Ghandar.
Ex. 1.3   *Paraselene. (unbarred).*.......................................218
Ex. 2.3   *The Earth Sings. (unbarred).*...............................218
Ex. 3.3   *Photophoresis. bars 40-43.*.................................218
Ex. 4.3   *Sinai Music. bar 18.*...219

G. Glynn.
Ex. 5.3   *Filigrees 2. bars 30-35.*......................................220

G. Hair.
Ex. 6.3   *Under Aldebaran. opening.*..................................222
Ex. 7.3   *Wild cherries and Honeycomb. opening.*............222

R. Smalley.
Ex. 8.3   *Variations on a Theme of Chopin. opening.*........224
Ex. 9.3   *Barcarolle. opening.*...225

A. Ford.
Ex. 10.3   *Portraits. bars 84-88.*.......................................227

T. Dargaville.
Ex. 11.3   *Alba. ending.*...229

M. Barkl.
Ex. 12.3   *Drumming. opening.*..230

R. Marcellino.
Ex. 13.3   *Dædalus Sequence III: The Riddle of the*
                  Sicilian Conch. bars 8-11...............................231

M. Whiticker.
Ex. 14.3   *The hands, the dream. bars 94-97.*....................233

W. Burt.
Ex. 15.3   *Aardvarks II: Mr. Natural Encounters*
                  Flakey Foont! opening....................................234

J. Yu.
Ex. 16.3   *Impromptu.* opening. 235

M. Pollard.
Ex. 17.3   *The Prayers of Tears.* bars 81-82. 236

M. Henderson.
Ex. 18.3   *Treadmill.* bars 209-212. 237

E. Kats-Chernin.
Ex. 19.3   *Sonata Lost and Found.* bars 18-22 (II). 245

M. Wesley-Smith.
Ex. 20.3   *On A. I. Petrof.* opening. 247
Ex. 21.3   *White Knight Waltz.* bars 9-15. 248

N. Westlake.
Ex. 22.3   *Piano Sonata.* bars 77-79. 248

W. Hiscocks.
Ex. 23.3   *Toccata.* opening. 250

A. Noble.
Ex. 24.3   *Fantasia "Panga Lingua" (Sonata No. 2).*
                opening. 256
Ex. 25.3   *Fantasia "Panga Lingua" (Sonata No. 2).*
                page 4 (unbarred). 256

Acknowledgments

Thanks to the Australian Research Council grants scheme, who made the whole project financially possible, and who are funding further flow-on research possibilities over the coming five years.

First and foremost I would like to acknowledge the work done by my researcher and current Ph.D. student Kate Bowan; without her this book would have taken so much longer and would be an inferior product. She has been tireless in locating material and ingenious in overcoming problems and bureaucratic obstacles. She is also responsible for the extensive database that will be found in the book as well as the bibliography. Kate has read my original text and suggested various improvements.

Judith Crispin, who came to the project a little later after completing her Ph.D., has been likewise invaluable in editing my impatient prose and setting out the many music examples, a very long and often tedious task; as well as tidying up my text and seeing the project through to its completion.

Thanks also to Ruth Martin and Jenny Gall who helped in the earlier stages of research. Particular thanks to Ruth for her participation in the preparation of the ARC grant application that allowed this project to go ahead.

Thanks are also due to:

All the staff at the Australian Music Centre, in particular the General Manager John Davis, Head Librarian Judith Foster and Michelle Kennedy, who massively assisted in voluminous and complex research.

The National Library of Australia, a veritable treasure trove of material on Australian Music; once again, many thanks to the staff of the Library in a number of areas who helped locate materials and information.

The librarians and archivists at the Mitchell Library, State Library of NSW, The State Library of Victoria, Gordon Abbott at the Barr Smith Library, University of Adelaide, Gionni di Gravio at the Archives at the University of Newcastle, Claire McCoy at the Sydney Conservatorium Library.

James Penberthy's son, David Reid for giving us complete access to his father's papers before lodging them at the National Library. Ian Shanahan for allowing us to examine the papers of Peter Platt. Pianist, David Bollard who sent us his private collection of Australian scores.

To all the composers and pianists who helped us by providing possible scores for study and perusal.

The School of Music, National Institute of the Arts, Australian National University for providing work spaces for this project and for supporting the concept right from the start. Special thanks to the two Directors, Nicolette Fraillon and Simon de Haan, for their continued and continuing personal support and encouragement.

Preface

The preparation for this book occupied a number of years in direct research, playing through hundreds of scores, including the massive holdings of Australian music in the National Library. The Library kindly provided an instrument and I sat there consuming score after score with my then assistant Ruth Martin groaning and developing headaches as kitsch after kitsch was revealed, while I confess that I got off on some of the awfulness. We also admired many of the covers. The occasional musical gems that appeared were even more lustrous in appearance in such a context. I remember Ruth being knocked out by the direct and dramatic beauty of Roy Agnew's *Deidre's Lament.*

It was with some mild surprise that I found myself well placed to author this book, having lived through half of the century as an active musician, and having continued parallel pursuits as a composer and pianist; indeed, on the way, finding myself also a writer on music almost by default. Thanks to such a diversity of activities, over the years I had become friends and acquaintance of most of the major figures discussed in this book and therefore knew them at first hand and had formed opinions about them and their music in general, but the piano music in particular. Within the text, the writing reveals personal contacts when I refer to composers in a familiar way using their first names; I trust I will be forgiven for this practice.

Not surprisingly, we found that composers who were also pianists themselves wrote the most effective and profound music for the piano. There are always exceptions to such statements, of course, but by and large Australian composers followed the universal pattern of music for the piano.

However, it should be noted that the mold is gradually falling apart in that the long genealogy of the pianist/composer is now somewhat weakened in a computer-driven society. The piano is no longer the predominant instrument and has given way at the least to the electronic keyboard and at the most to the computer keyboard. This is not to say that there will no longer be major or meaningful music composed for the piano, but it is now less likely to be written by a pianist/composer.

There was the thorny and potentially embarrassing question of my own contribution to Australian piano repertoire. This was resolved by Roger Woodward's essay. Within it, he addresses many matters outside of my own music: artistic issues pertinent to Australia; cultural displacement, now so common in this country and its policy of multiculturalism; other composers active at the same time. Woodward, who must be Australia's most famous pianist and widely respected internationally, delivered a piece that, quite obviously I did not attempt to control or to influence.

Viewing the 20th century in retrospect, some clear tendencies emerge. Paradoxically, the Australian 'identity', of so much evident concern to some composers, was in fact in the end most protected by those composers who seemed least concerned about it, simply by living and working in this country and by pushing their personal boundaries. These composers form a kind of modernist stream in Australian music and are responsible for a solid tradition of high quality art music for the instrument. They are the very composers who attracted most of our attention and whose work we value the highest.

The second strand was the one of using the piano in a more conservative manner to write pieces with titles that connected them directly and strongly with the past; in other words a strand that was softer in sound and intent, appealing to a wider public while still retaining some aspects of high art.

The third strand we have identified and isolated are composers who have met head on, and dealt with in their own ways, the question of a distinctively 'Australian' music. This concern with Australian national identity, as in all the art forms, has also been present since the turn of the last century. Interestingly it forms a very small part of the whole output for piano. One could argue that many more composers, than the ones we have chosen have concerned themselves with this issue. For example, is Hector Maclean's *Sun Music* any more or less Australian because of its title and the traditional notion of Australia being a sunburnt country?

For further comments on these movements within Australian music, and on what I perceive as non-art masquerading as art, see the Conclusion.

There is of course an additional strand that falls for the most part outside the scope of this research. It is also of some lineage and treats the piano unashamedly as a parlor instrument. The heritage of this strand is well established and colourful. Many of the productions of this type lavished time and money on elaborate art works for the covers; many were very popular hits and sold multiple editions. Quite often the contents (i.e. the music) did not match the promise of the cover. The evolution of the first strand, our primary interest, is largely what this book is about. Beginning with isolated individuals working by themselves, this strand gathered momentum and volume as the century flowed on, become increasingly diverse and complex, a sign of a healthy culture.

There were at least two important areas of discovery in the preparation of his volume. One was the unveiling and study of valuable materials still in manuscript form and an attempt to place these composers into the perspectives of the first strand. It was not so much that we uncovered composers hitherto unknown, but rather, that we blew the cobwebs away from much music that was known to exist but had not been seriously addressed. That in itself was for me enough justification for the whole project.

The second was confirmation that this first strand had always been there, and that Australian modernism and art music was not an invention of the last thirty or forty years of the 20th century but had roots from much earlier on. This to some extent flies in the face of popular wisdom on such matters. Unfortunately, serious study of Australian music is a relatively new phenomenon and so various mythologies enshrined in the writings of earlier writers had been accepted without question for, it seems to me, too long. What is uncovered here is a new look at our first strand, which was more substantial than some of us suspected.

The book is lavish in its use of musical examples. It is my simple and fairly obvious belief that quotes that are typical of the composer and that support the text are a thousand times more evocative than paragraphs of dry text. It has always been my aim to stimulate the reader to go out and find the music for further exploration.

It is my hope that books will follow this book on Australian piano music in due course, on other aspects of our musical culture.

Part 1: The First Generation

(i)   Composers of Their Time: Early Modernists and Neoclassicists

Pianists

Hooper Brewster-Jones (1887-1949)

Along the thin tracks that mark Australia's path of modernism, the name of Brewster-Jones is of the highest importance. It is a measure of the general conservatism of Australian music and society that right up to the moment when this book is about to go into print, one of the most innovative and adventurous of our composers is still almost totally unknown and unpublished; and indeed when known, then known for his most conventional and least interesting music.

This composer's biography is yet to be researched and written; when this occurs, it will fill a most important hiatus in Australian music history

One of the difficulties with the Brewster-Jones output is that the most valuable pieces are precisely the ones that do not seem to exist in fine copy. It is as if the composer is saying: "these were composed by me for my own edification, nobody is interested in them, they will never be performed, so what is the point of me slaving over a fine copy?" It is a fact that the works that exist in clearly decipherable manuscripts are those that Brewster-Jones put out into the world and probably those that have at least some measure of performance acceptability.

The archive contains much material for chamber forces as well as voice and piano. The composer was clearly an accomplished pianist; we even have a copy of the radio announcement surrounding his performance of the solo part of his Concerto, which was broadcast only in a two-piano version, unfortunately. As well, there is some music for two pianos, all outside the scope of this book.

One of the most intriguing works in the archive is the *Formula Series* of pieces, which are probably the first non-tonal works written in Australia. The title, suggesting a scientific approach – later beloved by the post-World War II avant garde - reveals a set of pieces which use a modernist approach to composition, systematically exploring a new world, opened by piling up different intervals. These pieces manifest themselves in the form of short preludes.

Thus, Prelude No.1 (dated 22/6/24) uses harmony of piled up thirds; the very first sound we hear is a ten-note chord with no doublings.

Ex. 1:1. H. Brewster-Jones. *Formula Series 1 - Prelude.* bars 1-5.

The second Prelude is built on quartal harmonies; it is dated 25/6/24. It very much looks as though these pieces were written at one sitting while the singular thought driving each prelude was fresh in the mind of the composer. Prelude No. 3 (9/7/24) pushes the intervallic vision into the realms of 5ths, and so on through the set of six. Preludes Nos. 4, 5 and 6 are dated 17/7/24, 20/10/24 and 12/11/24 respectively. Prelude No.6 exists in a good copy and is an interesting essay in the superimposition of pentatonic patterns resulting in a kind of bi-pentatonicism.

Ex. 2:1. H. Brewster-Jones. *Formula Series 6 - Prelude.* bars 5-7.

The publication of these and other pieces like them must now be given the highest priority. The *Formula Series* were by no means isolated experiments.

There are, for example, the remarkable series of *Bird Call Impressions* pieces written the year before in 1923. The titles sound like something from Messiaen, but this is years before the Frenchman. We give a complete list of the titles below, not just for the sake of completeness, or to illustrate Brewster-Jones' obvious love and knowledge of birds, but more as an indication of the possible excitement in the discovery of these works. The whole series needs detailed and expert editing, as it exists in a complete but quite often rough form. Brewster-Jones obviously valued these pieces, as he carefully assembled them into the Books as given below, and each of these short pieces is initialled by the composer, usually with the precise date, sometimes even giving commencement and completion dates.

Book I:
1. *Dance of the White Browed Babblers.* (9/8/23)
2. *Boom of the Bronzewing Pigeon.* (9/8/23)
3. *Song of the Grey Shrike Thrush.* (9/8/23)
4. *White Shafted Fantail.* (16/8/23)
5. *Bronze-wing's Mating Song.* (19/8/23)
6. *Black Swans Flying.* (15/8/23)
7. *Tree Creeper.* (10/8/23)
8. *Quarrelsome Blue Wrens.* (13/8/23)
9. *Wattle Bird.* (12/8/23)
10. *Song of the Brown Treecreeper at Heysens.* (10/8/23)
11. *Song of the Yellow-Breasted Shrike Tit.* (10/8/23)
12. *Shrike Thrush.* (13/8/23)
13. *Pallid Cuckoo at Dusk.* (23/9/23)

Book II:
14. *Magpy in the Air.* (13/8/23)
15. *Mudlark or the Magpie Lark.* (15/8/23)
16. *Shrike Thrush at the Window.* (22/8/23)
17. *White Shafted Fantail.* (16/8/23)
18. *Red Wattle Bird.* (22/8/23)
19. *Crescent Honeyeater* (Egypt). (23/8/23)
20. *Honey Eater (In the Heather).* No date
21. *Shrike Thrush (Morning at Glen Osmond).* (3/10/23)
22. *Shrike Thrush (Calm after Rain).* (18/9/23)
23. *Love Calls of the Tawny Crowned Honey Eater.* (19/9/23)
24. *Jolly Superb Warblers.* (24/8/23)

Book III:
25. *Golden Breasted Whistler.* 21/9/23
26. *Call of the White Nuped Honeyeater.* 20/8/23

27. *Bronzewing and a Wet Dawn.* 19/9/23
28. *Rosellas' Wooing.* 20/9/23
29. *Calm after Rain (Shrike Thrush series).* 18/9/23
30. *Blackbird in the Olives.* 13/10/23
31. *Blackbird in the Garden.* 30/10/23
32. *Superb Warbler.* 24/8/23
33. *Shrike Thrush at Long Gully Station.* 30/10/23
34. *Shrike Thrush in the Spring Shower at Dawn.* 18/9/23
35. *Shrike Thrush in the Saplings (at Ambleside).* 17/10/23
36. *The Cooing Pigeon.* 12/10/23

Book IV:
37. *Shrike Thrush (by the River).* (23/9/23)
38a. *The Skylark in Australia.* (23/9/23)
38b. *The Reed Warbler.* No date.
39. *Scarlet Breasted Robin.* (11/10/23)
40. *The Magpie in the Tree.* (31/10/23)
41. *Two Captive Magpies.* (16/10/23)
42. *Rosellas in the Misty Morning.* (17/10/23)
43. *Greenie.* (25/10/23)
44. *Blackbird (call).* (26/10/23)
45a and b. *Golden Breasted Whistler.* (16/10/23) (23 corrected in pencil to 24)
46. *Golden Breasted Whistler.* (dates as above)
46b. *Madame Golden Breasted Whistler*

Book V:
47. *Mopok.* (9/12/24)
48. *Wattle Bird in the Gardens*
49. *The Captive Magpie originally titled The Distant Magpie.*(29/10/21) The manuscript labels this piece as also *Rustic Sketches No.1*
50. *Shrike Thrush*
51. *Calls of the Bell Bird.* (15/7/24)
52. *The Spotted Padalote on High.* (13/8/24)
53. *Tom Tit*
54. *Calls of the Pallid Cuckoo.*
55. *The Peaceful Dove.* (27/3/26)
56. *Blackbird at Rose Park.* (13/11/25)
57. *Crescent Honey Eater.* (26/8/24)

Book VI:
58. *The Bird by the Brook.* (16/11/21)
59. *The Spotted Padalote on High* (same as No.52). (13/8/24)
60. *The Yellow Tailed Padalote.* (15/7/24)
61. *The Fighting Fantails.* (16/9/24)
62. *Tawny Crowned Honey Eater.* (19/11/24)

63. *Diamond Firetail.* (28/11/24)
64. *Shrike Thrush Call 7.* (15/8/23)
65. *Shrike Thrush in the Fog.* (16/7/24)
66. *Striped Honey-eater.* (16/7/24)
67. *Mysterious Mopoke.* (14/9/26)
68. *Jacky Winter Enlivens the Farmyard.* (no date)
69. *Wattle Bird at Noon.* (29/7/24)
70. *Blackbird in the St. John's Tree.* 17/11/ ?

To illustrate the world of these pieces, here are a few examples of the opening of pieces Nos. 5, 9, 11, 13, 25, 27, 29, 47 and 67.

Ex. 3:1. H. Brewster-Jones. *Bronzewing's mating song.* bars 1-5.

Ex. 4:1. H. Brewster-Jones. *Wattle Bird.* bars 1-6.

Ex. 5:1. H. Brewster-Jones. *Song of the Yellow-Breasted Shrike Tit.* bars 1-4.

Ex. 6:1. H. Brewster-Jones. *Pallid Cuckoo at Dawn.* bars 1-4.

Ex. 7:1. H. Brewster-Jones. *Golden Breasted Whistler*. bars 1-4.

Ex. 8:1. H. Brewster-Jones. *Bronzewing and a Wet Dawn*. bars 1-7.

Ex. 9:1. H. Brewster-Jones. *Calm after Rain*. bars 1-4.

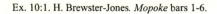

Ex. 10:1. H. Brewster-Jones. *Mopoke* bars 1-6.

Ex. 11:1. H. Brewster-Jones. *Mysterious Mopoke* bars 1-4.

Apropos, there is also a set of three bird pieces for two pianos. They are, in an order given by the composer, 1. *Impressions of the South. The Crow's Nest .* (4/2/29. 2). *Calls of the Pallid Cuckoo.* (18/10/23 or 25) 3. *Shrike Thrush by the River.* (23/9/23) These are in fine copy.

Another interesting series of pieces is entitled *Horse Rhythms* in which each miniature fixates on a particular rhythm or combination/superimposition of rhythms. These also come from that same very fertile period of the early and mid 20s. The titles are just as evocative as in the prior set of pieces; but this time we will merely list them without the dates.

1. *The Brown Nag;*
2. *Jacky Winter and the Pony;*
3. *The Toiling Crock;*
4. *The Old Moke;*
5. *Dobbin Walks Leisurely;*
5a. *Horses;*
6. *The Aimless Jockey takes his Horse Awalking;*
7. *The Trotting Pony;*
8. *A Horse with High Action;*
9. *A Pair of Horses;*
10. *The Restive Racehorse;*
11. *Australian 'Coster' and his Pony and Donkey Card;*
12. *The Crock in the Creaky Cart;*
13. *The Brown Horse;*
14. *Several Military Officers on Horseback;*
15. *A Quiet Walk on Sunday Morning;*
16. *The Canter;*
17. *Three Racehorses at 6a.m. (Cold and Frosty);*
18. *Two Racehorses Walking;*
19. *Two Horses Galloping;*
20. *A Pair of Horses;*
21. *Horse Jumping;*
22. *The Boy on the Pony.*

Because these are largely studies in rhythm, ostinato plays a very important, and a Bartókian atmosphere is often built up as a result:

Ex. 12:1. H. Brewster-Jones. *The Aimless Jockey takes his Horse Awalking.* bars 1-6.

Ex. 13:1. H. Brewster-Jones. *The Trotting Pony.* bars 1-6.

Ex. 14:1. H. Brewster-Jones. *A Horse with High Action.* bars 1-3.

Ex. 15:1. H. Brewster-Jones *A Pair of Horses.* bars 1-4.

These 'horse' pieces, like the 'bird' pieces, tend to concentrate on a single compositional aspect. The composer treats these with the same care and assembles them with dates and signature, as described earlier. Perhaps he hoped that sometime in the future it would be important for someone and finally be taken seriously as a genuine excursion into modernism. How right he was, and how sad that it has taken so long.

His book of the almost Satie-esque *Portrait Waltzes* is preceded by the strict injunction "not to be played in public!" Yet there are some genuinely whimsical and sometimes quirky pieces here, with humour and lightness. Many of the thematic cores of these little pieces are based on the letters from the names of the dedicatee. One of them, "To Brewster", has 7/8 in the right hand against 3/4 in the left. Did he deem these to be too irreverent for the public to hear? Or was quoting "God Save the King" in waltz-time too dastardly an act? Was tapping on the wood of the piano not done in public?

The same notebook that contains these *Portrait Waltzes* also has, at the back nineteen *Nursery Rhymes*. The composer says on the title page to the notebook with regard to these: "Rough Notes Only", but such a comment applies to the majority of his most interesting pieces and we should not allow that comment to deter us. The short settings seem to be complete and contain some delightful touches.

In 1924-25, Brewster-Jones composed a set of forty *Ballet-Preludes*, yet another set of pieces that are complete, but in rough manuscript form. They, too, appear as interesting and worthwhile pieces that should be rescued from oblivion. The manuscript suggests that some of these were initially just 'Preludes' and subsequently the word 'Ballet' or 'Dance' was added to the title. But a few have an extra word in the title; No.4 is also designated a *Valse*. A few have been neatly copied and were perhaps performed. Some have fingering added. No.12 is a *Doll's Chorus*. Nos.14, 15 , 19 and 30 have the word 'Nature' added at the top. Perhaps a series of 'Nature' pieces was originally intended? No.17 is a Waltz, an essay in bitonality combining E major and Eb major, including the final cadence. No.23 is subtitled both 'Nature' and 'Daybreak', No.24, on the other hand is subtitled 'Nature' and 'Valse'. No.27 asks for 'Pedal sustained throughout'. No.28 has 'Doll'. No.35 is intriguingly called "Mrs Tutankhamen"! No.36 has the word 'Epyptian' scrawled upon it. At the bottom of this one, it also says 'C. Scott. The piper in the Desert', no doubt referring to the composer Cyril Scott and then there is a scale construct given and some of the figures derived from it. The more one examines these manuscripts, the more one realizes that we have here a kind of Charles Ives case, a composer who was doing interesting things but seems to have been almost completely ignored not only during his lifetime, but now, eighty years later!

The Twenty Studies are another of the composer's collection of short pieces, veering between quite conventional to less conventional. These, too, are in very rough form, but could probably be deciphered and thus brought to the public. They seem to be not so much studies for piano playing as studies in some aspects of composition. No titles are used, with the exception of *No.19*, which is a *Frog Etude*, the crushed minor seconds of which depict jumping frogs:

Ex. 16:1. H. Brewster-Jones *Frog Etude.* bars 1-5.

The manuscript dates them in 1925, so they do belong to the period when Brewster-Jones was experiencing a great surge of creativity.

There is another set of Ten Etudes, from a few years on, in a much more adventurous idiom, and therefore, almost by definition, much harder to decipher. It is as though Brewster-Jones was so convinced that nobody would be interested in these pieces, that he considered it hardly worth writing them out properly and enough to just throw them onto the page. Nevertheless they are complete, signed and sometimes dated: No.1 and No.2 were written on the 21/2/28, No.6, "Variations Etude" on 27/2/28, No.7 on 18/3/28, No.8 on 30/9/28, and No.10, 'for Edith' (presumably Edith Piper) on 30/4/29. This set features whole tone constructs, piled up fifths, arpeggios in fifths and tritones, movement in ninths, parallel sevenths and tonal instability. Again, a painstaking job is required here, but a very rewarding outcome resulting.

Once again, there is clear evidence of the amazing speed with which the composer worked, even if one considers only the piano output. It would be fascinating to create a list of the complete works with dates thus giving us a very clear picture of this aspect of Brewster-Jones' work.

Opening the music of the sonatinas, I must admit that I expected to find easy and pretty pieces written for pedagogic purposes - there are so many examples of this kind of sonatina in the Australian piano music world. But I was very pleasantly wrong. The *First Sonatina* is in three movements; it was composed over a few days in 1924. The first movement for example was done between 20th and 23rd of January; the 2nd movement, in the form of a short Minuet, on the 28th of February with the last movement commenced on the same day.

The Third Sonatina, dedicated to Nadra Penalurick, exists in fine copy, but carries no date The copyist has included fingering so was probably working from a composer's copy that had already been fingered and possibly performed. The Thematic Catalogue attached to the manuscript bears a note which says "This Sonatina is elswhere known as *Sonatina No.3*"; in this catalogue the work is described as Sonatina No.2. So did the copyist simply put a wrong number and there is not in fact a Third Sonatina?

Both Sonatinas are certainly compact, especially the second one (timings in the scores give 8.5 and 5 minutes respectively), but within their fairly simple linearity they are also surprisingly gritty and would not have been out of place in the contemporary neoclassic output of a European composer.

Nadra Penalurick's copy of the *Valse Insouciance* is now part of the composer's archive. This piece, dated 17/9/26 consists of just two harmonies, one based on Db and one on Ab, and gently floats through its course vacillating between the two slightly ambiguous and unresolved harmonies. Similarly refined and delicate is *"Tes cheveux descendent vers moi!"* (21.6.27) The two could easily be bracketed together in a recital. The *Song of the Moonbeam* (19/11/24) also belongs in this class of miniatures; it consists of a freely melodic line in the left hand with a G#/A pedal serenely floating over it throughout the duration of the one page.

Intermezzo No.5 is a strange, troubled piece built of augmented chords floating without resolution, in atmosphere like a late Liszt piece. Apparently Intermezzi Nos.3 and 4 are lost, which is a shame; but the first two, which are extant, are early and not really characteristic of the mature composer.

There exists a set of twelve preludes, numbered and grouped by the composer, dating from the end of 1923 and the beginning of 1924, and, as usual written in one or (maximum) two days - sometimes more than one in a day. No.9 is currently missing from the archive. These are really exploratory pieces and yet again represent a lot of restorative work for someone who needs to take time and effort to decipher the scribbled notation, but the result will, as with other material from this period, well worth the effort.

In addition, and incredibly, there are a further number of some sixteen Preludes from the twenties, not apparently intended as a set of any kind, but all worth enshrining in print. Some of them are clearly copied. As usual, the most tantalizing are the sketchiest!

Ex. 17:1. H. Brewster-Jones *Prelude - Poingnoi.* bars 1-3.

Ex. 18:1. H. Brewster-Jones *Prelude – to John Jeffreys.* bars 1-4.

Ex. 19:1. H. Brewster-Jones *Prelude – marked 'Largo'.* bars 1-4.

There is a late set of preludes in fine copy written twenty years after his flurry of activity in the first part of the 1920s. *Extase* (10/1/44), *Meditation* (2/2/44), *Desolation* (7/3/45), another two unnamed, (4/11/45 and 29/3/45) and *Le Soir*, (15/3/45), grouped in the archive with a little waltz which doesn't seem to fit; these late *Preludes* exist in a world somewhere between the Cyril Scott of *Lotus Land* and some remote Scriabin. They are world-weary aphoristic pieces, possibly brought on by the exhaustion of the World War. This means that there exist over thirty *Preludes* by Brewster-Jones that could be assembled into a fine volume and published for the first time.

Ex. 20:1. H. Brewster-Jones *Le Soir.* bars 1-5.

Sitting somewhere halfway in style - that is, not as experimental as some, but not quite conventional either - are the *Five Impressions*. They consist of *Impression Russe* (21/1/21), *Dirge* (22/1/21), *The Waves Lap Idly on the Moonlit Strand* (no date), *Will-O-the-Wisp* (18/9/21).

There is also a set of *Three Impressions*, from 1922-1924, which would need a fair amount of work to decipher. Two of them have titles: *Under the Pine* and *By the Tanunda Fountain*.

The sonatas are yet another example of the extraordinary neglect of this composer. The series is constituted thus:

Sonata No.1.

> Complete. Ab Major. 24/10/15. 35 pages of ms. 1. Allegro Guisto 2. Andantino Grazioso. Elusion. 3. No tempo marking given, but an obviously energetic Finale.

Sonata No.2.

> Complete. F Minor. The first few pages also exist in fine copy 1. Allegro Moderato.4/1/21. 2. Scherzo. 28/12/20. 3. Andante Con Moto. 27/12/20. 4. Finale, No date. There is another Finale, perhaps composed as an alternative. It is in rougher form than the Finale, but also complete. It is given as Allegro Vivace, and the pages are numbered so that it clearly belongs to this Sonata. At the end of this 2nd Finale, it says '20 minutes'. It is hard to imagine anyone but the

composer being able to play from the messy manuscript, so this might have been merely a guess at the overall duration of the Sonata. When this work goes into print, both Finales will have to be printed.

Sonata No.3:
Incomplete. E Minor. (23/1/21). No numbering on the score, and there is some confusion on this issue. Incomplete. Just over 3 pages of ms.

Sonata No.4.
Incomplete. Eb Major. 1. Lento. Written between 6 and 7/1/22, revised 15/1/22. 2. Andante Con Moto. 7/1/22. 3. No tempo is given, but it appears to be dance-like. MS says 'commenced Wed.' 4. Caprice. In 5/8. Much material, but some of it very sketchy and the work appears to be not quite complete.

Sonata No.5.
Incomplete. The composer has written 'Commenced 1908? Finished 4/8/22. Part of the work is in fine copy. It appears to be a one movement work in Db Major, with the latter part of the work in rough form, requiring much editorial consideration and perhaps some compositional intervention.

Sonata No.6.
Incomplete. No key given, but in E Minor. 1. Crotchet speed of 140 is asked for. 11/1/24. 2. No speed indication, but evidently the slow movement. 3. Scherzo. 17/1/24. Finale in 7/4. 19/1/24. There is probably enough material in this yet again unfinished last movement to reconstruct it.

Sonata No.7.
27/9/28. Breaks off at the bottom of the fifth page. Rough but complete up to that point.

There are, in addition to the sonatas, several suites. These, like the sonatas, are written in a more conservative musical language.

Suite No.1:
Prelude, Sarabande, Bourée, Air, Minuet, Gavotte and Musette, Gigue. Written between December 31/12/21 and 1/1/22.

Suite No.2:
Almaine, Corrente and Courante (with an apparently obbligato cello part) Sarabande ('to be transposed into the key of F', says a note from the composer), March, Rigaudon, Minuet, Gigue. Written between 3-5/1/22.

Suite No.3:

> Prelude, Courante (both movements written on 26/11/21), Sarabande I (8/7/22) and II (24/11/21), East Minuet, Gavotte and Musette (4/3/21), Gigue. After the Gigue, the manuscript contains a *Waltz* (2/12/21) written in the same key; sketchy but complete, possibly also meant for this Suite?

Suite No.4:

> Prelude (16/2/25), Pavan, Galliard, Minuet (9/11/21), Gigue (27/11/21), Finale. The Minuet and Gigue are in fine copy, but also in an earlier style. The rest of the Suite is in rough, but complete and in a more advanced idiom. The Minuet was also intended for a String Quartet, from marks on the score.

There is also an early and quite passionate *Rhapsodie*, but in a derivative style; and a number of other early pieces which I have not written about, especially in view of the riches which are contained in the later music.

What emerges is that the miniatures are the most interesting works in his output, delving into areas that would have been considered experimental for their time, especially in Adelaide. My feeling is that concerning all of these miniatures is that, when they are all finally printed in a form that will allow for performance and recording, what will be concluded will be that the weakness in all these works is that the exploration is almost all in the realm of pitch; there is some tentative venture into the world of rhythms and ostinati, but almost none, it seems to me, in the world of structure. These short pieces are put together in a very classically conventional way, many of them tending to repetitions with codas attached after the second time round. This in no way negates the value and importance of the output or the amazing phenomenon of what occurred to Brewster-Jones during the 1920s. I could be very wrong, too, given the difficulty of playing through these hardly legible scores and being unable to get any real sense of continuity. Even the tempi of many of these works will be purely conjectural, let alone finer points of expression.

So ends the sad saga of the Brewster-Jones' music for piano. Much here that is ready to go into print, but also much that would require a huge effort to bring to publishable stage. The composer was obviously a highly creative talent, engaged in many activities and one can't help wondering whether performance ventures were more immediately gratifying and therefore seductive. Given that many of the works are in rough, it could be that the indifference shown to Brewster-Jones in Adelaide in the twenties mitigated against him completing and polishing many of his works, especially works in large forms. Paradoxically, the sonatas are non-threatening, yet still remained unpublished. The dates on all the manuscripts are revealing in that they do demonstrate that Brewster-Jones had the capacity to work very quickly and produce at high intensity, so completing miniatures was no problem, since I suspect that most of them were done at a single sitting. The sonatas, in general, are much more conservative than many of the works described above, harking back to late romantic gestures and tonally stable melodic lines, even in the late ones, by which time we know that he had worked on all those adventurous miniatures. At this remove, it is hard to know how he thought of the bird and horse pieces. Were they merely a personal indulgence in his mind, quite distinct from his other output?

There is no doubt that Hooper Brewster-Jones is a composer whose eventual publication will prove to be a revelation to many who have a particular view of Australian music of the twenties.

Roy Agnew (1891 – 1944)

Roy Agnew represents a special stature and achievement in the annals of Australian piano music: he is truly an archetypal composer-pianist. Most of his output is for solo piano; apart from this, there are only a handful of other pieces or songs, and only one surviving orchestral work. It seems curious to me that there was no concerto; Agnew certainly spoke of having written or of writing one, in a number of newspaper and journal interviews.

It is possible that it was lost; but probably more likely that Agnew's orchestral skills were not developed sufficiently for the task. His teacher, Emanuel de Beaupuis, no doubt gave him a foundation, but Beaupuis himself was a fairly lightweight, though skilled composer and pianist. Additionally, there would have been little point in working at a piano concerto, for where were the orchestras and possibilities of performance in Australia? There is much about Agnew's life that is still under-researched; we are uncertain how he spent his time during his trips abroad to England and the U.S.A. Some publications and possible commissions were outcomes, almost certainly, as well as contacts with some top pianists of the day such as fellow-Australian William Murdoch and piano greats such as Benno Moiseiwitsch. We know that he kept abreast of new developments in world music and that he played and later broadcast new music on the fledgling Australian Broadcasting Corporation, which included problematic composers such as Busoni and Scriabin and even some of the Second Viennese School.

Sydney during the first third of the twentieth century was not the place for a burgeoning composer, and Agnew had little choice but to support himself by suburban teaching. It was only in the last year of his life that he acquired a teaching position, he otherwise taught privately.

The output is two-pronged. There is a body of music written for young students and in a fairly conventional and acceptable idiom; had he stopped there, we would not be discussing him at all at this juncture. Then, there is a kind of intermediate number of pieces, still much in an English idiom; works such as the lovely *Diedre's Lament, Pangbourne Fields, Rhapsodie* and *Rabbit Hill.*

Some truly stretch the pianist and are evidence of Agnew;'s own pianistic prowess: there still exist a fair number of recordings from the 1930s, carried out for the A.B.C. and archived on large transcription discs that were used for broadcast before the days of reel to reel tape. Here we find virtuoso works such a *Concert Etude*, the *Toccata Tragica* and *Sea-Surge.*

Ex. 21:1. R. Agnew. *Étude.* bars 1-3.

Ex. 22:1. R. Agnew. *Toccata Tragica.* bars 1-3.

Ex. 23:1. R. Agnew. *Sea-Surge.* bars 1-3.

But Agnew's importance really rests on his series of *Sonatas* for the piano: there is nothing in Australian music of the time quite like it, in terms of consistency, advanced language and volume. There are six sonatas in all. Only three of them appeared in print during Agnew's lifetime. Two early sonatas seem to have vanished; only a fragment of one survives in the Agnew archive at the Mitchell Library in Sydney.

All the sonatas are in one movement and seem to have grown out of an appreciation of the Lisztian symphonic poem, encompassing a variety of moods within a single movement, but not always restricting oneself in terms of the number of themes; and Agnew must have had a working knowledge of the Scriabin sonatas, themselves examples of a Lisztian descent.

In my earlier article "The Piano Sonatas of Roy Agnew" (*One Hand On The Manuscript*, eds.Nicholas Brown et al, Canberra: The Humanities Research Centre, The Australian National University, 1995) I have written of an apparent tendency in the Agnew sonatas towards an economy of themes and expression; but with this also came an apparent shift towards a more conventional language. Did the conservatism around him eventually wear him down? His teachers (de Beaupuis and Alfred Hill) were certainly so inclined; but then, so were his pupils (Hutchens and Holland); all of these composers were successful in their own way, whilst Agnew had to struggle. It is entirely feasible that, willingly or unwillingly, he was forced to rethink his aesthetic position. By the time writers put pen to paper to deal with Australian music, Agnew was a forgotten figure and what little survived in the musical memory had to do more with *Rabbit Hill*, a polished and witty but entirely conventional little piece played and often destroyed by a few generations of young pianists, and almost nothing to do with adventurous works such as the *Sonata 1929*.

The *Sonata Fantasie* was published in 1927 (Augener, London) and dedicated to the famous pianist William Murdoch, who played the work a number of times during his London concerts. It was well received by the critics, though it does have a Scriabinesque feel about it. Scriabin was hardly the darling of conservative English music; his forays into the jungle of the Theosophical movement and the minefield of an occult programme hidden behind the sounds was widely thought of as dangerously eccentric. Agnew achieves a tumultuous atmosphere by constant changes of meter and mood. The Sonata is one of the longest in the series and employs the device of a complete recapitulation, possibly since the writing is dense and involved and the composer might have felt that repetition was desirable, possibly Agnew felt more comfortable with a pre-ordained structure, as this seems to have been his first foray into a large scale work. The *Sonata Fantasie* was Agnew's entrée into the world of international music. Winifred Burston (eminent pianist and friend of the composer) told me that Agnew considered the sonata to have four distance subjects. After a shimmering introduction featuring trills and tremolos, these subjects are introduced in quick succession. First, an upward thrusting idea, marked 'with exaltation':

Ex. 24:1. R. Agnew. *Sonata Fantasie.* bars 20-22.

This could have come directly from a Scriabin score, and, together with the performance instruction, is one of those themes that the Russian master designated to mean something like 'the urge towards the light'. Then, a more growly, threatening gesture in the lower reaches of the piano:

Ex. 25:1. R. Agnew. *Sonata Fantasie.* bars 33-35.

The dotted figure is characteristic of much of Agnew's later music. It might have initially sprung from a less turbulent English source, but its placement in the lower reaches of the piano and its insistent repetitiveness give it a special agitated feel. The third subject takes the notion of soft semiquaver tremolo from the introduction as background and is intervallically more spacious:

Ex. 26:1. R. Agnew. *Sonata Fantasie.* bars 53-55.

This owes less to Scriabin and more to late Liszt in its layout, although the harmony is more advanced. The final subject is a serene progression of chords, a bow in the direction of John Ireland:

Ex. 27:1. R. Agnew. *Sonata Fantasie.* bars 100-105.

The subjects have links between themselves too, and the recapitulation, though strict, does present these ideas in a different order. At the very end, a triumphant coda with tremolos in alternating hand chords balances the opening Introduction structurally.

The *Sonata Poème* was published in 1936 (Allan & Co., Melbourne) and was dedicated to Thorold Waters, an influential writer on music during this time. Since composers rarely dedicate music to critics, Agnew must have held him in high esteem; some research on Waters would not go astray either, if we are to more fully understand the period. A note at the end of the score proclaims that the work was completed in July of 1935, but we know that Agnew had played it at least six years earlier. Like many composer-pianists, Agnew constantly chipped away at his creations, touching up details, experimenting with different passage figurations. Some of these variants were preserved in manuscripts, or passed down through an oral tradition. The *Sonata Poème* is the most lyrical of the series and concentrates on line rather than chord work for its effect. The thematic material is more economical than in the *Sonata Fantasie*; according to Burston, Agnew talked about three themes. The predominant mood is inward and reflective, although Agnew cannot resist at least two impassioned outbursts in the work. The main theme is heard right at the start:

Ex. 28:1. R. Agnew. *Sonata Poème.* opening.

A series of descending chords constitutes the second seminal idea:

Ex. 29:1. R. Agnew. *Sonata Poème*. bars 32-37.

And a bell-like repeated figure is the third important motive:

Ex. 30:1. R. Agnew. *Sonata Poème*. bars 41-45.

The rest is rhythmic and intervallic transformation. Agnew is already heading towards greater economy, depending on inversions, rhythmic transformations and semiotic techniques for cohesion.

The *Sonata Ballade* was written in January of 1938 and dedicated to the composer and pianist Frank Hutchens. Agnew finished it in time to enter the Sesquicentenary Competition run by the NSW Music Association, a competition in which he won two prizes, one for this sonata and one for his *Cradle Song*. The prize included publication and, until very recently, one could purchase the score through the office of the self-same Association.

I still treasure such a score, moreover one in which some of Agnew's alterations and indications were written in by Winifred Burston. The work, apart from being my favourite from the sonatas, has very pleasant personal memories. I performed the work at least twice in the presence of Mrs. Agnew, who expressed approval and predicted a 'brilliant future' for me as a musician. I don't know whether the prediction was accurate, but it was nice to hear nevertheless. It also gave me an opportunity of speaking with Agnew's widow, a chance to understand something about him as a composer, a chance that, in hindsight, I squandered. I should have asked her what music Roy had at home, what manuscript works, which books, who were his favourite composers for the piano, etcetera; instead, we talked about cats (!) and Agnew's love of them. But it is easy to be wise thirty years later. As for Mrs Agnew approving my interpretation, it is no wonder: not only did Winifred Burston teach me the piece, having heard Roy play it any times, but, as well, I had (and still have) a copy of the 78 rpm recording that Agnew did for Australia Columbia.

The freedom and elasticity of the playing were a revelation, but I also remember Agnew racing through some bits to make sure it fitted on the disc: not more than four a side, and the sonata lasts, in performance, a trifle longer than that. For the record, as it were, I would like it confirmed here that Agnew said as much to a number of people.

The compositional technique is here further refined: we now have two themes, as in a classical sonata, and Agnew constantly develops these two ideas, using interval manipulation in a quite complex manner. The work is intensely dramatic. I recall playing it for Egon Petri, who liked it very much and said that it sounded like a cross between Scriabin and Ireland; quite an accurate summation of the sound world of the piece. Petri, a great master pianist and Busoni's favorite disciple, was a very fine Liszt player and instinctively felt drawn to those aspects of Agnew which derived from late Liszt and Busoni. His summation also suggested to me recognition of Agnew's internationalism.

Examining the two themes in question, the first is heard as both ostinato bass and melody, and is subject to almost instant inversion:

Ex. 31:1. R. Agnew. *Sonata Ballade.* Opening

While the second is a more undulating figure:

Ex. 32:1. R. Agnew. *Sonata Ballade.* bars 29-32.

This second idea undergoes a very lovely transformation in the middle of the sonata.

If the *Sonata Fantasie* had four themes, the *Sonata Poème* had three, the *Sonata Ballade* had two, then it would be logical to assume that the next work from Agnew's pen would be monothematic, and that is exactly what occurred in the case of *Sonata Legend ('Capricornia')*. The sonata did not achieve publication until 1949, five years after the composer's death, although he certainly performed it a number of times. The subtitle, suggesting that the Sonata has a hidden programme based on the Xavier Herbert novel, is not to be taken too literally. Agnew often said that tiles were appended after the work was composed. He was in no sense a programmatic composer, although it was probably the violent mood of the Herbert novel that gripped his imagination. The theme of the work gives perhaps a false impression of conservatism.

Ex. 33:1. R. Agnew. *Sonata Legend.* opening.

The *Sonata Legend* is the most compressed of the series, partly due to the use of just one theme, but also because the compression process was continuing its work in Agnew's compositional technique. The sonata is intense and emotionally draining to perform. It is a kind of antithesis of the *Sonata Poème*, being largely chordal in texture and consisting of varying statements of the one theme; there is no repetition and, in some ways this is a very stable sonata tonally, beginning and ending firmly in the key of E-flat minor.

Both Mrs Agnew and Winifred Burston had mentioned in passing that Agnew's manuscripts were in the Mitchell Library in Sydney. At that time, the import of that information did not sink in and was overtaken by personal events and interests. It was not until a few years ago that I finally investigated just what was in the Agnew archive and discovered, to my great joy, two large-scale piano compositions, worthy of a place beside the four published sonatas. It was a musicologist's dream to come across such a find. There were also some smaller unpublished pieces.

The first of these is simply entitled 'Sonata' on the manuscript; lower down the page is written 'April, 1929'. For the sake of uniformity of nomenclature in Agnew's output, I propose calling this work *Sonata 1929*. Often composers' unpublished works are inferior and forced into the public arena by scholars and performers for reasons more sentimental than musical. Naturally, I feared this, but am now quite convinced that the *Sonata 1929* probably did not achieve publication due to its progressive language. Rich in changes of texture and tempo, with a wide sweeping use of the keyboard, the work could also be labeled as a 'Sonata Rondo', because the little five-note motive that is heard at the very outset of the work is reiterated during the piece and serves the function of compositional glue in much the same way as a classical rondo theme. Like all the other sonatas, this is in one movement, with a massively climactic coda, just before the quiet ending. Here is the opening:

Ex. 34:1. R. Agnew. *Sonata 1929.* opening.

The debt to Scriabin in this sonata is more obvious than in others. Many of my compositional colleagues feel this work to be the best of the Agnew sonatas.

The second unpublished work has a variety of attempted titles: 'Poem sonata', with 'sonata' then scribbled out. "La belle dame sans merci (Keats)'; on another page, both of these one under the other; finally 'Symphonic Poem'. Quite understandably, 'Poem' seemed a necessity to Agnew, one way or another. No doubt various portions of the work can be related to the Keats poem. In my mind, again for the sake of uniformity, I call this piece *Sonata Symphonique*, not because it is any more massive than others in the series, but because a kind of rather delicate orchestral colouration seems to permeate the piece. In one passage, Agnew writes; 'Like flutes'; in an interview he refers to an orchestral composition by the title of 'Symphonic Poem'; no such work exists, as far as we know. Perhaps he intended to score this piano piece. The model now seems closer to Ravel than to Scriabin. Again a harmonic audacity is perpetrated, and possibly stopped the work being published. The main theme of the piece is a succession of descending chromatic ninths; at the very outset of the work they are marked 'very cold and desolate', and they lend a very special harmonic feel to the work.

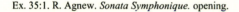

Ex. 35:1. R. Agnew. *Sonata Symphonique.* opening.

There is no date on the manuscript, but I surmise that the work predates 1920, as it is mentioned in an interview published during that year.

A more detailed chronology of the sonatas is available in Rita Crew's essay "Roy Agnew: The Man and his Music" and some additional personal comments on compositional aspects of these works are made by myself in "The Piano Sonatas Of Roy Agnew" so I will not repeat them here. But what may be worth mentioning is Agnew's strongly thematic technique coupled with a chromatic language and a developed pianism. The composer strove throughout his life for a logical yet colourful palette and in the progression of the sonatas there is a tendency to limit and shorten the material so that the great exuberance of the *Fantasie Sonata* gives way to the far more compressed expressivity of the *Sonata Legend*, inspired by the Xavier Herbert novel *Capricornia*. The luminescent, explosive codas of the *Fantasie Sonata* and the *Sonata 1929* owe something to Scriabin, but there is also a very personal economy, especially evident in the 1929 work, which, together with the *Symphonic Poem* had to wait many long years for publication.

Agnew's cycles of preludes and poems are also important additions to the Australian repertoire and make fine impressions in concert programmes. Of the poems, there is the linear and beautifully expressive *Poem No.1* from 1922, as well as the fiery *Poeme Tragique*, also published as the *Toccata Tragica*. The preludes, almost always in an advanced harmonic idiom, include one subtitled *The Wind*, also conjuring up most vividly the composer at the keyboard:

Ex. 36:1. R. Agnew. *The Wind.* bars 1-3.

In the smaller works, extremes of mood are to be found, from stillness, as in *Drifting Mists*:

Ex. 37:1. R. Agnew. *Drifting Mists.* bars 1-3.

to frenetic activity, as in *Exaltation*:

Ex. 38:1. R. Agnew. *Exaltation.* bars 1-3.

Diedre's Lament is unusual in that the left hand consist of constantly reiterated F octaves throughout the piece, with a moving outcome, encompassing a wide range of mood within one short work.

Then, there is the extraordinary *Dance of the Wild Men* from 1919, wherein Agnew asks the pianist to play "fiercely, with the utmost intensity', "furiously" and to "bang". At the end, a kind of limit is reached:

Ex. 39:1. R. Agnew. *Dance of the Wild Men.* ending.

Agnew made a lasting contribution to Australian piano music early in the twentieth century and for those of us who may be somewhat embarrassed by the thought of Percy Grainger as our founding father, Agnew may be a worthwhile substitute.

Margaret Sutherland (1897 – 1984)

Although belatedly recognized during her lifetime, and almost universally admired after her death, Margaret Sutherland had to struggle throughout her life as a composer. She fought with the musical establishment in her hometown of Melbourne, she had to survive a difficult marriage (and this is not the place to tell this sad story) and she had to grapple with ill-health, eventually badly affecting her eyesight and her ability to physically notate her own music. Her late scores are almost impossible to read and thankfully have now been transcribed and published.

Although a fine pianist herself, there are not as many works for solo piano as one would have wished for or expected, nor is there a work for piano and orchestra. It's possible that Sutherland did not see herself as a soloist and therefore the finest works are rather more inward looking than vehicles for her own prowess. The output is diverse and changing, culminating in a very important set of pieces from mid-century and on.

Going against the current of the time to produce soft and fluffy music for the piano, Sutherland's earliest published efforts are already lean and quite muscular, with a neoclassic bent in both form and expression. Thus, the *Sonatina* (1939):

Ex. 40:1. M. Sutherland. *Sonatina.* bars 27-29 of III.

Or, in the same work, the somewhat acid but very characteristic counterpoint and suggestion of bitonality:

Ex. 41:1. M. Sutherland. *Sonatina.* bars 50-53 of I.

and the conclusion to the slow movement with its unresolved false tonality:

Ex. 42:1. M. Sutherland. *Sonatina.* bars 18-20 of III.

The avoidance of overblown romantic gesture and richness is also evident in the lovely *Two Chorale Preludes,* which won a prize in a competition conducted by the A.B.C. in 1935. The settings were published the following year and the score proudly proclaims that the competition was adjudicated by John Ireland, as though that somehow lent it credibility and authority. So, even here, where pianistic tradition almost demands fullness of treatment, Sutherland writes:

Ex. 43:1. M. Sutherland. *Two Choral Preludes.* bars 3-4 of I.

There are pieces, too, which fall into that grey area between easy pedagogically inclined works and miniatures. These are rarely performed and Sutherland's reputation certainly does not rest upon them; they include a *Miniature Sonata*; (Sutherland writes on the score: "This little work is designed as a clear and concise introduction to classical sonata form for the young student") as well as two short Suites of four movements each (Suite No.1: *The Adventurer, The Dreamer, The Bustler, The Humorist* and Suite No. 2: *Chorale Prelude, Mirage, Lavender Girl, The Quest*). I list these because only a hop and a skip away are important works such as the *Valse Descant* and the wonderfully evocative *Six Profiles.*

The first is a shortish concert waltz, and the second a set of contrasting pieces. Do they depict profiles of actual people? Are they purely musical profiles? We don't seem to know, but they are certainly a most effective set of pieces. Most of them are but two pages each. They contain the already quoted ambiguity of tonal centre:

Ex. 44:1. M. Sutherland. *Six Profiles for Piano Solo*. bars 48-53 of III.

At times a scurrying busyness:

Ex. 45:1. M. Sutherland. *Six Profiles for Piano Solo*. bars 1-5 of IV.

and sometimes a quite savage intensity:

Ex. 46:1. M. Sutherland. *Six Profiles for Piano Solo*. bars 39-41 of VI.

The *Profiles* lead very naturally into those extraordinary works from Sutherland's final years, now widely admired: *Voices I* and *II*, *Chiaroscuro I* and *II* and *Extension*. (1967–68)

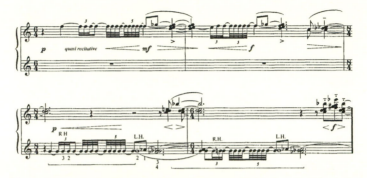

Ex. 47:1. M. Sutherland. *Chiaroscuro I.* bars 1-4.

Much of the material is sonic in that sense rather than thematic in the older sense, and the electronic reverberation is what is constant in this piece. *Chiaroscuro II* is more athletic and occasionally harks back to her older linear way of writing. But like *Chiaroscuro I*, it is economical and tense with its raw materials and usage:

Ex. 48:1. M. Sutherland. *Chiaroscuro II.* bars 1-4.

Extension also depends on a very simple rhythmic cell given at the start, and referred to throughout. In all these late works Sutherland largely abandons conventional tonality and even when she employs pedal tones, they largely pull against each other:

Ex. 49:1. M. Sutherland. *Extension.* bars 32-34.

Voices I uses extensive pile-ups of tones and semitones, tending towards cluster sounds

Ex. 50:1. M. Sutherland. *Voices 1*. bars 74-75.

Finally, *Voices II* is distinguished by a clarity of texture:

Ex. 51:1. M. Sutherland. *Voices II*. bars 88-90.

Margaret Sutherland is, without a doubt, an important Australian composer for the piano, with an output that acutely mirrors her stylistic changes over a long creative life and with an inherent understanding, from personal experience, of the piano and its capabilities. I am confident that her cycles of *Profiles*, *Voices* and *Chiaroscuro* will be increasingly heard in piano recitals in the future.

Raymond Hanson (1913 – 1976)

In the memory of any of us who were fortunate enough to have studied with and known Raymond Hanson ("Ray" to his friends), there is an image of a man who was kind, honest, full of integrity and humility and a man who cared for his pupils and for the future of music this country. Hanson was unlucky enough to have been in the 'in between' generation, i.e. he had shifted away from his conservative roots and teachers, but he hadn't shifted far enough in some ways, so that when there was a sudden surge of support and activity for Australian music during the sixties and seventies, he was somehow overlooked as being part of a past generation. It is only now, far too late for Ray, that we are looking at his contribution.

Part of Ray's bad luck was to have fallen within the clutches of a mini-McCarthyism in Australia; because of his genuine desire to bring art music to the trade union movement, to form an orchestra from trade union levies, to exchange culture with Russia, to regard music as a universal way of uniting people - for all these reasons, Hanson came to be seen as at least 'pink', if not outright 'red'. It affected his compositional prospects.

His piano music is clearly by a man who knows the keyboard. Hanson gave piano recitals and played standard repertoire as well as his own music. He had an easy, natural technique, without any undue movement or exaggerated mannerisms. Possessing a very fine ear, his playing constantly involved orchestration at the keyboard; one can hear this colouristic propensity at work in, for example his very fine set of *Preludes Op.11* with their word-paintings incorporated in the score (incidentally, the words in the manuscript score are somewhat more elaborate than the words in the published score). Since there was no composition tuition at the State Conservatorium in Sydney in those days, Hanson was employed to teach harmony and aural training; he spent hours at the keyboard playing aural drill to students, mildly puzzled at how bad some people's ears were!

Later in his career, he was allowed to teach what was then considered composition, but in reality was a historically driven style of harmony and counterpoint, as well as orchestration. Hanson had discovered the Hindemith text books and writings and for him this was a way into a contemporary sound world without throwing away his tonal roots. Not that Hanson's music sounds like Hindemith; not at all; it was actually closer to composers such as Prokofiev in his approach to the piano. Like many of his generation, one wishes that the output was larger, but teachers at the Conservatorium were paid for actual hours taught at that time; they were not salaried staff and had no superannuation benefits or anything else of that kind. It was really tough being a music teacher, even though superficially one had the status of being on the staff of a prestigious institution. Such matters did not change until the (late) sixties, after which time it became quite fashionable to actually employ composers as composers, instead of getting them there but using them as aural drill teachers. Nevertheless, some miniatures and teaching pieces apart, Hanson's contribution to piano repertoire is very solid: apart from the above-mentioned set of Preludes, which are large scale virtuoso pieces and which work brilliantly as a cycle, there is fairly big Sonatina and a very fine Sonata, plus a set of *Variations* (Hanson calls them *Episodes on Tarry Trowsers*).

Hanson's music is rugged (the parents, incidentally, were of English stock) and reflects his difficult boyhood and the privations of the Great Depression; his first paycheck was at the age of 28, from the Army. Until then, he did odd and often unpleasant jobs, including being a sanitary carter in early twentieth-century Sydney. His early compositions were from self-teaching, using his ear to remember his mother playing Bach and Chaminade. Apparently most of this juvenilia is lost, something that Ray would not have rued; he was always saying that young composers were far too eager to leap into print and get performed immediately.

He never had any truck with being labeled 'Australian': he claimed not to know what this meant. However, the Preludes were certainly inspired by a particular and specific landscape of the Burragorang Valley; whether this makes it Australian or not is a debatable point; the Preludes would still be very fine example of the genre without such knowledge. What is certain that, stated or not, is that Hanson was imbued with a deep spirituality - at one time in his life he even wanted to go to India as a missionary; the piano music might not be the most obvious manifestation of such feeling, but it is there nevertheless. With it, there is a strong sense of a very flexible rhythm and Hanson's affection for jazz manifests itself this way, not that the music ever sounds like jazz in the accepted sense; but there is an attempt by the composer to write a music that sounds spontaneous and never rigid in terms of beats. This fluidity is a strong core element of Hanson's music. He was certainly aware of the post-war avant-garde but did not wish to move in that direction; to him, much of what was occurring was more in the realms of noise and technology than what he perceived as music; he couldn't accept serialism for a variety of reasons at a time when it was considered the only way forward. Ironically, he was instinctively correct, and the style pundits were wrong.

Although recognition, commissions, recordings and awards came late in his life, at least Hanson lived to experience them, unlike the generation immediately before him.

The Preludes Op.11 written in the Burragorang Valley of the Blue Mountains of New South Wales between December 1940 and January 1941 have, in retrospect survived very well. In the early days they were played by the composer and then by some of his friends and acquaintances; the set was eventually published in 1975 and since then this set of six Preludes has been fairly regularly performed and recorded. Like the Sonata which immediately followed it in initial completion, these pieces certainly establish Hanson as an individual voice in Australian piano music from the huge resonances of the second *Prelude*:

Ex. 52:1. R. Hanson. *Preludes Op.11.* bars 44-47 of II.

through the assymetric groupings of No.3:

Ex. 53:1. R. Hanson. *Preludes Op.11.* bars 5-7 of II.

to the storm of No.4 in the key of Bb Major, the same as the Sonatina and the Sonata:

Ex. 54:1. R. Hanson. *Preludes Op.11.* bars 43-45 of IV.

There are still a few piano works of Hanson's that are unpublished and it is time that they achieved print. Works such as *Procrastination* a complex and serious three-part polyphonic work and *Quizzic*, somewhat lighter in vein with quirky outbursts of dance. Other short works are now difficult to obtain and perhaps a album of such works can now be issued. The amiable *Idylle* can be included; a composition awarded the prize donated by the Australasian Performing Right Association in a competition conducted by the New South Wales branch of the Guild of Australian Composers. A similar short work is *On Holidays*, Hanson's Op.1 No.1, which sits somewhere on the narrow border between a teaching piece and a concert work, with its open texture, cheerful mood and clear tonality.

The *Sonatina Op.24* was probably submitted for a competition at some stage. In the manuscript copy given to me by the composer, it is described as having been written by 'Sagittarius', a good pseudonym for such an event! I am uncertain as to whether he had any success in the aforesaid lottery. The work is a dramatic, one movement affair lasting, according to the composer's own timing 'between 11.30 and 11.45 minutes. The name should not imply anything light; it was simply Ray's way of denoting that this was not a fully-fledged sonata in shape; like the Banks and Meale Sonatinas, there is nothing frivolous here. Largely, in the Australian piano world, the titled 'sonatina' has implied a pedagogic, often thin-textured and light-hearted piece. Like its longer counterpart, the Sonata, the Sonatina is also, curiously, in Bb major, with a strong ending in this key:

Ex. 55:1. R. Hanson. *Sonatina for Pianoforte Op. 24.* ending.

The *Sonata Op.12* was, to quote the composer, 'sketched and written in 1938-1940; revised and completed in 1963. On the published score (finally achieved in 1976) the composer has also added: "I wish to express my gratitude to a fierce advocate of this Sonata, my friend Igor Hmelnitsky, an outstanding pianist and pedagogue. His dedication and stimulating support created for me the necessary inspiration to revise and complete this work". Hanson used to play bits of this work to interested students during my time with him in the 1950s, so it was obviously very much a work in progress for a long time.

The world of the *Preludes Op.11* is very evident here, as well as the Hansonian habit of departing strongly away from a key only to confirm it at some crucial point. If anything, this almost Hindemithian gesture is stronger in the Sonata than in the Preludes and therefore lends it a more conventional air. It is possible that this occurs because the composer felt that the tonal signposts were more critical and important. Thematicism is the basis for most of the work, as it is with most Hanson, who was a lyrical composer and who therefore thought naturally in evolving lines and in lines that repeated themselves sometimes with elaborations and sometimes in different harmonic settings.

The Sonata is a dark and powerful work and its mood is given out at the very opening with strongly suggested bitonality:

Ex. 56:1. R. Hanson. *Piano Sonata Op. 12.* bars 1-3.

The huge texture of *Prelude No.2* written on multiple staves is here revisited, just like the fifth Prelude has a connection with the slow movement of the Sonata. The harmonic movement of the last movement has close connections with the fourth Prelude moving powerfully away from and to the home key. The Sonata ends with this idea pushed to a kind of keyboard ultimate:

Ex. 57:1. R. Hanson. *Piano Sonata Op. 12.* ending.

The Sonata is the most important of Hanson's works for solo piano. It is in some ways a piece parallel to the Prokofiev *War Sonatas*, as it too was inspired by the Second World War. Is this connection reinforced by the Bb major key signature? At any rate, it must rank with the very best major works produced by Australian composers during the past century.

Dulcie Holland (1913 – 2000)

This composer, over a long life, had a remarkable career in that probably every young musician in the country knows her name through her many publications encompassing theory, pieces for young pianists, duets, etc. Dulcie studied with composers written about elsewhere in this book: Frank Hutchens, Alfred Hill and Roy Agnew, followed by studies in England with John Ireland and, after World War II, with Matyas Seiber. Dulcie was also active as an arranger and a film composer and it is little wonder that the output for the piano – her own instrument – is not as extensive as it could have been. Dulcie Holland, therefore, is somewhat of a parallel case with Miriam Hyde, although her language is somewhat different and, as in the powerful Sonata, she proved that she can speak to a contemporary audience even though she was always very firmly anchored in a tonal and conventional world.

Having said this, there is nevertheless a small corpus of works for the piano which is distinct from the hundreds of pieces written for children.

Concert Study No.2 (1920), signed Dulcie Cohen.
Green Lizards (1936)
A Song Remembering (1937)
Lyric Piece (1937)
The Lake (1940)
The Sandman Comes (1944)
The End of Summer (1946)
Nocturne (1947)
Autumn Piece (1947)
Serious Procession (1949)
Asterisk (1950)
Sonata (1952)
Christmas Greeting, being a Variation on Two Carols. For Moneta Eagles (1956)
Dreamy John (1957)
Hornpipe (1960)
Tribute to Clem Hosking (1965)
Prelude I: *The Stones Cry Out* (1980)
Prelude III: *In Resignation* (1980)

Cat-Walk (1985)
Valse Ironic (1986)
The Dry West (1986) (This is virtually the same as Prelude I)
Bagatelle for Selma (1986)
Unanswered Question (1986)
Toccatina (1986)
The Scattering of Leaves (1986)
Retrospect (1991)
Shade of Summer (1992)
Sonatina (1993)
Autumn Gold (1993)
Three Dances for a New Doll (1942, revised 1994). 1. *Serenade.*
    2. *Quick Step.*   3. *Rig-A-Jig*
Farewell, My Friend (1994)
Fairy Penguins (1994)
At the Fountain (1995)
Autumn Pastorale (1995)
Bird at the Window (1995)
Northbridge Sketches (1995). Three movements:
    I: *Twin Towers;*
    II: *Valley Below;*
    III: *Weekend*
Four Aspects (1996)
Winter Lament (1996)
Piano Rag (1996)

This list is probably incomplete. There are many works still in manuscript, and many of these need to be published. There are also a number of works which are in that no-man's land between concert and educational. Dulcie Holland suffered from being typecast in a certain role, and it always seems to evoke surprise when it is discovered that she actually wrote seriously for the piano. Dulcie was both pianist and organist and so her approach to the instrument is certainly from a performer's point of view.

The language didn't seem to change much over the years. Early pieces such as *The Lake* and *Autumn Gold* are always lurking close to the whole-tone scale:

Ex. 58:1. D. Holland. *The Lake.* bars 1-6.

although, sometimes there is a drift towards bi-tonality:

Ex. 59:1. D. Holland. *Autumn Gold.* bars 25-28.

Like Miriam Hyde, Dulcie Holland seems to have found her approach early and never really left it. Her pianistic demands are, in general, less stringent than Hyde's, who was using Rachmaninov as a model.

Holland's world is closer to Hutchens; it is melodic, optimistic and sunny; and darker forces driving Agnew's music only surface occasionally in the music of Dulcie Holland; perhaps Agnew taught her something about colour and chromaticism. But in general, Holland is a more positive composer. The autumnal mood of her late pieces is still gentle and lyrical.   Perhaps the performing indication in her early *The End of Summer* describes her music rather well: "Reflectively (not fast) and with much expression".

Holland is also fond of the pentatonic scale with its built-in ambiguities and the possibilities thus given to modulate to unexpected keys. Many pieces at least begin like harmonization of chorale melodies before gradually shifting to some arpeggiation in the left hand, but retaining the feel of part writing:

Gently expressive and at a moderate speed

Ex. 60:1. D. Holland. *Dreamy John.* bars 1-7.

The unstable world of late Liszt is sometimes visited by the composer in works such as *Prelude III*:

Ex. 61:1. D. Holland. *Prelude III.* bars 24-27.

Prelude I is in a similar vein and seems close to those strange last pieces of Margaret Sutherland, a solipsistic universe that speaks to us all in certain moods:

Ex. 62:1. D. Holland. *Prelude I.* bars 29-38

But she is capable of using the natural configuration of the keyboard to move towards an approximation of clusters by having black notes in one hand and white in another:

Ex. 63:1. D. Holland. *Asterisk*. bars 1-6.

See also the opening of *Farewell, My Friend*, where the technique is applied in a more elegiac mood, or the *Valse Ironic*, where a harder edge is present. This is extended into a quasi-Prokofievan piece in *At the Fountain*:

Ex. 64:1. D. Holland. *At the Fountain*. bars 1-7.

The weakness is many of these pieces lies in the predictable phrase lengths, which go exactly where one anticipates; even the more adventurous pieces suffer from this.

The best work for piano from Dulcie Holland is doubtless the fine Sonata in three movements. From the brooding opening, suggesting somewhat unstable tonality:

Ex. 65:1. D. Holland. *Sonata.* bars 1-6 of I.

to the sometimes triumphant finale reminiscent of an orchestral Vaughan Williams.

Ex. 66:1. D. Holland. *Sonata.* bars 192-7 of III.

The Sonata maintains interest throughout and lies well under the hands, although in performance and recording I felt I had to amplify the texture somewhat. It is undoubtedly a landmark work in the Australian oeuvre.

Moneta Eagles (1924 –2003)

Moneta Eagles, after winning a number of prizes and commissions in the concert music world (including an important prize for her Sonatina for piano) moved towards composing music for films.

Most of her piano music is from her earlier years and to a certain extent are more indicators of what might have been rather than records of mature achievement. But it must be said that even with such qualification, the writing is clearly that of someone who understands the piano well and is obviously by a pianist. The music is never short of ideas and contains both structural and keyboard elegance. Eagles appeared a soloist under Eugene Goossens in her own work *Diversions* as well as in standard repertoire. Another contemporary of her time at the Sydney Conservatorium and also working with Goossens, was Malcolm Williamson. She studied at the Conservatorium with Alex Burnard, and like Don Banks, worked with Matyas Seiber in England. The earliest of her piano works that we found was a *Passacaglia*. The manuscript has on the title page *Theme and Variations – Passacaglia. Composed in 1948-1949.*

The title page implies that the composer wasn't certain whether she should call the work a "Theme & Variations" or a "Passacaglia". In truth, it partakes of some characteristics of both, but is closer to the second. The piece consists of an eight-bar theme, set out like a ground bass, followed by seven variations (not so identified by the composer however) that become increasingly more dense and dramatic

Ex. 67:1. M. Eagles *Theme and Variations – Passacaglia.* bars 95-96.

and ending in a grandiose restatement of the opening idea.

There is also an Impromptu in G from 1949, in a similar vein.

The *Poetic Fragment* comes from 1950. A two-page piece containing interesting quartal harmonies, it, like all the unpublished Eagles, should be brought into print.

Ex. 68:1. M. Eagles *Poetic Fragment.* bars 1-7.

Two other pieces from 1950 were written as a result of Gyorgy Sandor showing some interest in Eagles' music. They are *Mirage* and *Whirlwind*, grouped under *Two Impressions for Piano.* We have not found any documentation from the period showing any evidence of the Hungarian pianist's continued promotion of Eagles' music.

The *Arabeske* from 1952 is only a little longer than the above, but is also a delicate essay with some spice in the harmony.

Moneta Eagles' *Sonatina for Piano* (1954) is the best known of her keyboard pieces. It was published and disseminated quite widely for a period, whereas her other piano music is still in manuscript. The Sonatina won an important prize, jointly awarded in a competition run by the ABC and APRA. It is in the usual three-movement format. The first movement is musically the most interesting and adventurous and bears some affinity with the sonatas of Roy Agnew who would have been Eagles' immediate predecessor in Sydney and no doubt well known to her through the Conservatorium of Music. Unlike most sonatinas of the period, meant for young players, and usually quite jolly, the Eagles Sonatina begins with quite a dark statement.

Ex. 69:1. M. Eagles. *Sonatina.* bars 1-5.

The other two movements are more conventional. The second is labeled *Pastorale* and is based on a simple, modally-inclined melody in the right hand, with a gently rocking bass in the left, in compound time. The last movement is more extrovert and virtuosic.

Aquarelles: this set of pieces was awarded 1st prize in 1962 in a competition run by the Musical Association of New South Wales. The work is set out in what the composer calls a 'Miniature Suite' and consists of a Quasi Minuet, a Nocturne and a Toccatina.

The Minuet is in a clean, neoclassic texture, tending towards ambiguity in the tonal centres, and sounding all the notes of the chromatic scale in the opening bars.

Ex. 70:1. M. Eagles *Quasi Minuet.* bars 1-5.

The Nocturne is not dissimilar in mood to the slow movement of the Sonatina, while the last movement again reverts to a slightly spiky linear writing:

Ex. 71:1. M. Eagles *Toccatina.* bars 1-4.

In summary, the music of Moneta Eagles for the piano shows a distinct talent at work, and an individual voice. Though coming from a period early in her career, the manuscript works should now be issued in print, as they are part of the thread uncovered and demonstrated in this book.

As a footnote to the above, I came across three pieces by Marjorie Fetter (*Namouna, Berceuse and Scherzo*), which in spirit have connections to Moneta Eagles. Neo-classic in outlook, these are linear pieces with some quite startling dissonances, given the extremely conservative trends in Australian music at the time (1953). These pieces, with music by other emerging composers, are heralding the changes that swept over the Establishment soon after.

Non-Pianists

Fritz Bennicke Hart (1874 – 1949)

Hart is obviously an important figure in early twentieth-century Australian music. For our purposes here, his huge creative impulses are less significant because they seem to lie more with vocal and operatic music than in music for the piano. Hart's pupils included Peggy Glanville-Hicks and Margaret Sutherland.

The piano music is all much of a muchness. We cannot claim to have examined all of it, as there is such a huge amount, but we have certainly looked at a representative selection of the Hart output. His musical thinking is strongly tied to writing for the voice so that almost inevitably the piano pieces all seem to have a melody with accompaniment texture. The melody is placed in the right hand, usually within a vocal range, while the left hand does what accompaniments usually do, that is, arpeggios and chords. It does not make for an interesting output. The harmonic language is in itself very conventional so that even works written late in his life still have a 19th century feel to them. Hart was also obviously attached to English folk tunes. There are many settings, all aimed at a young market and therefore of easy to intermediate technical difficulty. The three books of *English Folk-Songs* published by Stainer & Bell contain an introduction written by Hart, addressed 'To the Young Musician' and extolling the virtues of Folk-Songs in general and English Folk-Songs in particular. At one point Hart makes a political point:

> ..they are all real English tunes, and so they belong as much to Australia, New Zealand and Canada as to England. French children have French folk-songs, Russian children have Russian folk-songs-indeed every nation has its own national music.

Hart's love of English folk-music extended to the composition of larger works such as *Strawberry Fair. Folk-Song Fantasy on the West Country Folk-Song* as well as *Cold Blows the Wind To-night, True Love. Folk-Song Fantasy on the Somerset Folk-Song*, both published in Australia in the early '20s. These, although obviously more ambitious than simple one or two page settings, are still, pianistically, of only moderate scope and interest and therefore only marginally more interesting.

There is, however, one set of piano pieces that seem to stand aside from the bulk of Hart's output for piano. This is a set of fourteen short pieces entitled *Fourteen Experiments* and dated 1917. Here Hart essentially tries his hand at assymetric bars and phrase constructions as well as occasionally delving into unrelated triads. As such, these pieces are important in the history of Australian piano music. True, what may have been experimental in Europe in 1917 is hardly that in Hart's hands. Nevertheless, this is a cycle of piano pieces that would work in a recital situation and that are worth publishing. We have a fine copy in Hart's hand. The pieces are mostly of one page duration.

1. Moderato. A kind of choral in 5/4.
2. Andante. A tranquillo piece with the time signature 3/4 4/4 (i.e. 7/4 consisting of 3+4)
3. Misurato. A piece in 5/4/ with the odd 4/4 bar insertion.
4. 4/4 3/4 time (i.e. 7/4 consisting of 4+3)
5. A piece in 4/4/ but experimenting with the harmony in a relatively mild fashion.
6. Moderato consisting of 6+4+3+6.
7. "The Travelling Man", bars of 4/4 and 5/4 intertwined.
8. Allegretto of 5+4
9. Moderato in 4/4 but using some unexpected harmonies, but firmly anchored in B Major.
10. Shifting harmonies, 4/4/ and 3/4 freely intermixed.
11. Lento, somewhat like the previous piece.
12. Quasi scherzando. Parallel 7th chords.

13.Superimposition of 5 and 4

14. Return to the mood of the first piece. 3,4 and 5 mixed.

The pieces are all of very moderate difficulty. Hart's complete piano legacy is still awaiting thorough exploration.

Dorian Le Gallienne (1915 –1963)

Le Gallienne was an influential teacher and was spoken of very highly and with great affection by all who worked with him at Melbourne University, including Don Banks, Keith Humble, James Penberthy and Helen Gifford. In his role as a music critic, he was acutely aware of the poor state of art music in Australia and of his responsibilities in that direction. He was a great lover of the Australian bush, but this love never appeared in his music as any obvious or cheap display of jingoism.

He suffered from poor health and died relatively young and resultantly his output is not large. The language is lean and muscular, with elements of tonal ambiguity and bitonality ever present, though usually strongly resolved. His command of larger forms, of which his Symphony is the prime example, is evident in the Sonata for piano. It must be said that Le Gallienne's inclusion in this book rests solely on his Sonata, for there is little else for the instrument.

The incidental music to Macbeth, written as a piano score, consists solely of beginnings and 'etc' signs. There is a charming *Nocture in C Sharp Minor*, which used to be widely played as it was published in an examination book by the A.M.E.B.. An unpublished *Symphonic Study for piano* (one of the manuscript copies has '1940' on it) actually supports an argument I make below about Le Gallienne's piano music: it is unusually sparse and austere as a purely pianistic work and almost looks to me as a short score of an unrealized orchestral work. Nevertheless, there is sufficient material in this manuscript to produce a performance copy of this work. Both here and in the Sonata and late Sonatina, Le Gallienne is the exception that proves the rule, for he writes successful music for the piano without being a pianist himself and without the music being particularly pianistic. Some short works held at the State Library of Victoria are omitted from the discussion below. There is also a set of Three Piano Pieces, from 1946, the first of which contains some seeds of the Sonata, with wide spaced texture,

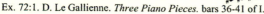

Ex. 72:1. D. Le Gallienne. *Three Piano Pieces*. bars 36-41 of I.

whilst the second utilizes counterpoint in which the lines are already doubled in major thirds.

Ex. 73:1. D. Le Gallienne. *Three Piano Pieces*. bars 3-6 of II.

The last piece of this set fills the complete spectrum of dynamics from a dead moment where the composer asks the pianist to play 'with no expression' to a full-blooded *ffff*.

Sonata for Piano (1951)

1. Allegro Moderato
2. Alla Marcia
3. Molto Lento

The composer Robert Hughes supplied this note for the sonata in the copy produced for the Australian Music Fund:

> The three movements of this sonata were composed during the latter part of 1950 and early in 1951. Although the composer had not written a finale, he permitted public performance of the completed movements as an unfinished sonata. David Fox played it at a concert of Le Gallienne's music in Melbourne on 9th July 1951. At that time, there was no doubt that he had planned a work in four movements, but there is no evidence that it was ever completed. No sketches for a finale could be found among the manuscripts collected after his death in 1963.

Le Gallienne wasn't a pianist and it is quite possible that he simply ran out of compositional steam, writing for an instrument that he perhaps didn't have a strong affinity with. The work functions surprisingly well in its incomplete state and lends a rather sombre air to the overall effect. The other factor might have been the substantial weight and nature of the second movement, meant originally to function as a scherzo, and which might have stolen the thunder from the originally planned finale.

The writing is clean and linear and almost suggests that an orchestral palette, with much implied doubling and colouristic venturing, was in the composer's inner ear when composing this piece. Some of the longer piano chords seem to be begging for orchestral crescendi and percussion rolls – but perhaps this is simply a peculiarity of my own inner ear.

The Sonata begins very simply in defining the thematic material.

Ex. 74:1. D. Le Gallienne. *Sonata.* bars 1-5 of I.

But this almost folksong like opening leads to quite violent outbursts soon after.

Ex. 75:1. D. Le Gallienne. *Sonata.* bars 29-32 of I.

and the raw material is piled up into quite tense contrapuntal overlays. There are orchestrally driven episodes reminiscent of Shostakovich, here and in the widely separated tessitura characteristic of the 2nd movement.

Ex. 76:1. D. Le Gallienne. *Sonata.* bars 189-192 of I.

This second movement consists of an angular march followed by a slightly slower 3/4 in which the right hand plays sometimes awkward parallel triads (in an imaginary trumpet section) while the left hand imitates pizzicato lower strings.

Ex. 77:1. D. Le Gallienne. *Sonata.* bars 34-36 of II.

There is a still slower central section, followed by a violent return to the two quicker ideas. This second movement is a large statement and made the composition of a finale a problematic proposition.

The third movement is another example of the composer's linear approach to the keyboard, this time in a very expressive mode:

Ex. 78:1. D. Le Gallienne. *Sonata.* bars 23-25 of III.

If to some ears this very fine Sonata ends somewhat unsatisfactorily, I suggest a solution below.

The *Sonatina (1962)* was written very close to the composer's death and represents his final thoughts on the piano. It is still unpublished and this needs to be rectified in the near future. On the manuscript there is a note by composer Robert Hughes, dated 1964, and obviously another result of his tidying up Le Gallienne's manuscripts:

> The passage contained within the brackets on page 5 is drawn from material in the pencil sketch and is inserted as a possible completion of the gap in the original manuscript. Bars five and six of this passage are not original but follow the material as a suitable bridge to Bar seven of the original pencil sketch.

For the moment, and until the pencil sketches can be restudied, we should accept Robert Hughes' solution. He knew La Gallienne well and presumably had insight into his colleague's methods. Besides, what he suggests works very well. The Sonatina begins, like the Sonata, very simply, with parallel movement in octaves.

Ex. 79:1. D. Le Gallienne. *Sonatina.* bars 1-6.

It continues in much the same linear vein, and in a style very close to that of the Sonata, both in subject matter as well as in the essentially two-part counterpoint, which constitutes much of the work. The Sonatina is in one movement. It is not a light piece meant for young players and is a serious and sometimes sombre essay gradually winding down via a Hindemithian path to a cadence in B flat major.

Ex. 80:1. D. Le Gallienne. *Sonatina.* bars 115-120.

It struck me, while playing through it, that this piece may well be the way to 'complete' the unfinished Sonata, if one wanted to somehow do so. The Sonatina certainly fits well stylistically into the world of the Sonata and returns to the mood and texture that opens the Sonata. It must at least be a possibility.

(ii) Composers Looking Back: Late Romantics and the Nineteenth-Century Legacy

Many of the composers from this early period such as Ernest Hutcheson, George Boyle, Percy Grainger, Frederick Septimus Kelly and Alfred Hill, like their English counterparts went to Germany to study. For slightly younger composers such as Frank Hutchens, Katharine Parker, Dulcie Holland, it then became the norm to study in England.

Throughout this book emerges the question of what an "Australian composer" actually is? Arthur Benjamin is a case in point. After leaving Australia for England he returned only once in 1950 for the premiere of his Piano Concerto; he nonetheless remained interested in Australian music as seen in his active promotion of Australian music through the organization of concerts at Australia House.

Pianists

Hutcheson and Boyle, although separated here for reasons of chronology are easily viewed as a pair due to the parallel nature of their careers and the fact that they were close friends who assisted each other during the course of their professional lives. Both studied in Germany and went on to build their careers in the United States never returning to Australia permanently. Both are now almost completely forgotten in Australia. Their stature in America can be seen in the premiere of Boyle's Piano Concerto with the New York Philharmonic. The composer played the solo part with Ernest Hutcheson conducting.

Ernest Hutcheson (1871 – 1956)

Ernest Hutcheson's career was roughly contemporaneous with that of Boyle. Teaching, just as Boyle, at the highest level of institutions in the United States, Hutcheson's career was more as a writer on music for the piano (the texts are still standard reference works to this day) and as an administrator rather than as a composer; among his appointments was a deanship and later presidency at Juilliard. Hutcheson's lineage is with Reinecke and the Leipzig Conservatorium. His graduation work included a performance of his own Piano Concerto. His output is smaller than Boyle's.

The music is very much of its time, as Hutcheson was by no means an innovator. Playing through *Four Pieces for Pianoforte Op.10* (Andante Tranquillo, Capriccio, Sarabande, Scherzo), *Two Pieces for Piano Op.11* (Prelude, Caprice) and *Three Piano Pieces Op.12* (Idyll, Humoresque, Album Leaf) one is struck, though, by its professional sheen, so often missing from Australian music of that same period back home. The Sarabande is very much a ninteteenth-century imagining of a faded but nostalgically desirable world, but the Prelude is still a strong piece today, an exercise of repeating a melodic idea with ever changing accompaniment:

Ex. 81:1. E.Hutcheson. *Four Pieces for Pianoforte Op. 10,* bars 46-49 (III).

The early Piano Sonata (Hutcheson was sixteen) does not strictly belong in this book; it was written in 1887 and has remained unpublished to this day. I suspect that this fate is deserved although the piece does show a fine command of the keyboard as well as a clear mind for form. Too much of the piece is routine passage work, but of the four movements, perhaps the slow one could be revived today, with its Schumanesque atmosphere:

Ex. 82:1. E.Hutcheson. *E Flat Major Sonata,* bars 53-58 (II).

Why did musicians of the high caliber of Boyle and Hutcheson leave their native land and work elsewhere? The answer in their case, and in the case of many other and later composers was simply lack of opportunity as well as, in the early days of the century, lack of training possibilities and lack of professional ensembles and orchestras. The first professional generation of Australian composers and pianists naturally felt this most keenly, and included apart from the two mentioned above, Grainger and Benjamin. As late as 1948, and thanks largely to the efforts of Louis Lavater, by then eighty two years old, efforts were still being made to create government subsidies to discourage the musical brain drain out of Australia. It was an ongoing problem for most of the twentieth century for Australian music. Many of these composers were 'acquired' by other countries as their own and it is common to see these names listed as American or English composers in various reference books, and of course in many ways this is correct.

Frederick Septimus Kelly (1881 – 1916)

One of the earliest examples of the Australian virtuoso pianist-composer, Frederick Septimus Kelly is largely an unknown figure in Australian music. The reasons for his obscurity are various. In addition to his musical activities, Kelly had significant athletic prowess and was, in fact, an Olympic level sculler and won a gold medal in 1908. Despite being active in the highest circles of music making, including musicians such as Casals, d'Aranyi, Tovey and Grainger, his sporting success and private means somehow guaranteed that he was not taken seriously as an artist by succeeding generations. In Australia's fledgling years as a nation, Kelly's social class caused him to naturally gravitate to England and to all intents and purposes he became an English musician; in fact, he barely thought of himself as an Australian. Perhaps this, more than any other factor, sealed Kelly's reputation in his native land. His meticulously kept diaries are a fascinating account of music in a particular time and place. Kelly was killed in action during World War I.

The *Waltz-Peagant Op.2b* is dedicated to Donald Tovey who was a friend of Kelly's for a period in England. The opus is really a set of separate waltzes, for which the obvious model seems to have been Brahms.

Ex. 83:1. F. S. Kelly, *Waltz-Pageant*. bars 1-4 of V.

Essentially there are nine discrete waltzes and at the end, the first waltz is recapitulated to round the cycle off. There is probably no reason why separate waltzes cannot be performed. An early work, even in Kelly's short life, these occasionally suffer from somewhat awkward modulations.

Schott published this opus as well as the one that followed it, the *Allegro de Concert, Op.3*. No other piano music appeared in print. The *Allegro de Concert* is dedicated to Grainger, and it is tempting to speculate what Percy thought of it, as it strongly suggests Chopin, who is by the far the most pervasive influence in Kelly's music; here, both the melodic substance as well as the pianistic figurations are both Chopinesque and the 3/4 time constantly suggests the waltzes of Chopin.

Among the other shorter works, is a manuscript inscribed "Scherzo Etude", but it cannot possibly refer to the piece under it, which is a fugue in Eb Major!

Ex. 84:1. F. S. Kelly, *Scherzo-Etude*. Fugue Exposition, bars 1-17.

Polyphony is a rarity in Kelly's output and this may be an interesting work to programme.

The *Irish Air & Variations* is very early (pre-20th century) and strictly outside the orbit of this book. Anyway, it is not very good, the variations tending to restate and restate the theme with varying elaborations around it. There are a few other manuscript trifles as well.

Kelly's reputation must rest on the two large cycles of pieces that remain. The first is the set of Twelve Studies, (labeled Op.9 on one of the manuscript copies). The Studies are modeled on Chopin in that they each seize upon a particular pianistic problem and then exploit it throughout the whole of the piece. There seem to be two copies of the Studies, one a more or less final copy, the other with more corrections and insertions. An edition incorporating all the ossias by the composer is readily achievable and should be done, as this is historically an Australian document of some value. The harking back to Chopin, rather than using Liszt as model for Studies seems a deliberate choice; Liszt of course used the genre of 'Studies' more as studies in composition than in piano playing; but there is some evidence to suggest that Kelly did not like the Liszt that he was exposed to, and thought that the music was vulgar and showy.

The Studies – technically – cover quite a wide gamut of pianistic activity:

#1: an obvious homage to Chopin's own first study.

#2: Scorrevole in running right hand semiquavers.
#3: a study in thirds
#4: this one features some wide stretches and is quite difficult. The raw idea is exploited in both hands and eventually simultaneously. It is one of the more interesting of the set.
#5: an Adagio trill study.
#6: A strongly melodic, impassioned etude:

Ex. 85:1. F. S. Kelly, *12 Studies for the Pianoforte, Op. 9. Study no. 6,* bars 1-10.

The sound world of the whole set can be gleaned from this quotation.
#7: a piece in which the right hand plays in 5/8, with the left hand in 3/4 at the same time:

Ex. 86:1. F. S. Kelly, *12 Studies for the Pianoforte, Op. 9. Study no. 7,* bars 1-8.

#8: this is quite like a Nocturne by John Field or Chopin, in layout as well as acoustic result.
#9: possibly the most difficult of the whole set, with contrary motion arpeggios and incessant passagework in both hands, *leggiero.*
#10: a chord study in very full sonority.
#11: an etude in alternate hand patterns.

#12: a fiery but conventional piece with many routine scale passages.

The *24 Monographs Op.11* is modeled on the Chopin Preludes, and really is another set of studies, but on a more miniaturistic scale. Sometimes Kelly casts the net wider, and we get echoes of Brahms as well. The cycle suffers from lack of memorable melodic material. But just sometimes – not often enough unfortunately – there are departures from the routine. #9, for example, uses 7-bar phrases as its building blocks.

Ex. 87:1. F. S. Kelly. *Twenty-four Monographs for Pianoforte Solo, Op. 11. No. 9,* bars 1-7.

When Kelly actually abandons his endless successions of triads and ventures into something more adventurous and tantalizing,

Ex. 88:1. F. S. Kelly. *Twenty-four Monographs for Pianoforte Solo, Op. 11. No. 16,* bars 32-34.

one deeply regrets that he didn't live long enough to explore this potential world in his music.

The Sonata is incomplete. The first two movements are complete, but the manuscript breaks off after a substantial portion of the Minuet, and I would have thought that a fourth movement was the original plan. The opening movement and subsequent slow movement contain all the notes, but almost no performance indications. These could be surmised and editorially reconstructed. Perhaps the two movements could be performed separately.

The Sonata, broken off as a result of Kelly's untimely death, illustrates Kelly's quandary most eloquently. Here we are, in 1916, the world is at war, European modernism has made a brilliant and exciting entry into the world of art-music; yet this composer chooses in his last work to produce something that sounds like early Chopin, and maybe even Hummel, with endless sequences, the very bane of the Kelly output.

Ex. 89:1. F. S. Kelly. *Sonata in F minor for Pianoforte,* bars 1-6.

Regrettably, one has to come to the conclusion that, interesting and important and fascinating as Francis Septimus Kelly's life was, in the end the product is closer to that of a very talented amateur/dilettante; but one that needs nonetheless to be studied, published and performed.

Judging by the dates on the manuscripts of this set, Kelly composed very quickly, quite possibly only writing each etude down after it was fully formed in his head and/or via improvisation.

Kelly's studies at the Frankfurt Conservatorium were with Ivan Knorr, who was regarded as a master of counterpoint. No doubt this accounts for Kelly's graduation piece being the "Theme, Variations and Fugue for Two Pianos".

Kelly was essentially a conservative composer, although we know that he was certainly aware of music by composers such as Schoenberg, Ornstein, Ravel, Debussy and Cyril Scott. Yet they do not appear as influences in his output at all.

Percy Grainger (1882 – 1961)

So much has been written about Grainger that one hesitates to add more, but no book on Australian piano music can be complete without some reflection on this strange figure.

For someone who on the surface seems to be a real model of the composer-pianist, additionally having even studied with a figure such as Ferruccio Busoni, Grainger has a small output of original music. Moreover, he had an instinctive distaste for the piano, which he saw as a really limited instrument, so all the 'dished-up' versions (Percy's own term) of works for solo piano were possibly done for commercial reasons.

There is firstly the question of all the folksong settings. How does one regard them? Are they sufficiently tempered with Grainger's own style to be listed as – at least partially – original works? If they are, why is Grainger constantly tampering with them and arranging them yet further, for various combinations of instruments? Was he dissatisfied with the piano versions? Was his aesthetic such that there was no such thing as a definitive piano version of a work, or definitive version in any arrangement? Was it a fixation on one piece for a while? Was it poverty of ideas? Most of the piano solos are in fact arrangements of works originally written for other instruments. There are a handful of pre-1900 pieces originally for piano.

One could further argue that some of Grainger's original music is very much like his folksong arrangements. Thus, is not the very popular and attractive *Colonial Song* very much like, say, the setting of *Danny Boy (Irish Tune from County Derry)?* where the original becomes a recreation of a sort of folk melody. Even the *Colonial Song* (sometimes listed as *Sentimentals No.1*), exists in multiple versions. The result is that there is almost no Grainger that is exclusively and recognizably for solo piano, a strange position for someone who was in his day a world-famous pianist! Another example might be *Handel in the Strand*, a very well-known piece; but it was composed as early as 1911, with the version for solo piano only appearing in 1930; originally called *Clog Dance* by Grainger, it is yet another instance of a composed quasi-folk piece. Clearly, however, black and white classification is difficult to achieve! The clunky chords predominant in this piece, and a defining feature of Grainger's approach to the piano, may also be found in the music of friends and imitators, such as Kitty Parker and Alex Burnard.

The British folksong settings are very well known: there is the ubiquitous *Country Gardens*, together with other *Morris Dances*. The settings tend to be very bouncy and quick or else somewhat slow and sentimental. A favourite device is to have short, full staccato chords under the melodic line. The printed scores still look fresh and idiosyncratic, with Grainger's rather quirky use of the English language and very precise pedaling instructions.

Ex. 90:1. P. Grainger. *Colonial Song,* bars 1-6.

Ex. 91:1. P. Grainger. *Irish Tune from County Derry,* bars 18-21.

In his *Lullaby from Tribute to Foster* uses the sostenuto pedal to create a harmonic resonance in the background of the piece:

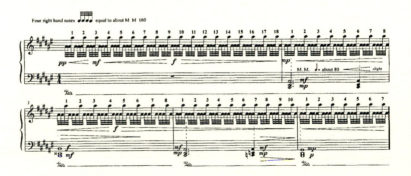

Ex. 92:1. P. Grainger. *Lullaby* from *Tribute to Foster,* bars 1-5.

The Foster melody is surrounded by a kind of gamelan-like haze throughout. As far as Grainger was concerned, setting a Foster melody was not unlike setting a 'real' folk-tune. He treated Gershwin and Brahms similarly, as great melodists and therefore grist for his compositional mill. There are also more conventional paraphrases from Tchaikovsky, Bach, Handel and Richard Strauss, that at least plug much more comfortably into the tradition of the great romantic pianist/transcribers. Some of these 'rambles' are deeply offensive today: a piece called *In Dahomey (Cakewalk Smasher)* says under the title: "Using tune from Darkie Comic Opera "In Dahomey" by Will Marion Cook and tunes from Arthur Pryor's *A coon band contest.*

The Immovable Do (or *The Cyphering C*) is an interesting concept and could have produced, in other hands, a far more interesting and adventurous piece; in Grainger's piano solo version – 'dished-up by the tone-wright' (i.e. composer) seven years after the original version, it turns out to be yet another folk-like piece saturated with four-bar phrases.

There are some musicians in Australia who look on Grainger as a kind of father figure, a parallel to Charles Ives. But Grainger is far too conventional a figure musically to be regarded in such a light. Playing through Grainger's complete pinao music, as I've done for this book, one is both exhilarated and depressed: exhilarated because the high latent energy in the music is still vibrantly there, as well as sheer exuberance of the settings and the comfortable and enjoyable use of the keyboard; depressing, because so much of it is numbingly the same, over and over again. And all of Grainger's piano works are essentially miniatures, only lasting a few minutes - he never attempted an original piano work in an extended form after 1900.

Grainger's colourful life has lent a kind of aura to his personality, and he himself regarded his sexual preferences as important to understanding his music. I am personally somewhat dubious about this level of self-absorption; moreover it is really difficult to regard Grainger as a founding father of Australian piano music, given his really awful racial theories, his various sado-masochistic practices and expressed preferences for incestuous love.

Katherine Parker (1886 – 1971)

Almost as a postscript to Grainger, one should say a few words about Katherine (Kitty) Parker, the Tasmanian-born composer and pianist, who studied first at the Melbourne Conservatorium and later became a student of Percy Grainger in London. Although obviously gifted both as pianist and composer, Parker's private life, from the little we know of it, was somewhat turbulent and unsuccessful; she eventually returned to Australia and taught in Tasmania for a number of years, slipping into almost total obscurity. Grainger thought highly of some of her pieces and even orchestrated one of them (*Down Longford Way*),

included in a recent *Anthology of Australian Piano Music* published by the
Australian Music Examinations Board, (which I happened to edit). It is not
especially surprising that Grainger approved of this piece, since it is so very like
his own music. Parker was published in England by six of the top publishers,
but somehow, neither this fact nor Percy's advocacy seem to have helped her
cause. She was apparently subject to depression and self-doubt as well as ill-
health, so sadly never realized her full potential.

The *Four Musical Sketches* (1928) consist of *: A Patchwork of Shadows; Down
Longford Way; The Red Admiral; and One Summer Day*. The piano writing is
extremely effective and felicitous and one gets some idea of how Parker played
the piano. The opening of *Down Longford Way* is as good an illustration as any
of this and of her link with Grainger:

Ex. 93:1. K. Parker. *Down Longford Way,* bars 1-3.

Of the remaining extant music (and it is entirely possible that she composed
more which is yet to be unearthed), there is only a Nocturne from 1925, which
exhudes a faded charm redolent more of John Field than Frederic Chopin, and
Arc-En-Ciel, Valse Ballet, from 1936. The latter is a kind of concert waltz,
which Kitty had hoped that Grainger would orchestrate for her; he refused,
either trying to goad her into doing it herself, or else because this piece was less
to his liking than the earlier music. Without making excessive demands, the
piece nevertheless expects a developed pianism to make its full effect. The
Waltz is a cross between film music and cocktail genre of the time.

George Boyle (1886 – 1948)

I have had to agonize over the perennial problem in writing this book: what to
include or exclude and on what basis? I am not talking about issues of quality,
which, though to some extent subjective, are at least fairly straightforward. No,
it is the thorny question of the expatriate composer that is the most difficult
question of all. Take the case of George Boyle, fairly typical of this problem.

Certainly, he was Australian born, a child prodigy who toured his native country
as a youth. But then, in 1905, at the age of nineteen, he left, never to return, and

made his career as a composer and concert pianist, largely in the United States. His studies with Busoni between 1905 and 1910 seem to have influenced his performance style much more than his approach to composition; possibly Busoni's cerebral and philosophic approach was daunting to the young student. But from Busoni he inherited the massively colouristic playing style and that, in turn, filtered into his music.

Boyle's compositional style, therefore, is in a grandiose late-romantic fashion. The output falls naturally into three categories: the large scale works which include a Sonata, a Ballade, a Suite for Two Pianos, and the Piano Concerto; pieces in smaller forms, but for concert use such as the *Habanera*, Nocturne, a *Marionette Suite* and many others; and finally, pedagogic pieces.

The Boyle works are now difficult to locate, but perhaps some of them are ripe for republication. The *Habanera* is an obvious candidate, beginning with major/minor ambiguity perhaps learnt from Busoni:

Ex. 94:1. G. Boyle. *Habanera,* bars 1-7.

an idea which is developed during this quite extensive piece.

Ex. 95:1. G. Boyle. *Habanera,* bars 80-84.

The *Three Short Pieces* are romantic miniatures, pleasant enough, but hardly substantial. The Gavotte is a very typical of its day in the way that older dance forms were treated as somehow quaint and adorned with various levels of virtuosity. So here Boyle treats the raw idea with an almost Rachmaninovian approach:

Ex. 96:1. G. Boyle. *Gavotte and Musette,* bars 31-34.

Similarly, the *Five Pieces for Piano* are a conglomerate of unrelated pieces. The first, *Summer* reminded me of Cyril Scott's *Lotus Land* in its languidity

Ex. 97:1. G. Boyle. *Five Piano Pieces,* bars 17-20.

and with some harmonic progressions close to Ravel. The Valsette is miniature only in mood and is light in tone, but in reality a concert waltz of some length. *Improvisation* is quite chromatic, and almost Scriabinesque at times in its approach to texture.

Ex. 98:1. G. Boyle. *Five Piano Pieces,* bars 1-4 of III.

The last two pieces are, I feel, less interesting. The Minuet is another example of old forms reused, described above, and *Cascade* is a virtuosic showpiece, without much substance. But the two large scale works of Boyle are another thing entirely. The Ballade written for Leopold Godowsky, is a big dramatic piece full of heroic gestures and orchestral pianism. It is twenty nine pages long, building to huge climaxes. The generally dark colour of the piece may gleaned from the very opening.

Ex. 99:1. G. Boyle. *Ballade,* bars 1-8.

The Sonata was dedicated to Ernest Hutcheson. A work in three movements, it is perhaps in a more optimistic mood than the Ballade. A dotted feeling of a march dominates much of the whole work. The first movement is a more stately tempo than the last, but both movements are linked by this dotted rhythm, which is also apparent in the slow movement. Here, the language is somewhat darker again

Ex. 100:1. G. Boyle. *Sonata for Piano,* bars 1-8 of II.

and moves to dissonances not usual in Boyle.

Ex. 101:1. G. Boyle. *Sonata for Piano,* bars 54-57 of II.

Both the first and last movements move into large expansive writing for the piano. In the last, brittle and aggressively virtuosic passages prevail, with sometimes wide spacing.

Ex. 102:1. G. Boyle. *Sonata for Piano,* bars 36-37 of III.

Like the Ballade, the palette is obviously orchestral and big pianism is required to bring this work off spanning over fifty six pages of shifting patterns and effects.

Ex. 103:1. G. Boyle. *Sonata for Piano,* bars 125-128 of I.

Arthur Benjamin (1893 – 1960)

Although Benjamin lived in London virtually all his professional life, he always regarded himself as an Australian composer. His desire to identify with his homeland manifested itself in activities that involved organizing concerts of Australian music and trying to assist Australian composers who came to

London. At the same time there is absolutely nothing in his output that is at all –
nor does he attempt to be – in any obvious sense Australian.

Arthur Benjamin was a fine pianist and his music for the instrument
demonstrates this. Plowing through reams and reams of Australian piano music
while working on this book, it was always clear that some music leapt out from
the page at the performer as quality piano music; and Benjamin's output
certainly does that. He tended to work at different levels of difficulty for his
potential markets. There are a number of compositions obviously pedagogic in
intent. For these he even sometimes wrote prefaces directed at young players.
Many of these works have appeared on examination lists in Australia and are
well known to teachers; over the years I remember editing pieces such as a
March and *Dance at Dawn* for various collections. Benjamin never wrote down
to children and his music for young players in not condescending or patronising.

Then there are intermediate level pieces. The publisher Winthrop Rogers
published so-called *Concert Series for Piano*, which actually favoured
intermediate difficulty music for student pianists. Benjamin was represented by
two works in this series: a *Scherzino* (played by hundreds of examination
candidates) and a *Chinoiserie (Gavotte & Musette)*. Of the latter, the only
Chinese aspect I could find was the odd exposed perfect fourth! On this level,
there is also a charming *Siciliana*, written for the pianist Lance Dossor.

There are two works that seriously represent Benjamin. The first is a Suite from
1926, written for Harriet Cohen, which demonstrates Benjamin's established
place in the English music. The Prelude is a quick-running piece that now and
then approaches bitonality:

Ex. 104:1. A. Benjamin. *Suite for Piano - Prelude*, bars 17-20.

The following Air is somewhat like Vaughan Williams in its use of modality
and in its large span chords in the left hand, almost begging for a string
orchestra scoring. Then there is a Toccata:

Ex. 105:1. A. Benjamin. *Suite for Piano - Toccata,* bars 16-18.

demonstrating the stretch of Benjamin's hand and momentary bitonality, which is as far as Benjamin was prepared to go. The Suite has the refinement of a Ravel, as well as the occasional bite of the then modernist harmony:

Ex. 106:1. A. Benjamin. *Suite for Piano - Toccata,* bars 75-76.

The Suite ends with an Epilogue, which is in reality a canon, almost all of which is on the white notes only.

The *Pastorale, Arioso and Finale* (1948) is Benjamin's major work for solo piano, running to twenty four printed pages. The opening Pastorale is not always 'English' or 'nice',

Ex. 107:1. A. Benjamin. *Pastorale, Arioso and Finale,* bars 31-36 of I.

indeed, it is sometimes polyphonic as well.

Ex. 108:1. A. Benjamin. *Pastorale, Arioso and Finale,* bars 86-89 of I.

The Pastorale even has a cadenza, lifting it well out of what one would expect. The following Arioso is not unlike the previously mentioned Aria, but this time the melodic line is in octaves and the texture is much denser; the left hand, once again, utilizes chords that are mostly fifths and tenths, but there is also a middle section in a faster tempo:

Ex. 109:1. A. Benjamin. *Pastorale, Arioso and Finale,* bars 29-30 of II.

The Finale is a fast Allegro. Here and elsewhere, I came to the conclusion that Benjamin must have had thin, slender hands, as the lines constantly interweave and such close crossover and interlacing is only possible for a pianist so equipped, but very awkward for players with bulkier apparatus. This movement is generally lighter and cleaner, somewhat like the Toccata from the Suite, but it does drift into a 5/8 sequence:

Ex. 110:1. A. Benjamin. *Pastorale, Arioso and Finale.* bars 8-11 of III.

This work is now largely forgotten, but is a major piano work by an Australian composer who lived most of his professional life as an English composer.

Alex Burnard (1900 – 1971)

Anyone who studied at the State Conservatorium of Music in Sydney during Burnard's teaching years there would vividly remember a kindly man with a pipe who took endless harmony and counterpoint classes to often unwilling or obtuse performance students. Composition as a subject was not available, and working with Burnard was often the closest that one could get to studying composition. Alex never pushed his own barrow as a composer, and the richly illustrated lessons with him were quotations not from his own works, but the works of composers he admired or knew personally, or had studied with: much from Peter Warlock (Philip Heseltine), whose music he knew well enough to regurgitate on the spot, sometimes from his mentor and teacher Vaughan Williams, occasionally from Delius and Grainger, and a huge amount from Bach, whose music he knew really well. I first became aware of Burnard as a composer when, during a piano recital given by Raymond Hanson, there was a bracket of chorale-preludes by Burnard, which Hanson introduced as " amongst the best chorale-preludes ever composed". Until that instance, I – and many of my student friends – had regarded Burnard as our harmony teacher, who might make some harmless jokes and puns and even flirt a little with his female students ("you can't be pure and interesting", he would say, and then add: "harmonically speaking, of course", followed by a couple of nervous puffs on his pipe). His teaching activity was not necessarily equated with being a composer; that was the tone and the culture of the day – mid-century Australia.

Alex had large hands, and his piano music demonstrates this quite clearly. In his *Further Scenes from Childhood* there is a *Walking Tune* dedicated to Miriam Hyde, who sent me a copy and commented that she could never perform it as the stretches were huge for her hands.

Many of the pieces are affectionately dedicated to friends and students, sometimes light-heartedly, sometimes heart-felt. His wit and wide conquest of technique thus appears in the *March Op.40*, No.8 – part of a Suite. The full title is *March of the Non-Dangerous Inmates* and the middle section is named *Revivalist Trio (incorporating a nauseating Quodlibet)*. Burnard's own piano playing was full of Scotch snaps, double dotting, spiky staccato and constantly mixed articulations (all this witnessed during his Bach demonstrations), and the piano music is full of these characteristics too.

A piece from late in his life, *Faschingschwank aus Salzburg (Andante senza Funicolare)* is dedicated to "the God-being, in recollection of a strenuous arthritic trudge (in midwinter, funicular not functioning) through snow and ice up the rough mountain road to the old Archiepiscopal castle – and to what a view!"

Or, at the head of one of the *Three Preludes & Fugues Op.48*: *Allegro Comodo un poco Buffo*; at the end of the *Prelude*, Burnard writes on his manuscript "The

Prelude acts the part of Court Jester to the Fugue's pompous Pontiff, but still
with an occasional contemptuous intellectual flick of the bladder (16.4.71)". The
following *Double Fugue* is marked '*Lento Pomposo, Ponteficoso*'. Both *Prelude
and Fugue* are meticulously fingered throughout, so Burnard must have either
performed or else practised the work. At the end of the score, the teacher in him
triumphed, as there is a quick kind of sketchy analysis of the counterpoint of the
work. The seeming anachronism of writing a *Prelude and Fugue* in a given key
in 1970 must have been uppermost in Burnard's mind, for at the opening of
another Prelude in this opus he writes "something NEW, now, is something
OLD'.

Burnard did not publish during his lifetime – at first it was probably impossibly
difficult, then the War made it seem frivolous, and finally his music became
anachronistic and old-fashioned. It is only now, in hindsight of the whole
century that it becomes possible to look at Burnard's output and appreciate the
many positive qualities in it, without futile discourse on style. (Style: one of the
great political frauds and disguiser of content).

I suspect that Burnard was, by inclination and training, a traditionalist. An early
work from 1928, *Three Experimental Preludes*, has a subtitle: "Voices from the
Past". One of the Preludes is a setting of a Hampshire folktune "I sowed the
seeds of Love". At this remove, it is difficult for us to understand what was
experimental about these pieces; one can only guess that it was the super-
saturated harmony:

Ex. 111:1. A. Burnard. *Three Experimental Preludes*, bars 55-57 of III.

But such progressions are there even in folksong settings, for example in
Farewell My Dearest Nancy

Ex. 112:1. A. Burnard. *Farewell, my dearest Nancy*, bars 17-22.

(An eccentricity of some of the instrumental music is that sequential movements are sometimes for different forces; for example, the *Prelude & Fugue* on 'Aus Tiefer Noth' has a Prelude apparently for piano, but the *Fugue* is clearly for flute, clarinet and bassoon; perhaps the *Prelude* is too – it's written in three parts).

The various and often quite complex contrapuntal works now need to be typeset and performed so that they can be revalued and considered as a serious part of the Australian art-music output for piano. Even Alex's highly developed contrapuntal skills sometimes led him into impossibilities. An incomplete *Fugue in G Major* has, at the breaking-off point: 'Gorn- leave it!' The completed fugues require some dexterity:

Ex. 113:1. A. Burnard. *Fugue* from *Prelude and Fugue in D major,* bars 16-20.

Simpler works, such as the *Twelve Folk-Songs Settings* (a rather Grainger-esque effort) written for the young pianist Gordon Watson, although virtually unreadable in their present form, could be realized fairly easily. One of the tunes in this collection, *Tarry Trowsers*, is the theme of an important set of *Variations* by Raymond Hanson, a student of Burnard.

Burnard, author of a fine textbook on harmony which was known and used by many a student, had a very tidy and organized mind; hence, it is hardly surprising that he was drawn to writing tightly controlled contrapuntal music, and it is on the success or failure of his fugues for piano that his reputation essentially rests, with folk settings, chorale preludes, suites and other pieces taking second place.

The music is strongly tonal and comes from the expected world of English music of the earlier part of the 20th century- the world of Vaughan Williams, Grainger, Delius, Warlock, always tempered by Burnard's contrapuntal skill:

Ex. 114:1. A. Burnard. *Brigg Fair*, bars 1-7.

At the same time, there is nothing soft-edged or pretty about a Burnard score. In its own terms, it is rigorous in its technical application and is devoid of nice effects for their own sake, or sentimentality; some of it sounds old-fashioned to our ear, and was probably already old-fashioned when it was written; but it has its own integrity and now needs to be viewed on its own terms.

The harmonic palette is rich and often dense:

Ex. 115:1. A. Burnard. *Fuga Elegiaca*, bars 1-14.

And the composer is very fond of cross-phrasing and mixed articulation, both used to separate the voices:

Ex. 116:1. A. Burnard. *Puck* from *Seven Piano Preludes,* bars 1-5.
(another work dedicated to Hanson)

Ex. 117:1. A. Burnard. *To Leone Stredwick* from *Seven Piano Preludes,*
bars 1-4.

Representing as it does a particular musical inheritance and mind, coupled with
a real understanding of the piano, this composer's music is ripe for rediscovery.
Most of Burnard's manuscripts, including his quite lengthy correspondence with
Vaughan Williams, reside in his archive at Newcastle University.

Mainly Miniaturists

Louis Lavater (1867 – 1953)

Lavater's name is currently almost completely forgotten, yet in his day he was
not only well known and published but also a respected figure in the literary
world as well as a writer on music himself.

That he was limited as a composer he knew himself; his compositions
demonstrate a technical deficiency that was in the end a fatal flaw, both in a
structural sense and in the sense of a limited harmonic vocabulary. But it must
also be said that the best of his music is grateful to play and graceful to the ear.
At its peak it was the kind of work that one would expect from a gifted amateur,
in the very best meaning of that word. Yes, it was sometimes dated and pretty
but Biddy Allen wrote "never without humour". In the same article Allen also
says that "Louis Lavater died neglected and disappointed...musical Australia
gave him a raw deal" (Composer file: Australian Music Centre).

Lavater's *Valse Elégante* describes the music well whilst showing a departure from mere parlour music in the wide melodic leaps:

Ex. 118:1. L. Lavater. *Valse Elégante,* bars 1-6.

I have performed this and the *Valse Capricieuse* in concert (and on CD) and can vouch for their charm. On the other hand, many of the other miniatures are simply not worth the effort, veering from predictability to banality.

Miniatures such as *A Passing Fancy* and *Hornpipe* used to feature in eisteddfods at the hands of young players, especially the latter, allowing for the display of a flashy technique; but they are literally a passing fancy now.

It should be noted that the *Hornpipe in G* was published in a simplified edition (which all the children played), but there is also an original edition that is more of a concert piece and requires a span of a tenth and some facility with double notes. Lavater also published a book of Twelve Preludes in various keys some of which could be revived.

I was intrigued to see the manuscript of the Sonata in A for Piano, subtitled 'The Awakening'. There is probably a hidden programme that drove this piece:

1. Rondo alla Gavotta (Youth)
2. Elegia (Grief)
3. Allegro Moderato (The Awakening)

The manuscript also has a quotation from Mary Gilmore: "Nurse no long grief, Lest thy heart flower no more, Grief builds no barns, Its plough rusts at the door". There is no date on the manuscript; but I suspect from the hand that this is an early opus. Indeed, all hope of discovering an early major work by an Australian composer was dashed, alas! Except for the slow movement that might be worth an occasional airing, all that this Sonata displayed was an inability to cope with a larger form. There is also another, unfinished Sonata.

There is a Lavater Manuscript Collection lodged in the State Library of Victoria. The composer Robert Hughes (who although well-known to the author is not represented in this book since he didn't write for the piano) was apparently

asked by the Library to put this collection into some order. He left the following
note in the archive:

> As Lavater seems to have made a practice of re-using a work, or a
> single movement of a work, with only minor textual changes, and
> giving these a new title, I considered it best to place all these related
> manuscripts together. In these instances, I have assumed the definitive
> title to be that under which a work was published; for example, the
> Preludes for Piano, one of which was originally entitled *Meditation*;
> but which, in turn is a movement of a Suite for Piano. In the case of
> unpublished work, I have taken the title apparently most favoured by
> the composer.
>
> Manuscript works by composers other than Lavater...as Lavater also
> used pseudonyms in his works for publication, some of these pieces
> could be original compositions. Allans Music Pty. Ltd. should be able
> to supply a list of these pen names.

Hughes then supplies a list of the piano compositions, totaling some four dozen
pieces, although some are gathered into collections of preludes and waltzes, as
well as some incomplete compositions. Detailed work on Lavater obviously still
remains to be carried out.

Alfred Hill (1870 – 1960)

Alfred Hill was an early Australian composer who chose to remain in residence
in this country – and in New Zealand – instead of Europe, with a huge
commitment to the establishment of training for musicians. He was one of the
very first composers in this country to show an interest in indigenous music and
both he and wife Mirrie Hill devoted some considerable time and energies in
pursuit of this interest. If Hill had not turned out to be a composer, he might
well have become an anthropologist or even an ethnomusicologist. He was
genuinely concerned that the culture of our indigenous peoples was rapidly
disappearing. In an interview (Sydney Morning Herald, 18 April 1950), Hill
talked about some recordings brought back from Arnhem Land by
C.P.Mountford:

> There is enough material in these recordings to start an entirely
> Australian school of music, as different in idiom as Vaughan Williams
> and the English school from anything else. It's a gold mine.

Hill was not a performing pianist and the instrument to him was more of a day-
to-day tool than a creative enterprise. Nevertheless, he must have felt reasonably
proficient and familiar with the piano, as there is a huge number of miniatures
for the instrument, written, one feels, very quickly, perhaps even in one sitting.

Playing through the huge amount of music, one is struck by the immobility of it. Pieces written forty years apart have little or no discernable difference in approach. If anything, the earlier music is more interesting, so there is even the possibility that Hill burnt himself out. When one reads that later in life he converted string quartets into symphonies, such a suspicion does not seem without foundation. The music is quite firmly rooted in the 19th century world of Dvorak, Grieg and the like. The interest in indigenous music did not seem to produce any shift in compositional direction.

Although extensively published during his lifetime, there is still much Alfred Hill in manuscript and no doubt some enterprising soul(s) will rectify this situation.

How can one summarize the unpublished material? There is a plethora of preludes, as well as dance pieces; pieces with quasi-programmatic titles: *Afterglow, Happy Hearts, The Poet Dreams, Rendezvous, The Woodpecker, Through a Veil of Mist* and so on. These are all descendants from the 19th century albumleaf genre and are hardly more adventurous or interesting than that. To find that some of them were still being written well after World War II is a cause for some concern.

I seized on a Sonatina, but only one movement was complete and at any rate it was a piece obviously aimed at an educational market. There is quite an attractive setting of the traditional tune *Early One Morning*. I also found an "Adagio for an unwritten Sonata".

Ex. 119:1. A. Hill. *Adagio for an unwritten Sonata,* bars 1-7.

There are some Fugal pieces; a *Moto Perpetuo*; pieces relating to hope and victory during the War.

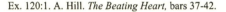

Ex. 120:1. A. Hill. *The Beating Heart,* bars 37-42.

Alfred never produced a major work for the piano – the closest one comes is a *Concert Waltz*, still unpublished, which is at least of some length, but alas, not substance. A piece written for Laurence Godfrey Smith, *A Day Dream* (6th August 1935) should see print. So should some of the folk settings.

Amongst the published works, apropos, there is one called *Highland Air (Waes for Me Charlie),* dedicated to Grainger, which is a masterly setting of this melody. There is another folk setting, *The Broken Ring" (Das zerbrochene Ringlein)* which is equally accomplished. If one adds little pieces such as Berceuse (also published in a slightly different form as *Slumber Music*), the *Valse Triste* from 1914 ,

Ex. 121:1. A. Hill. *Valse Triste,* bars 1-5.

Doves (dedicated to Frank Hutchens), *One Came Fluting* and *Retrospect,* there is a respectable body of music already in print. One perhaps needs to augment this body with some judicious selection from the manuscripts.

What is tantalizing, too, is the fact that there seems to be no reason why some works appeared in print and others did not. Perhaps the publishers couldn't cope with the sheer volume of output, especially as it became so predictable. If one ignores some of the dates on the compositions – that is, if one ignores the historical context, then it is possible to say that Hill represents a late romantic vestige in Australia, a sort of post-Dvorak idiom, created by somebody with a reliable and fluent technique, but little flexibility or capacity to change and evolve.

I suspect that Alfred Hill's ultimate importance is not so much as a pioneer composer in Australia but more as a foundation educationalist who was truly concerned with establishing proper professional practice in this country; equally admirable is his concern and interest in indigenous music and its preservation; he and his wife Mirrie were very early propagandists of such a notion, although it was Mirrie who did more for such a cause here; Alfred wrote more music linked to the New Zealand Maori culture.

The scholar Allan Stiles is currently carrying out a massive project on Alfred Hill, which will include a bio-bibliography and a complete listing of all of unpublished material. As this book goes to press, he has informed me that there is an Alfred Hill Piano Sonata, which he is publishing.

Frank Hutchens (1892 – 1965)

For many years, the names of Lindley Evans and Frank Hutchens were linked in the perception of the public. Both taught at the Conservatorium of Music in Sydney, both were composers, both were well known as pianists, teachers and adjudicators. Moreover, they had formed a two-piano team which stayed together for many years and for which both wrote music, contributing to the repertoire for two pianos as well as two pianos and orchestra.

Even the output for solo piano was not significantly different in style. Hutchens was certainly far more prolific than Evans and therefore contributed more music for young players as well. It is impossible to estimate how many children played *At the Bathing Pool*, just as one instance (incidentally, dedicated to Laurence Godfrey Smith who taught both Mirrie Hill and Donald Hollier). Many Hutchens pieces fall into that category of pieces that were used for teaching, certainly, but could also be regarded as legitimate, if miniature, concert works.

For some reason, many works by Frank Hutchens have a water or island connection. Perhaps a Freudian would make something of this, but I rather think that it more likely represents the comfortable feeling of post-colonial Australia – a huge island, far away from most of the world, peaceful and unthreatened. It was perhaps an age of innocence and many of Hutchens' pieces have an air of softness and even languidity about them.

Ex. 122:1. F. Hutchens. *The Enchanted Isle,* bars 17-19.

The names say it all: *The Island, Fairy Ships, The Enchanted Isle, At the Bathing Pool, In a Boat, Sea Music, The Voyage, Sea Fantasy, Lord Howe Island, The Surfer, Ship Ahoy, The Smuggler's Cave, By the River, Weeping Mist.* It seems obsessive.

The style is always strongly tonal, the harmonies obviously late romantic, with just a hint of sanitized impressionism, all of which coloured much Australian piano music in the first half of the twentieth century.

Hutchens was widely published in Australia with publishers with head offices in England. He was obviously in demand; yet there is a sizable folio of unpublished material that should be looked into. Some of this material contains no surprises, but merely confirms that Hutchens was essentially a miniaturist and harmonically quite timid and soft; indeed some of the unpublished pieces would not be astray in a cocktail lounge. But occasionally another side of the Hutchens persona peeks out. For example, a C major *Concert Prelude*, in rough but complete form, could make quite a stormy appearance in a programme. There is a *Ballade* from 1939 that runs to seven pages and contains some grander gestures from the Hutchens norm. A Toccata in the obligatory perpetual motion of semiquavers, which, if not flashy, is at least amiably busy. Among the papers, strangely enough there is a copied out item from Schumann's *Carnaval* - the *Paganini* movement. Does this bear some connection to one of the pieces? At this juncture we don't know.

The sea pieces seem to engender a more epic style. In the unpublished manuscripts there is a *Sea Fantasy*, similar in scope to the slightly enlarged canvas of *The Voyage* and *Sea Music*; although a similar larger use of the keyboard is also evident in the *Prelude Romantique* and the *Gavotte Brillante*:

Ex. 123:1. F. Hutchens. *Gavotte Brilliante*, bars 1-3.

The *Gavotte* also suggests that a more acidic almost 'Prokofievan' Hutchens could have emerged in a different musical environment. Among all these pieces there is a novelty of a work for right hand alone - a fairly rare occurrence in the piano literature generally. This is a piece called *Vienna Interlude* and is, predictably, in waltz rhythm, requiring some dash and agility.

Iris de Cairos-Rego (1894 – 1987)

Iris de Cairos-Rego, a child prodigy, was largely educated in Germany and England; she had the beginnings of a career in London and on the continent but returned to Australia because of lack of money. She was by all accounts a gifted pianist with a huge repertoire, which even included Gershwin, but was largely devoted to Liszt, Chopin, Rubinstein, Moszkowski, Grieg, Jonas, and other similar romantics.

Iris developed very early as a pianist and worked at the Conservatorium in Sydney during the thirties. At this time she moved to the Frensham (a prestigious private girl's school) School in Mittagong the stayed there for the rest of her professional life.

Unlike other members of her family, Iris managed to elevate an essentially salon style towards the concert platform. No doubt mirroring her own pianistic abilities (Alex Burnard dedicated a work to her), some of her pieces require a reasonable level of keyboard dexterity and control. The English publishers Chappell issued most of her music. Although her pieces are much closer to mainstream art music than other de Regos, she allowed Chappell to advertise her pieces as: *Meritorious and Melodious Teaching Pieces for Pianoforte.*

There are no large-scale works that we could discover, The connection with Great Britain is strong and pieces with titles such as *English June, Tarrel (A Highland Song), Graneen Vale* and *Country Dance* all support this view. Most of the other pieces are dance-like or song-like in character (*Canzonetta, Waltz Caprice,* Waltz, Arabesque) with a few descriptive 'character-pieces' such as *Firelight, Clouds* and *Albatross.* In the right setting, some of these pieces work in concert; I can vouch for this, having played and recorded a few of Iris' solo pieces. There is also a Toccata (The Train) with the obligatory starting and stopping and shrill whistle to indicate 'go' from the platform.

Rex and George de Cairos-Rego

Two family members of Iris also composed, their output was, however a markedly inferior quality to that Iris's. Still extant are Iris' brother Rex's *Two Intermezzi*, which are like pale copies of Schumann, while the Nocturne pays a similar homage to Chopin. Like some other music I have come across from very early in the century, these pieces were copyrighted in the U.S.A., but published in England, probably saying something about the immediate post-colonial period in Australia. The Nocturne was originally one of a set of pieces for violin and piano, Op.1. I have sighted two pieces by Iris's father George, the *Moment Musicale* and *La Cascade (Caprice)*: both are rather simple and puerile. The habit of giving grand-sounding names to fluffy pieces has persisted well into our own times.

Lindley Evans (1895 – 1982)

For someone who was very well known as a pianist and accompanist and who appeared on national television every week over a long span of years as Mr. Music Man, tickling the ivories in a show for children, Lindley Evans composed remarkably little piano music. There was a time – and perhaps it is still the case – when every young pianist competing in eisteddfods or sitting for public examinations run by the Australian Music Examinations Board would perform Evans pieces such as *Tally-Ho!* and *Merrythought*. The titles give a very clear impression of what such pieces were like – it was that very thoroughly explored idiom almost endemic in Australian piano music which allowed young pianists to play 'jolly' pieces without ever running the risk of too much emotional involvement or of having to grapple with any challenging musical ideas other than purely digital ones. These pieces are outside the scope of this book, as is Evans' *Waltz for Two Pianos,* which is actually a fairly substantial piece, written for Evans and his musical partner Frank Hutchens.

This leaves us with a handful of medium difficulty fairly short solo pieces, all in an amiable idiom veering extremely close to outright sentimentality.

Vignette: *Fragrance*, a prize winning composition in the Australian Broadcasting Commission's Composition Competition of 1935; *Lavender Time,* which just squeaks in here, a piece aimed at the pedagogic market; and a *Berceuse (for a sleeping sand baby)* published in a small anthology of Australian piano music entitled *Four Original Australian Tone Poems*. There is in fact only one substantial piano work, which is a little more dramatic and effective and leaves one wondering why Evans did not develop this side of his compositional persona. It is the *Rhapsody*.

Evans, a very modest man, never big-noted himself as a composer and was perfectly well aware that his contribution to the genre was of a very soft and gentle kind, skirting very close to parlour music.

Non-Pianists

Ernest Wunderlich (1859 – 1945)

This name is well known in commercial Australia, as Ernest Wunderlich founded a very successful roof tile manufacturing company; this gave him the capital to privately print his own music as he chose. These publications are now very rare and scarce. Handsomely presented, they declaim "Privately printed, not for sale", whilst elsewhere: "With the author's compliments". Wunderlich had the music engraved and printed in Leipzig by the prestigious firm of Breitkopf & Haertel, no doubt at some expense.

This says much about the difficulty of getting serious music published in Australia at the time - and Wunderlich was certainly a serious composer. By this I mean to say that there was nothing frivolous about his music; like his name, it was earnest, perhaps overly so. It is also, uncharacteristically for most of what was going on round him, fundamentally Germanic in outlook.

The *Theme and Variations* for example are consistently Brahmsian in outlook with the occasional harking back to Bachian sequences and counterpoint:

Ex. 124:1. E. Wunderlich. *Theme and Variations,* bars 37-40 of XX

As far as I know, there were three series (sets) of Variations. Series No.2 was for 4-Hands, but Series No.3 reverted to solo piano. Here, as in other of his music, a classical presence reminiscent of some Beethoven is always about:

Ex. 125:1. E. Wunderlich. *Theme and Variations, Third series.* bars 1-4 of VII.

Wunderlich obviously laid great store in contrapuntal skills. Variation 15 from this set is not an isolated sample:

Ex. 126:1. E. Wunderlich. *Theme and Variations, Third series.* bars 1-4 of XV.

Apart from these two sets of variations, which could well represent Wunderlich's major contributions to the piano repertoire, he also published *8 Pieces in Fugal Style, Six Characteristic Pieces* and *Twelve Miscellaneous Pieces.* There are also some vocal compositions, all privately printed.

The *Twelve Small Pianoforte Pieces* were published by W.H. Paling and Co., Ltd., in Australia, but even here the music was "engraved and printed in Belgium", whilst "All monies derived from the sale of these Compositions will be given to the Red Cross Fund". The year of publication is 1919. One could easily point out various deficiencies in these and other Wunderlich works: the square rhythms, the backward looking language. In this set of twelve, one also discerns the influence of the Rubinstein *Barcarolles*; there is another piece with echoes of a plaintive Tchaikovsky. No.6 could almost have come from a Bach Suite:

Ex. 127:1. E. Wunderlich. *Twelve Small Pianoforte Pieces*. bars 1-12 of VI.

Wunderlich thus represents a kind of European classicism in Australian piano music.

G. W. L. Marshall-Hall (1862 – 1915)

The name of this flamboyant composer, conductor, poet and music educator from very early in the 20th century is well-known to Australian scholars and to some music-lovers. His reputation largely rests on his output of operas and orchestral works. He taught Margaret Sutherland, one of our most important composers. For the piano, we could only find one lone piece, *Jubilum Amoris*, in reality a concert waltz at the head of which it says *Allegro molto e brioso* and then "Hambourgisch!" In the middle of the fairly extensive piece there is another reference to Hambourg after a Molto Animato: "Mit Hambourgischer Electricitat". Another curiosity of the piece is that at one point, over a melodic line, Marshall-Hall has written:

(She): Lo! as the moonbeams kiss the sea, Thou, O Beloved, Kiss Thou Me! As rocks the sea, mew on the sea's breast, O, on thy bosom let me rest!

Whether this may be a quote of an aria from one of his operas or whether he expected the pianist to break into song, is unclear. Musically, the waltz is not of any great interest, although the piece could be effective in the right hands, given the occasional flashy passage-work and cadenzas which periodically occur.

Arundel Orchard (1867 – 1961)

Orchard had a distinguished career as a music educator in Australia's earlier music history and served as director of the Sydney Conservatorium. As a composer, the case is somewhat less strong. For the piano, there is very little, and perhaps also a reflection of his own pianistic limitations.

Orchard's *Toccata* written as late as 1943 sounds like a faithful copy of an non-existent piece by Bach or Scarlatti. Marked *Allegretto Con Moto,* it is a genteel English gentleman's foray into the genre, complete with some discreet non-threatening hand crossing and firmly rooted in A Minor. It represents the values, which were imported into our culture by a certain kind of English musician, no matter how well intentioned they were. This sort of imported conservatism meant that any modernism in Australia prior to mid-century was only there hanging by a slender, if golden thread. There is a Concert Study from this same year, which we have not seen.

But if it is anything like *Ariel* (also 1943), I doubt that it would be gripping. Perhaps *Ariel* was only meant as a mid-level teaching piece, but the Shakespearean character and the storm are in a teacup with a nicely curved little finger.

There is also, in like mode, a *Scherzo in E Mino*r which, too, lives in that no-man's land between good student medium difficulty piece and concert work. The Scherzo is light without being witty.

The *Rhapsody in A Minor* is a slightly more ambitious venture, but only in duration, not in scope or flair. Orchard must have been only a very fair pianist; there is nothing in the music that challenges musically or technically. Because of his standing in the musical community, all of these light-weight pieces were published, while serious composers, written about elsewhere in this book, had the devil's own time surviving.

Adolphe Beutler (1882 – 1927)

Just as this book was about to go to press, the National Library of Australia acquired material relating to a composer named Adolph Beutler, which had sat in a box and had been kept by his son for decades. The story of the music's survival is quite romantic and inspired television coverage in the series "Australian Story" on the national network. I was involved in the filming of the story and asked to comment on the music. Beutler, who worked closely with the artist family of the Lindsays until there was a falling out, left a very respectable body of work, including an opera and a number of songs, all with a strong German tradition driving the music.

Like Wunderlich, Beutler discovered very quickly that Australia in the opening years of the 20th century was not particularly interested in supporting composers; and, like Wunderlich, he had to earn his keep and support his family by going into business rather than having time to practice and perfect his craft. His extant diaries and some letters vividly describe his dilemma and pain. Beutler died at a fairly early age, and almost nothing ever achieved publication.

The piano music that I have seen and played through includes Preludes in a quasi-Bachian style and a conservative harmonic language. The piano music in general does not move into more chromatic realms that can be found in some of the songs and in the opera, the little of them that I glimpsed. A modest *Rhapsodie Hongroise* (modest in terms of technical difficulty) derives from Brahms rather than Liszt, just as the opera is surely from Wagner. The *Rhapsodie* (1911) is complete and in fair copy but lacks dynamics. One gets the impression with some of this music that the composer gave up for lack of interest and support. Whether he was a good enough pianist to play his own scores I simply don't know. A set of *Variations and Fugue* subtitled "Gilderoy" presents a theme in block chords followed by eight variations in a Brahmsian cast and a quite elaborate fugue. Again, dynamics are absent, and the restatement of the theme at the end is not quite complete and simply breaks off in mid-stream. This work from 1914 probably deserves revival, but will need sympathetic editing.

There is another set of *Variationen über einem Choral von Sebastian Bach* in a similar mode (1912) which is more complete and encompasses six fairly dense and busy variations. They are not easy and require good octaves and chords. Much slighter is a set of three pieces, *Arabian Scenes* (*The passing of the Caravan*; *Nocturne*; and *Dance*) from 1914: a very European view of what constitutes the East, with what is by now a clichéd way of describing it. I sight-read the *Nocturne* for the TV show and it seemed to have a kind of faded charm.

Finally, a bigger piece: *Hyperion, Tone Poem for Piano after the poem by Keats* (1926), dedicated to his doctor and written shortly before his death. This work is clearly also inspired by Beutler's association with the Lindsays, as it is full of classical allusions, with various passages treated programmatically and discriptively, almost like a script for a silent movie of the time. Thus: 'satyr'; 'here comes the faun'; 'chorus of Gods'; 'nymphs and sirens chatting'; 'centaur' etc etc So the score progresses, with these 'explanations' for every few bars of music. There is even a very Norman Lindsay-like 'bachanalia'. The musical model here is Beethoven rather than Brahms and moreover the Beethoven of the *Pastorale* Symphony rather than anything later or more difficult. It may be that a performance would amuse a contemporary audience of today if staged appropriately and with the words perhaps on a screen behind the pianist, as though it is a silent film unfolding; possibly some stills from Lindsay would further enhance such a performance?

The Beutler manuscripts are unlikely to change our view of Australian piano music or indeed of Australian music, but they do add a poignant reminder of the fragility of the compositional art as well as the utter dependence of the composer on support from the community.

Edgar Bainton (1880 – 1956)

Bainton was an important figure in music education in Australia and came here from England for a period as director of the Sydney Conservatorium. Whether as a composer he is of importance now, to Australians, is dubious. The piano music includes a salon-like *Shadowy Woodlands* (1915), one of a set of *Four Tone Pictures*, the others being *Humoresque, Nocturne* and *Still Waters*. The landscapes portrayed, inasmuch as one can portray landscape in music, seem, on the basis of the cover picture, to be English rather than Australian anyway; fair enough too, since they were written before he came here. A few years later, Bainton's *Capriccio in G Minor* was included in an important series of piano music by *Modern British Composers* issued by Ascherberg, Horwood and Crew, with photographs of the composers on the very distinctive covers. Bainton's inclusion in this set underlines his growing reputation as a composer. At about the same time his *White Hyacinth* (1925) was included in the Oxford Piano Series. This is the most substantial piano piece from his pen that I have seen, with florid and chromatic passages of at least moderate difficulty; there is still, however, a whiff (pardon the pun) of the salon present. A more serious work, published in Australia is *Visions* (1941), exploring chromaticism akin to other British composers of the era such as Ireland.

Esther Rofe (1904 – 2000)

Like Marshall-Hall, Esther Rofe's reputation rests on her work in the theatre. She composed principally ballets and also worked professionally as an arranger. As a result, her small output for the piano can only be regarded as quite marginal to her long life's work in theatre and film. She composed for voice and voices as well as for small chamber ensembles. A child prodigy on the violin and piano, studying the two instruments from the age of four, Rofe lived to the age of ninety six. Her life story is a biography just waiting to be written.

Most of the piano music is too slight to be considered in the present context, though one work. *The Island* (composed in 1938 and revised in 1993) is a moderate length, medium difficulty that could take its place in the concert repertoire, with its slightly diffuse harmonies and hints of bitonality:

Ex. 128:1. E. Rofe. *The Island.* bars 1-4.

Horace Perkins (1901–1986)

The presence of Horace Perkins in this book is to some extent peripheral. He is best remembered now for his orchestral music and for some of his chamber music. Although he contributed much to the musical life of this country and of his native state of South Australia especially, his connection with piano music is less vital and important. The approximately two dozen works that make up his output for solo piano are all still in manuscript form, some of it not even in fine copy and would require some dedicated editing for revival.

Many of the smaller works sit in that uneasy world of almost-salon and would have been called 'real nice' by Charles Ives' imaginary character Rollo. A few settings of folksong might be worth considering worthy of revival for intermediate level students; in general, the technical difficulty of all the piano music is quite moderate. We can probably deduce that Perkins was not a virtuoso or solo pianist. Quite a number of the short pieces also seem to lack a title, so we cannot be certain whether they were part of a larger composition such as a suite or were meant to be left self-sufficient.

The pieces tend to be interrupted by cadenza passages, but these are so timid and predictable that they are a mere semblance of a cadenza and only lend a rather dated parlor music character to the music.

Apart from the almost compulsory elves and fairies that appear in much Australian music of the time, the manuscripts contain short preludes and romances. A Rondo, with subtitles such as *Australian piece No.1* and *Bush Stroll* is in truth much more like an amble down an English country lane. Many of the works lack a title altogether. There is a work assembled by the accretion of seven short pieces: the collection is called *Legends from a far Country* and consists of 1. The Troubadour, 2. The Sailor Boy, 3. Lullaby, 4. In an Old Castle, 5. The Jester, 6. Reconciliation 7. The Bridal Morn. In the midst of all this prettiness there is a *Prelude on a Bach Chorale*.

There is a Ballade which surprisingly, actually contains some grit and conflict; perhaps an overdose of melodramatic chromatic scales, as well, but nevertheless a piece that is worth considering reviving. Perkins never seemed to have produced a fine copy, but the manuscript shows work and is complete.

The opening suggests what is to come:

Ex. 129:1. H. Perkins. *Ballade,* bars 1-4.

The only other exception to these rather negative impressions is a fairly meaty *Legend for Piano*, which runs to fifteen pages of manuscript and encompasses a variety of episodes; it also pushes the pianist further than in other of his pieces. Perkins did not date his manuscripts neither do we know who this was meant for to play; the *Legend* also contains metrical variety that suggests both rhetoric and improvisation. But it must be said in the end that both the Ballad*e* as well as the *Legend* are uneven pieces. They contain seeds of development that never occurred in Perkins' piano music, but at their best, they have that sense of temperamental letting go which is so much missing in most of his work.

Salon Music Composers

Marjorie Hesse (1911 – 1986), Una Bourne (1882 – 1974), Henry Stewart (1885 – 1930), Frederick Hall (1878 – 1956), Emanuel de Beaupuis (1860 – 1913)

There was much music written by pianists, who kept alive the nineteenth century tradition of performers composing. Often such pieces were either for themselves to perform, or, more frequently, they served a double function as teaching pieces for moderate and advanced students. A typical example, which I just happened to have in my personal library, is Marjorie Hesse's (1911 – 1986) *All Suddenly the Wind Comes Soft* (the line is from a Rupert Brooke's poem *Song*). Hesse also composed a *Romance*, included in an early anthology. A more prolific example of such is from the pen of Una Bourne (1882 – 1974), who had a solid international career as a performer, and who still has a scholarship named after her at Melbourne University. Bourne's output was light and dainty, not even showy. The dates are from between the two World Wars. It included pieces like *Gavotte, Humoresque, By Sunny Streamlet* etc. *Wiegenlied* was dedicated to Melba. *Petite Valse Caprice* is closer to being a true concert piece and was no doubt performed by the composer. There is also a *Marche Grotesque* fitting neatly into the imps/gnomes genre indicated by the cover picture.

Another composer who should be mentioned here is Henry Stewart (1885 – 1930), writing prolifically for the market and supplying, like many, many others, supposedly serious art music, full of all the outward identifying marks of the genre, but inwardly vapid and shallow. This kind of piano music, which I identify with the anti-composer elsewhere in the book, has always been with us, and this form of kitsch has been and still is, alive and well. I have before me, as a sample, Stewart's *Musette (Rhapsodie)* from 1920. Note the pretentious spelling of rhapsody, thus implying a serious intent, a technique that has continued to be employed. Stewart published lots of piano music, including titles such as *March Humoresque, Tarantelle, Repentance, Silver Stream, Silvery Shadows (Barcarolle)* etc.

Frederick Hall (1878 – 1956), a powerful figure in Australian publishing, was another composer who churned out quasi-music with all the correct titles to suggest real music. Thus: *Chanson d'Autumn, Intermezzo Brillante, Consolation* (perhaps suggesting a link with Liszt?), *The Evening Prayer* (with a biblical scene on the cover; the covers were often the best part of the package), *A Venetian Reverie* (two cultural references in one title), *English Country Dance* (reference to the mother country), and then a swag of 'little' pieces: *A Little Waltz, A Little Gavotte, A little Minuet, A Little March, A Little Barcarolle.* 'Little' was and is a favoured fallback position for the anti-composer (see last chapter): it suggests cuteness, amiability and usually contains within the title a reference to a preexisting art form, thus also adding legitimacy to the piece, which is almost inevitably kitsch.

The last composers mentioned, with the exceptions of Hesse and Bourne, were not, as far as I know, performing pianists, but I have lumped all of these together because of the similarity in their output. My personal library contains literally hundreds of examples of this type of piano music written by Australians, and so the above can only be regarded as samples (of the better albeit more pretentious kind) rather than any attempt to be comprehensive. The music also begins to shift towards programmatic parlour-music and, frankly, (though this latter class might be more honest) I don't want to go there!

Emanuel de Beaupuis (1860–1913), Roy Agnew's teacher, needs mention in this book because he lived in this country for a while and was involved in concertizing, composing and teaching. I have collected Australian piano music for many years, and have managed to gather together a reasonable number of Beaupuis' compositions. His full story is yet to be written and much research needs to be done. Beaupuis was obviously a brilliant concert pianist, playing major works by Liszt and Chopin. In a rave review from the Melbourne *Argus*, we learn that he played the Beethoven *Waldstein* Sonata as well as the Liszt-Wagner *Tannhaeuser Overture*. His works, known to me, are listed below:

> *Valse Impromptu in Db*
> *Valse Caprice*
> *Muriel- Graceful Dance*
> *Irresistible- Gavotte*
> *Flight from Pompeii- Galop*
> *Stella- Mazurka Elegante*
> *Evening Bells- Nocturne*
> *Menuet Fantastique*
> *Pensée fugitive*
> *Bolero*
> *Troiseme Valse de Concert*
> *Sur la Mer- Etude Caractéristique*
> *Hygeia- Valse*
> *Marche Hongroise*
> *Valse Impromptu Op.15*
> *Menuet a l'antique Op.14*
> *The Merry Peasant- Morceau de Salon*
> *Twilight Reveries*
> *Chant de la Nuit*
> *Premiere Mazurka*
> *Deuxieme Mazurka*
> *Dors, mon enfant- Berceuse*
> *Prelude in a Major*
> *Le Chant du Berger*
> *Irish Airs* (arranged)
> *The Queen's Reign- March*
> *Edward Hoffman's "The Mocking Bird", Air & Variations,* edited by Beaupuis

The publishers range from Glasgow, Melbourne, Milan, and Sydney. This is not a complete list, only what I have located thus far – there is no doubt more out there, and there may be an archive in a library somewhere. Beaupuis, from even the titles of the pieces listed above, is clearly inclined to write quasi-salon music, with an eye on the market. However, the catch is that technically many of his pieces would have been beyond the range of the amateurs who were the main target in the marketing.

In the course of preparing this book, I can safely say that I have played through hundreds of pieces, and the marketing was clear and cunning: exciting packaging (covers often in colour), free advertising on the front and back covers for like pieces, technical demands moderate at best, appearance of high art in the titles (often not in the music, so what has changed?), reference to other exotic cultures, including the mysterious Orient (so what has changed?), political correctness (ditto). Beaupuis fulfils all the criteria except the one of moderate technical difficulty.

I think when we learn the full story about this man, he may well emerge as a kind of Gottschalk figure on the Australian scene. At this stage, we don't even know whether he wrote exclusively for the piano or not, or whether there are more musically ambitious compositions.

(iii) The "Australian" Composers

Pianists

Mirrie Hill (1892 –1986)

As a composer, it is a sad fact that Mirrie Hill's music was, during her lifetime, completely overshadowed by that of her husband Alfred Hill. Hill was one of her teachers; she married him in 1921 and traveled with him a number of times to Europe and New Zealand, possibly, as a result acquiring cultural exposure and ideas. Because she seemed to have been completely subservient to Alfred, at this remove one gets an impression of a compositional career and development that was stultified and only very partially realized. I have a sneaking feeling that she was actually more gifted than Alfred and arrived at such a point of view after reflection and performance of a few of her piano works as well as some exposure to her other music. Unfortunately, there is little to write about. There are plenty of very simple miniatures for young players, and they certainly do not excite one's curiosity to look further, being exactly what one would expect from the times they were published and the illustrations on the cover.

Originally Mirrie Irma Solomon, Mirrie Hill was brought up in a cultured Jewish household with the music of the German romantics such as Schubert, Schumann, Wolf and Richard Strauss well to the fore – a very typical European Jewish view of culture imported into Australia. What is curious is that later in her life, partly thanks to C. P. Mountford (an early anthropologist and photographer) and also to her husband's interest in Maori music of New Zealand, she in turn became fascinated by Australian Aboriginal music, especially music from Arnhem Land.

Was this a member of one persecuted minority being drawn to that of another similarly afflicted group of people? It certainly was not from some idea of founding a typically Australian school of composition. She said herself (Composer file, Australian Music Centre):

I think the feeling of most of us is that we prefer to be without a label. It's the old story that people have an idea that nothing good can come out of our own country. They hear 'Australian music' and switch off the radio. Quite apart from that we're not writing in any Australian idiom or in any Australian tradition so why label? Put our music with the other if it's good it will be accepted and if it's bad - well, it still shouldn't be labeled Australian.

Elsewhere, Mirrie Hill also made clear that apart from attempting to get some rhythmic ideas notated accurately, it was impossible to notate in our tunings and in equal temperament the inflections of Aboriginal music that she heard on tapes apparently supplied to her by Mountford.

Nevertheless, in the *Three Aboriginal Dances* for solo piano, there is a successful capture of some elements of tribal music on a quite inappropriate instrument such as the piano. (It is interesting that at the head of the score, the composer writes "composed and arranged by Mirrie Hill") Although treated very conventionally in a harmonized Western fashion, there are effective and affecting moments, such the opening of *BROLGA (The Dancer):*

Ex. 130:1. M. Hill. *Brolga.* bars 5-10.

The suggestion of dance in *The Kunkarunka Women*:

Ex. 131:1. M. Hill. *The Kunkarunkara Women.* bars 6-9.

or the vast expanse of the bush in *Nalda of the Echo*:

Ex. 132:1. M. Hill. *Nalda of the Echo.* bars 44-48.

Mirrie Hill also tackled another indigenous culture in a work rather grandly entitled *A Maori Rhapsody* but disappointingly this merely produced a rather feeble and conventional Waltz. Indeed many of her miniatures intending for young players were in dance rhythms and tending towards that rather coy cuteness that has characterised much of Australian piano music sitting on that side of the fence with an eye to populism and genteel appeal. For example, Mirrie Hill's *Willow Wind*, published as late as 1973 moves beyond the realms of easy pedagogic material towards a concert piece, but still retains that element of pictorial depiction so obvious in much of our music for children. *Willow Wind* is an essentially pentatonic work rooted on Eb full of aeolian harp wind chime effects. In her early *Three Miniature Pieces for the Piano*, dedicated to her teacher Laurence Godfrey Smith, Hill is actually more ambitious, still publishing under her maiden name of Mirrie Solomon (1911). But the titles suggest that much the same of aesthetic is at work here: *Will O' the Wisp* and just *Fun*. *The Leafy Lanes of Kent* falls somewhere within the same realm expressing that yearning towards the mother country England that was so much a part of the Australian ethos in at least the first half of the twentieth century.

It is only when we explore the still unpublished manuscripts of Mirrie Hill that we catch a glimpse of a more serious composer. Setting aside more children's pieces, one comes across things such as The *Wonder of Night* (recorded by the well-known Australian pianist Eunice Gardiner), *The Sea*, *The Unquiet Ocean* and *Rotha's Lament*, all suggesting that there was a side to Mirrie Hill that was largely hidden and either refused publication, or else subsumed by her subservience to her far more famous husband Alfred Hill and probably desire not to be seen to be in competition with him. Ironically and in hindsight it seems that she was potentially at least his equal if not his better, at times displaying a passion and natural flow that is often absent in Alfred's more Germanic output. Other pieces found in her archive include an *Improvisation*, a witty and exuberant *Do You Remember an Inn, Miranda* (after a poem by Belloc) and *In a Reflective Mood*. The *Rhapsody*- as distinct from the *Maori Rhapsody* is a strong six page work of orchestral texture and scope and must be another candidate for revival:

Ex. 133:1. M. Hill. *Rhapsody for Piano.* bars 29-31.

Among the papers: a version of *Brolga the Dancer*, the first of the three *Aboriginal Dances*, but this time for piano and a cymbal apparently played by the pianist. This version also differs slightly in other respects from the printed score. Other quite unknown music surfaced here: some pieces based on Aboriginal motives that are certainly worthy of publication. Especially prominent among this category is a piece called *Odnyamatana Rhythm*, in another version titled *Aboriginal Song to the Whirlwind*.

Ex. 134:1. M. Hill. *Aboriginal Song to the Whirlwind.* bars 1-4.

This was based on a tape supplied by Mountford. There are a number of manuscript copies of this fairly extended piano piece and a performing edition should be prepared soon.

Among the manuscripts there are also piano versions of dances from her own *Cinderella Suite*, an early *Concert Etude*, a quite powerful but short *Lament*.

Some of her other miniatures lend themselves to the concert stage in the right setting and possibly with some little elaboration. I believe that I have successfully achieved this with her three page Waltz (on my CD "Retrospect").

Non-Pianists

Henry Tate (1873 – 1926)

Henry Tate's *Morning in the Gully* was, as far as I know, his only piano piece.
Tate no doubt dreamt of creating an 'Australian' music based on our own bird
calls and experiences of nature. This little three-page piece certainly doesn't
come anywhere close to achieving such a goal. It is probably a historically
curious example of early nationalistic kitsch, with its clumsy chromatic scale
cadenzas and its attempt to evoke the waking calls of birds and other life; but
placed correctly in a programme it could survive some hearings, even if only in
a historical context.

Arthur S. Loam (1896 - ?)

A like-minded composition from a somewhat later date is *Maranoa, Fantasy for
Piano on an Australian Aboriginal Theme* (1938) by Arthur S. Loam. It is
dedicated "To the last of his Tribe", and a note by the composer says: "This
Fantasy, while interpolating an Australian aboriginal melody, seeks to express
something of the feelings of one who belongs to a vanishing race, and who feels
the tragedy of fate. Other than using the melody as a beginning and ending, no
attempt has been made to include any other aboriginal tune. Except for the short
aboriginal theme the music is the composer's own.

The Maranoa tune is a lullaby to which the mother rocked her baby to sleep in
the bark cradle, using her foot to avoid stooping. It is from the book of
"*Australian Aboriginal Songs* collected by Dr. H. O. Lethbridge from the
Maranoa district, Queensland, and arranged by Arthur S. Loam".

Like the Henry Tate, this fantasy is now more of a curiosity than anything else,
but it is nevertheless a genuine attempt to use Aboriginal materials in a piano
concert work. The theme on its first appearance sounds more like Dvorak than
authentic Aboriginal music, but this is almost the inevitable result of using the
piano in such fashion:

Ex. 135:1. A. S. Loam. *Maranoa*, bars 13-16.

Part 2: The Second Generation

(i) Post-1945 Modernism Arrives in Australia

Post World War II modernism arrived in Australia in the early 1960s with pivotal events such as the first Conference of Australian Composers held in Hobart in 1963. It became clear that composers were shifting away from an Anglo-centric view of their heritage and adopting cultures from a wider Europe and America. Prominent composers were being appointed as teachers in Australia's main universities, and performances of their music became a more routine occurrence, inserted into mainstream concerts. The Australian Contemporary Music Ensemble appeared, ancestor to later reincarnations of a similar nature. For a while, the Australian Broadcasting Commission was active in its promotion of new Australian music; and a new generation of composers arrived in Australia from European countries. Consequently, the term 'Australian composer' acquired an expanded meaning.

Pianists

Felix Werder (1922)

Werder occupies an interesting place in the scheme of Australian music. In Melbourne, where he has lived most of his professional life, he has been a kind of founding figure of the post-war avant-garde, a rallying point for the new generation of the then emerging composers as well as one of the first composers to openly confront the Establishment. As such, he must certainly be considered an important figure. Given his strongly European background and views it is no surprise that he sees himself as in the line of descent from a long succession of central European – and probably essentially German composers. There has always been a strong connection with Schoenberg and it has manifested itself in his piano music over many years. Indeed, the connection with Schoenberg was a family connection, and Werder's psyche includes writing about music, being a published music critic and philosopher.

The big difference between Werder amd Schoenberg is that Schoenberg's quest was always for unity, whereas Werder has declared on numerous occasions that his music is misunderstood because he has always sought the opposite - discontinuity. He seems also to reject the process of development and therefore the logical arrival at some musical point as a relic of the past. The music flickers and shifts like some sort of elusive film without a storyline and with the images not necessarily logically linked. Thus, his *Piano Music Op.97* (1968) whips through seven movements in the space of twelve pages. The language is more like Webern than Schoenberg, but the serial rigour is either missing or else not immediately perceivable, although conglomerates of all twelve notes are all certainly present. The *Sonata No.4* from 1973, in two movements, may be regarded as a companion piece to the above.

Werder must be one of our most prolific composers: his output is huge and encompasses all instruments and forces. Although he knows his way around a keyboard, he is not a performer in the sense of a soloist, and to him the piano is a working instrument.

Regrettably, Werder's early piano music appears to be lost. The composer insists that he destroyed it himself since there was no interest in it. I have no way of corroborating this, but have no reason to doubt it either. The surviving piano music can best be described as post Second Viennese School, as the gestures and economies of harmony stem from that source.

The *Sonata No.5* is in conventional three movement form, with the slow movement in the middle, but most convention stops there. The music consists of short, isolated events separated by silence. Use of the sustaining pedal is strictly controlled to ensure that the gaps are maintained. The approach to the keyboard is to a great extent single note strands, sometimes dry, sometimes pedaled to build up sonorities:

Ex 1:2 F. Werder. *Sonata No. 5*. bars 56-61.

The effect is that of music from a forgotten time, with fleeting reference to what might be a thematic piece, be it a tritonal gestures, or a pattern of repeated notes. When the music erupts, it tends to be quite violent:

Ex 2:2 F. Werder. *Sonata No. 5*. bars 95-99.

In the last movement, the idea of repeated notes dominates for a while, almost like a partially controlled improvisation. Long silences, or long held chords are another feature of this Sonata.

In *A Little Night Music*, Werder makes his discontinuity a little more orderly by actually numbering the various fragments and interspersing a series of "WHIM"s (the composer's word) into the text of the music. The effect is not unlike a baroque form of contrasting tempi rapidly succeeding each other in 'movements' that are no more than seconds long.

A late work, *Monogragh* is in a more flowing style and even contains vestiges of thematicism, such as the nervous little triplet figure that opens the work followed by the grace figure encompassing a third:

Ex 3:2 F. Werder. *Monograph.* bars 1-3.

The last movement hints at an almost Bartókian assymetric dance feel with some affinity to Bulgarian rhythm:

Ex 4:2 F. Werder. *Monograph.* bars 1-3 of III.

Werder's *Blake's Songs of Innocence and Experience*, (1985) strings of single note strands over the score in a fairly relentless way, almost suggest that Werder at times is edging towards the New Complexity in terms of style and if so, it is surprising that he still regards the piano as a viable outlet for his music rather than some electroacoustic means of accurate reproduction. Successions of repeated thirds, reminiscent of one of Schoenberg's short piano pieces, once more hint that there is some level of organization behind the seemingly illogical facade.

Don Banks (1923 – 1980)

The well-known Australian composer Don Banks left his native country in 1950. He felt he had to go abroad to discover what being a composer meant. Arthur Benjamin, some years before had had a similar experience when he left Australia; Benjamin had been told (in Australia) that all composers were dead and there were no live composers! Banks' father was a very versatile jazz performer and accounts for the pervasive jazz feel in most of Banks' music. Much of Don's early experience was as a performer and improviser in jazz bands, an activity that gravitated towards jazz arranging for various bands of various sizes. When he went to the Melbourne Conservatorium, one of the chief inspirations was the composer Dorian Le Gallienne.

The *Sonatina in C# minor* dates from the period just before Banks left Australia to study abroad. It is a student work, but fascinating as it foreshadows many of the traits of the mature composer: fastidious craftsmanship, careful control over form and the presence of a jazz beat, lurking somewhere behind the facade of even the most complex work. Don gave the first performance of the *Sonatina*, composed in 1948, at a concert of the New Music Society in Melbourne in 1949.

The first movement is in a five-part form – the first two ideas of the work are in *Allegro* and *Andante* and therefore aurally simple to place. In the middle, the tempo speeds up into a *vivace* and then, via a *cantabile*, the first idea and tempo reappear. The main subject cries out for a big band colouration:

Ex 5:2 D. Banks. *Sonatina in C# Minor*. Bars 75-78.

It is clearly a kind of simplified sonata form notion. The second movement is in a free-flowing counterpoint, suggesting solo instruments and strongly reminiscent of the kind of jazz piano that Banks himself played at the time.

Ex 6:2 D. Banks. *Sonatina in C# Minor*. Bars 36-39 of II.

The last movement is closer to a rondo form in that the opening idea reappears between incursions of other contrasting episodes; here classical counterpoint and jazz rub shoulders with a short venture into something approaching a Webernian sparseness.

Ex 7:2 D. Banks. *Sonatina in C# Minor*. Bars 87-89 of III.

The *Sonatina* is quite expansive and could almost be labeled a sonata in its scope. It is currently still unpublished.

It is quite telling that even after the turn of the half-century (1956), Don's important work, *Pezzo Dramatico* appeared in a volume called *Contemporary British Piano Music*. The whole angst associated with being an expatriate was still going on, not to dwindle until the last quarter of the century.

Pezzo Dramatico is the clear result of the intense work carried out by Don under the tutelage of people like Matyas Seiber, Milton Babbitt and Luigi Dallapiccola, work which involved refining the use of the twelve-tone system and eventually making it his own, the Banks version being smoothly linear, clean, with articulated pulsing and a soft, expressive *cantabile* in place within the rigour that is also ever present. One of Don's great talents was the ability to reconcile seemingly divergent ideas in music, and *Pezzo* is a fine example of this. It is not a long piece (as Don said: "I'm all for the concise in art"), but manages to encompass a variety of moods and tempi from the quasi-orchestral opening flourish.

Ex 8:2 D. Banks. *Pezzo Dramatico*. opening.

through a progessive jazz feel in twelve-tone language:

Ex 9:2 D. Banks. *Pezzo Dramatico*. bars 85-88.

to an almost trademark Banks lyricism.

Ex 10:2 D. Banks. *Pezzo Dramatico*. bars 56-60.

Pezzo Dramatico is one of the landmarks of Australian piano music. Because Don wrote so little for the piano, and although it does not strictly fit the framework of this book, I would like to mention in passing a work that was originally for piano and two-channel tape (1971). Late in his life and before his final illness prevented any serious work from being carried out, Don and I spoke of recreating *Commentary* (the work in question) as a solo piece. Don was generally in favour, but it was never done. The point of my suggestion, having performed the work many times, was that the spoken words on the tape (including the sound of Don's voice) lent a humorous air to the piece, often quite at odds with a very substantial and serious solo piano part. The electronic component is not large and by now is extremely dated and to our ears of the twenty first century, rather primitive. This is not without its own charm, but the whole system of reel-to-reel technology is gone and this will inevitably restrict performances of this very fine piece.

Don Banks was generous with his the time he allocated to what he called 'fighting the good fight', i.e. the cause of Australian music and Australian music education. While abroad he and Margaret Sutherland co-founded the Australian Music Association. In Australia he chaired the Music Board of the Australia Council and sat on many committees (probably too many), all assisting the cause. Banks was an important figure in Australian music in as much as he expended considerable energy making it possible for Australian composers to exist professionally rather than in an amateur capacity in this country.

Keith Humble (1927 –1995)

Like his Friend Don Banks, Keith Humble was a tireless fighter for Australian music and Australian composers, not to mention performing standards within the Australian context.

Humble is an seminal figure in terms of this book because he continued, throughout his life, to write for the piano and moreover was, all his days, an exponent on the instrument, performing his own and other composers' music. I can only describe Keith's style at the piano as "white": that is, a way of playing that was no nonsense, no histrionics, no excess movement, little pedal, dynamics always reigned in, a sense of delicacy and elegance ever present, understated with that curious detachment that is quite often 'the composer at the keyboard', as though what meant most to the creator at the time of creation was now viewed with some critical detachment.

Keith Humble was also significant because as an educator he, for a time, exerted an ideology and idealism that was important for Australian music. He was there because he believed in what he was doing, not because he had an eye out for the main chance. It was this idealism that led to the formation of the Australian Contemporary Music Ensemble and which was the daddy of much subsequent performance of new music in this country. But that is a story that needs to be told elsewhere. Within the activities of ACME, Keith Humble also acted as conductor and one of the artistic directors.

Throughout his life, Humble followed, to a stricter or looser extent, the aesthetics of the Second Viennese School; but the lean sound of Schoenberg's and Webern's piano music is ever present in the Humble scores, right from the very early *Three Little Pieces* through to the late *Bagatelles*.

Having said that, I need to qualify it by pointing out that there are some early Humble pieces which do establish a beginning in tonality. From 1947, a set of three pieces called *Childhood Tunes*: 1. Teddy Bear; 2. The Wind; and 3. A Dream – Bewilderment. The last is somewhat less tonal than its predecessors, playing on the tritonal pull between B and F. The last two pieces are somewhat reworked and combined into a *Prelude* also dated 1947. Two Preludes (F Minor and F# Major) were written in 1948. The harmony is well-defined not only by the key signature but also by the strong writing, although the second prelude is shifting towards some added notes in the chords; this prelude features alternate hand chords for most of its texture. An *Essay for the Piano* was composed in 1949 and explores chords in piled-up fifths, although still within well-marked tonal boundaries of Bb minor-major. An *Etude* from 1952 owes something to the first Debussy Etude with a similar humorous reference to the elementary five-finger pattern on white notes superimposed with black notes foreign to the implied harmony. The manuscript now names Paris instead of Melbourne as a location. From the same place come the *Three Album Leaves* (1954). The tonal centres are now weaker and the writing closer to Humble's later aphoristic style. In a similar vein is *The First Day of Spring* (dated somewhat prematurely 23/2/54; perhaps an early onset that year?); this charming miniature is dedicated *To Jill*, presumably the same Jill that was to be his wife of many years. All of this early music is unpublished, like so much of Humble and has become available only very recently with the establishment of the Humble archive at the National Libary of Australia. To complete this list from earlier years, I should add the *Three Statements for Piano* (Overture, Improvisation and Finale) from 1967, the whole only taking up two pages of manuscript and now in a confirmed and confident Second Viennese School approach. Finally, two incomplete works: *Loose Leaves* (date difficult to decipher, but could be 1989), of which only the first is complete, and the second breaks off. Similarly, *Miniatures* (1994) with one completed piece followed by a detailed scheme of pitch rotation. The single first pieces of *Loose Leaves* and *Miniatures* could conceivably be published together.

There are four sonatas and in a way they characterize all of Humble's music for the piano. Keith was a composer who found his personal language very early and never deviated from it, at least not to any significant extent, and he was content to stay within this framework. He used the twelve-tone system in his own way, subdividing the row in various ways – not always in equal subdivisions – and treating the material at times as a main cell and a subsidiary cell of notes. But the resultant textures and expressive devices rarely shifted from a world defined earlier by Webern and Schoenberg.

Sonata I (1953) already has within it the characteristics of later Humble:

Ex 11:2 K. Humble. *Sonata I*. opening.

Both movements are in this telegraphic style, and it is not until the coda that some hint of a warmer world manifests itself with some tremolo pedals.

Sonata II (1977) is a fiercer, more aggressive work; in it Humble works his raw material in a more chordal and polyphonically denser fashion than in *Sonata I* and so forces the performer to extend the dynamic range due to close proximity of changes and moods and the need to delineate them, often harshly.

Ex 12:2 K. Humble. *Sonata II*. Bars 17-20.

Nevertheless, there still is room for gentler moments in the coda near the end, as before in Sonata *I*, where a Schoenbergian mood and texture momentarily holds sway:

Ex 13:2 K. Humble. *Sonata II*. Bars 67-69

The sonatas are all short. For example *Sonata III* (1985), in Keith 's sprawling calligraphy, still only runs to ten manuscript pages. Whatever one feels about the music and its unvarying style, Keith had the courage to stick to his guns and an even greater courage, not possessed by many composers to put a full-stop when he had said what he wanted to say. The works have no excess fat on them, no room for trimming – it is all spare and essential. A volume gathering all the sonatas together should be a publishing priority.

Sonata III, like its predecessor, is a continuous work, but the composer does divide it into smaller sections; an Epilogue of a more extended and gentler nature sums up the qualities of the Sonata:

Ex 14:2 K. Humble. *Sonata III*. opening of *Epilogue*.

Sonata IV (1990) is Humble's last major work for piano – it is eight pages of manuscript and although no new expressive ground is covered here, what is evident is a higher level of control over the technique and a refined language. Once again, the composer ends the Sonata with a gentle coda. Here is how *Sonata IV* opens, a composite world of what was experienced in the first and second sonatas:

Ex 15:2 K. Humble. *Sonata IV*. opening.

The set of *Bagatelles* (1992), eight in all, is Humble's last work for piano. I had the privilege of hearing Keith perform these short pieces and to my ears they are a beautiful summation of his musical journey, with gentle reference to some of the major influences on his style and piano playing.

In 1969 he wrote this note in connection with his piano piece *Arcade II*:

> The sound material of *Arcade II* is derived from a recent computer research programme which was conducted at the University of Melbourne. It appears from the results of this programme that there are but four 12-tone rows (out of a possibility of millions of combinations) in which all of the 12 distinct trichords appear. Consequently, I have used each of these rows as a basis for each section of *Arcade*.

Humble's restless and probing curiosity, his pianism, his love/hate relationship with Australia, his refusal to concern himself with current fashions - all produced music of high integrity and value. His uncompromising honesty is all too often missing from our compositional scene.

Malcolm Williamson (1931 - 2003)

Australia has always seemingly had a problem with its expatriate composers. Are they truly Australian? Why don't they live here with us? How dare they leave us! All these questions – and there are many more – seem to me to be part of that Australian identity quest which was once of burning importance and now seems quite trivial. The fact is that Williamson, together with other composers of his generation like Banks and Lumsdaine, simply had to go abroad as there was little for them to do in their own country. Some happened to return and reestablish themselves in Australia; some never did. Some seemed to become more and more English as they became older – a crime in some eyes. Williamson was of course appointed Master of the Queen's Music, which is a kind of ultimate accolade, but it didn't seem to bring happiness in its wake. Malcolm was a complex character and no doubt his story will be told in due course. His relationship with his own country and especially with Australian composers was patchy at best. Most of his return visits were at the height of the avant-garde period in Australia; in that kind of context, he was seen as old-fashioned and passé.

In *Australian Composition in the Twentieth Century* (Melbourne: Oxford University Press, 1978, eds. Frank Callaway and David Tunley) he is quoted as saying "When I think about it, I am certain that my music is characteristically Australian, although I have never tried to make it so". The same article by Brian Chatterton also quotes some fascinating divergent views on the first *Sonata*, discussed below.

Williamson was an accomplished pianist and a thorough professional. He had facility and technique to burn. He could and did perform his own music.

Sonata No. 1 is linear and clean, with a muscular drive not unlike a combination of Copland and Stravinsky. We know that he studied with people like Eugene Goossens, Erwin Stein and Elizabeth Lutyens, and it seems to me that the discipline of these teachers emerges in this work.

In three movements, the middle slow movement is still to some extent tonal and gravitates about F sharp minor. But in the fast outer movements, tonality is much less clear and the beat often assymetric. Some compositional procedures in the work are a result of Williamson's study of Messiaen.

Ex 16:2 M. Williamson. *Sonata I*. bars 21-24 of III.

Sonata No. 2, written in memory of the British composer Gerald Finzi is a bigger piece, with two slow movements and breaking out into a jagged Allegro Assai only in the last movement. The middle movement again, has key signatures, whilst the third movement is, yet again, extremely linear and angular. The first movement is strongly thematic and has moved closer to the language of someone like Michael Tippett:

Ex 17:2 M. Williamson. *Sonata II.* bars 74-76 of I.

Much of the Sonata as a whole lies in the lower registers of the piano, giving it an overall darkness.

The numerous short pieces such as the collection of *Travel Diaries* depicting various scenes of famous cities as well as publications like *Five Preludes for Piano* with their semi-programmatic titles, all illustrate Williamson's facility and technical command, perhaps without moving us emotionally. They illustrate his openness to new influences as well as his harking back to the past when it suits him. Thus, the Preludes subtitles are: *Ships, Towers, Domes, Theatres* and *Temples,* whilst the various *Travel Diaries* are even more specific and actually name tourist hot-spots as the inspirations for the pieces, such as Eiffel Tower, Notre Dame Cathedral, St. Paul's Cathedral, Mt. Vesuvius, etc. I suspect that we are witnessing here is the two-sided Williamson persona; pieces such as the sonatas are the more serious side, the others are more in the nature of Gebrauchmusik, written for a perceived market, slick rather than profound: witness, for example, his impression of Sydney's King's Cross – "The Bohemian, cosmopolitan, night-club district"

Ex 18:2 M. Williamson. *King's Cross.* opening.

Part of Williamson's war with critics and colleagues alike has no doubt been his ready shift to populism, his refusal to be pigeonholed as only having one 'style'.

Richard Meale (1932)

Meale was largely self-taught as a composer. However, while at the State Conservatorium in Sydney, he was encouraged by his piano teacher Winifred Burston and by composers such as Raymond Hanson and Alex Burnard. Richard has always had a restless enquiring mind constantly seeking new possibilities and to some extent, therefore, new role models. Looking back over his compositional life, one can see very clearly that there is a pattern of various musical and non-musical influences occurring, all of which shape the work under consideration. Meale has never hidden or disguised such external factors; indeed, he has openly spoken of them. As a pianist he was more active earlier in his career, but nevertheless performed many new and difficult works spanning the gamut from Vaughan Williams to Messiaen and a number of European avant - garde in the sixties and seventies such as Bussotti, Castiglioni and Boulez. His knowledge and feel for the piano is consequently extensive and deeply ingrained.

His early *Sonatina Patetica* demonstrates this affinity. The movements are:

1. *Molto Moderato*
2. *Recitativo- Adagio ad libitum*
3. *Tempo Comodo*

The manuscript bears no date, but stems from Meale's student days and was composed in ca.1952. I think I gave the first performance in a radio broadcast.

The *Sonatina Patetica* is an attempt to write a medium size work in a consistent mood and with strong thematic connections between the movements. Meale, at that time, was imbued with the ideas of Hindemith and there is a Hindemithian touch too in much of the counterpoint and even the melodic construction. The writing is mostly spare and linear.

Ex 19:2 R. Meale. *Sonatina Patetica*. bars 1-4.

The sustaining of a single mood throughout the piece is possibly a weakness, but also an achievement, giving this early work unity and logic. As such, it is certainly the precursor of much of Meale's mature music.

The early *Four Bagatelles* are in a similar style and are laid out thus:

1. *Andante;* 2. *Moderato;* 3. *Flowing;* 4. *Cantabile.*

The *Four Bagatelles* began life as *Two Bagatelles* and were then expanded into four. They date from the same period as the *Sonatina Patetica,* however, the first two Bagatelles preceded the *Sonatina.* Although student works, the *Bagatelles* are highly polished miniatures with their own harmonic world. Each of them is based on a simple idea that is then thoroughly explored. The harmonies are tonal but Meale is beginning to explore shifts into unrelated triads. The second bagatelle plays with bar durations involving five and seven.

Ex 20:2 R. Meale. *Bagatelle No. 2.* opening.

The third is canonic, built on a four note descending figure and ending with four voices.

Ex 21:2 R. Meale. *Bagatelle No.3.* opening.

The last *Bagatelle* is the most substantial of the set and possibly the most melodic.

Another early work, *Orenda* (1959), immediately precedes Meale's first acknowledged work, which happened to be a *Flute Sonata* (1960). *Orenda* used, in its first movement, a notion of a series of chords with constantly expanding durations. Both Meale and some of his performers now consider *Orenda* structurally flawed, and so, like these other early works, it has largely been forgotten. All of these works are still in manuscript, but hopefully will soon achieve publication.

Meale's major work for the piano is *Coruscations*, a brilliant evocation of the Aurora Borealis (hence the title). Behind the highly virtuosic flashes and gestures at speed, which is what the pianist is required to deliver, lies a complex web of organization, no doubt inspired by Richard's then - interest in Boulez and his explorations of ways to manipulate pitch and other parameters of piano sound. For those interested in such analytical matters, please see *Australian Music in the Twentieth Century* (ed. Callaway). Here it is important to note that in the right hands, *Coruscations* can be a dazzling experience, as witness performances by the dedicatee of the piece, Roger Woodward.

On the question of a distinct Australian musical style, Meale has said:

> It's an unavoidable question. And I dare say that in a country that boasts of being multicultural, how dare we inflict our concept of Australiawhich has been formed by a white, English-based people? ....
> I think it's a big illusion and a sentimental approach that we have to have an Australian music. I don't think it's eventually a constructive view, because it is false. We are trying to define the thing before it has happened; we are trying to reverse a natural historic process.
> (Composer file, Australian Music Centre)

Donald Hollier (1934)

Hollier's career has encompassed a number of activities, all of them impinging on his compositional approach to the piano. He is a concert organist as well as a concert pianist; he has written for the theatre and directed opera; he has conducted, including oratorios; he has toured as an accompanist and has had a long and distinguished career as a teacher. An altogether flamboyant personality has merged all these activities in his music for the piano.

Returning to Australia from England in the 1960s after completing a Doctorate at the University of London, Hollier represents an interesting amalgamation of academic and experimental thinking; his performance background imbues his music with the freedoms learnt from early music ornamentation and romantic music's rubato and soloistic cadenza. Eventually this led him towards various types of controlled aleatoricism. Thus, it is not untypical to find, in the same piece, strict fugue and mirror fugue combined with great freedom of notes and structure including some measure of improvisation. This last no doubt comes from Hollier's organ practice, probably the only classical instrument on which improvisation is still taught today. The resultant mix of very strict and free is what gives Hollier's music its special flavour and grand dramatic gesture.

The actual appearance of a Hollier score is the first impression one gets. Many of the larger works are also written in a format that demands large size paper, given the system of notation. This works against the composer, as the scores become difficult to reproduce, carry around, and even place on a music stand. The presentation of the scores possibly has an effect on the potential number of performances. Generally, Hollier prefers to rule his own paper and set out the page exactly as it suits him. The visual impact of his scores has some connection, I feel, with his theatrical flair and sense of the dramatic.

This kind of impracticality illustrates some of the immediate problems of approaching a Hollier score. It is possible that some of the music, at least, could be presented in a different way in print, but so far, almost all of it is still in manuscript form.

Like Burnard, Hollier comes from the English tradition and prides himself in his abilities to harmonize chorales, write fugues and canons and subject music to his keenly critical gaze. He favours set forms, or invents new forms to suit himself. His harmonic language, often wild and unrestrained, is perhaps best demonstrated in his cycle of Sonnets for piano.

Ex 22:2 D. Hollier. *Sonnet No. 6.* opening.

The required pianism is of a virtuosic order:

Ex 23:2 D. Hollier. *Sonnet No.4.* opening.

The difficulties are not merely motoric or those of learning an often dense, chromatically saturated score. They also involve the ability to use all three pedals skillfully, to learn to play on the keyboard and inside the grand piano sometimes simultaneously, to juggle and superimpose different tempi and moods, to gauge the silences, to make informed choices when they are asked for to create a viable structure for the listener to follow and last but certainly not least, to understand the raw emotion driving these pieces.

The cycle of *Sonnets* for piano are probably the most important set of pieces so far produced in this country, for their extensive and consistently imaginative use of the instrument, the huge range of emotions displayed and the wedding of sound and intent. They represent the elements of Hollier's personalities (I use the plural deliberately) in their most successful exposition. The *Sonnets*, like Shakespeare's, are very personal utterances directed at specific but unknown people (Oral History interview NLA). I have provided the dates of composition as they appear on the manuscripts. They give some indication of the white heat at which these works were written. The plan of the cycle is:

SONNET I: August-January '76-'77
> The cycle opens ominously and dramatically with constant shifts between fragments marked *Mesto* and *Scherzo*. The *Mesto* fragments ask for controlled rise and fall of dynamics within repeated notes or chords, creating an atmosphere of slow and hypnotic chant. There is also some choice allowed as to order of events. The contrasts are extreme.

SONNET II. (Spring '62). June 1976. For Keith
> The date of composition is the second date. The first refers to events. The performing direction is *Molto Appassionate*. The left hand is utilized throughout to play up/down quasi arpeggio patterns, giving a turbulent undercurrent to the whole sonnet.

SONNET III (the manuscript mistakenly has 'sonata' not sonnet). August-January '76-'77
> Features a *Tranquillo Quasi Chorale* at the end. Again, choices on the spokes of wheels. Hollier writes here : "start anywhere and proceed in any direction. Play only once". This leaves open some ambiguity in other *Sonnets* with similar wheel layouts - that is, is it permissible to play more than once? This Sonnet features strumming chords inside the piano, like in Henry Cowell's *Aeolian Harp*.

SONNET IV. 15/8/76
> One of the more difficult of the series, with frequent markings such as 'Frenetic' and 'Violent'. Consistently non-legato, this also contains a gesture at the end that the composer wants repeated fourteen times! It is marked 'sinister'. Hollier adopts the most simple notation that he can in terms of the durations of the notes, allowing, throughout the cycle, the many gaps between gestures to constantly play with the perception of beats and time.

SONNET V. (Summer '48). 25/8/76.
> The date of composition is the second one. Pianist is asked to play 'Very intense but always hushed'. This is the most atomized of the

series, with long silences. Hollier destroys the mood at the end with a violent outburst. The long succession of low chords has each to be held until it disappears into silence.

SONNET VI. 25/8/76. SONG OF RESIGNATION.

Juxtaposition of varying tempi. Some passages consist of the simultaneous and rapid sounding of passages with its own inversion. Strumming and keyboard playing combined. (Hollier is tall and has long arms, and so to him such a request does not sound in any way excessive! But I stress it is all eminently possible).

SONNET VII. 18/7/75

The score consists of three blocks of events marked A, B and C. Instructions are: "A, B, C may be played in any order. D (which in the score is a blank block with four 'spokes') is the recapitualtion of A or B or C. The sentences within each box may also be played in any order. But no sentence should be repeated." A 12-note chord that appears in other *Sonnets* is here caught on the third pedal. It is possible that the pitch choices have some symbolic meaning.

SONNET VIII. 24/7/75. AUTUMN '75

Order of events is fixed. A combination of notes played on the keyboard with notes plucked inside the piano. Third pedal is used to sustain a 12-note chord throughout the piece. Most durations are rhapsodically free.

SONNET IX. 235/5/75

This is a continuous piece which the composer asks to be played "as rapidly and quietly as possible with both pedals down. The score is arranged like a giant wheel and the player has a choice as to which fragment comes first and then whether to move clockwise or anticlockwise. There is a violent coda at the close.

SONNET X. August '76-January '77.

This is marked 'Monotonous'. The player is given some choice for a series of end-gestures described as 'refrains' and is asked to pick which refrains are heard. As the title might suggest, this is predominantly made up of slow chords.

SONNET XI. Winter '59-'59. June-January '76-'77.
The second date is the date of composition. The first must refer to the date of events in the composer's life.

The sonnet is marked *Molto Appasionate*. A powerful, relentless piece, the left hand of which provides a constant and inexorable drum beat using black and white note glissandi in the lowest reaches of the piano. The huge score is divided into time spans marked by the funereal beat of the left hand, within which the right hand plays at consistently high intensity. This sonnet is played all on the keyboard in the conventional manner.

SONNET XII.January 1977.
    The heading is 'Desolate'. Most of the Sonnet is arpeggiated patterns with controlled up/down dynamics and silences, giving an overwhelming sensation of sighing passages. As once before, Hollier tends to destroy any feeling of peace or tranquility with a powerful succession of very loud chords at the end.

It should be said that what might first sound like gimmickry – the plucking of notes, the glissandi inside the piano, the big clusters, even the visual impact of the huge score soon settles down into 'normal' acceptable language and one is then free to immerse oneself in the actual musical world of these pieces. Because structurally the *Sonnets* are by their nature fragmentary, it requires a performer to cope with this plethora of beginnings and endings by varying the length of the gaps and building these silences into the fabric of the works. It is only when the fragments are allowed to begin to sound predictable in length and in duration of the breaks between them that the cycle could falter. The whole huge edifice of the *Sonnets* is predicated on a violent rhapsodism in which consistent but controlled structural freedoms predominate and give a unifying voice.

They are heavily emotional works, charged with outbursts of energy. It is of course possible to play individual *Sonnets*, or a number of them as a bracket, but the huge impact of the cycle can only be experienced by a complete performance of the whole work. The visual appearance of the *Sonnets* on paper only confirms the aural impression, but Donald's presentation of the *Sonnets* on out-size paper has mitigated against them becoming better known. It seems to me that much of the music could be typeset in a more accessible way on ordinary sized paper and presented to the public anew; perhaps now is the time for this to occur; perhaps the presentation in the way the composer chose was part of the ethos of the then avant-garde and is no longer vital today?

Since much of Hollier's orientation as a musician has to do with the human voice (even the use of the title *Sonnets*), the cantabile aspect of writing for the piano is ever present:

Ex 24:2 D. Hollier. *Sonnet No.3.* opening of Quasi Chorale section.

The *Sonatina for piano* (1971) is a much more accessible and lighthearted piece, in the traditional three movement format, and although there are some aspects of serialism, everything is treated lightly and with humour, includes such – by now – well-worn techniques as plucking the piano strings and wedging keys down to create sympathetic resonance. This short work, although not easy, is nevertheless an excellent introduction to techniques of the time; it is an effective concert work, and an almost essential stepping stone to the much darker world of the *Sonnets*.

Other works for solo piano by this composer were not available to us at the time of writing this book. Some of these works may be lost.

Bozidar Kos (1934)

Kos used to play the piano professionally in his younger years, when he was involved in jazz performance. His use of the keyboard shows someone who is familiar with piano geography and whose experience manifests itself in his piano music. His approach to the keyboard is, as he himself says, 'traditional' (Composer questionnaire) and he regards the piano and the piano repertoire as very important 'within the context of contemporary music in general'.

Kos's *Reflections* (1976), dedicated to Richard Meale has an obvious kinship to Meale's *Coruscations* in the busy piano figurations of the opening, and the subsequent development of those figures as well as in some of the more explosive moments.

Ex 25:2 B. Kos. *Reflections*. bars 3-4.

However, the Kos piece is less violent, and the quaver movement is spaced more closely on the keyboard and in the end, reduces to a murmur that dies away. There is also what Kos calls a 'proportional distribution' of notes with square note-heads, which introduce an element of aleatoricism in the durations of these notes.

Ex 26:2 B. Kos. *Reflections*. bars 19-21

Though not easy, *Reflections* is marked by clarity of thought and texture, something of a trademark in Kos's approach to the piano.

Kolo (1984) in fact begins very much like *Reflections*, with rapid assymetric figurations, which are subjected to additive processing. Concerning these assymetric groups, which in this work are barred and given slight accentuation, Kos prefaces the work with the following explanation:

> Kolo is a common name for various folk dances of Yugoslavia. They are usually danced by a larger group of dancers, holding hands and forming an open or closed circle. There exist a large variety of these dances with respect to steps, direction of movement, character of music, etc... Musically this work relates to folk dances only through the use of additive rhythms and assymetric metric pulsations, which are characteristic particularly for kolo dances of Southern Yugoslavia.

Thus, just about every bar of *Kolo* has a differing assymetric breakdown. *Kolo* fluctuates between a slow and a fast tempo, but all of it is unmistakably dance –

based, and the constantly irregular beats, lightly accented, give the work a somewhat dizzying flavour.

Ex 27:2 B. Kos. *Kolo*. opening.

Concerning the *Piano Sonata* (1981), the composer writes in his score:

> This is a single-movement sonata consisting of several contrasting musical ideas. Successions of vigorous *marcato* chords, for example, ranging in length from very short staccato bursts to longer sustained durations, are often juxtaposed with very rapid scurrying patterns that in turn may be followed by 'cantabile' type of homophony, or very light and airy pianissimo figures, superimposed on long sustained static harmony. These diverse ideas are then further contrasted either by slow, tranquil polyphonic textures, or by bright and fast sections, based on assymetric additive rhythms, strengthened by accents. These contrasting musical ideas are then subjected, during the process of composition, to a number of transformations and repeated several times, each time in different juxtapositions to each other, yet there exist various underlying factors that unify these diverse materials. Contrasting ideas, for example, often complement each other, thus forming larger unified groups. They are also closely related through the use of common pitch and other material.

The restlessness already evident in prior works as well as the clash of greatly contrasting ideas are here given full play, but are also totally controlled by the composer:

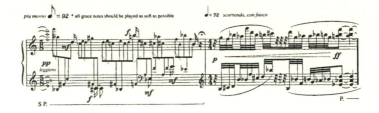

Ex 28:2 B. Kos. *Piano Sonata*. bars 28-29.

The achievement of this *Sonata* is not just the logical connection of various disparate elements, but ultimately, the resolution of these seemingly clashing elements at the very end of the piece. This is clearly an important work in the Australian context.

Kos's music shows diverse influences: his background as a jazz player and arranger, his study and awareness of the European avant-garde, including Boulez, as well as his own search for logic and coherence. The piano music displays an impressive clarity and even elegance, with its own stylistic logic, which the composer inevitably attempts to resolve and display by the end of each piece.

Nigel Butterley (1935)

Nigel Butterley has been a consistent and distinguished presence on the Australian musical scene for a number of decades. As a pianist he has performed his own and other composers' music and although he would be the last person to describe himself as a touring virtuoso, he is certainly very much at home at the keyboard and therefore some important and seminal works of the Australian repertoire have come from his pen. The music is always highly crafted and worked in some detail; furthermore, his connections with the past are clear from the earliest pieces. For example, a short *Arioso* from the 1960s is an obviously neo-Bachian piece; there is an even earlier unpublished Toccata (1960), lasting just over a minute, with similar references to an earlier keyboard style, but already exhibiting that spare and muscular linearity that is characteristic of Nigel's keyboard approach. Similarly, *Comment on a Popular Song* (1960) is also in a spare, somewhat bouncy idiom with assymetric groups of lines and chords.

In an early review of an LP, Butterley declares that he is "allergic to Liszt", an interesting declaration that informs us to some extent that his keyboard writing will tend to avoid flashy gestures, which indeed it does (I am certain that not all of Liszt would be included in Butterley's statement).

In another issue of the same magazine (Composer file, Australian Music Centre) Butterley declares a different sort of creed which encompasses much of his mature music:

> .... I think we will find...that the world's really great music, including that by composers of unorthodox or nebulous religious views, is fired with some kind of mysticism or spiritual quality. And if we today want to reject this kind of mysticism, our world of music will be a very bare, empty one.

Butterley expands on this idea and on his religious interests in the aural history tapes held at the National Library of Australia. Looking at Butterley's output now, it seems to me that the mystical aspect of music which is so important to him, emerges more in the vocal and choral works, as well as in the orchestral works rather than the works for piano; these last show another persona of the composer. What this may be is hard to put into words, but the piano music seems more dispassionate somehow, more concerned with craft.

Butterley, in correspondence we had during the writing of this book, does say that the piano has always been central to his thinking; but goes on to say that he hasn't written much for the instrument because he finds it difficult to write something grateful and to avoid clichés. For this reason, a desire to compose a piano concerto has never been realized.

Like most of the composers of his generation, Butterley was to some extent self-taught, although he lists Noel Nickson and Raymond Hanson as teachers; Hanson was at that time imbued with Hindemith's theories and so Nigel was taught to think of chords as manifesting varying degrees of tension and resolution.

Concerning the work *Letter from Hardy's Bay* (1971), Butterley writes:

> Hardy's Bay is an inlet in Brisbane Water, north of Sydney, a few miles from the place where I often go to write music. As writing music is such a solitary thing one's mind tends to be over-active, and filled with all sorts of questions, relevant or irrelevant to the job in hand. I've walked to Hardy's Bay in this frame of mind, and the place has a strong personal significance. In a modest way this piece and its title are in line with what Aaron Copland said - "Every new work is in part an answer to the question 'who am I?'". I suppose the recurring gong-like chord, which halts the flow of the piece every time it appears, is like an idea which keeps coming to the surface of one's train of thought, no matter how much one tries to get away from it.

Butterley's approach to this 'landscape piece' is thus a very personal reaction to a place and a state of mind, with nothing obviously 'Australian' about it. *Hardy's*

Bay could be anywhere. Butterley asks for four notes to be 'prepared' by inserting eight metal bolts between the strings. The pianist is also asked to pluck some strings and play harmonics directly on the strings. The gong-like chord appears at the very opening, and a typical example of it interrupting the flow of the music occurs soon after:

Ex 29:2 N. Butterley. *Letter from Hardy's Bay*. end of section A.

Parts of this piece use proportional notation, but generally Butterley does not relinquish any control over the durations of his notes.

Butterley has said this of *Lawrence Hargrave Flying Alone* (1981):

> The idea and title of this piece, and of the two-act opera of the same name completed seven years later, came from a series of sculptures by Peter Taylor, based on the Australian aviation pioneer Lawrence Hargrave (1850-1915). Taylor sees Hargrave as a hero-figure, with a vision incapable of fulfillment in his own lifetime and environment.

> Hargrave had a vision of flying, but for all his years of planning, inventing and model-making, he himself only ever left the ground for a minute or so - suspended by four box-kites. But his ideas and inventions, including the box kite, contributed vitally to the success of others. Hargrave's striving to reach his vision of flight is clearly the motivation behind the upward-reaching lines of the music – often faltering, sometimes succeeding.

> His theory of what he called trochoid motion, demonstrated most clearly in the way a snake moves, as well as by insects, birds and fish, is represented musically by a series of chords which increase and decrease (in both duration and the number of notes), as well as by two lines of single notes heard simultaneously, one getting faster and the other slower. The idea of this curve is behind many of the musical shapes in this work, and affects pitch, dynamics, duration and chordal density. Some of the musical material was arrived at with the aid of note-rows and cryptography.

> (Composer file, Australian Music Centre)

Much of the texture of this most interesting work is widely spaced two part polyphony, at times giving way to a single line widely spaced all over the keyboard:

Ex 30:2 N. Butterley. *Lawrence Hargrave Flying Alone*. bars 41-45 .

Ex 31:2 N. Butterley. *Lawrence Hargrave Flying Alone*. bars 51-52 .

In my mind, Butterley's other major composition *Uttering Joyous Leaves* is related to the Hargrave piece – not in any musical or thematic sense but simply by the uniformity of approach to writing for the piano. This important work is preceded by a quotation from Walt Whitman:

> ...and though the live-oak glistens there in Louisiana
> solitary in wide flat space.
> Uttering joyous leaves all its life without a friend a lover near,
> I know very well I could not.

Butterley structured this work in a manner similar to Tippett, a composer he greatly admires. There are three thematic groups and three different tempi, and *Uttering Joyous Leaves* involves restating this material´in different order and with variations each time. It is not an easy piece to learn or to indeed to play, but proceeds with a wonderful inevitability and has a really strong and individual sound world all its own. The first appearances of the three groups give the flavour of the entire score:

Ex 32:2 N. Butterley. *Uttering Joyous Leaves*. bars 1-3 .

Ex 33:2 N. Butterley. *Uttering Joyous Leaves*. bars 8-9 .

Ex 34:2 N. Butterley. *Uttering Joyous Leaves*. bars 10-11 .

Grevillea was first written in 1962, but revised in 1985. Its approach to the piano is characteristic Butterley, right from the start.

Ex 35:2 N. Butterley. *Grevillea*. bars 1-4 .

Like the *Hargrave* piece, it too examines very wide spacing on the keyboard. *Hargrave* and *Uttering Joyous Leaves*, and indeed, *Il Gubbo* (see below), *Grevillea* ends with an upward swoop on the piano, a gesture that is a Butterley signature.

Nigel's love of the dry piano sound is taken to its logical conclusion in a miniature named *Il Gubbo* (The Hunchback), in which no pedal at all is used and the pianist has to develop a technique of changing fingers on the same note as well as silently take over notes from one hand to another. This little three-page piece was part of a *Bicentennial Piano Album* issued by Allans Publishing, to celebrate Australia's Bicentenary in 1988. The idea of the piece came to Nigel from a church figure in Verona. Butterley is an enthusiastic lover of architecture and painting.

Although the actual output for the piano is not large, it is significant and distinctive and a rich contribution by the composer to the genre.

Non-Pianists

Meta Overman (1907–1993)

Although Meta Overman's *Sonata II* (1953) won an APRA prize (judged by Lindley Evans and Alex Burnard), and although she was a pianist, her output for piano was quite limited and she is now remembered chiefly as a music theatre composer. The piano writing, which began while the composer was still in Holland and studying with Pijper, is very much in the European neoclassic mold of the time, with clean lines and occasional deviations from a strongly stated tonality. Of the two sonatas I have played through, the second is a more powerful and rugged work, especially in its opening movement, with a more dramatic and darker colour than in the first. The pianism required to play Overman's music is of moderate difficulty and it is surprising that one doesn't hear more performances of her sonatas and other piano music. Perhaps some of this may be ascribed to her quite long absence from Australia for a while, as well as her post-war arrival and struggle to make herself heard in the early years, with a long history of frustration connected to the mounting of her music theatre piece *Psyche*. There was a period in Melbourne when she worked in the music mainstream and was friendly with composers such as Le Gallienne, Sutherland and Humble. Her full story is yet to be told and her piano music yet to acquire a sympathetic performer. Some of her very late piano music such as *Tristan Images* (1986), *Tristan Variations* (1988) and *Tristan Sonatina* (1989), were written for her grandson, and being music for beginners, is outside the scope of this book. In these works she introduces young pianists to a non-tonal language.

Peter Platt (1924 –2000)

Peter Platt was Professor of Music at the University of Sydney for many years. He was primarily a musicologist with early twentieth century music the focus of his research. There does not appear to be much piano music, although his personal papers have yet to be catalogued.

Two Views of Eternity, Fritzi Raubitschek in memoriam (1997): This curious but very lyrical piece by Platt combines his own music with music by Bach. The texture is largely governed by the quotations from J.S.Bach: the *Courante* from the French Suite in Eb No. 4. a general tempo "roughly that of a serene performance of *Jesu Joy of Man's Desiring*" and a short quote from the Debussy Prelude No. 6, with interludes of a rather dreamy nature by Platt. The composer says:

> The idea is that...two visions of eternity (Bach's and mine) are going on simultaneously - only while one vision is playing, you can't physically hear the other (though there is a brief dialogue between them at the end).

Platt has also written two pieces for left hand alone: *Andante Lirico* and *Cantilena*; there is no indication in the manuscript copies whether these are related pieces meant to be played together, although a letter attached to the *Cantilena* refers to it as the 'second' piece. There is also, among the papers, a short Largo in a quasi-Bach style. Some of these manuscript works are carefully and meticulously fingered, suggesting that Platt intended them for his own performance, perhaps even domestic performance. Peter had some piano lessons with me and never pretended to be a solo performer.

More interesting and harmonically adventurous is a short work called *A thoughtful piece for Eric*, from 1991:

Ex 36:2 P. Platt. *A thoughtful piece for Eric*. bars 1-3.

Platt also apparently planned a set of twelve pieces, possibly entitled *Boulez Notations*, or else just simply *Notations*. The first four have so far been found, dated 1995. They are in rough but complete form and could make a complete bracket on their own.

Harold Allen (1930–1983)

There is a composition prize in Harold Allen's name at the School of Music of the Australian National University. He has written two piano works and it seemed appropriate to say a few words about the music.

Since he trained with Peter Racine Fricker and then Elizabeth Lutyens, it was inevitable that some serial method would appear in Allen's work, although he treats it freely and regards it as a device for a certain mode of expression rather than a rigid technique. In his output he favoured small groups and solo instruments.

The *8 Episodes for Piano* are a set of serial aphorisms, matching Webern in brevity and with carefully constructed gestures and dynamics as compositional hallmarks. They would only last approximately six minutes in total, and our information is that they were written in 1966, even though the manuscript is undated.

Tristram Cary (1925)

Cary's place in Australian music is assured through his important pioneering work in electronics as well as his work for film. He taught composition for many years at the University of Adelaide.

Tristram's *Polly Fillers* (1989) just sneaks into this book. It is described as of 'moderate technical difficulty' and for 'adult learners', but the composer later admitted that he pitched the difficulty too high. These pieces can be played as a cycle or separately. The album comprises:

1. *Grand Gesture (Sort of Fantasia style)*
2. *Petite Valse des Téléphones*
3. *Micropassacaglia*
4. *Calm Chorale*
5. *Small Dance*
6. *Brick Lane Blues (also issued separately as "Tandoori Blues")*
7. *Fugue à 3 (Polly takes tea in old Leipzig)*

The pieces were written for Tristram's friend the painter Polly Hope, in exchange for a portrait. The title is of course a pun and suggests that these pieces can be played at any time of the day, to fill in the odd moment. The pieces are an ideal illustration and encapsulation of Cary's eclecticism, command of technique and sense of humour, the last a fairly rare attribute in the music we are surveying. The opening piece is built up of fourths and fifths; although fully barred, in experienced hands it could well be performed like a baroque unbarred fantasia. The ensuing *Valse* uses telephone numbers to create themes as a starting point. The *Micropassacaglia* has, in the words of the composer, 'interchangeable sections', 'so you can design your own piece'. The composer in his notes for the performer at the back of the volume is constantly encouraging the player to add, ornament and improvise. The *Chorale* does what the title states. *Small Dance* is a short exploration of assymetric beats. *Brick Lane Blues* introduces an old Indian melody in its middle section (Brick Lane is what Cary calls *Little India* in London) and so effectively mixes East and West in a non-ponderous unpretentious manner. Both the opening Fantasia and the Fugue are in F and so could be performed as a Prelude & Fugue - which works very well. The Fugue is lighthearted but complete, with the nursery rhyme 'Polly put the kettle on, we'll all have tea' woven into the polyphonic texture. It is interesting that some of Cary's earliest listed piano pieces are a set of fugues (1952) as well as an early *Partita* (1947).

Concerning the work *Strange Places* (1992), the composer writes:

> This piece can be regarded as normal abstract music with no programmatic content – for example as a five movement sonata. The idea behind it, however, is to mirror the astonishing unity within complexity that is evident in the natural world around us. Both in the inanimate world of rocks, hills and bodies of water, and in the vast diversity of plants and animals, one is constantly struck with a sense of ordered randomness, of purposeful chaos, which I have tried to capture by finding a musical analogy for the phenomenon.
>
> Outside the familiar modes of tonal music there are many other possible scale formations, still using whole and semitones but differently arranged to make scales of anything from seven to ten notes per octave. *Strange Places* explores a musical outback of nineteen scales, which with transposed versions is presented as 141 different pitch formations.
>
> Imagine that the explorer has arrived at a site with 141 similar but different features, and intends to investigate and map this apparently random arrangement of locations. Dividing the site into three sections to organize the search, the first two movements cover two of these contrasting frames of mind (*Site Surveys 1 & 2*). Following this a first complete *Tour (141A)* is made, and afterwards the third section is seen again from a different angle *(Site Survey 3)*. Finally, in the light of previous experience, a second *Tour (141B)* re-explores the whole site in a more intense way, making a third visit to each location.
> (Composer file, Australian Music Centre)

The score of the work actually lists all the scale patterns that are used, making clearer the text above. Although the scales (modes) are used for both horizontal and vertical construction, it is almost inevitable that the essentially linear thinking will produce a predominantly linear piece, although harmonies are built up by using the sustaining pedal and by holding notes down. Unlike *Polly Fillers*, this is a pianistically demanding work.

Peter Tahourdin (1928)

Tahourdin is a distinguished composer with many large scale works in his catalogue. His output for the piano is small.

The composer's note to *Exposé* (1995) reads:

> *Exposé* was written for the French pianist, Alain Raës. The title has a dual meaning, referring both to a verbal or visual statement or exposure, and to the term 'exposition' - an unfolding and revelation of purely musical material.
>
> The two bar opening gesture is the springboard that initiates that unfolding and, together with the slow-moving, lyrical phrases that follow, forms the basis of the subsequent activity. In addition, it serves as a link between the two more playful, faster episodes and provides the material for the short coda that takes the work back to its origins and brings it to a quiet close.

Like all of Tahourdin's music, this is delicately crafted, very clean in texture, with the composer vary much in control of the materials:

Ex 37:2 P. Tahourdin. *Exposé*. bars 1-3.

Lawrence Whiffin (1930)

Lawrence Whiffin (Laurie to his friends), who I have known for a good number of years, was trained as a pianist in Melbourne, initially with the well-known teacher Roy Shepherd, who incidentally also taught Keith Humble; and like Humble, Whiffin went on to study with the Schoenberg disciple René Leibowitz. Whiffin's writing for the piano is strong and sits comfortably for the performer, whilst sometimes offering technical challenges. But as with all successful piano music, the challenges are well worth meeting and conquering.

Perhaps in passing, I will mention a little suite of six pieces, more closely akin
to teaching material, that constitute what Whiffin titles *The Garfield Suite*, no
doubt inspired by that well-known cartoon character, since each of the small
movements have cat-related titles: I. *Bite, Scratch and Purr*; II. *Old Tom's
Mooch;* III. *Funny Cat*; IV. *Pas de Chat*; V. *Sleepy Fat Cat* and VI. *Tom
Foolery*.

I first came across Laurie's music as a pianist whilst recording the *La Trobe
Anthology of Australian piano music* during the 1980s. The *Prelude's* complex
weave of sound fascinated me, and it is true but curious that after recording it in
a rather free flowing rhapsodic fashion, Laurie told me that he had always
imagined the piece played strictly! I came to the conclusion that good music is
susceptible to and survives sometimes opposite treatments. Concerning the
Prelude, the composer writes:

> The *Prelude* is in ABA, the second A of which is, until the Coda, an
> exact mirror of the first. The Coda is short and reveals how the initial
> idea is based on a 1940 popular tune, disguised by extreme
> chromaticism. The composition's pitch organization depends on the
> cyclic unfolding of a transposing chord sequence; a technique derived
> from the procedures of late tonal composers. The sound in the
> "Prelude" is, however, very different from that of the Romantics since
> the chord sequence is constantly used simultaneously with its
> inversion.

Ex 38:2 L. Whiffin. *Prelude.* bars 32-33.

There is also a *Sonatina* that lies somewhere between *The Garfield Suite* and the
Prelude in terms of difficulty. Laurie here demonstrates his experience as a film
composer and arranger by providing a piece that is lighter in substance and
texture than his more extended compositions. The *Sonatina*, like the later
Sonata, is in a one-movement format, so the Lisztian model lives on into
modern times.

Whiffin's serious venture into a large-scale piece for the piano is described by
the composer himself:

Mechanical Mirrors is a one movement sonata for piano consisting of four large sections replacing the traditional four movements. The first large section representing the sonata 'allegro' is followed without interruption by a second slower section which leads in turn to the third and fourth sections. The one-movement form develops its own particular requirements resulting, in the present work, in the replacing of the traditional *minuet* or *scherzo*, by a third large section elaborating ideas from the first. In the second large section, an undeclared theme and variations, an ancient technique used by Handel (among others), is used. This consists of halving the initial slow note values then halving them again, resulting each time in increased agitation and doubling of the tempo. The piano is treated almost orchestrally in much of this second section, with three independent voices in different registers unfolding simultaneously. Just as the third section develops first section ideas, so the fourth section repeats and develops a good-humoured tune taken from the second section. Its good humour soon changes, however, as the tune turns grotesque via the previously mentioned technique of halving the note values, the increased speed provoking a fortissimo climax and final coda based on brief flashbacks to the first and second large sections.

The Sonata is a virtuosic work written by a composer who knows and understands the piano. Although only lasting just over a quarter-hour, it is intense, packed to the rafters with material and ideas. The writing is not just idiomatic- it is consistently clean and effective, no matter what the level of difficulty:

Ex 39:2 L. Whiffin. *Mechanical Mirrors*. bars 323-325.

The Whiffin Sonata is another example of a finely wrought Australian work for the concert piano that has yet to make its place in the repertoire.

David Lumsdaine (1931)

Lumsdaine falls into that somewhat unclear group of Australian composers who have lived most of their life outside of this country and therefore do not appear to have actively contributed to our musical culture. Additionally - for the purposes of this book, Lumsdaine is not an active pianist and his contribution to the piano genre has been restricted to a handful of pieces, albeit significant ones. Lumsdaine is a complex example of a composer – his influences are diverse and his responses to various composers interact in ways not immediately clear to the listener. Although he hasn't lived in Australia for a long time, the composer has many pieces which use Australian landscape or history in its titles and the vast stillness of the Australian bush is in much of his music. Lumsdaine is an ornithologist and the music has shifted towards the use of electronics to capture and encapsulate natural landscape. Like his friend Don Banks, Lumsdaine had to leave Australia to discover what it meant to be a composer, and like Banks, Lumsdaine's Australianism is not of the obvious kind, but is deeply ingrained and deeply felt.

The composer's *Kelly Ground*, the survivor of a planned opera on Ned Kelly, which was finally aborted, is a serially based work that uses quite complicated pulses superimposed in a number of ratios. The composer explains further in the preface to the score, which is dedicated to Don Banks. The piece, which David regards as his first mature work, comes from 1966. It is organized in cycles and strophes and to a certain extent is a child of its time, i.e. the post-war European avant-garde.

Ex 40:2 D. Lumsdaine. *Kelly Ground*. bars 12-15 .

Concerning his next major piano work, *Ruhe sanfte, sanfte ruh* (1974), Lumsdaine has written that this

> ...is a meditation on the last chorus of Bach's *St. Matthew Passion*...Bach's music is never stated explicitly but it creates a motivic and harmonic web out of which the music grows. A gently rocking refrain opens the work, and articulates an extended rondo structure. Each section grows out of its successor and, unlike a classical rondo, encompasses a longer stretch of time. I imagined the

shape as a helix, with the refrain marking the beginning of each circuit.

Roger Woodward commissioned the work and Lumsdaine wrote it as a memoriam to a close friend who died just as the composer commenced work on the piece. Like *Kelly Ground*, this too seems haunted by the sound of bells. It begins and ends with Bach's C minor chord, but that is not to say that what transpires between these chords is related to functional tonality. The work is marked by use of the extreme registers of the piano, quite often together and sometimes harshly:

Ex 41:2 D. Lumsdaine. *Ruhe sanfte, sanfte ruh.* circa bar 33 .

Cambewarra (1980) is somewhat kinder to the performer than the two prior works. Once again, Lumsdaine writes a preface that gives background to the music. However, here it is possible to also create shorter versions of the given piece, which extends over twenty seven pages and is in three movements. Lumsdaine gives the performer some possible ways to play these shorter versions, but the tone of the preface doesn't seem to indicate that the composer would be over-concerned, should other versions occur to the pianist.

Each of the three movements commences with a fairly free section, which is described as 'toccata-like'. In the first movement, a chorale is interspersed in this free-flowing texture and is marked in the score as '1st verse', '2nd verse' etc. The toccata-like sections are more open and cleaner than in *Kelly Ground*:

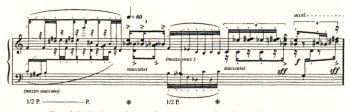

Ex 42:2 D. Lumsdaine. *Cambewarra*. circa bar 46 .

The second movement presents a more rhythmic approach to the piano and contains passages specifically marked 'cadenza' that are closer to a more traditionally *brillante* approach to piano writing, utilizing *martellato* in percussive alternating hand effects.

Ex 43:2 D. Lumsdaine. *Cambewarra*. circa bar 218 .

The last movement gives the listener more obvious repetitions of patterns to orientate themselves. At the end, after pushing towards a flashy finish, the composer asks the performer to 'play the silence!' at the end of the work.

Lumsdaine's output for the piano, though relatively small, represents three substantial pieces which, in this country at least, have yet to be given their due recognition.

Helen Gifford (1935)

The composer writes:

> The piano has always been of prime importance to me... but I have always found it the most difficult of instruments to write for. This I see as a general problem for composers of the mid-twentieth century and beyond, mostly to do with the inflexible tonality of its tuning and its unvarying timbre, compared with other instruments. Even so, the piano still provides me with potentially the most satisfaction and greatest challenge to compose. (Composer questionnaire)

Gifford is not a performing pianist, but grew up with the instrument and is so familiar with it that she has written two major and significant works for it. She regards herself as primarily a composer for the theatre, yet apparently Chopin is her favourite composer. Not a fervent admirer of academia and of theoretical speculation about music, Gifford nevertheless completed a music degree at Melbourne University in the late 1950s, majoring in piano. Dorian Le Gallienne was a composer who encouraged her in her early years; otherwise she is largely self-taught. Her biographer, Zoe Sweett, writing the preface to a recent edition of Gifford's piano music and therefore probably making statements approved by the composer herself, describes the *Piano Sonata* from 1960 as being primarily inspired by Prokofiev and Bartók. That may very well be true, but this three-movement work also displays an economy of gesture and notes which is very much Helen's own approach to the piano, so that the energy is constantly tempered by refinement:

Ex. 44:2 H. Gifford. *Piano Sonata*. bars 86-91.

Even the ending is relatively subdued, though dramatic:

Ex 45:2 H. Gifford. *Piano Sonata*. ending.

The next two works are smaller in scope, and both date from the 1960s. *Catalysis* (1963) is a six-page work that takes the incipient refinement of the Sonata a step further and delicately explores the great variety of touches and dynamics, pedaled and unpedaled, available on the piano. All this is achieved with largely single and double strands of voices:

Ex 46:2 H. Gifford. *Catalysis*. Bars 46-47.

There is hardly a chord in the whole piece.

Three Pieces (1966) are miniatures of two pages duration each. They push the refinement already seen in *Catalysis* a step further. Thus, *Cantillation* is obviously a melodically inspired work, though the line is spread all over the keyboard, and beats tend to be assymetric, mostly seven divided into four and three:

Ex 47:2 H. Gifford. *Cantillation*. bars 13-17.

The Spell is a static piece capturing a moment of enchantment. It is written on three staves and although Gifford doesn't indicate pedal at all, I used to enjoy playing it with much pedal, increasing the sense of stillness:

Ex 48:2 H. Gifford. *The Spell*. bars 4-6.

Finally, *Waltz* retains but a vestige of dance, as though heard very softly from a great distance:

Ex 49:2 H. Gifford. *Waltz*. bars 20-23.

Helen's most important work for piano holds an exciting place in the Australian repertoire. *Toccata Attacco* was written in 1990 and was the happy result of a commission by the pianist Sally Mays. The *Toccata* assumes a position in a long pianistic tradition of display pieces using a driving, percussive approach, interrupted twice by contrasting episodes, somewhat in the manner of a baroque toccata. The two interludes are not unrelated to the earlier *The Spell*. Written on three staves, this time Gifford actually suggests that both pedals may be kept down through out the whole episode of sixteen bars.

Ex 50:2 H. Gifford. *Toccata Attacco*. bars 24-28.

But the bulk of the *Toccata* is taken up by ostinato-like patterns and repeated chords:

Ex 51:2 H. Gifford. *Toccata Attacco*. bar 44.

The *Toccata* actually winds down dynamically as though suffering from exhaustion and ends on a *ppp*.

For an adventurous and uninhibited pianist, there is also *as foretold to Khayya'm*, wherein the player has to sing and do vocal effects on specified pitches:

Ex 52:2 H. Gifford. *As foretold to Khayyám.* bars 17-21.

Gifford is a distinguished Australian composer with a valuable contribution to our piano literature.

Derek Strahan (1935)

No book on Australian piano music would be complete without some mention of Derek Strahan and his *Atlantis Variations* (1992) for solo piano. This huge cycle of pieces is a semi-programmatic work inspired by the Atlantis legend and apparently largely based on Otto Heinrich Muck's book *The Secret of Atlantis*. The score of the work is preceded by an essay on the subject of Atlantis as well as explaining the musical symbolism of the work and the sequence of depicted cataclysmic cosmic events. Strahan has also composed other instrumental works which are all part of the Atlantis cycle, and which develop thematic material in common. It appears that the culmination of this Atlantis composition will be an epic cycle of four operas. One cannot help being reminded of Nicholas Obukhov and his *Book of Life* project which was planned along similar massive lines and which apparently he never lived to complete (it might have been just as well, for Obukhov's prediction was that when *The Book of Life* was finished, Nicholas II of Russia would come back from the dead!). Derek Strahan makes no prediction for the completion of his opera cycle. His *Atlantis Variations* take about fifty three to fifty four minutes to perform, according to his own estimate on the score. I am unaware of a performance, although the composer has certainly recorded large sections of the work, which falls into thirteen sections. I presume that the work is programmatic to the extent that the composer himself, in his notes refers to "The Program" and to a "musical narrative". It's not easy to write about this huge piece: there is some connection to the world of Messiaen and therefore also to the obsessive repetition of ideas and motives. But the style of writing is eclectic as well, and Strahan has obviously made choices motivated by his own considerations. It seems to me that the central issue is the point at which the composer forgets about Atlantis and allows the purely musical aspects of his raw materials to govern the evolution of his work. The procedure is fraught with danger in this respect: if the mythology of Atlantis and the details of its destruction - all of which is shot through with number symbolism as well as graphic representation - if these are allowed to take front rank over musical considerations, then the argument of the piece, in a purely sonic sense, will be obstructed and flawed; structure will become subservient to extra-musical codes. It is also likely that the music will be discontinuous as a result since the driving force behind the unfolding of sound events is actually a vivid 'picture'. So unless such 'pictures' accompany the musical performance, the 'meaning' of each event will be obscure or blank, even though in the mind of the composer each sonic occurrence was no doubt clearly linked to a non-musical idea. One needs to reserve judgment until the work as a whole can be experienced. At this stage, I have played through the entire score and am voicing some possible concerns and reservations about the music; but would love to hear the work as a whole from some enterprising pianist.

Jennifer Fowler (1939)

Fowler is an Australian composer, who, after studies with Peter Maxwell-Davies, chose to remain in England.

Fowler, in her own words finds the piano to be "rather a problem" (Composer questionnaire). She has written very little for solo piano, but has, in her own words, "less problem about including the piano in an ensemble piece, but even there, I am mainly responding to the instrumentation of particular ensembles rather than choosing to include it". Elsewhere in correspondence to us, the composer makes clear that she thinks mainly horizontally, and this, to my mind, creates yet another problem for the composer, almost fighting against the very nature of the piano.

The earliest available work is *Piece for an Opera House* (1973). The score outlines three performing possibilities:

       1. for two pianists, two pianos
       2. for one pianist who pre-records Piano I part on tape and plays Piano II part live with the tape
       3. for solo pianist who plays Piano I part only

The first possibilities are outside the coverage of this book. The third option of just playing *Piano I* as a solo is possible but musically unconvincing, as much of the interest generated by the piece is in the contrapuntal interplay of the two pianos and the rippling almost electronic echo created in this fashion. The writing for the pianos is quite sparse and the stereophonic effect is, in my view, central to the working of the piece – this effect would of course be lost by performing *Piano I* as a solo.

In her notes to this work, Fowler writes:

The music is based on three different "Scales" of fixed pitches, which extend over the whole keyboard. (The word "Scale" is in inverted commas because in these scales, every octave is different from its neighbours). Some sections of the piece are based on the main "cadential scale" and here the progress is directional towards and around three specific notes or nodal points; one in the lower, one in the middle, and one in the upper register. In between these sections are sandwiched material based on the other two scales, which result in a free-er, more rhapsodic, and less purposeful mood.

This concept of using the piano in such a manner was clearly of interest to the composer because in 1980, when she composed *Music for Piano - Ascending and Descending*, she was still exploring this idea. Once again, from the composer's programme notes:

The range of available notes on the piano were formed into two (non-repeating) scales: an ascending scale and a descending scale. These scales were divided into sections of differing lengths, and during the piece the music progresses from one of these to another. Only one section is ever used at any moment i.e. although there are some quick alternations between sections, they are never used simultaneously. If a section of the ascending scale is used, the music reflects this by being predominantly upward moving; and similarly if a section of the descending scale is used, the music is downward in emphasis.

The composer then goes on to explain some other considerations to do with other possible parameters.

Because of this approach, much of the piece is written on one stave.

Ex 53:2 J. Fowler. *Music for Piano – Ascending and Descending.* (unbarred)

There is also Fowler's *Piece for E.L.,* written the following year (1981) for the 75th birthday celebrations of the composer Elizabeth Lutyens. We have not seen this composition.

Hellgart Mahler

Hellgart Mahler is Gustav Mahler 's great grandniece, if I have understood the family connection correctly. She has lived her professional life in Tasmania and is yet another example of imported European culture arriving and mixing with the Australian scene. Her output for the piano is not large, though a number of her piano works are quite well known due to repeated exposure such as *Photons* and *Three Galactic Fragments*. They are good examples of her approach to the keyboard. She says of this last: "The most persistent characteristic of my music is my use of the greatest possible variety of changes in articulation, intensity and timbral quality". She then goes on to talk about the "greater flexibility and the inclusion of improvisatory episodes" in her more recent music. This has resulted in a piano music that is elusive, fleeting, scattered over the whole keyboard and seemingly springing to life in front of the listener.

John Exton (1933)

British-born composer John Exton came to Australia in 1966 to assume the position of Senior Lecturer at the University of Western Australia. His formative influences were almost parallel to the Australian Don Banks in that he was also taught by Matyas Seiber and Luigi Dallapiccola. His *Give or take a few dB* (1975), composed for David Bollard (distinguished pianist and a recipient of many awards) is a set of five short pieces in a kind of quirky Morton Feldman-like style, with great sensitivity to the overtones of any given sound or combination of sounds. David Bollard's timing for these pieces is just over seven minutes, and this little cycle is well worth inclusion in a concert programme. Exton is a string player, so it's possible that the piano holds little attraction for him.

Stuart Davies-Slate

In a very similar vein are the set of *Four Piano Pieces* (1984-86) also written for David Bollard and also by a composer from Western Australia: Stuart Davies-Slate. The set is comprised of *Chant No.1*, *'Vidimus Stellam'*, *Chant No.2*, and finally, *Two-Part Invention*. The writing is sparse and linear, which is not surprising as the composer quotes the post-World-War period as the one influencing him the most. Davies-Slate studied with both Don Banks and David Lumsdaine. Most of his mature output is in theatre. (There is also *Two Movements for Unaccompanied Piano* (1971), which we have not seen.)

Stuart Hille

To these sets of pieces from Western Australia written for David Bollard, who taught for many years at the University there, perhaps I should add another set of *Five Little Piano Pieces* by Stuart Hille (1978): also spare, aphoristic pieces, which David inspired possibly due to his highly refined way with the piano.

(ii) Retrospective Composers

Pianists

Miriam Hyde (1913)

By her own admission, Miriam Hyde was deeply influenced by the example of the great Sergey Rachmaninov, both at the keyboard and as a composer. She defines seeing and hearing him in the flesh as one of the most important moments of her life. The role model of the composer-pianist has dominated her own musical life and she has, throughout her long public career, sought to pursue both composition and piano playing, as well as being a busy teacher.

She plays her own more virtuosic works in public and since her output is primarily for the piano, it has never lacked an exponent, as she is a very fine pianist and indeed had not the World War broken out when it did, its quite feasible that she would have remained in Europe and forged a performing career for herself.

Like Frank Hutchens, Miriam Hyde seems haunted by water imagery, and many of her pieces have such an association, readily perceived by referring to the database in this book.

Moreover, unlike Hutchens, the musical structure has programmatic connotations which one recognizes when the composer speaks of particular works. For example, here she is writing concerning *Grey Foreshore*. The piece was inspired by a received Christmas card, which depicted a sea scene:

> The sea is subdued, under a cloudy sky. The first change to four flats
> suggests the warmer tones of golden sand and brown earth at the cliff's
> base. From bar 41 there is a bigger amplitude; one's thoughts go out to
> the ocean's depths and the romance of a passing ship. The new figure
> in fourths (bar 61) conveys the gentle pattern of waves in a nearby
> inlet, etc

As further illustration of the programmatic inclination, two other water-based pieces, *Wet Night on the Highway* and *Reflected Reeds* are both published with a paragraph at the head of the score giving as precise sources Sydney scenes for the inspirations behind these pieces.

These are not an isolated examples, neither is this kind of 'explanation' of the music limited to scapes, as the composer also applies such descriptions to other works which operate on a more personal emotional level. For instance, the composer sent me a page long description of *The Spring of Joy*, which deals exclusively with her inner states at the end of World War II.

Is this naive? Do we need to know such matters? Many composers have their own inner springboards that trigger pieces, but they may choose to keep these sources to themselves, whether they be landscapes, or emotional states, or philosophies, or mythologies, or mathematics; many elect partial unveiling, leaving the listener and performer with only a few clues. It is interesting that some such clues or even lengthy prefaces to pieces can be seen to be politically correct, or even profound and various posturing composers have used them in such a fashion. Hyde simply chooses to reveal openly what her triggers happen to be, and therefore leaves herself open to labeling. All of these pieces could have had a very sober and possibly less interesting existence as a set of preludes. The other pertinent aspect to Hyde's output is that she chose to ignore almost all the musical developments of the twentieth century happening around her and remained firmly rooted in the late nineteenth and early twentieth century as though nothing had moved since then. In an interview with her that I conducted for the National Library, I asked her about this and she replied that she had attempted, together with another composer, Marjorie Hesse to use a more contemporary idiom even involving tone rows, but had found that it seemed so utterly alien that she abandoned the experiment and decided to continue writing as she felt most comfortable.

Perhaps, rather than viewing her as an anachronistic figure, it would be more fair to see her as a representative of a nineteenth century inheritance in Australian music: even though historically, Australian music essentially sprang to life in the twentieth century without much preamble. Consequently, there could have been little reaction to the nineteenth century, when in effect, it hardly happened here! Hyde's model Rachmaninov was himself an anachronistic figure in his time and we have managed to view him in a certain way and appreciate his qualities even though they are startlingly out of their own time.

In due course, this out of phase effect in Australian music - romanticism and mild impressionism happening later here than anywhere else, also caused an upheaval in the latter half of the century, when a fully formed avant-garde movement seemingly arose out of a late romantic environment.

The music is, therefore, unashamedly romantic and many of the gestures are directly from composers such as Chopin. Witness for example, the opening of one of the unpublished etudes:

Ex 54:2 M. Hyde. *Study for Left Hand Tenths*. bars 1-3.

Or the Lisztian ghost behind *The Fountain:*

Ex 55:2 M. Hyde. *The Fountain*. bars 1-3.

Or this Rachmaninovian episode from her second *Rhapsody:*

Ex 56:2 M. Hyde. *Rhapsody No. 2. A minor*. bars 1-3.

In *Valley of Rocks* a somewhat darker side of Miriam Hyde is shown, inspired by the Valley of Rocks near Lyunton in North Devon:

Ex 57:2 M. Hyde. *Valley of Rocks*. bars 1-5.

Hyde's output is far too large for me to comment on every work, neither is it
necessary, for the approach to the piano and the harmonic and technical
language has remained consistent and unchanged over many years. Perhaps
Evening in Cordoba should be mentioned here in passing; a piece from the late
1980s, it allows the occasional improvisation by a castanets player to be added
to the solo part, if so desired (there are some other Spanish inspired pieces as
well). The work itself is highly reminiscent of Albeniz, a composer who is no
doubt familiar to Hyde the pianist. The *Humoresque*, dedicated to Frank
Hutchens, but more virtuosic than anything that Hutchens produced, also has a
hint of a Rachmaninovian connection:

Ex 58:2 M. Hyde. *Humoresque*. bars 30-35.

Tap Tune is an effective encore piece. The title has nothing to do with foot
tapping, rather with a faulty bathroom appliance! *Firewheel* (a native Australian
tree) is another piece demonstrating Miriam's own prowess at the piano over
nine pages of *vivace* semiquavers.

Ex 59:2 M. Hyde. *Firewheel*. bars 53-54.

In a similar vein are the *Three Concert Studies*, stemming from the 1930s. The
first concentrates on broken octaves, mostly in the right hand, the second looks
at double notes and the third is a study in alternation of hands. This is the most
difficult of the three, and Hyde refers to Arthur Benjamin's style of playing as
having influenced the piece. These studies make very clear Hyde's lineage, and
the fact that she composed these at the piano and wrote them down later only
underlines the lineage. Together with the *Sonata*, the *Studies* represent Hyde's
most substantial contribution to the repertoire. To these *Concert Studies* should
be added *Study in Blue, White and Gold, Study in A Flat* and a *Rhapsodic Study
for Left Hand alone*. A *Burlesque*, alternating 4/4 and 3/4, an unusual procedure

for Hyde, probably also belongs to this group of pieces, but has yet to be published.

Variations in C Minor, on a theme by Hyde's mother is a large scale, student work, written when Miriam Hyde was presenting her final recitals for her Bachelor of Music in Adelaide. Though rather academic and strict in its form, it nevertheless does demonstrate Hyde's early mastery at the keyboard.

Her major work for piano is undoubtedly the *Sonata in G Minor*. The sonata was recently published and there is quite a long descriptive note by the composer, which relates the work to her memories and experiences during World War II, during which she was separated from her husband for five and a half years. A spacious work in three movements, this Sonata, whilst not saying anything new either for its time, or terms of what has already been described above, nevertheless is a fine representation of a certain kind of Australian music at the time of the second World War. Unlike other composers at the time and certainly after the War, Hyde did not react to the obviously changing world; the music belongs to a time past, possibly quite a long time past. Like her ideal, Sergei Rachmaninov, Hyde therefore is an example of a composer-pianist who belongs to the nineteenth century in spirit and musical outpouring.

Eric Gross (1926)

Sydney composer Eric Gross is almost impossible to pigeonhole. He is a complete musician and within his substantial output, Eric has encompassed everything from light and film music to avant-garde solo pieces; he has played piano in jazz ensembles and in theatre pits; he has taught composition at a tertiary level for nigh onto forty years; he is also a scholar of certain schools of early music! Eric says that he is impatient with the piano because he learnt to improvise early in his career and so is often bored by the whole business of notation; he also adds that because he has always played the piano, trifles come easily to him and so he has written a substantial number of them. The latter are easy to identify, as Eric tends to give the game away by his names. Thus, we know that we are dealing with music easy on the ear when we see titles such as *Moon Interlude, Nostalgic Interlude, Op.209* (the opus number gives a quick notion of how much music Gross has put out), *Thanksgiving, Op.149, Rondino Tranquillo Op.34 No.2, Miniature for Ray Op.195, Pensive Prelude Op.208, Habanera-Serenade Op.31 No.2, Glebe Island Minuet Op.20.*

There are little descriptive pieces like the ones that make up his Op.169: 1. *Lonely Desert*; 2. *Alone and Sad*; 3. *Meandering in series*; 4. *Sydney Harbour Blues*, and 5. *Little Jazzeroo.* Then, there are somewhat weightier pieces with a more serious intent. Here I would list *Toccata Op.184/2A, An Idyll for Idil Op.244, Sally in the Mallee, Interlude for Piano Op.250, Minuetto Capriccioso Op.238A, Toccata: No Piano at Three Op.226A* and *Sonata Piccola Op.188 (in four movements).* These are tougher technically than the first group and are often written for particular performers. Working at this book, I've played through many many scores that are verging on impossibility, or are musically obscure. Eric always writes music that works on the instrument and even at its most difficult, there is never any doubt as to the intent. The writing is often spiky and strongly rhythmic; piled up fourths, bitonality and time changes abound.

It's interesting that Gross' most serious works for the piano have a German name. The *Klavierstücke I-IV* represent his most substantial contribution to the genre. The chronology is as follows: *Klavierstücke I Op.120* (1983); *Klavierstücke II Op.127* (1983); *Klavierstücke III: Op.150* (1986); *Klavierstücke IV: Op.225* (1998). Although the pieces were composed separately and can certainly be performed separately, they now form a unified set and it should tempt a pianist somewhere to present them in this fashion. The *Klavierstücke* have similar structural and stylistic characteristics. They are strongly thematic and Gross is constantly manipulating and juxtaposing well-defined and easily heard motivic cells. The principle of constant variation is always at work here, coming not just from Eric's jazz background, but surely also from the Germanic tradition of the variation form symbolising some of the highest compositional achievements by the great masters. Schoenberg's twelve-tone dictum was also one of constant variation. It is my feeling that all these forces are at work in the Gross cycle. The logic is sometimes extended to allow huge arpeggio-like patterns spread over the keyboard to create a neo-romantic often quite lush sound. Eric also uses breaks or changes of tempo to shift toward new combinations of cells. The set is an important addition to our piano music; regrettably, the third of the series has not yet been typeset.

Ex 60:2 E. Gross. *Klavierstück III*. opening.

Mary Mageau (1934)

American born and educated, Mageau settled in Brisbane. In the score of *Ragtime* for solo piano, the composer writes in 1977:

> During the past year I have been exploring the school of classical ragtime piano with avid interest, and when I was asked to write a new piano work I decided on an experiment, - an integration of bits and pieces of Scott Joplin's *Missouri Rags* with my own idea of a contemporary keyboard sound. The result is *RAGTIME* for solo piano.

The three movements that make up this work are: 1. *Elite Syncopations*; 2. *Bethena*; and 3. *Cascades*. This 'experiment' from Mageau succeeds because her own approach to the keyboard is refined and clean so that the shift from Joplin's music to her own does not result in a nasty bump. *Elite Syncopations* in particular is a most attractive piece. I remember that while recording it, the boundaries between Mageau and Joplin almost disappeared in my mind and a rather satisfying whole emerged. In concert, the Joplin piece *Bethena* is meant to precede *Elite Syncopations*; *Bethena* is a gently nostalgic concert waltz

Mageau returned to the rag idiom in her *Ragtime Remembered* (2000), which consists of three movements: *The Samford Rag, Two to Tango* and *A Rollicking Rag*. These are cooler rags than the Elena Kats-Chernin variety (discussed below), but closer to the original roots.

The same somewhat detached approach to the piano permeates another set of pieces named *Cityscapes*: *High Street, Noon - Cathedral Square, Rendezvous, Rain,* and *Homeward*. These are simpler, cleaner pieces than the *Ragtime Remembered* set, which asks for double notes on a regular basis. *Soliloquy, Dance Piece 1* (1980) has a similarly open texture; some of it is printed on three staves. However, Mageau's *Etude* (1970) is a study in octaves, many of them alternating between the hands and often in asymmetric groups – it is an altogether fiercer piece. This *Etude* also serves as *Entrance Piece* in Mageau's *Cycles and Series* from the same year. The work asks for some activity under the lid involving plucking, stopping the string, clusters etc. Later Mageau doesn't go for these effects; this is clearly a younger and more experimental composer here. The movements after *Entrance Piece* include a most atmospheric *Night Music* followed by *Cycle Complete*, a showier piece with repeated chords and toccata-like figurations. In more recent times, Mageau espouses a more elegant and refined music and her piano writing is probably coloured by her liking for the harpsichord, as in the concerto discussed below.

Michael Bertram (1935)

Michael Bertram, domiciled in Melbourne, writes fierce but exciting piano music. I first looked at his *Sonatina Op.2* (1977), which was premiered by Keith Humble. The first movement is mostly a single line scattered all over the piano, apparently played *secco*. The second has heavily pedaled fast alternating hand outbursts, eventually and quickly building to *fff* and leading to the third movement which offers choices of material of a very circumscribed nature - all soft. The last movement reverts to some extent to the patterns of the second movement, but not as aggressively. The piece ends very quietly. It is an impressive early work.

The next piano work is *Five Pieces Op.9* from 1984. The score quotes from Roy Campbell:

> The sap is music, the stem is the flute, and the leaves are the wings of
> the seraph I shape who dances, who springs in a golden escape, out of
> the dust...

The five pieces constituting the work seem to me to make up a whole and should not therefore be performed separately: *Rumelia, Ingenu, Kinetic, Violet* and *Iconoclast. Rumelia* is a tamer version of the opening of the earlier *Sonatina*, although there are other features such as short trills, time measured rests and repeated patterns, before the movement is brought to a close with a strange recitative. *Ingenu* asks for many simple triads in the left hand while the right hands twitters incomplete triplets that eventually peter out inconclusively. *Kinetic* is largely often repeated patterns or widespread arpeggios, all at great speed. *Violet* is largely bursts of double octaves with rests in between only alleviated by some soft scalar figures which, too, don't seem to want to go anywhere. Finally, *Iconoclast* uses piano vamping as its basis with the most cliched left hand supporting plaintive melodic meanderings in the right. In some respects, in this work Bertram has rediscovered triadic sounds, although they are not used as functional harmony. His Op.9 is witty and arresting, but there is a feeling of exhaustion and perhaps of dubious searching for something.

The *Fantasie-Sonata* (1999) is a massively ambitious work. The composer's timing suggests that the Sonata lasts for over forty minutes, and the various pianistic devices played with in the previous works now seem to be securely in place and used with great confidence. Common triads now appear with more frequency and the sounds evoked have more than hints of Messiaen and Debussy, to name but two. There is also a brand of self-belief that reminds one of Scriabin. Music as Symbolism is very strong in this piece. I am not saying that I like it all, but I have a feeling that the composer has something to say and is not afraid to say it in the face of current fashions, which I find admirable. The often huge blocks of unrelated triads conjure up the brass chords of a Vaughan Williams. The concept of the work is on a grand romantic scale, though many devices are those of the twentieth century. In the hands of the right pianist, I believe that this piece can be made to work. I attach, in full, the composer's programme note.

> The Sonata is in three movements. Each movement is built around a literary text and represents a journey, viz. through a Celtic phantasmagoria; from innocence to disillusion; and finally through darkness to light.
>
> First
> "And then lost Niamh murmured, 'Love, we go
> to the Island of Forgetfulness, and lo!
> The Islands of Dancing and of Victories are empty of all power'
> 'And which of these is the Island of Content?'
> 'None know' she said"
>
> The overall plan is an arch with a G sharp-G natural motif at the beginning, towards the centre and at the end. Within this arch are a number of tone-rows and other episodic material. A secondary theme (employing the same motif) builds to an avowedly romantic climax shortly before the conclusion.
>
> Second
> "We have an interval and then our place knows us no more"
>
> A set of five variations on the theme ABCD, portraying a progression from ingenuousness to the dissolving of dreams. Some of the music in this 'life story' is intentionally prosaic.
>
> Third
> "...Man, in imitation of his Creator,...wanted to
> reproduce the continuity of Cosmic Time..."
>
> A contrast between 'darkness' and 'light', the first represented by an extended series of synthetic (ie devised) scales which slowly transmogrify; the latter by ever mounting sequences of repeated notes and chords which, finally victorious, recede into the infinite. All that has gone before is now resolved.

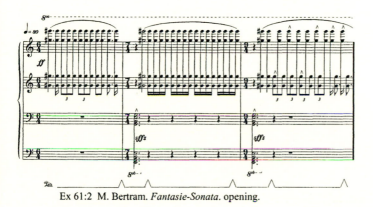

Ex 61:2 M. Bertram. *Fantasie-Sonata*. opening.

Richard Peter Maddox (1936)

Just looking at Richard Peter Maddox's scores, one can instantly tell that he must
be an accomplished pianist. The *Toccata* requires a fiery *martellato* touch and
later, chords in piled-up fourths on both black and white keys - sometimes
alternating between the hands. The scores also tell us that he is content with
older rhythms and techniques. The use of variation form in *Tyringham
Mailboxes* (2000) is almost classical in its austerity. Beginning with a *Theme* set
out in four-part harmony, the six variations gain in rumbustiousness and finally
generate a stately Finale, almost Brahmsian in its approach. Similarly, the Four
Fugues display someone who understands the keyboard and how to write for it.
The first Sonata, in four movements subtitled *Winter*, is equally conservative in
outlook. Maddox was a pupil of Frank Hutchens at the start of his career: I
mention this only becasue Hutchens' music is not noted for the very features that
seem to fascinate Maddox, that is, working within rigid forms.

Non-Pianists

Lloyd Vick (1915)

Vick turned out to be a Brisbane version of Alex Burnard, with a similar
background, teaching similar subjects and even some similarities in the
compositional output. There are a number of works for solo piano, which Lloyd,
like Alex, played mostly in class. Like Alex, he has a well-developed sense of
humour. Witness for example, a work written for me in 1963, consisting of a
splashy *Adagio*, acting like a prelude to an angular and syncopated fugue, which
eventually transmutes into a quirky *Cafe Piece*, which ends this three-movement
work.

Lloyd went on to write a considerable body of piano music. Some of it was written after 2000, but for the sake of completeness I am mentioning them here.

A Noise that Annoys (2002) is almost like a reincarnation of the Bartók *Diary of a Fly*, except that here the beast is considerably larger, the piece lasts longer, and the texture is almost unrelieved octaves with added grace notes with added seconds within them. The piece is fast and loud, and Vick sometimes utilises a kind of mirroring at cadential-like gestures (he calls this "invertability") that probably came from his contrapuntal training and was a staple in a much older music. The subtle rhythmic shifts and the din of the quasi-octaves show some adherence to the Bartok of the 1920s.

Related pieces are the set labelled *Short, Sharp and Shiny* (2001-2002). The composer calls them 'fun-pieces', and there are four of them. Like the work described above, these are all in very similar vein and pianistic demand. Sometimes pure triadic fanfares interrupt the jangle of octaves; these lend an air of burlesque and even coarseness to the pieces, which are all exuberant, brash and tend toward vulgarity – again, perhaps, by compositional intent.

I next looked at *Dream Cycles* (2000-2001) and, given the title, was expecting something quite different. But these pieces are all most similar in their approach to the piano. There are some significant departures from the above, however. Firstly, the muddied octaves are now more often complete triads and so, when the counterpoint in applied, we have triadic shifts in contrary motion. Secondly, there are slow episodes in this cycle, and the huge momentum of the other pieces is now interrupted by a softer music. Sometimes the sound seems to hark back to that of Ralph Vaughan Williams, for whom we know Vick has a great affection. Even the jolliness of the Lloyd Vick output has a kind of English Falstaffian exuberance about it. The composer deliberately calls these pieces *Pianoforte Recital Works*.

More of the same may be gleaned from *Sound Shapes* (1999). Here he even gives the fingering for the enriched octaves. The music does not break new ground from his other piano music.

In May-June of 1999, Lloyd wrote a *Fantasia*. Here the inevitable octaves are interrupted by some difficult trills; the example below will show these are also perhaps give a taste of the sound world of Vick's music:

Ex 62:2 L. Vick. *Fantasia*. bars 40-42.

What the composer calls 'powerful dissonance' is merely a momentary clash of triads:

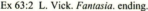

Ex 63:2 L. Vick. *Fantasia*. ending.

From this same late period comes *A Group of Three*, a set of works also written for Piers Lane. Here, finally, a richer and more diverse approach is evident. The three movements are: *Domenico's Here!, For the Peerless- from Moto Perpetuo* and *Final*. The second is a strict canon. The music is perhaps light in spirit but demands complete pianism and control. Unlike some of the music above, much of this is soft and scampers all over the keyboard. In a letter to me, Lloyd describes the first movement as 'fun'. But the playful mood that the composer wishes can only be achieved by a fine pianist. Most of the three pieces are fast and require drive. The canon is in two parts, but sometimes these are octaves. The last movement requires both good trills as well as octaves. These three pieces are probably the most likely as candidates for a bracket in a concert. *Group of Three* covers fifty six pages. There is nothing in the manuscript that says that the pieces cannot be played separately.

I would stress that all of this music is in manuscript, and if we are to savour the spices of a canon that goes for sixteen pages non-stop, a performance score would be an attractive proposition. There is much that is similar and repetitive in Lloyd Vick's music, but individually the pieces – especially the shorter ones – have attractive features.

It's interesting to see Lloyd Vick's arrival point given his departure point. There is an early *Modal Suite for Hapsichord* (1954). The composers says 'for

Pianoforte' on the manuscript, but this is clearly a harpsichord-intended work. It consists *of Prelude, Scherzo I, Aria, Burla, Scherzo II* and *Gigue* and is a neo-classic excursion. It is also clear that what surfaces in the late pieces is residual counterpoint often disguised by huge octaves and chords, although the middle movement of *Group of Three* allows the purest form of counterpoint, the canon, to come through.

Ex 64:2 L. Vick. *Group of Three.* opening of *Canon*.

Noel Nickson (1919)

Noel Nickson, who tried to teach me harmony is one of the many harmony/counterpoint teachers who would on occasion, when time allowed, publish a piece. There are other examples, but I chose this one as typical of a kind of writing in mid-century Australia. Nickson's *Sonatina* (1956) shows a slightly tart harmony combined with very spare lines and most often two planes of activity. The intention behind the composition of many like works was to get them published and included in examination lists for medium to advanced young pianists to play. Sonatinas were less threatening than sonatas and more likely to achieve this objective. This one is in the almost compulsory three-movement format.

Ex 65:2 N. Nickson. *Sonatina.* opening.

Geoffrey Allen (1927)

This composer began quite late in life when he founded a publishing firm and began to issue his own music as well as the music of many other Australian composers. The Keys Press specialises in piano music as well as some chamber music. Currently it must be the largest publisher of Australian music in this country.

Geof's music looks conventional until one tries to play it, and then the pianist discovers that the patterns are quite unpredictable and don't lead where one thinks they will go. Geof has never been a performing pianist, but he does play the instrument and composes at the piano; he always says that he can play everything he writes, but not at tempo! Sometimes the piano works do mirror his own pianistic limitations and there is a sense in which all the sonatas and various other pieces exist in a very circumscribed world that is, I suspect, Geof's pianistic ability.

The gestures that make up Geof's piano music are largely very familiar, and he himself says that they come from Delius and Bax, although I am often hard pressed to find that special link. For example, the second Sonata is inspired by Spain and certainly there are flashes of what we normally associate with Spanish music, but then Allen moves away into his own world. The piano output, which is fairly large, is basically the result of the last ten years of the twentieth century, after Geof retired from his job as librarian.

Tonality is always lurking in his music and is sometimes explicit in cadential moments, but otherwise quite elusive. As much as anything else, the old gestures and the old rhythm leads one to expect tonality at some point; but this expectation is not always met. However, the music is certainly not atonal either, or serial in any sense. It is organic and usually grows from primary ideas stated un the beginning of a work.

For example, near the start of his fourth Sonata, the initial material looks like English pastoral music:

Ex 66:2 G. Allen. *Piano Sonata no. 4*. bars 212-214.

But this is only a starting point and the text moves a long way away from this style.

Geof's texture is almost always melody and accompaniment in one form or another and is therefore essentially a lyrically flowing line. He tends to like the multi-movement sonata structure. In the fifth Sonata, unusually, the piece begins with a chord progression and much of the subsequent material is derived from this opening gesture. There are occasions when Allen abandons the melodic flow and lashes out, uncharacteristically, as in the sixth Sonata that was inspired by violent events in Kosovo and Timor. There are verbal introductions to some of the works that tie them with specific events. Sonata no.7, which still carries over some of the sombre mood of No.6, has a long introductory note:

Ex 67:2 G. Allen. *Piano Sonata no. 7.* bars 13-16 of II.

Allen's music is full of sequences, which are of course a tonal device, but here they are constantly frustrated, dashing tonal expectations. The series of sonatas continues into the twenty first century and therefore outside the scope of this book. In No.8, for example, Allen experiments with the idea of all the movements being in 3/4.

There are quite a number of other solo piano compositions. Amongst them: a substantial *Variations and Fantasia* Op. 28, three impressionistic Impromptus with debts to various composers including Scriabin (see Allen's note at the opening of the score); and *After the Rapture* dedicated to Marjorie Beer, Roy Agnew's youngest sister.

Geof Allen has become a significant figure in Australian piano music by virtue of his extensive publishing as well as his contribution to the genre.

May Howlett (1931)

There are two sets of pieces by May Howlett that we found: *Stimmungen* and *Kryptiques* (dedicated to me). Howlett tends to write short atmospheric piano pieces essentially for young pianists, although there are usually some twists in the tail, i.e. they are not always predictable, neither are they obvious. We have therefore listed them as a concert possibility; Howlett likes quirky rhythms and time signatures as well.

Ralph Middenway (1932)

There are two sonatas by this Adelaide composer. The first, *Sonata Capricciosa* (undated) is curious because apparently it "is a piano version of a sonata written for solo percussion". I'm not certain how that works, and can only assume that quite a few notes have been added to what might have been largely a marimba solo – but this is pure conjecture on my part. The work has lots of time changes, and the manuscript has an irritating way of breaking the stave lines completely to insert a new time signature between bars, which gives the work a really discontinuous appearance. Middenway's harmonies are strongly triadic, although he also enjoys juxtaposing different triads, which we witness right at the opening bar of the piece; he is also very fond of assymetric rhythms, and *Danza*, the first movement, is full of them. The second movement is an *Aria*, with most of the left hand in open fifths suggesting strong tonal centres once more. The last movement, *Gioco*, is a rondo, with the constituent parts of the form ABACA2DACA2BACoda written out as separate fragments. Much of this movement is in 5/8. I suppose that the origins of this work forced a very lean texture upon it, and a predominantly melodic aspect.

The other sonata is a real piano piece: *Toyokawa - East River - Piano Sonata* (1990). The composer has supplied a long introduction, and I will quote from part of it. After some material on the place named Toyokawa and on its Shinto shrines, Middenway writes:

> In early 1990, to my almost total incredulity, I found myself, one of the first international guests in Japan for the Lafcadio Hearn Centenary Year, being very solemnly, very noisily, and comprehensively blessed by the most charming Precentor, with a huge cohort of choristers, drummers, bell-ringers and various other instrumentalists in front of a substantial congregation.

> The strong, eccentric Rhythmic pattern forming the basis of the first movement of the *Sonata* formed the basis of the music of that ceremony. A couple of other rhythmic patterns in the piece were also used on the same occasion. The thematic material is not Japanese.

> The *Sonata* is constructed using the age-old, three-part, Japanese jo ha kyu pattern - "introduction, scattering, rushing" are the usual English terms. Plays, pieces of music and all sorts of artistic creations can often, on reflection, be seen to consist of a tiered mosaic of three-part sections, whose overall tendency seems to be one of increasing urgency, and, sometimes, as in many popular Bunraku and Kabuki pieces, increasing cheerfulness...

Surprisingly, the writing for piano in this sonata is not greatly different from the other one! So it seems that a very spare linear approach, with many octaves and octave transpositions for the melodic line, is simply the way that Middenway deals with the keyboard. The three sections run into each other, so this turns out to be quite a solid non-stop piece, covering thirty pages. The middle section is a rather plaintive quasi-choral alternating between 3/4 and 5/8, with chromatically descending harmonies. The outer movements are dance-like, especially the last, and tend to be dramatically declamatory.

David Morgan (1932)

I remember David Morgan well from my student days at the Sydney Conservatorium. He was a little older than me and many of us looked up to him as an already accomplished composer. He is another example of a composer who found his personal language and style early and does not seem to have deviated from it to any great extent. His *Sonata No.1* (1948, rev.1997-98) was written at the age of sixteen. I don't know how extensive these revisions might have been, but the work comes across as a very sophisticated composition for one so young. The last movement is a Theme followed by five variations and a finale. As with later music by David, everything is well crafted and in its proper place. The rhythm is for me the least interesting aspect of his music and I find the emotional temperature fairly low, but that could just be my Slavonic nature.

His *Divers Paces* (1999), a suite for piano is a large-scale work, each movement preceded by a literary allusion and all of them dealing with our concept of time. At the head of the score: *"Time travels in divers paces..." (Shakespeare)*. The first movement is called *Palindrome*: *"Time will run back" (John Milton)*. The movement truly reverses and runs backward from bar thirty seven, on a C minor chord. The second movement has two quotations: *"The silence...in the starry sky" (Wordsworth)* and *"The silence...of pure innocence" (Shakespeare)*. Not unexpectedly, this is the slow movement. The third movement has another Shakespearean quote from *Romeo and Juliet*, referring to Queen Mab, "the fairies' midwife" whose "chariot is an empty hazel-nut", drawn by "a team of little atomies". The music here is a very fast 6/8 and serves as the Scherzo; the Trio of the Scherzo is a succession of soft four-part chords. Movement Four is another slowish section, prefaced by *"For You and I are past our dancing days"*, also from *Romeo and Juliet*. The last, fifth movement is a Toccata: *"Melodious birds sing madrigals"* (Christopher Marlowe, *"The Passionate Shepherd"*). Here Morgan begins by notating two birdcalls - the Grass Parrot and the Wattlebird - and then proceeds to treat the calls in various contrapuntal ways, including close canons. *Divers Paces* may be yet another representation of a trend I have written about elsewhere, suggesting that with post-modernity, the interlacing of literature and music may prove once again to be acceptable and indeed fruitful.

Colin Brumby (1933)

In all ages there have been composers who either began as avant-garde and then turned their back on it, or else chose never to go that way, because they were satisfied with their current mode of expression. Some deliberately go back to an earlier time for inspiration and technique. Others perceive it as a quicker road to success. The tendency itself cannot be judged and I certainly don't necessarily see it as a pejorative exercise.

The Queensland composer Colin Brumby provides a kind of barometer of changing fashions and directions in new music in Australia, as well as the pressures exerted on composers. Thus, we firstly have a well-made Theme and Variations (1963), an early work, showing fluency and a fine set of construction throughout the eight variations. Colin is not a concert pianist, so the keyboard music is not central to his output, and makes sporadic appearances amongst his prolific compositions. From the next decade we have *Antistrophe* (1976), mirroring the height and prestige of the avant-garde movement. In 1980, Brumby wrote *Demotica* in which the sevenths and ninths have largely given way to fourths and tritones. This fairly extensive piece of over twenty pages is already harking back to a much more conservative way of approaching the piano, including arpeggiated harmonies, octaves, and split octaves. The transition is completed with a *Romance in C Major* which could have very well been composed at the end of the nineteenth century

Ann Carr-Boyd (1938)

Like recent Brumby, Ann Carr-Boyd works in an unabashedly quasi-popular idiom. Her list of pieces is fairly extensive (see database) and she carries on a long Australian tradition of writing short character pieces often inspired by particular landscapes and places. Even her *Perpetual Motion*: (1979 rev.1992) which I thought would be an 'abstract' piece was actually an adaptation for piano of an organ piece and was originally called *The Bells of Sydney Harbour*. The score contains annotations suggesting 'waves' and a 'peal of bells'. Most of the writing is of moderate difficulty.

Sven Libaek (1938)

Sven Libaek is a composer in a very similar mode to Ann Carr-Boyd. A prolific composer of film and light music, Libaek also responds to descriptive romantic miniatures. Like Carr-Boyd, who is fond of the harpsichord, Libaek writes some pieces in a quasi-Bach manner; witness his *Two Baroque Preludes,* Op. 30 and the *Toccata in D Minor,* Op. 4. These are not complex contrapuntal works, but rather a popular evocation of what Bach might sound like if he wrote light music. Actually, the second of the *Baroque Preludes* is more classical in style, replete with Alberti bass. The *Nocturne* Op. 2 on the other hand harks back to Chopin, at least to begin with, but the melody is not single notes but chords with added notes. There is also a set of Etudes for piano concentrating, like the Romantics on special technical difficulties such as octaves or double notes. The composer runs his own press and so disseminates his music from his desktop publishing, an increasingly viable solution today to the perennial problem facing all composers.

Philip Bracanin (1942)

Philip Bracanin is an interesting case of a composer who began as a graduant in both music and mathematics and then went on to study techniques of the composers Seiber and Webern. Ironically, his own musical style moved him away from any form of 12-tone or serialism and he began to compose - for the piano, at any rate - in a very French neo-classic way, with regular rhythms and very clean lines. I have seen the Seven Bagatelles (1982), which as Philip himself says, is an intentionally eclectic collection of pieces, designed to extract maximum contrast in performance. There is also his *Sonata Mescolanza* (1978). The Sonata opens with a *Presto* involving very secure 3/8 rhythm and much parallel handwriting, almost like a slightly demented Poulenc. The second movement is a melodic allegro, also with much parallel chord writing and a slow inner section. The third is a scherzo set out like a two part invention. And the last is a theme presented in octaves followed by a set of seven variations. I don't get the impression that the piano is close to Bracanin's heart; there has been nothing for twenty years.

(iii) More "Australian" Composers

Non-Pianists

James Penberthy (1917 - 1999)

Penberthy was one of Australia's most prolific and an indefatigable fighter for this country's composers, willing to take on the whole panoply of Establishment. Penberthy has to be regarded as a pioneer is this area and in Australian culture; he had a vision of Australia's possible future and was one of the first composers to proclaim loudly that we not longer need to go abroad to train our new composers, that we can do it right here. (He himself had studied with Nadia Boulanger at a time when it was considered essential to finish one's education abroad).

Like most of his generation, Penberthy was affected by the Great Depression and had to toughen himself to survive; like many others, he served in the armed forces and then trained at a tertiary institution – in his case Melbourne

University. He was well-traveled and international in outlook, but at the same time fiercely Australian. He had extensive experience in the theatre world, especially as a ballet conductor.

Although not a performing pianist, Penberthy obviously had a working knowledge of the instrument and the output for the piano confirms this, as well as the number of piano concerti. But I suspect that Penberthy's most personal pieces are rather for instruments such as strings than the keyboard.

He was a pupil of Dorian le Gallienne and so falls within that particular (non-pianistic) tradition. The works for solo piano represent therefore only occasional and often sketch-like pieces. Thus, *Trivial Pursuit* is a miniature and quite traditional in its use of the keyboard; the *Three Happenings* are completely untraditional, but still slight; many short pieces lie somewhere in between. Penberthy clearly comes from a conventional background, but has the temperament and will to break out, as it were, when he chooses. The more massive piled-up harmonies that one finds in some of his music are not unrelated to music by Ruggles and sometimes Ives; there is the same mix of primitivism, naiveté and ruggedness. Some are clearly linked to his balletic work, such as the *Pieces* Op. 53, with depictions of the Brolga; the manuscript here even contains some instructions in Russian, no doubt put there by his first wife; similarly, a piece described on the first page as '12-tone' entitled *Hans and Roosters* is equally dancelike and sparse, sometimes evoking the sound-world of Satie.

Undoubtedly, the two most successful works for piano are, firstly, *Clocks*, written for the Sydney International Piano Competition and consisting of a set of short pieces played as one, with a hypnotically reappearing C# (sometimes Db), and which has a final say:

Ex 68:2 J. Penberthy. *Clocks*. ending.

The second is the *Earth Mother Fantasy*, a mythological figure close to Penberthy's heart and which reappears in various guises in his music, proclaiming the composer's closeness to the land. James regarded this work as his best piece for piano; it contains all of the characteristics already given above, and the primitivism manifests itself in quite unabashed and insistent use of chromatic scale as well as in superimposed open fifths and octaves, suggesting bitonality. Like Le Gallienne's piano music, so Penberthy's is almost like a sketch for an ultimately orchestral work.

Among Penberthy's papers, there exists a little gem – a two-page piece called *Sad Music for Thursday*. It is dated 1985 and dedicated to I.D.A. I have no idea what happened on Thursday, but it inspired a moving encore piece:

Ex 69:2 J. Penberthy. *Sad Music for Thursday*. opening.

Peter Sculthorpe (1929)

Sculthorpe's output for the piano is rather small and the music tends to wards miniatuarism.

The subtitle to the *Sonatina* reads: "For the journey of Yoonecara to the land of his forefathers, and the return to his tribe". This Australianism aside, the music sounds like simplified and dessicated Bartók, with quite strong tonal centres and gestures and many minor seconds used like delicate percussion. The short melodic snatches are repetitive and sound like so many middle-European neo-classic easy to moderate pieces, with a mild sprinkle of modernism to spice up the harmony. The use of the keyboard is timid and unadventurous.

There are a further number of short piano works of moderate difficulty utilising Aboriginal fragments and names. *Djilile* (1989), for example, adapts a melody collected by A. P. Elkin and Trevor Jones. But the modest and simple piano treatment of the melody makes it sound more Spanish than anything else! *Callabonna* (1963) is a place-name, and is slightly more interesting harmonically. Like most of Sculthorpe's music, it is slow and often static. In *Simori* (1985), Sculthorpe sets some melodies from Papua New Guinea, again very simply and repetitively. Some of the settings are faster than the works mentioned above, but even then, the rhythmic ideas are static and unchanging. *Simori* consists of brief fragments of these New Guinea songs, put together to make a larger piece. These three works are published as *Three Pieces for Piano*.

There are more pieces with Aboriginal associations in *A Little Book of Hours*; but these, like *Night Pieces* and *Two Easy Pieces*, are essentially teaching material and outside the scope of this book. The little piece *Stars* is fairly effective, using the upper portion of the piano to suggest twinkling stars.

Music that does not allude to Aboriginal culture includes a two-page piece called *Night*, which is in the range of easy teaching material. (*Night* also appears within the collection called *Night Pieces*, see above) The sound world is similar to the *Sonatina*. *Mountains* is a slightly more ambitious piece. It begins with a series of split chord patterns that sets up a repetitive harmonic progression in the lower range of the piano. This waxes and wanes, and the composer adds some higher flourishes. The middle section is marked *estatico*, although the composer doesn't seem to provide the requisite materials for achieving that state, the writing for the instrument rather conservative and tentative. The piece ends with a return to the opening ideas. The only other composition for solo piano is *Nocturnal* (1989) a slow dreamy piece based on repetition, with some elaborations of a rather simple modally inclined pattern. The piece tends towards minimalism. The harmony tends to be quiescent, a feature of this composer's piano music.

Betty Beath (1932)

Betty Beath, the Queensland composer, studied with Frank Hutchens for a time in Sydney and has to some extent inherited the Hutchens approach to the piano. She writes music that is essentially atmospheric, reacting to the world that she got to know during her life that included a dash of Eastern (Indonesian) music. Her piano writing is often pentatonic and also uses the whole tone scale to some extent. The result is warm and often sentimental, with much pedal overlay. Although a trained pianist, her pieces lie in that area between educational music and concert music. Most of the pieces are smallish and she emerges, in my view, as a minituarist for the instrument. Some of the piano music also exists in orchestral versions.

Don Kay (1933)

Don Kay has for many years been the outstanding composer in Tasmania. A true gentleman by nature, his music mirrors his personal traits, and is always refined and well thought out. The late Gwen Harwood, famous poet and librettist to many Australian composers, wrote, on the occasion of Kay's 60th birthday:

> ...Music itself is speaking of what your life has been, your long devotion to realising, in the world of sound, the world we share. You speak for all who live or ever have lived in this lovely island.

His *Sonatina* is a case in point. Don regards the sonatina form as a somewhat less demanding version of the sonata, so indeed, the work, in three movements is elegantly crafted without becoming a grand opera in the process. The spare linear and harmonic content sometimes reminds of Stravinsky, especially when the rhythm becomes somewhat quirky:

Ex 70:2 D. Kay. *Sonatina*. bars 186-188.

A similar refinement permeates the world of *Dance Rituals* (1997), written for the famous fortepianist and my ex-pupil Geoffrey Lancaster. The style is admirably suited to Geoffrey's way of playing: suave, clean, devoid of bombast, and with fleeting figurations that of course accompany Geoffrey's performances of early keyboard music:

Ex 71:2 D. Kay. *Dance Rituals*. bars 1-2.

The *Legend* from 1993 is constructed like a ballade, with the 'story' unfolding right from the start without preamble:

Ex 72:2 D. Kay. *Legend*. bars 1-4.

Kay does not reveal which legend is here being portrayed – perhaps there isn't one – but in his *Bird Chants* (1998-1999), he is very clear. The score says:

> A variety of birds singing together can generate an atmosphere in which time seems to stand still, with a prevailing sense of heightened enchantment. With my short piano solos, 'Bird chants', I have aimed to suggest something of such an atmosphere.

There are two pieces in all and they are inscribed "antipodean homage to Olivier Messiaen". Kay does not identify any of the bird calls by name, as what interests him is not any particular bird but rather the effect of all of them together; the piece is therefore atmospheric and strongly harmonic, and obviously related to his dwelling place in Taroona, Tasmania.

A reworked early piece is called *Looking north from Tier Hill* (1999), originally entitled *Looking out to Sea* and once again Don cements his connection with Tasmanian places. This one happens to be his birthplace in Smithton, and the view was out over Bass Strait. This is probably a less accomplished piece because of all the relics from his youthful work. But a more recent piece is much more successful: *Blue sky through still trees* (1999), an archetypal Australian image. The result is a haiku-like piece, in which the tritone G-C# floats without resolution although some strong cadential references are made underneath it.

Different worlds (1999) is dedicated to David Bollard. It consists of two movements. The score says: "In this world I have explored, on the one hand, the lyrical and textural; on the other, the mechanical and repetitive". Thus the two movements of this effective work are contrasts between a still, meditative first movement and a robotic, somewhat twitchy second, with some aspects of minimalism in the repetition of patterns.

Don Kay's biggest work for piano is the Sonata from 1998. The composer adheres to the three-movement format and the writing is like the earlier *Sonatina* but on a bigger scale. Kay does not write massively for the piano, so the neoclassic cleanliness is present right from the start:

Ex 73:2 D. Kay. *Sonata*. bars 1-4.

The piece, though in three movements, uses thematic references throughout the piece to unify the work. The second movement is in the key of E major and some if it, at any rate, is set out like a chorale, although it departs from this mood in the middle; the last movement comes back to some extent to the mood of the opening, with its open fifths reminiscent of Copland. I suspect that the this Sonata has not yet made its way into the repertoire of Australian sonatas because it is lean, and not a showy piece; but this may well be its hidden strength.

Sitsky's Keyboard Music: *Si Yeoo Ki*

Roger Woodward

I

In 1951 a sixteen-year-old boy, the son of Russian-Jewish parents, arrived in Australia. His family's possessions had been confiscated and they had one hundred dollars to their name after fleeing from north China, narrowly avoiding repatriation to Stalin's Russia. This boy was Lazar (Larry) Sitsky. Throughout the 1950's, he studied in Sydney, then in San Francisco, returned to Australia in 1962 to commence work in Brisbane, then settled in Canberra in 1965. Between 1977 and 1983, he made several journeys, which enabled him to understand his cultural roots and arrive at a sense of self. The first was to the Soviet Union before he returned to China thus enabling him to discover within himself a legacy of unconnected cultures to provide an unusual blend of idioms. It also shaped a personal quest to understand human values and his own destiny, and became the force which linked his work, his life and the world into which he was born. Whilst in some respects this is perhaps self evident, it is important because in Larry Sitsky's story, attempts to explain some myths of childhood, and the journey to self-realization of adulthood are representative of the age-old experience of cultural displacement.

To elucidate this dynamic, it is necessary to consider the turbulent aftermath of the October 1917 Revolution, when Sitsky's parents, still children, left Irkutsk and Vladivostok with their families and crossed the Chinese border into the Russian enclave of Harbin. However, it was in the nearby French concession of Tientsin where the family eventually resettled, and Lazar was born on

September 10th 1934 – the first day of the Jewish New Year. Until 1949, the strategic Chinese port was one of many such commercial concessions held by foreign interests. Tientsin was proud of its cosmopolitan cultural life and young Lazar performed with the city orchestra on many occasions. He attended the Jewish School in the British concession, and was a regular visitor to the Chinese opera. He took his first piano lessons from his mother, from Moscow and St. Petersburg Conservatory graduates, and from the formidable Madame Khokhlachkina, a memorable disciplinarian and pupil of Safonov, amongst others. In 1941, the seven-year-old composed his first work, a Fugato, during the Japanese Occupation when singing the Japanese national anthem was compulsory every morning at school. In 1944, a Pushkin Setting for voice, piano and solo violin followed while news reached the young composer of the premieres of Sergey Prokofiev's *Sixth, Seventh and Eight Piano Sonatas* and collaboration with Richter on the *Fifth Piano Concerto*. News also filtered through to distant Tientsin of Prokofiev's collaboration with David Oistrakh, Sergey Eisenstein and Vsevolod Meyerhold, as well as the scandal which followed the premiere of Dmitri Shostakovich's *Lady Macbeth of Mtensk*.

While Sitsky's parents had headed further East with their families at the time of the October Revolution, Lenin and his alert cultural commissar Anatoly Lunacharsky had championed young iconoclasts of the post-Skryabin *avant-garde* by providing contracts for them to have their works published by the Universal Edition, Vienna. Roslavetz, Mosolov, Krein, Feinberg, Schillinger, Golyshchev, Shcherbachev, Obukhov, Vyshnegradzky, Vogel, Kriukov, Polovinkin, Myaskovsky, Melkikh, Prokofiev, Shostakovich, Liatoshinsky, Deshevov, Popov, Protopopov, Lopatnikov and Lourié, among others, were wholeheartedly supported by the Bolshevik State.

However, in the period following Lenin's death, government control of artistic thought focused increasingly on censorship. The first show trials of 1928 were followed barely a year later by a series of repressive decrees that outlawed experimental music and exacerbated the position of creative artists in the Soviet Union until Andrei Zhdanov's death in 1948. Musical and other works of art not ideologically approved by the State were publicly condemned as counter-revolutionary. At the time of Sitsky's birth, the dogma of Socialist Realism was declared by Maxim Gorky, Nikolai Ivanovich Bukharin and Andrei Zhdanov at a Soviet Writer's Conference. Russians who lived in neighboring border enclaves had little in common with daily life in the Soviet Union, but such perceptions of life under the Soviets persisted until Tientsin was *liberated* by Mao Tse Dong's victorious Communist troops in 1949.

Once again, the pain of migrations experienced thirty years earlier befell Sitsky's parents, as White-Russian families and creative artists were forcibly repatriated to a culture into which the phenomenal movement that had been so vigorously supported by Lenin and Lunarcharsky had vanished. The Silver Age mysticism of Aleksandr Skryabin and Kandinsky's *Spiritual in Art* fell foul of planners in a Soviet Union in which intense nationalism, xenophobia and anti-Semitism widespread. Political intransigence concerning the reorganization of post-Leninist cultural policies, complete with inward-looking centralization and discrimination, had considerable bearing on the overall orientation of emerging composers and the contributions that they could make.

> We knew or suspected what was going on, although of course everything was controlled, especially the flow of information; there were always friends or relatives in the USSR, and therefore sporadic contact. Attending mass meetings with gigantic pictures of Stalin was viewed with a certain cynicism. At the same time, the propaganda was so ubiquitous and all-pervasive that one eventually began to doubt what was true and what wasn't. Russia had just defeated fascism, so as Jews, we had to feel some kind of gratitude. Many Jews, despite the known antisemitism, were Russophobes and absolutely loved the Russian culture. There's a paradox for you! Tientsin was not only Russian centred, but also a diverse post-boxer international society. I thought the whole world lived like this, and so arriving in a narrowly-focused Anglo-Saxon Sydney of 1951 was a kind of culture shock. The big plus was that no one cared what books you read, what films you saw, what radio stations you tuned into; Policemen couldn't just barge into your home to check things out. (LS)

An increasing sense of cultural loss and sacrifice of personal liberty, including the loss of freedom of movement to travel even within the Soviet Union, became a matter for concern. The oppression of artists that had taken place from 1928 on became well known to Russians everywhere, and the upheavals in China at the end of the 1940's combined with the specter of repatriation to Stalin's Russia confirmed the Sitsky family's decision to flee. It was, therefore, to the Australian Government's credit that the family was granted refugee status as late as 1951.

Ever since his arrival in Sydney, Sitsky remained in close touch with developments in the Soviet Union until his first official visit there in 1977. In this sense, his work may be seen as either developing to, or from, that point. Among the many strong impressions it made, his visit confirmed the existence of out-of-sight-out-of-mind-politically-approved performances that had become enshrined rituals behind closed doors. These were the only places that *modern* music by Arnold Schoenberg, Anton Webern, Alban Berg, Edgar Varèse, John Cage, Morton Feldman, Olivier Messiaen, Iannis Xenakis, Karl Heinz Stockhausen, Luciano Berio, Pierre Boulez, Jean Barraqué and others, could ever be heard. Although the pace of the Soviet cultural thaw that began taking place in the 1970's could only be described as glacial, it resulted in a progressive return to democratic change and experiment. By the 1990's this movement had made considerable strides towards establishing the tolerance of experimental music and free creative thought, for which Sitsky's ground-breaking research into early Soviet Music helped pave the way.

Through several decades of Stalin's ideological reorganization of creative arts, the *big three* of Soviet Music: Sergei Prokofiev, Dmitri Shostakovich and Aram Khatchaturian had constantly battled against overwhelming political odds in their attempts to persuade conservative Soviet planners and administrators to adopt more liberal attitudes towards experimental Art. Following Vladimir Mayakovsky's suicide and the murders of Meyerhold and Raikh, the bravery of musicians such as Sviatoslav Richter and Mstislav Rostropovich deeply impressed Sitsky. Their stand was shared by many others, such as Andrei Tarkovsky and Andrei Sakharov who were intimidated and harassed for speaking out, while Alexander Solzhenitsyn and Lina Lluberra Prokofieva were sentenced to long terms in labor camps. It was a period in which Sitsky also witnessed what happened to human rights supporters in the apparent safety of Western democracies, who did not escape the wrath of far-reaching Soviet influence through long-established spheres of Soviet political and media influence. Events in the Soviet Union continued to make a deep impression on Sitsky, evident throughout his keyboard music, which served increasingly as catalyst for ambitious symphonic and operatic designs.

> Life is very short, and it ought not to be spent crawling at the feet of miserable scoundrels. (Stendahl)

To Sitsky's amazement, his 1977 visit to Brezhnyev's Soviet Union revealed that most administrators still vigorously denied even the existence of works composed by the celebrated experimental *avant-garde* from sixty years earlier. Time and again, his research unearthed treasures which had at best been suppressed or neglected, and at worst, been lost or destroyed. Little did he realize the extent to which he was to rediscover his own cultural roots, not only as one who was creatively close to post-Silver Age Russian Art, but even closer to the achievements of giants who had vanished from an ancestral lineage to which he felt he belonged. Research into the keyboard works of this lost *avant-garde* touched his soul, and its influence is abundant throughout his keyboard works. Perhaps in contrast to biographical descriptions that constantly emphasize his inheritance of a Liszt-Busoni tradition, Sitsky's return to Russia in 1977 and to China in 1983 completed a *gestalt* of rediscovered artistic identity after the torment of a lifetime of cultural dislocation. Although to a large extent these biographical claims are true, such interpretations of Sitsky's artistic make-up often do not sufficiently take into account those powerful Hebraic, Russian and Chinese forces that had also shaped his creative idiom during the first sixteen years of his life.

On arrival in Australia, it was decided to enroll him at the School of Engineering, at the University of Sydney, but within the year, he had abandoned Engineering to seek out Alexander Sverjensky at the Sydney Conservatorium.

Sverjensky spoke nine languages and was an accomplished, if conservative, White Russian, steeped in cultural traditions of the kind cherished by the Sitsky family from major centers of musical excellence in St. Petersburg and Harbin. He knew the music of Rakhmaninov, Skryabin and Prokofiev as intimately as the keyboard works of their more radical contemporaries. As fate would have it, he was firmly put in his place by the older, more experienced, Rakhmaninov /Siloti student and the audition ended abruptly. Did Sverjensky's first meeting with the young prodigy revive memories of Madame Khokhlachkina, or was it possible that the spirited sixteen-year-old spoke out of turn?

But fate lent a hand and guided the controversial young pianist-composer to the mentorship of Winifred Burston, who had been a founding member of the Sydney Conservatorium in 1915. She was a close colleague of Sverjensky, as well as venerated Ferruccio Busoni/Egon Petri student, she had remained a fervent advocate of new music, and she was infinitely patient and kind. Burston persevered with her brilliant pupil for seven years, opening his eyes to a completely different musical world from the Russian musical traditions into which he had been born and trained. She propelled the teenager forward into a highly productive period of creative growth, which proved to be a revelation, and transformed his entire perception of art-music.

He studied the *avant-garde* of the time as promulgated by Sir Eugene Goossens, then the Director of the Sydney Conservatorium and principal conductor of the Sydney Symphony Orchestra throughout Sydney's Golden Age 1947-1956. It was in the second half of the miraculous Goossens directorship that Sitsky established a lifelong relationship with the works of Schoenberg, Webern, Berg, Bloch and other seminal, early-Twentieth-Century figures such as Claude Debussy, Igor Stravinsky, Busoni, Béla Bartók and Hindemith. Goossens introduced the works of most of these seminal figures to Australian audiences. Sitsky already knew Rakhmaninov, Skryabin, Prokofiev, Shostakovich and the works of most Russian composers, but was also drawn to Bartók and Bloch.

In Burston's studio sometime towards the end of 1951, Sitsky befriended another phenomenon of the time, Richard Meale, equally destined to provide leadership for Australian music.

> We were very close friends and saw each other virtually every day
> during the period . (LS in conversation with RW, June, 2003)

The two friends dedicated themselves to a long and impressive series of premieres in which they were joined in the mid-1950's by a third pianist-composer, Nigel Butterley. The three became more closely acquainted with the works of Messiaen and the celebrated students of his Paris class of the early 1950's such as Amy, Boulez, Barraqué, Berio, Stockhausen and Xenakis. He became more familiar with North-American composers such as Charles Ives, Varèse, Henry Cowell, Milton Babbit, Aaron Copland, Elliott Carter, Cage,

Stepan Wolpe and Morton Feldman. After Goossens' removal the performances of experimental music given by Sitsky, Meale and Butterley throughout the late 1950's and 1960's, were tantamount to the founding of an alternative culture, especially when compared to the bedeviled, embarrassing annual turnover officially offered by the conservative, narrowly-focused music Establishment, which had mired itself in the scandal resulting from the ouster of Eugene Goossens from the prudish society of the time.

Without realizing it, the Three, Australia's unknown but most brilliant emerging composer-pianists, began providing strong national direction for music to continue in times that were otherwise considered by many to be a vacuum after Goossens' demise had been engineered by ambitious amateurs who lacked the necessary vision and expertise to provide even adequate leadership, but who had, nevertheless, hijacked government Arts funding sources and derailed the management and direction of art- music throughout Australia. The Herculean task that faced Meale, Butterley and Sitsky to continue staging their unique if controversial series of new music concerts was daunting, but their commitment remained unwavering at a time when true leadership was desperately needed. Perhaps more than in any other period during the past fifty years, such inspired leadership-by-example bears testimony to what could only be described as the genesis of an authentic Australian School of new music performance and composition as the direct result of the Goossens inheritance. After Goossens, the burden of pioneering new music was considerable. However, the integrity and open quality of musical leadership provided by Sitsky, Meale and Butterley continued the Goossens renaissance which welcomed all participants. It displayed a kind of commitment inherited from the courageous stand made possible not only by Goossens' legendary, exacting standards, but also by the forward-looking example shown by the pianist-composer Percy Grainger.

Both Goossens and Grainger were highly venerated outside Australia as advocates of experimental music. However, both had alienated Australia's *Yellow Peril* political Establishment together with its deeply conservative, Anglo-centric *arrière-garde* composers, performers and critics. They were as suspicious of Goossens' investigations of black magic sources for exotic opera themes as the Soviets were of Shostakovich's *Lady Macbeth of Mtensk*. Few such Australian musical luminaries welcomed the new music of an emerging Australian, or any other, *avant-garde*.

Sitsky understood the isolationist mentality behind the Soviet system as well as Australia's geopolitical view of its neighbors which was, at that stage, still very much oriented from Whitehall and from the maintenance of British interests. The challenge of those interests, even culturally, by Goossens' and Grainger's artistic beliefs, made them a liability to the Australian Establishment of the time in a relationship exacerbated by persistent encouragement given young musicians to look north and to reach out to the ancient cultures of Japan, China, South-East Asia, to the Gamelan orchestras of Indonesia, Chinese Opera,

Japanese Noh theatre, and Buddhist temples of the Orient, which had so fascinated Debussy decades earlier. Such highly controversial views ultimately contributed to Goossens' expulsion and Grainger's progressive alienation. Both musicians were harassed, compromised, and publicly humiliated before being hounded out of Australian society.

Amid the Cold War's Soviet and McCarthyist excesses, Sitsky became an Australian citizen in 1954, the year of the infamous Petrov Affair, in which the Soviet Ambassador had requested political asylum in Australia. In the political furor that followed between Soviet and Australian authorities, xenophobia was bolstered in a scenario well known to the Sitsky family involving intolerance of refugees, censorship of *modern* music and free thought, intolerance of non-English-speaking religions, foreign accents, films, books and clothing (even footwear) - a panoply of intolerance totally unexpected by those who had fled to a safe haven of much-publicized freedoms in the New World from the ideological excesses of Central and Eastern Europe.

Sitsky's graduation from the Sydney Conservatorium in 1956 witnessed the spiritual crippling of Australia's foremost musicians similar to that which had been taking place in the Soviet Union.

> We were shattered by the Goossens affair; it was all downhill after
> that. (LS)

Little did Sitsky realize that it was only the beginning of a half-century of obsessive repression of talent that refused to endorse the mediocrity that had dismissed Goossens while holding management hostage for another half-century with its constantly growing army of ambitious, but often poorly-trained, administrative personnel renowned for showing little empathy with creative artists. *Arrière-garde* divide-and-rule tactics split Australian art-music in two, and the Meale-Butterley-Sitsky *avant-garde* was progressively relegated a back seat as closely-guarded *arrière-garde* policies and appointments consolidated its ill-gained authority. Alleged *reforms* in which artists had little or nothing to say about the running of their own affairs, except in a token way, were universally despised. For the first few decades after the *arrière-garde* coup it was impossible to utter Goossens' name (for decades) for fear of possibly attracting unfavorable professional repercussions from those directly responsible for compromising him.

The discreet breed of tyrannical new Australian cultural commissar covertly advised culturally uninterested politicians in successive Australian governments how to allocate Arts funds. The dove-grey suit era of the benign musical amateur had begun. Although in many respects, it gave the impression of being well-intentioned, it was, nevertheless, prone to discriminating against the many who believed in Goossens and spoke well of his achievements. Hand-in-glove with musical mediocrity, the Australian commissar, who was a classical music lover himself, ensured obstruction of artistic excellence loyal to Goossens, including Australia's daring *avant-garde,* which had begun providing such high-octane musical leadership. As a result, valuable opportunities for artistic growth and musical investment were lost, as unknown, second-rate composers and conductors mushroomed in government advisory positions, influential academic posts, key planning and funding bodies and media and management positions connected with the nation 's art-music. The new administrative breed, while outwardly pretending to empathize with Grainger's and Goossens' ideals, consolidated its grip on the nation's cultural affairs by stealth and manipulation. The effects on keyboard music were immediately apparent. Generous *arrière-garde* commissions were channeled towards much-publicized, but mediocre, new-breed composers, which resulted in all-pervasive distribution of derivative, commercially-orientated, simplistic piano music, while keyboard art-music of an experimental nature, including Sitsky's work, was rarely commissioned or published.

Sitsky felt increasingly excluded from a privileged community of musicians who had formed the equivalent of an Anglo-Saxon-oriented club, which, while protesting equality of opportunity, discriminated against followers of Goossens and foreigners (which usually meant non Anglo-Saxons). Sitsky had the perspicacity to sign a publishing contract with *Seesaw* Music Publishers (New York); Meale signed with Boosey & Hawkes (London), then Universal (London) and Butterley with Ricordi (Milano). The post-Goossens period witnessed an officially-cultivated imbalance of commission and performance opportunities wrested from an *avant-garde* which, although it provided true leadership, was seen as having been tainted by association with Goossens. Opportunities for composing serious art-music of any kind, including keyboard music, over the past half-century should be viewed against such a background.

With the suppression of Goossens and the emerging *avant-garde* which followed him, the standing of Australia's art-music deteriorated rapidly. The standing of the creative artist also dropped from pride of place to that of *artiste* – a dismissive term, matched only by similar pejorative use of *intellectual.* Public and government apathy, together with organized *arrière-garde* obstruction, exacerbated discrimination and a progressive dumbing-down of the national culture. Australia lost international cultural standing while the cream of its emerging talent abandoned hope of ever achieving an international reputation from a home-base of artistic excellence.

With Goossens' departure, Sitsky saw a promising Golden Age in which Australia could have played a more significant role, as active participant on the world stage, brought to a swift end, from Goossens' dynamic, cosmopolitan home base. An alarming exodus began, which continued for nearly fifty years, to witness the nation's finest talents perpetuate the quality of musical life elsewhere, beginning with the emigration of musicians of the stature of Roy Agnew, Percy Grainger, Charles Mackerras, Geoffrey Parsons, Don Banks,

Malcolm Williamson and David Lumsdaine. Other composers, such as Raymond Hanson and Dorian le Gallienne, who had been promised commissions and/or performances by the National Radio Orchestras (funded by State and Federal government entities), and publishing support by the post-Goossens Establishment, were persuaded to stay. However, they experienced difficulties. As the result of his questioning discrimination and administrative excesses in Australia's post-McCarthy years, towards the end of his life, Hanson admitted to close colleagues that he had not received anywhere near the kind of support promised in return for not joining the exodus.

In the unending struggle between artist and system, the vindictive personal agendas of ambitious or corrupt Arts *apparatchiks* triggered the emigration of high-caliber artists.

Although of course the system was completely different in Australia, creative artists were as effectively intimidated and isolated as they were in the Soviet Union. Whereas the Soviets tended to banish artists who were considered politically incorrect to periods of internal exile or hard labor, Australian bureaucrats pretended to be more democratic or even empathetic. Whilst praising their victims publicly, the politically incorrect were hounded into exile abroad by covert slander campaigns accompanied by the systematic removal of professional opportunities. Australian émigrés fled to the UK where, if they renounced their Australian citizenship, they became part of the British system, or else progressively disappeared into grand isolation or obscurity. In all systems, whatever the justification for discrimination for bringing creative artists to heel, the reasons remained the same. Perhaps it was only the methods (of manipulation and harassment) which differed in order to achieve the desired goals.

> Leopards break into the temple and drink to the dregs what is in the
> sacrificial pitchers; this is repeated over and over again; finally it can
> be calculated in advance and it becomes part of the ceremony. (Kafka)

In order to provide leadership equivalent to that of Goossens, Sitsky and the emerging *avant-garde* of the 1950's knew, therefore, that they would have to travel abroad if Australia was to replace vital cultural gaps necessary to keep pace with the European and American *avant-garde*.

> The atmosphere in Sydney was not overtly repressive, naturally,
> although in actual fact it was. New music ended with the funny sounds
> that people like Debussy made. Everything after that was not even
> mentioned let alone taught. The composers on the staff did not teach
> new music. (LS)

It was not until the end of the Twentieth Century that keyboard art-music in the parochial institutions of the former Soviet Union and Australia ended with

Debussy or Prokofiev, who, to all intents and purposes, were considered *modern* composers in the syllabuses of such Academies and Conservatoria. Despite the existence of a magnificent *alternative* culture in Australia's musical life, by the turn of century an *avant-garde* Sitsky, Meale and Butterley had studied at the Sydney Conservatorium in the 1950's, was still considered *modern* by most Australian heads of keyboard departments. Perhaps this was inevitable, given the quality of the legacy inherited by the generations of the past half-century from the hands of those who had ousted Goossens and systematically eradicated his influence from Australian cultural life over fifty years. In a young, dynamic culture like Australia's works such as Xenakis' *Eonta*, *Mists*, *Evryali* and his works for piano and orchestra; Stockhausen's Sixth and Tenth Piano pieces, *Kontakte* or *Mantra*; Boulez's *Structures* ; Dillon's piano works; Cage's and Feldman's major keyboard works; Barraqué's *Sonate* ; the Sitsky *Concerto for Two Solo Pianos* and other such keyboard works, are still rarely performed. The national cultural awakening and coming-of-age promised throughout the miraculous Golden Age of 1946-56 was not realized.

It was during Australia's McCarthyist period that Burston suggested Lazar change his name to Larry in order to ease his passage through the institutions of the 'Fifties. Correctly, she had read the writing on the wall of the Sydney Establishment of the time, and made arrangements for Sitsky to study on scholarship with Egon Petri in San Francisco. Meale traveled to Spain and the US, Butterley to the UK ,and Sitsky came to the USA, after which the Three returned to rebuild music in their country. In 1961, Sitsky assumed his first professional appointment at the Brisbane Conservatorium as lecturer in Keyboard Music, and in the 1960's Meale and Butterley took up positions at the Australian Broadcasting Commission's Federal Concert Music Department, planning for annual orchestral subscription concerts. The Three remained legendary advocates for new music, often programming highly committed performances of their own compositions side by side with the (then) recent European, North American and Japanese repertoire. Their concerts were not only the highlight of Australian art-music's emerging *alternative* culture at the time, but were welcomed, inspirational events that provided longed-for, clear direction so keenly sought by talented composers and performers.

> I don't think that any of us thought of ourselves as pioneers; we just did what we did and it included trying to inform the public of what was happening in the world. (LS)

As cultural displacement and subsequent migration from one culture greatly enriched another, so too did Australia benefit from a foreign policy that tried to attract a quota of distinguished immigrants, many of whom were World War II survivors from societies reputedly less tolerant than Australia's. Eminent musicians included Robert Pikler, Georg Tintner, Florent Hoogstoel, Leo Demant, Jan Sedivka, Jiri Tancibudek, Alexander Sverjensky, George Dreyfus, Felix Werder, Werner Baer, Richard Goldner, Ignazy Friedmann, and young

Larry Sitsky. Vital artistic renewal was thus provided mostly during the Goossens years by refugees who completely transformed the stagnant musical training ground of the Conservatoria into powerhouses of emerging talent. At that stage, university music departments were molded very much according to the British system. Strictly academic courses became the priority of Universities, while the Conservatoria specialized in Performance.

From its inception, Sitsky understood that the directorship of the fledgling Sydney Conservatorium had, in the year of Skryabin's death, fallen into the hands of a series of second-rate appointees of which Maurice Ravel was just one of the many unsuccessful applicants. A succession of play-safe directors suppressed modernistic tendencies with Australian composers up until the World War II. Keyboard music was affected. It was a time when heroes, including cultural heroes, traditionally, needed first to be approved by the British in their colonial sphere of interest. Australian keyboard music tended to emulate British achievements. After all. Australian society was, at that time, more openly dominated by British interests, including British cultural interests and its priorities.

The enormous groundswell for change and the outburst of optimism that immediately followed the end of the war, together with the dynamic leadership from the unknown but brilliant young Australian *avant-garde*, were not dissimilar to the expectations of creative optimists in the Russia of 1917, when a young but unknown *avant-garde* had emerged with equal promise after Skryabin's death, albeit as part of the Bolshevik dream to reconstruct a culture intended to provide international leadership. In 1947, musicians of the caliber of Georg Szell vied for the chief conductorship of the Sydney Symphony Orchestra and directorship of the Sydney Conservatorium, although another composer-conductor of similar stature, Sir Eugene Goossens, who was Igor Stravinsky's preferred director for key works, was appointed to the position, for which sweeping change was required. For those who studied at the Sydney Conservatorium during this period, it was an unforgettable Golden Age that inspired and maintained the highest musical standards. As a result, Sydney at that time became a serious international musical center of excellence, widely venerated abroad. Australian musical leadership promised a coming of age in the pursuit of its own cultural destiny. Fifty years later, in the national interest, a return to the artistic excellence and cultural priorities of the Goossens times is necessary if Australian Music, particularly keyboard music, is to be taken seriously on the world stage. After Goossens' demise, the much-publicized series of artistic successes by the coup's new breed composers did little to regain this lost reputation.

> Although Sydney was known to be provincial, I remember the excitement when Goossens premiered *The Rite of Spring* during the Fifties. (LS)

The consequential events of 1956 convinced Sitsky how efficiently the Australian Establishment, like its Soviet counterpart, could, manipulate, isolate and punish those who dared to question the abuses and excesses of administrators. In retrospect, it is interesting to observe how a series of administrative coups that had been brought about in Russia by an equally conservative *arrière-garde* torpedoed the very same cultural vision and promise shown by a similarly inspired emerging *avant-garde* that should have provided strong leadership. It was a time when Sitsky looked back not only at the misfortunes of Soviet composers as a result of the reorganization of musical life in Russia but as a new Australian, the misfortunes of politically incorrect figures such as Agnew, Grainger and Goossens. In apprehension he considered what might happen to Hanson and to others as the result of the enforced reorganization of Australia's cultural life. His fears were confirmed by the kinds of discriminatory decisions that were subsequently made behind closed doors to affect the quality of commissions, performances, recordings and government-funded special projects. As he pondered the price of free cultural expression in the new world, his concern for its welfare was confirmed by the continual exodus of a significant group of composers and performers.

At a time when the Sitsky family, already under considerable pressure, began reconsidering their options, the twenty-two-year-old pianist-composer displayed exemplary loyalty to his new country, as well as tenacity and artistic integrity. Whilst Sitsky's artistic contribution celebrated Russia's Silver Age and the spiritual in Art, it also provided a musical bulwark for the new world of his time. Sitsky's enormous output of keyboard music – the most prolific of any composer in Australia since the end of World War II – in which his keyboard compositions play a pivotal role, should be examined in this historical context. Works of creative keyboard experiment and maturity fall into three periods, the first two from 1959-77 and 1977-1985.

II

Seven large branches of the Sitsky keyboard tree spread out with eight *Fantasias* for solo piano on one side, representing the present while, in part, paying homage to the past. While painting expressionistic portraits of pianistic or compositional dedicatees, they are organic, unbroken single-movement, operatic/symphonic legends constructed on the single-movement piano sonata model of Liszt, inherited by Skryabin and Busoni with the exception of *Sharagan: Fantasia No. 5* , a multi-movement format based on Armenian influences. Rhapsodic in nature and steeped in Russian keyboard traditions, in many ways they remain a vocal preparation for the operatic *cantilena* of Sitsky's six operas on librettos by Gwen Harwood as well as providing the *cantilena* that eventually dominated his five Violin Concertos dedicated to Jan Sedivka.

On the other hand, is an abstruse, less predictable, futuristic non-*Fantasia* output with origins in unorthodox, experimental keyboard miniatures, four of which contain some of Sitsky's finest musical thought including *Petra, Nocturne Canonique, The Great Search* and more recently, a forty-minute, magnum Opus entitled *The Way of the Seeker*. The remaining two of these six pieces are the declamatory *Twelve Mystical Preludes* and the aleatoric *Foucault's Pendulum*. With the possible exception of the latter, all are inspired by an eclectic range of mystical beliefs and are dominated by a less restrictive aesthetic than the more orthodox procedures evident in the *Fantasias*. Experimenting with massed sound densities and textural saturation, the scope and design of the (above four) non-*Fantasia* pieces verge on the symphonic and multiple piano effects Beethoven worked on in the piano sonatas Opp.27 no.2, 53, 57, 101, 106, 110 and 111, which were exploited in Liszt's symphonic piano writing before being overhauled by Debussy, Skryabin, Ives and Cowell; redefined by Obukhov, Vyshnegradzky, Mosolov and late Messiaen, Stockhausen, Xenakis, Feldman, Takemitsu and more recently, Dillon. These four non-*Fantasia* pieces are completely different from any of the *Fantasias* or other Sitsky works. Indebted to Beethoven and the visions of Sitsky's early Soviet heritage, they are lost in a rampage of unrelenting violence and abandoned to an uncompromising category that certainly does not aim to please. Their savage aural discomfort would alienate a well-intentioned music lover were it not for their hypnotic tenderness, fragile strength, glimmering, luminous qualities and their dark, wild, spirit.

The remaining five branches of the Sitsky tree include two major works for piano and orchestra; a prolific series of transcriptions for solo piano and works involving the piano in chamber music combinations; experimental keyboard works such as: *Dimensions for Piano and Two Tape Recorders, Improvisation for Harpsichord, Concerto for Two Solo Pianos, Seven Meditations on Symbolist Art* for Organ; and two carillon works: *Eleven Abstractions* (on Paganini's *La Campanella*), and *Peal*.

In 1958, four years after the Petrov Affair when Sitsky had completed his post-graduate studies with Burston, the celebrated Soviet violinist, David Oistrakh was sent on a tour of Australia by the Soviet Ministry of Culture. A Conservatorium packed to the rafters witnessed his historic Sydney recital in the Verbrugghen Hall. For young Sitsky it was an electrifying and inspirational musical event and the beginning of a twenty-year pilgrimage ending in his first visit to the Soviet Union. Significantly, it triggered the gestation of Sitsky's first mature work – a homage to Bartók entitled *Unaccompanied Sonata for Violin* described by the composer as his Opus 1. 1958 was the year that Sitsky crafted an exquisite *Little Suite* (1958) followed two years later by a *Sonatina Formalis*, both significant in that they link high-grade Juvenalia to a mature creative output.

Sitsky's early solo piano miniatures were an attempt to integrate new-found Busoni/Liszt and Russian traditions with a highly personal keyboard idiom which combined formative experiences of his Russian/Tientsin upbringing with the Faustian European-*avant-garde* impact of Burston, distilled by Meale. Given the problems traditionally associated with piano construction and rapid sonority decay, composers of original keyboard art-music for children, such as Debussy, Bartók, and Prokofiev, had waited until mid-career before tackling the stylistic imperative of clarifying complex procedures in succinct, imaginative presentations mindful of the proverbial limitations inherent with sustaining sound.

The pianistic compendium contained in Larry Sitsky's *Little Suite* (1958) also touched upon the intimacy of his relationship with the pianist Magda Wlczek who became his wife and mother of their children, Petra and David. Based on perfect fourths, five pieces were constructed on the five letters which formed Magda's name to provide an improvisation in the form of a Jazz Waltz, a Russian folk song recalling Stravinsky's *Petrouschka*, a lyric *Nocturne* for the work's central arch, a two-part *invention,* and a closing *Elegy.*

Ex. 1: 4. L. Sitsky. *Little Suite for Piano (IV): Two part invention on a name.* (explanatory note).

Egon Petri's name provided the key to four movements that constituted the *Sonatina Formalis.* After Sitsky completed his first mature work for unaccompanied violin, he followed it with an unaccompanied sonata for flute, for which the *Sonatina Formalis,* like the *Little Suite,* paved the way, although both keyboard works properly belong to his Juvenalia. *The Sonatina Formalis* opens with *Melody with Accompaniment.* It is followed by *Canon at the Tritone* with sensual combinations of E major with E minor in *Preludio* to predict *The Lovers'* rendezvous thirty years later on the sixth path of the Tarot in his *Piano Concerto* (in G) and in the piano writing of his the two *Lotus* pieces. At a time when young Sitsky was overwhelmed by Busoni's *Fantasia Contrappuntistica,* it is difficult to imagine that similar configurations that open the *Presto* section of Busoni's opening *Preludio Corale* were not in some way destined to provide an ongoing, constructive influence. The *Preludio* of Sitsky's *Sonatina Formalis* is followed by a thirty-bar, two-voice *Fuga* to close the work, the derivation of the subject for both of which is E-G-O-N + P-E-T-R-I

Ex. 2: 4. L. Sitsky. *Sonatina Formalis*. explanatory note.

In 1990, the *Fantasia no.8* also extended constructions according to musical codes using the letters D-B-A-S from Don Banks' name.

Stringent economy, neo-classic simplicity and unorthodox linear applications of Sitsky's early keyboard miniature-art confirmed a technical and stylistic criteria evident in the creation of his cycle of 154 pieces of graded difficulty assembled between 1973-90 entitled *Century*. The challenge of such children's pieces refined Sitsky's emerging vocabulary, language and technique in readiness for the *Fantasias* (1962-1996) and two works for piano and orchestra (1991-2003).

A transcription for two pianos of the early version of Liszt's *'Etudes Transcendentales'* (incomplete) (1959-61) opens Sitsky's first mature period; transcription of Gershwin's *Summertime* from *'Porgy and Bess'* (1962); *Fantasia No. 1 in Memory of Egon Petri* (1962); *Dimensions for Piano and Two Tape Recorders* (1964); *Seven Statements* for solo piano (1964); *Improvisation* for Harpsichord (1965), adapted for use as the Overture to the opera *Fall of the House of Usher* with the addition of flute and pre-recorded voices); *Concerto for Two Solo Pianos* (1967); *Petra* for solo piano (1971); Seventeen *Bagatelles for Petra* (eventually incorporated into *Century*) (1973); *Twelve Mystical Preludes* on ancient Assyrian magic after the *Nuctemeron of Appollonius of Tyana* for solo piano (1973); *Eighteen Pieces for Young Pianists* (1974), later incorporated into *Century* (1973-90); *Nocturne Canonique* (1974); *Eleven Abstractions for Electronic Carillon* (on Paganini's *La Campanella*) (1974); *Seven Meditations on Symbolist Art* for organ (1974)

By 1959, Sitsky had already embarked upon a lifelong Bach-Busoni odyssey, which continued with his arrangement of J.S.Bach's *Chaconne* from the D minor Violin *Partita*. This left-hand piano *Etude* was followed by a transcription of Busoni's *Second Sonatina*, and a work entitled *Encore Piece* for two pianos, an arrangement for two pianos of J.S. Bach's *D major Prelude and Fugue* Book I from *The Well-Tempered Clavier* with the *Prelude* played simultaneously with the *Fugue*. Other works in this idiom include *Sonatina nach Bach-Busoni*, transcribed for strings and trumpet; Busoni's *Sonatina* transcribed for chamber ensemble; three works from Busoni's *Fantasia Contrappuntistica*: for solo piano, for two pianos and a *Concerto for Orchestra*; Bach's *Chromatic Fantasia and Fugue* in D minor BWV 903, for woodwind quintet.

Arriving in San Francisco in 1959, Sitsky embarked on the impressive trilogy of his first mature works with the completion of an *Unaccompanied Sonata for Violin*. It received approval from Szigeti and was followed by a *Sonata for Unaccompanied flute,* which immediately established itself as a repertoire classic. Egon Petri's death in May, 1962, triggered Sitsky's first mature solo keyboard work, the most significant of this masterful early trilogy, composed in homage to the Busoni tradition and entitled *Fantasia No.1 in Memory of Egon Petri*

> The Fantasia is the first real 'me'; all else that comes after it proves that statement: its intense expressionistic style, the improvisatory aspects, the ejaculatory phrases, the abrupt changes of dynamics with its associate expressiveness, all characteristics of my recent music are there in the Fantasia. ("Sitsky on Sitsky", Music Now, April 1971, p.7.)

Sitsky's earliest piano writing offers an expectation vindicated in applications of organic *cantilena* for the *Fantasia No.1*, pieced together in fragmented phrases with musical emphases dependent on a successful fusion of linear and contrapuntal elements. Deployment of intervals, especially fourths, tritones and minor and major seconds; uses of clusters as melody; and an unusual use of ornaments and phrase lengths enabled him to explore wider emotional parameters than in either of the earlier two unaccompanied sonatas. Precise indications of touch, attack and uses of standard, terraced, layered and *subito* dynamics; contrasting juxtapositions of sonorities involving a variety of clusters, have their origins in the *avant-garde* reading techniques and notation with unbarred phrases and unusual uses of time controls and accidentals notated in the early miniatures which constitute the *Little Suite* and *Sonatina Formalis*.

Musical trace elements abundant in earlier pieces reappear with sharply-defined authority for the finest of the Sitsky *Fantasias*, a work which has successfully withstood the trials of style and time over the past forty years. Tritonal, chromatic and cluster-cell references supplement Busoni motifs and delayed *cantilena* fragments form a gestalt and organic unity of dark grandeur as the rhapsody's mysterious energy illuminates spiritual journeys out of darkness into light, hope and renewal. Dedicated to Anna Rickard, the *Fantasia No.1 in Memory of Egon Petri* is divided into two main parts, the second is divided into a further three.

Ex. 3: 4. L. Sitsky. *Fantasia No. 1 in memory of Egon Petri*. bar 37.

In the *Fantasia No. 1,* a subtly concealed linguistic development unfolds through melodic motifs based on cellular techniques observed by the young pianist-composer in his studies and performances of Busoni's piano music. The principal theme of Sitsky's first part, the work's contrapuntal ingenuity and haunting chorale theme of the second, are built on three principal motifs: a cluster of minor seconds – A + G sharp + F sharp + G+ B (beginning/ending); signatory tritone motifs: B – F (Busoni) and E flat – A (Sitsky); a three-pitch chromatic cell: E + F+ F sharp. The idea returns for the third and final section of a second part to exploit the fragile strength of a palette of bell-like sonorities exploited in ancient patterns, sound codes and sacred chord progressions that survived the Pogroms, and which were handed down through generations of pianist-composers and teachers, some of whom, eventually who studied with Liszt or, like Feldman's and Sitsky's piano teachers, with Skryabin and Busoni. Such bell-like   progressions occur throughout the piano music of Rakhmaninov and Obukhov, and as the direct result of the migrations that followed the October Revolution, they eventually reached young Messiaen and his celebrated class of the early fifties. They are sounds that had completely mesmerized the young Russian-Jewish refugee in north China before he settled in Australia.

Ex. 4: 4. L. Sitsky. *Fantasia No. 1 in memory of Egon Petri*. bar 38.

Except for one page, the entire piece is scored without time signature and bar lines. Its rhythmic freedom propels intense musical emphases onto fragmented phrase lengths, including a reference to Busoni's *Fantasia in Memory of my Father*. Five years later, this fragmentation process intensified to near-Brechtian proportions by the time it reached the *Concerto for Two Solo Pianos*, although after Sitsky returned from his native Russia in 1977, he progressively abandoned fragmentation of the *cantilena* in favor of extensions of it as part of a major change in style, interpreted by some critics as exhibiting greater expressive and structural freedom and others as abandoning himself to traditional romanticism. At about the same time in the mid-late 1970's, both Meale and Butterley also experienced significant changes of style, at least according to the edicts of emerging composers who were committed to writing in the more romantic veins of Xenakis, Dillon, Stockhausen, Ligeti and Radulescu, although some of the more ideologically-orientated and opinionated who had discussed such major changes of style concerning Meale, Butterley or Sitsky were themselves espousing the importance of *New-Romanticism*.

Ex. 5: 4. L. Sitsky. *Fantasia No. 1 in memory of Egon Petri.* bar 3.

Come, follow me into the realm of music...Do you hear the depths and the heights? They are as immeasurable as space and as endless as numbers. Unthought-of scales extend like bands from one world to another, stationary and yet eternally in motion. Every tone is the centre of immeasurable circles. Innumerable are its voices... If you focus your attention on one of them you perceive how it [melody] is connected with all the others, how it is combined with all the rhythms, colored by all kinds of sounds, accompanied by all harmonies, down to unfathomable depths and up to the vaulted roof of heaven. Now you realize how planets and hearts are one, that nowhere can there be an end or an obstacle, that infinity lives in the spirit of all beings; that each being is illimitably great and illimitably small: the greatest expansion is like a point; and that light, sound, movement and power are identical, and each separate and all united, they are life.
(*The Realm of Music: An Epilogue to the New Aesthetic* – letter from Busoni to his wife 3rd March, 1910).

Following his first three mature works for solo instruments (1959-62), Sitsky composed two experimental works: the *Woodwind Quartet* (1963) and *Dimensions for piano and two tape recorders* (1964), which extended the *Fantasia No.1* by primitive electronic means. The *Woodwind Quartet* had been publicly derided at the inaugural Australian Composers' Seminar in Hobart and mercilessly attacked by *arrière-garde* critics. Undeterred, the composer continued a new, experimental piano piece with electronic participants. *Dimensions* was performed at a memorable Brisbane Conservatorium graduation ceremony for an invited audience intended to be seated in an open triangular acoustic space. Student performers used the piano and two speakers to create a form of *musique-concrète* with pre-recorded piano sounds played back aleatorically as two 'live' components of three freely-performed sound layers. Works in this genre from the 1950's and early 1960's composed by Cage, Takemitsu and the Messiaen students - Boulez, Barraqué, Stockhausen, Xenakis and Berio were almost unknown in Australia at that time, which in some ways accounts for the disturbing, parochial reaction to the thirty-year-old's work on the occasion of its premiere.

A ritual to political correctness was enshrined at the Conservatorium graduation ceremony as proud musical participants, graduates, and their families were reassured by outraged Directors of Education and the Conservatorium that steps would be taken immediately to ensure that such works would never again be performed at their institution. Although they were true to their word in the years that followed, the confrontation only made the young composer resolved to defend experimental music more than ever, and to take steps necessary to protect his compositional integrity from the deeply conservative Brisbane Establishment of the time, which had been so destructive of his hard-won artistic achievements and professional reputation. Within a year, he left Brisbane for Canberra, although, like the more-established serial composers, Barraqué and Boulez, Sitsky eventually abandoned loosely-structured *musique-concrète* and aleatoric procedures out of a desire to exercise greater control over his musical design. The compendium of possibilities that *Dimensions* presented in respect to textures, sonorities, and expressive attacks, were reworked more successfully nearly thirty years later in a succinct, multi-purpose, aleatoric mobile for solo piano entitled *Foucault's Pendulum* (1992).

1964 was the year that Sitsky returned to a rigorous, epigrammatic serial notation for solo piano entitled *Seven Statements*, in which finely-sculpted essays created the overall impression of an uninterrupted improvisation looking restlessly out to untamed vistas from the safety of the cultivated serial hedgerows of the time. A progression of metered phrase lengths (Statements I and IV) are juxtaposed against un-metered phrase lengths (Statements II, III, V, VI) around loosely-structured rhythmic freedom evident in the *Fantasia No.1* while Statement VII combines both metered and un-metered phrase lengths to offer grandstand views of the preceding six, as Sitsky codas increasingly took on the notion of retrospect.

The stage was set for Sitsky's first two major works in 1965 with the composition of his opera *Fall of the House of Usher,* and *Concerto for Two Solo Pianos* in 1967. In 1965, an *Improvisation for Harpsichord* was composed and immediately seized upon to provide the Opera's Overture with flute and pre-recorded voices. In the same year, he accepted a grant from the Myer Foundation to conduct research into the music of Ferruccio Busoni, the result of which was a twenty-year study published by the Greenwood Press, USA, entitled *Busoni and the Piano: The Works, the Writings and the Recordings.*

In 1965, Sitsky moved to Canberra and became Head of Keyboard Studies at the newly founded Canberra School of Music, where he became Head of Composition in 1978, and a full Professor in 1994. He had kept in close contact with the brilliant Brisbane husband and wife duo-piano team Max and Pam Olding, for whom he composed his torrential *Concerto for Two Solo Pianos* (1967). In constantly unrolling variation form using four themes, the *Concerto for Two Solo Pianos* belongs to a decade of intense creativity that preceded his inspirational visit to the Soviet Union in 1977, when he first heard the bells of Russia. It was a long-dreamt encounter which completely transformed his art, first apparent in the miraculous song cycle for soprano and eight players, *Music in the Mirabell Garden* (1977) – an intimate, ecstatic, Universalist vision that attested to a joyously reclaimed destiny after decades of cultural displacement.

Sitsky's epic *Concerto for Two Solo Pianos* explores the organic development of his *Fantasia No.1* and *Seven Statements,* while developing complex contrapuntal relationships. Precisely-articulated, four-hand part-writing dominates five stages of cellular growth with tightly-knit motifs of clusters of seconds, tritones and pivotal intervallic relationships to extend intensive fragmentation of phrase-lengths. A highly-intimate dialogue between the two soloists exchanges chord progressions from antiquity as thematic legend is swept into a broad vortex of energy streams, treacherous undercurrents, and side-eddies of sound, before being engulfed. Eleven Variations and a Fugue flow past the reaches of an estuary, Cadenza, further set of Variations (12-18), second Cadenza before the ascent into foothills, third set of Variations (19-23) and a closing ritual of joyous songs on craggy heights.

> The fact that time flows the same way in all heads proves more
> conclusively than anything else that we are all dreaming the same
> dream; more than that: all who dream that dream are one and the same
> being. (Schopenhauer)

Four years later, four important works were written for piano, Richard Meale's *Coruscations* and Ross Edwards' *Monos II* in 1971 and Anne Boyd's mesmeric *Angklung* in 1973. The remaining stride forward from this disparate group of masterpieces was the first of Larry Sitsky's experimental works, also from 1971, a deceptively fragile and impressionistic piano piece dedicated to *Little Petra,* the result of her father's reading T.E. Lawrence's *Seven Pillars of Wisdom*. The *yin* quality of *Petra*'s understated but penetrating narrative seemed to portray Larry and Magda Sitsky's daughter less as Beethoven's Fraulein Maximiliana Brentano from the Opus 109 Piano Sonata but perhaps more as some kind of polaric opposite to the *yang* of *Petra*'s expressionist twin, the *Fantasia No.1*. A subtle blending of sonorities was achieved by the uncompromising use of sustaining pedal, held down throughout the entire piece without ever being lifted. The historic precedent invoked recalled thirty-year-old Beethoven's identical *"experiment"*, a term used by the thirty-year-old composer to describe his C sharp minor *Fantasy-Sonata* Op.27 no.2 in which the sustaining pedal is held throughout the whole of its opening *Adagio sostenuto*. It was a conception which was inspired by Haydn's sturdy *Longman & Broderip*, which he had brought back with him from England in 1794 and with which young Beethoven had completely fallen in love. The instrument's celebrated *sopra una corda* and ethereal timbre had proven ideally suited to the *delicatissimamente* textures of Beethoven's *Adagio sostenuto*, which sounded as crystal clear without the dampers in the 1990's as they evidently did at the time. Using the instrument's sustaining pedal to simultaneously create a maximum sound saturation, the young composer sought an ethereal transformation of filtered sounds over sixty-nine bars of an opening movement which, nearly two centuries later, managed to sweep young Sitsky off his feet.

Perhaps Sitsky is one of few composer-pianists who realized Beethoven's bold experimental intention and sought to extend its possibilities, albeit in an entirely different musical context. Sitsky's hushed palette of luminous sonorities develops an *agitato*, hinted at by Beethoven, mid-development, on an extended dominant pedal point immediately preceding the reprise in the *Adagio sostenuto* of Op. 27 no.2. In *Petra*, Sitsky extends the idea of such a central *agitato*, as he does again fourteen years later, but more fully, in the giant slabs of his masterful *Si Yeoo Ki*.

There are moments in which the textural densities of both works sound as though they were conceived for multiple keyboards and in others, perhaps for orchestra, because of the dimensional effect caused by the sustaining pedal's overwhelming saturation on the modern-day instrument. Unorthodox sustaining techniques evident in Beethoven's pedal experiments maintained throughout the first movement of his C sharp minor *Sonata–Fantasy*; in the extended impressionistic phrases of the *Allegretto moderato* Op. 53 and throughout the Sonatas Opp. 57, 101, 106,110 and 111, all created similar saturated textures to achieve ethereal, quartet-like or symphonic effects intended to defeat the ever-present problem of rapid sound decay so typical of keyboard instruments and the inherent problems of sustaining sound when faced with a fundamental construction so limited by such rapid decay. Multiple piano, orchestral and saturated textures were exploited by Liszt, and in the Twentieth Century by Debussy and particularly by Feldman, using two, three, four and even five keyboard extensions to achieve dimensional symphonic grandeur. It was a journey also made by Xenakis in his *'clouds of sound'*, at times written across ten staves in the pianist's part of *Synaphai,* and in the pages of Xenakis' other masterpieces for keyboard such as *Eonta, Mists* and *Keqrops.* Sitsky, however, returned to the Beethoven, Liszt and Busoni tradition, and extensions of the celebrated *sopra una corda* and ethereal timbre of the Haydn instrument proved ideally suited to the *delicatissimamente* of the Beethoven textures, which were crystal clear without the dampers at the time of the post-Russian Silver Age experiments of Vyshnegradzky.

Ex. 6: 4. L. Sitsky. *Petra.* bars 55-57.

Petra's giant wash of sound, translucent textures and uncompromising juxtaposition of harmonies confront the listener with blurred sound densities. In chords or their components as part of larger harmonic references, fleeting moments pass from one area of the work to another through uses of subtly-placed harmonic macro-pivots and the constant movement of intervallic dissonances, false relations and suspensions. The totality takes on an aural impact of colliding galaxies in a distant spectacle of awesome, majestic ferocity. Attaching meaning to such sound events is offered through the subtle underlying presence of an ongoing *cantilena* almost as a haunting chorale, offset by stringent use of dynamics to produce the same spectral grandeur, heightened intimacy and repressed violence of Beethoven's *Adagio sostenuto* Op. 27 no.2. Hidden in the tranquil mists of the work's opening, arcane, veiled thematic references envelop the piercing vocal narrative as it departs with five questions left unanswered.

> We had at last reached the mysterious city of Petra, a city deserted
> and lost to history for one thousand four hundred years. (Lowell
> Thomas: *With Lawrence in Arabia*)

In 1973, I received Anne Boyd's timeless *Angklung* for solo piano, based on the elusive tintinnabulations of Indonesian instruments, whose aesthetic and achievement subtly redefined known parameters of the octave. In the same year, Sitsky composed seventeen pedagogical *Bagatelles for Petra,* and the following year added *Eighteen Pieces for Young Pianists* to offer a compelling update to

Bartók's *Mikrokosmos*. Entitled *Century*, each piece is more or less of one page duration, designed to introduce new reading techniques and notations concerned with key signatures, accidentals, dynamics, harmonics, scattered pitches, time and meter functions, control of *accelerando*, *rallentando*, free durations, the role of the *fermata* and *agogic,* and other expressive accents, *rubato*, altered rhythmic lengths, removal of bar lines, extensions of conventional hand and palm clusters to include elbows, uses of three pedals and a wide variety of unorthodox keyboard techniques

> ... to introduce [children] to the sight and sounds of contemporary music, to encourage them to play freely and at times to improvise. (LS)

In 1973, Sitsky composed *Twelve Mystical Preludes after the Nuctemeron of Apollonius of Tyana,* dedicated to Beryl Sedivka.

> When the ABC approached me with the commission for [Roger Woodward's recital in the inaugural series of concerts of] the Sydney Opera House and mentioned twelve minutes as a duration for a work, I immediately thought not only of the twelve hours of the Nuctemeron but also of twelve in musical terms... Thus, three uses of the number twelve brought the work into being. (Larry Sitsky interviewed by JM Penny, 1978)

In many ways, Sitsky's *Twelve Mystical Preludes* provides a comprehensive aesthetic preparation for the *Piano Concerto: Twenty-two Paths of the Tarot,* composed nearly twenty years later. As the result of a childhood spent absorbing culturally diverse influences, all his creative life, Sitsky has been preoccupied with inspirations from a wide variety of mystical sources, including The Kabbalah, I-Ching, Egyptian and Tibetan Books of the Dead, Hindu, Sufist, Armenian, and the Russian-Universalist concepts of Gurdjieff, Blavatsky and the Medieval Tarot. However, his composition of the *Twelve Mystical Preludes* by a mid-nineteenth century French Rosicrucian's translation of ancient Assyrian magic, the *Nuctemeron* by Eliphas Levi Zahed, resulted in a work dedicated to the sacred ritual of raising the spirit (Apollonius') out of darkness into light. It was an aesthetic pursued by many composers for entirely different artistic reasons including Stockhausen, Xenakis and Barraqué in his formidable early *Sonate* (1950-52), in which the progression is from light into darkness. Movement towards white, shining light crops up often enough in the works of Silver Age Russian composers such as Skryabin and Obukhov, who were devoted to such Universalist visions. Sitsky's *Preludes* depict spiritual growth through twelve mystical steps, a concept that had also been one of the most meaningful inspirations behind the composer's life and work at many levels:

> Music is to me a mystic experience, in the broadest understanding of
> that word; the mystic state can be achieved, even within music, in a
> number of ways. Taken in such a light, my compositions can then be
> regarded as biographical milestones on the road to self-awareness.
> (LS)

Sitsky's *Twelve Mystical Preludes* and *Piano Concerto* are pieced together using
colorful visual and rhythmic images to serve a more complex play of subtle,
ritualistic associations notated in classical, declamatory pianism. Vivid linguistic
symbolism, wider emotional parameters, extended dynamic scope and dense
chord structures extend horizontal procedures in precisely-articulated,
fragmented *cantilena* in the Fifth and Tenth Preludes, recreated for the main
theme of the *Piano Concerto* (1991).

Ex. 7: 4. L. Sitsky. *Concerto for Piano and Orchestra.* opening.

Unlike the *Twenty-two Paths* of the *Piano Concerto*, each of the *Twelve
Mystical Preludes* is preceded by apocalyptic descriptions such as:

> In The Eleventh Hour the wings of the genii move with a mysterious
> and deep murmur; they fly from sphere to sphere, and bear the
> messages of God from world to world.

The pianism of the Twelfth Prelude and Fifteenth Path of the *Piano Concerto*
have much in common, as do the pianistic shapes throughout the First Prelude
with the Second Path. In homage to Skryabin, the Tenth Prelude evokes a
longing of the soul throughout the central section of the Fifth Path with its
loving distribution of opaline sonorities and *appels mysterieux* scored over three
registers and use of three pedals.

The Tenth Hour is the key of the astronomical cycle and of the circular movement of human life.

Ex. 8: 4. L. Sitsky. *Twelve Mystical Preludes (after the Nuctemeron of Apollonius of Tyana).* opening of The Tenth Hour.

Indications ranging from *vertigineux en délire* in Prelude 7, and *radieux* in Prelude 10; the idea of subterranean voices in Prelude 2, *estatico* in Prelude 5, and similar expressionist visions from Skryabin, Obukhov and Vyshnegradzky, led Sitsky early in life to Russian-Universalist philosophy. They also inspired the Messiaen students Karl Heinz Stockhausen and Yannis Xenakis, composers with whom Sitsky otherwise had little in common through the post-Silver Age migrations of composers like Obukhov and Vyshnegradzky.

Ex. 9: 4. L. Sitsky. *Twelve Mystical Preludes (after the Nuctemeron of Apollonius of Tyana).* bars 10-11 of The Fifth Hour.

The opening and closing of the Eighth Hour recall *The Golem* as well as the opening of *The Tower* in the *Piano Concerto,* in which identical pitches and registers predict or recall cataclysm.

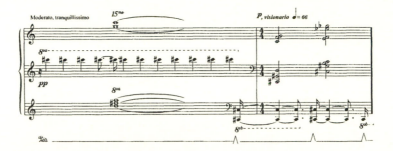

Ex. 10:4. L. Sitsky. *Twelve Mystical Preludes (after the Nuctemeron of Apollonius of Tyana).* opening of The Eighth Hour.

Asymmetric rhythmic groupings of chords in Prelude 7 reappear in Paths 8 and 9 of the *Piano Concerto*.

Ex. 11: 4. L. Sitsky. *Concerto for Piano and Orchestra.* ending of The Hermit.

I find that my compositions are constantly being affected by my other lives as a performer, researcher and teacher. (*Sitsky on Sitsky*, Music Now, April, 1971)

The result of the gift of a carillon to the city of Canberra by Her Majesty Queen Elizabeth II, Sitsky composed a violent, cluster-based work in 1974 entitled *Eleven Abstractions* based on Paganini's *La Campanella*. It was followed twenty six years later by an ecstatic occasional piece entitled *Peal* to celebrate his son's marriage in an intimate Canberra lakeside setting.

In 1974, Sitsky revisited *Petra* with his composition of a lyric night fantasy which in many ways recalls the black, suppressed violence of Mosolov's *Nocturnes* and Beethoven's prodigious *Adagio sostenuto* Op. 27 no.2. However, it also recalls Debussy's crystalline *Et la lune descend sur la temple qui fût* perhaps in a place like Petra, and similarly abandoned without explanation to the ravages of time, in which wistful memories of childrens' games linger throughout empty, moonlit ruins. An absolute gem in Sitsky's creative output, the *Nocturne Canonique's* succinct, three-part writing and symmetrical rise and fall predict the masterful experimental piano piece: *Si Yeoo Ki* (1985) while glimmering, luminous sonorities and a searing, fragmented *cantilena* veil a passionate outpouring in the composer's richest contrapuntal vein. Torn by memories of lost chorales, dreams, tears, love lost and the specter of death, its dithyrambs are consumed by a black longing that dominates the *Fantasia no.8 on D-B-A-S* (1990).

> We are tormented by our inability to know the truth. But there is no
> need to know it! We need to love. And to believe. (Dostoyevsky)

Ex. 12: 4. L. Sitsky. *Nocturne Canonique.* bars 9-12.

In 1975, Sitsky presented the works of seven Symbolist painters combined with experimental textures based on clusters in a lengthy, pragmatic conception entitled *Seven Meditations on Symbolist Art* for organ played with slides shown simultaneously of seven paintings by Munch, von Stuck, Delville, Khnopff, Kupka, Redon and Rosetti. In many ways, it continues the cluster vocabulary of *Eleven Abstractions* and saturation techniques of *Petra,* while offering a halfway house between the *Twelve Mystical Preludes* and *Piano Concerto* . A complexity of massive chord progressions open and close the work, interrupted at salient points by dense, cluster-orientated improvisations as heavy lead weights are placed or removed from the keyboards or pedals for extended periods. When asked about the programmatic aspects of the work the composer replied:

> The whole idea of programme music is naïve – it holds no interest for
> me whatsoever. I merely reacted to the Symbolist paintings.

Sitsky's reaction is not far removed from Beethoven's when asked to explain the meaning of descriptive titles which precede the movements of his *Pastorale* Symphony:

> Not painting, but the expression of feeling

However, Sitsky's synaesthesia probably has less to do with Beethoven than with Skryabin since his expressionist statement of sound and visual images remained very much part of the traditions that he inherited from visionary Russian Silver Age multi-media masterpieces such as Skryabin's *Poem of Fire* (1910) and sketches for *The Mysterium* (1915).

III

In 1975, Sitsky co-founded the Composer's Guild of Australia together with James Penberthy, and in 1976 he established the Australian Contemporary Music Ensemble with Keith Humble and Don Banks, which did much to promote Australia internationally. In 1977, the Australian Department of Foreign Affairs offered Sitsky a Composition Fellowship as part of its inaugural Cultural Exchange programme with the Soviet Union. The composer used the opportunity to rediscover his personal and musical relationship with a culture that remained native to him, but in which fellow composers had struggled or vanished as the result of ideological edicts. The project proved to be the turning point of his life following many rehearsals in a role Sitsky knew well. A ten-year period of frenzied research into the fate of the lost Soviet *avant-garde* ensued that had followed Skryabin, published in 1991 by the USA Greenwood Press, and entitled *Music of the Repressed Russian Avant-garde 1900-29*.

This profoundly moving classic in the field was re-released four times in the space of a decade, and presented the life and work of musical giants who, after Skryabin, as a result of political incorrectness, disappeared at the hands of commissars and administrators into obscurity, cultural dislocation or worse. These unrecognized musicians helped establish the foundations and *lingua franca* of a phenomenal *avant-garde* that was later exploited by Western composers in the latter part of the Twentieth Century, including the illustrious, celebrated young composers who emerged from Messiaen's Paris class of the early 1950's.

Face to face with destiny, the historic visit also enabled Sitsky to understand what Busoni had before him, that it was, fundamentally, not Liszt but Anton Rubinstein, one of the main founders of the Russian School of Piano Playing, who had in fact provided the main role model for him as a pianist. Although Sitsky's well-intentioned biographers often seem to dwell on the impact of his

Busoni-Liszt inheritance they sometimes neglect the deeper significance of his cultural displacement and the full meaning of the impact of his historic 1977 visit to the Soviet Union which confirmed, more than ever, his possession of two entirely separate musical traditions. The first was the Russian tradition into which he had been born and raised as a child, handed down from Rubinstein through Rakhmaninov, Skryabin and his teachers from the Moscow and St. Petersburg Conservatories then nurtured throughout the first sixteen years of his life. The second was his Liszt/Busoni scholarship, acquired through Petri and Burston.

As he came face to face with his past in 1977, the realization of the significance of what he held in his grasp triggered an implosion responsible for the richest period of creative growth to date. The series of visits he made to the Soviet Union and his return to China in 1983 witnessed his creative style move further away from granitic tensions of serialist formulas towards lush, mystical textures of a non-Western sound world, equally impossible to forget even though he had always remained first a Russian. This change became evident with a return to the long-abandoned percussion timbres of Chinese opera from childhood which had taken up permanent residence in his musician's inner ear over decades, and which had haunted and resonated throughout his musical being with their pervasive magic. Between 1977 and 1983, Sitsky's coming to terms with his Russian emigré childhood spent in China and realizing all that his Russian cultural inheritance meant to him marked this significant turning point as the imperative to rationalise a complexity of Faustian, Silver Age, Chinese and Hebraic traditions became an imperative that ultimately revitalized his art and life.

Keyboard works from the period include an *Encore Piece* for two pianos, an arrangement of J.S.Bach's *D major Prelude and Fugue* No. 5 from Book 1 of *The Well-Tempered Clavier* (1980); *Fantasia No. 4: Arch* (1980); *Fantasia No. 2 in Memory of Winifred Burston* (December, 1980); *Two (Armenian) Folk-Settings for Piano Ensemble* transcribed for electric pianos (1981); *Century* (1973-1990) (154 pieces of graded difficulty for young players, including the *Seventeen Bagatelles for Petra* (1973) & *Eighteen Pieces for Young Pianists* (1974); transcriptions completed for solo and 2 pianos of Busoni's *Fantasia Contrappuntistica*.

> Towards the end of 1980, I was working on two separate commissions. One was a test piece for the Sydney International Piano Competition and the result of that was ARCH: Fantasia No.4 [dedicated to Geoffrey Lancaster] a simple - structured neo-romantic piece based on the tritonal pull between E flat and A which two notes feature prominently in it. When I completed ARCH, it seemed to me that various ideas embodied in it had further possibilities. And so Fantasia No.2 in Memory of Winifred Burston [dedicated to John

> Luxton] came into being. It amused me to use the same basic materials
> as in ARCH resulting in quite a different work. (LS)

In single-movement works, the principle of intervallic oscillation, inversion and transposition exploiting linear, chord and tritone motifs developed in conjunction with discordant ostinato figures, chromaticism, wide octave displacements and statements of themes in constant rhythmic variation, evolving gradually – the classic hallmarks of the Sitsky *Fantasias*.

In 1980, Sitsky composed *An Encore Piece for Two Pianos* (after Bach-Busoni) once again for the Brisbane piano duo – Max and Pam Olding, based on J.S. Bach's D major Prelude and Fugue Book 1 in D major from *The Well-Tempered Clavier* based on an idea propounded by Busoni in his *Well-Tempered Clavier* Edition, where he wrote about thematic unity in Bach. While Piano I performs the complete Prelude, Piano II simultaneously commences the Fugue.

> I hear this piece as fast, witty and light but, like all Bach, it seems
> open to other possibilities.

In 1981, Anne Boyd made a significant contribution to piano literature with her juxtaposition of rich, hanging-garden sonorities notated across ten multiple staves and entitled *Book of the Bells*. It was the year that Sitsky was commissioned by Narrabundah College, Canberra, to compose a pedagogical piece for a group of six piano students to perform in a class laboratory situation. Six-part pieces entitled *Piano Ensemble* (1982) were set for electric pianos based on Armenian folksongs. Within the year, Sitsky had fallen completely in love with Armenian music, resulting in a prolific creative outpouring. In an interview he gave *The Canberra Times* he declared Armenian music to be "melodically rich, highly ornate and rhythmically, very interesting."

Indefatigable research into his Russian inheritance intensified, while the China of his youth kept revealing its secrets. Ongoing scholarly visits became increasingly responsible for journeys to a wider range of mystical destinations to inspire *Si Yeoo Ki*; *Fantasia No. 7* on a theme of Liszt; Transcription of *Perele's Song* from *The Golem*; *Fantasia no. 8 on D-B-A-S*; *Concerto for Piano and Orchestra*: *The Twenty two Paths of the Tarot*; *Foucault's Pendulum*; Fantasia no. 10 (for double-keyboard piano); *Lotus I* (opening of incidental music to *Faust*); *Lotus II* (closing of incidental music to Faust); *The Seven Spells* (Transcription of incidental Music to *Faust*); Beethoven's *Für Elise* edited for student pianists; Transcription for solo piano of Rachmaninov's *18th Variation* from the *Rhapsody on a theme by Paganini* for piano and orchestra; Transcription for solo piano of a *Pachelbel Canon*; *Fantasia no.11* (incorporating "E" and "E II"). Sitsky's recent *Second Symphony* for Piano and Orchestra and magnum opus major for solo piano based on Sufist philosophy, entitled *The Way of the Seeker,* places him at the beginning of an entirely new period of creative growth.

1983 was the year that Sitsky completed a sixteen-minute piano piece in four movements entitled *Sharagan: Fantasia No. 5*, dedicated to his student Robert Zocchi. It opens with an un-metered first movement of pure Armenian folk song, scored exclusively in bass registers and played

> Majestically, with much freedom, occasionally erupting into violence. Always moving, rarely still, with a restless undercurrent. (LS)

to which most of a metred fourth movement returns.

Ex. 13: 4. L. Sitsky. *Sharagan: Fantasia No. 5.* top of page 7 (unbarred).

> Sharagan is Armenian for 'ancient song' thus encapsulating two dominant features of this composition: the strongly melodic thrust of the music and the debt to Armenian folk music. Both aspects emerged strongly in my music in 1983 and 1984. Although Sharagan is in four movements I did not choose to call it anything formal like 'sonata', which to my mind conjures up a tightly structured edifice. Sharagan is rhapsodic and improvisatory and so joins my other Fantasias. The first movement concentrates on the dark, low register of the piano; it broods but tends to erupt into occasional violence. The second movement is in a strict 4/4 throughout, with the left hand marking the beat unrelentingly. The third is slow and remote whilst the fourth's principal character is the use of asymmetric beats in a Presto ending in a sweeping gesture after a movement of non-stop repeated notes. (LS)

The end product of this most decisive period in Sitsky's creative development is the composition *Si Yeoo Ki* (*The Great Search*) which, alongside *Petra* and *Nocturne Canonique* is arguably his finest keyboard work. It could easily be called *The Great Wave* since it is the tsunami unleashed and extends structural, textural densities and saturation techniques for which *Petra* and *Nocturne Canonique* were preparatory models. In an uninterrupted *crescendo e accelerando* similar to the overall construction of the movements in Beethoven's C sharp minor *Fantasy-Sonata* and in an ambitious time-frame of similar duration, the physical impact of *Si Yeoo Ki's* massive blocs of sound unleash awe-inspiring energies in macro extensions of unpredictable terraced dynamics that completely overwhelm the listener. Diatonic in orientation, *Si Yeoo Ki* opens *Lento occulto – pianississimo*. Fragile sonorities mass towards an *Allegro fortissimo* as *appassionato, con molto agitato* seize control in restless, unwieldy terraced waves until the highest dramatic point, *martellato fortissimo*, devastates *Fantastico, precipitato* at the work's summit. The maelstrom abates mid-page 10, in stages: *pianissimo, misterioso, andantino,* before *fortississimo furioso, presto* (pages 11-12) subside *pianissimo* and finally *Adagio, pallido*.

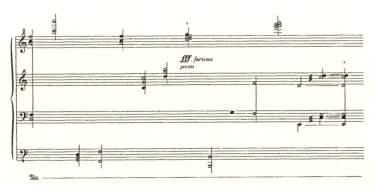

Ex. 14: 4. L. Sitsky. *Si Yeoo Ki.* (unbarred).

Sitsky's four-stave notation partly pays homage to a stage of Schillinger's five and six-stave notation from his *Heroic Poem* Op. 12 no.1 (1922) except, in Sitsky's case, for the decision to remove all bar lines. The highest stave reads an octave higher and bottom, an octave lower with the sustaining pedal perpetuating the crucial role it had played in the uncompromising wash of sound throughout *Petra*. In *Si Yeoo Ki*, the sustaining pedal is held down without being released at all for the first three and final four pages, intermittently for two pages and not at all for only one other. The degree of difficulty in performing a work which is so close to nature, to master its sense of flow and massive tidal movements and achieve a sense of spacious aerial freedom is a challenge alongside other Sitsky keyboard works such as the *Concerto for Two Solo Pianos, Petra, Nocturne Canonique* and *The Way of the Seeker. Si Yeoo Ki* has less in common with the formal compositional achievements of the *Fantasias* and in a certain sense, even his other experimental piano works. If it is the least played of Sitsky's keyboard works at the time of this writing, perhaps it is Sitsky's most challenging keyboard work to date.

> Music, to me, is a mystical journey, and one learns from the various
> gurus that are encountered along the way of the Great Search. Without
> the mystical reason for its existence, music, for me, loses its point. The
> mere desire to please or amuse holds no abiding value in my eyes.
> (LS)

IV

In late 1985, Sitsky's great search continued with a returned to orthodox traditions with the *Fantasia* side of his keyboard writing when the Liszt Society commissioned a new *Hexameron* for the centenary of the composer's death dedicated to the pianist Geoffrey Tozer. In accessible textures closer to predictable pianism, Sitsky called upon his Bach-Busoni inheritance to develop a new form of Prelude and Fugue based on Liszt's fourteenth Hungarian Rhapsody. *Fantasia No.7, on a theme of Liszt* (1985) is signed by the composer's characteristic E flat-A tritone initials evident in earlier *Fantasias*, while contrapuntal ingenuity is supplemented by a fascinating *ossia* to predict the dying measures of the *Piano Concerto* perhaps as some kind of baroque *Echo* by way of a Graingeresque postscript to "play the last nine bars of Liszt's theme pianissimo, far away, like a distant Bach choral". (LS)

Ex. 15: 4. L. Sitsky. *Fantasy no.7 on a theme of Liszt.* ossia at end of score.

In 1986, Sitsky composed *The Secret Gates of the House of Osiris* based on the Egyptian *Book of the Dead*, and in 1987, arranged a solo piano version of *Perele's Song* from his operatic masterpiece *The Golem*. Loving *fioritura* of a *berceuse*-like *cantilena* prepares an Aria with accompaniment for the elegant nocturnal lyricism of his *Third Violin Concerto*, which followed in the same year. In 1982, *Century* was completed, after which the Australian National Library commissioned a piano work to commemorate the tenth anniversary of the death of the composer Don Banks: *Fantasy no.8 on D-B-A-S* which Sitsky dedicated to his piano student Kate Bowan.

Ex. 16: 4. L. Sitsky. *Fantasy no.8 on D-B-A-S.* preface to score.

From the outset, the inventive role of the lone, unorthodox E flat of the key signature establishes a mood of unrelenting sorrow and despair in the poignant *cantilena* of this fierce Litany. Underpinned by Banks' and Sitsky's overlapping signatures E flat (Es=S) – A, a musical code to friendship is solemnly inscribed on the same monument that the composer had dedicated to Magda and Petri thirty years earlier. From the outset, homage and separation are stated by the *Largo's* four isolated pitches. With an impact of B-A-C-H or perhaps the catastrophic four-pitches which open Bach's A minor Fugue Book 2, Skryabinic *appels mysterieux*, fanfares and a protrusion of trills parade this bleak pageant from the end of pages 1 and 2 before their return in the latter part of the *Piano Concerto*. Progressions of diminished, perfect and augmented fourths also recall Skryabin's intervallic progressions in fourths from his *Eighth and Ninth Sonatas*.

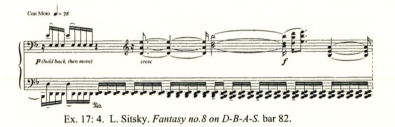

Ex. 17: 4. L. Sitsky. *Fantasy no.8 on D-B-A-S.* bar 82.

In an inventive exploration of four pitches, contrapuntal ingenuity pierced by anguished cries, closes the work in descending bravura octaves E flat-D-B-A, *feroce*, reminiscent of the violent clusters in Sitsky's first carillon piece. Throughout Sitsky's keyboard writing, there are many Bach and Bach-Busoni references that evolved naturally, endlessly evolving, to eventually form an integral part of his musical language. In this sense, the final descent of octaves in the *Eighth Fantasia* brings to mind, at least for some performers, the trampling out of death in the final pedal passage of J.S.Bach's *Heut Triumphiret Gottes Sohn* .

In 1988, Sitsky was awarded a Travelling-Research Scholarship by the USSR Union of Composers and the Ministry of Culture to participate in the Third International Festival in Leningrad and conduct research into early Soviet music. The same year, he received a two-year Fullbright Australian-American Fellowship, and in 1989, the Greenwood Press, USA, published two volumes of his *Index of the Classical Reproducing Piano Roll*.

In 1990, after reading *A New Model of the Universe* (1914) by the Russian philosopher P.D. Ouspensky with a chapter devoted to *The Symbolism of the Tarot* and Ouspensky's ordering of cards in the form of a prose poem, Sitsky discerned an order and meaning of meditation that inspired his *Piano Concerto*

(1991) linked to Ouspensky's publication and ideas surrounding the twenty two cards which constitute the Tarot's major Arcana.

> Some mystical teachings link each of the cards with a Hebrew letter; a further link with Jewish mysticism is via the Cabbalistic tree of Life, which comprises the Ten Sephiroth, or emanations of God; there are twenty two paths linking the ten emanations. In the end, of course, the music takes over and makes its own piece with its own rules; the cards then recede as mere props, a poetic point of departure for the work. (LS)

Having commissioned Sitsky's *Piano Concerto*, my initial impression of its rich orchestration, joyous and tolling bells and the trance-like, shimmering textures and *appels mysterieux* of its opening bars gave the impression of an evocation from the furnace of the Australian bush as much as programmatic associations of the major Arcana. Whatever the origin, it was an intriguing process to try to discover the work's hidden arc and design, the secrets of its musical flow and linguistic patterns behind musical dialogue. I returned to The Kabbalah, to Dürer, Dali, Egyptian maps of the unconscious and looked into meditative practices adopted by medieval Europeans, but the work seemed to be hermetically sealed. Not to be deterred by mystical forces which had allegedly shaped the destinies of so many other elusive Sitsky works, I toyed with the multiple possibilities offered by the permutations and their transformations to piece together a convenient work plan of 6+6+2+7+1 divisions.

An exposition of six divisions was followed by a two-part central development of fifteen (VII-XII + XIII-XXI) divisions, a plan that allowed the structural span to open three stages of mounting dramatic intensity: to the point of the major cadenza at XIII (Death) with symphonic extension at XIV (Temperance); to the impenetrable darkness. At XVIII (The Tower) and ascent to XX (Judgement), where invisible deities render the work asunder. A progressive scaling down from this point takes the form of retrospect with further cadenzas and thematic flashbacks until the final path chosen for The Fool, wisest of all major arcane presences. A succinct reprise with coda provides distant memories of the opening theme as it recedes into the mists of time and silence, recalling the hypnotic, Graingeresque ossia from *Fantasia No.7* surrounded by the Coptic light of the *Nocturne Canonique* and abandoned ruins of *Petra*.

Ex. 18: 4. L. Sitsky. *Concerto for Piano and Orchestra.* cadenza opening (XIII).

> Music interests me as a primal force, owing its origins to ritual, magic
> and mysticism. It is this hidden (occult) power of music that is my
> chief concern. (LS)

The freedoms that

> Sitsky is prepared to give performers in altering the score to suit their
> own desires and interpretation, and the frustration Sitsky suffers when
> a performer feels the need to seek permission for every small change

mentioned in the 1977 Robyn Holmes (Patricia Shaw and Peter Campbell)
Sitsky Bio-Biography published by the Greenwood Press (page 16) are a matter
with which many composers throughout history were well versed when they
arranged other music to suit their musical needs. Sitsky's many transcriptions
and adaptations are no exception.

The earliest ideas about the work discussed when I was commissioning the work
continued when I received the incomplete and then completed score, and right
through my own preparations. In regard to for the first performance and
generous admonitions given me by the composer, I would not wish Ms. Holmes'
reference to my collaboration with Sitsky to pass without reference to the
alleged freedoms to which Ms. Holmes alludes. Sitsky's fascination with the
freedom of interpretation, evident in early sound recordings, and his
encouragement of performers to respond freely to his notation despite the
personalized nature of his writing are mentioned in the recent Grove entry about
him. To translate generic statements into terms of clarifying such a precisely
notated score as the *Piano Concerto*, however, becomes marginal when dealing
with the practicalities of having to learn and perform a notated score. Although
marginal, the *ossias* certainly do offer a limited scope for freedom of
interpretation as do sections of Path XV, although I was encouraged to write
ossias of my own for parts of the work, omitted during the recording sessions.

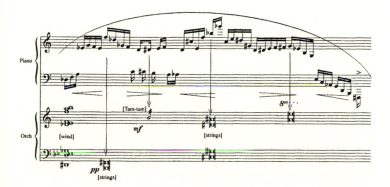

Ex. 19:4. L. Sitsky. *Concerto for Piano and Orchestra.* from XV (unbarred).

There remains an ongoing moral imperative to be faithful to a text, especially a text that is so precisely notated, and in this case, which necessitated clarifying structural movement as well as hundreds of imprecise details over a prolonged period of time with a composer who was reluctant to discuss "*old works*" whilst involved with new projects. The moral imperative remains, nevertheless, all the more if the composer is alive as evidenced by the Rakhmaninov/Horowitz, Prokofiev/Richter, Bartók/Menuhin, Walton/Heifetz collaborations etc...Many such discussions, which are a normal matter of course for any artist learning a new work, took place with the composer before the premiere. While at times it may have been frustrating for the composer, for the performer they frequently took on the appearance of a discourse with someone who seemed to struggle remembering his own name. During this process, Sitsky, like most composers who seek a performance of commitment, may, at least in this respect, have imparted an incomplete or confusing impression to his biographer concerning basic matters of accountability which, traditionally, have, since time immemorial been respected between composers and performers. During a prolonged early collaboration, it was Kuzmin who provided reassurance during the correspondence:

> Whether your soul is unscathed or broken in two...I beg you to be logical – and may I be forgiven this cry from my heart ! – logical in plan and structure, in syntax ...be a master architect in detail as in the whole ....let there be story in narrative and action in drama, keep lyricism for verses, love words as Flaubert did, be economical with your means and parsimonious with words, precise and genuine; then you will discover the secret of something wonderful – that exquisite lucidity which I would call – 'clarism'.

At the end of the preparation period, I remained curious to see how far Sitsky's interpretative freedoms might extend since there had always been loose talk about feeling "free to make the work your own", even though the work was precisely notated. So I decided to put his allegedly liberal attitudes to the test during the limited time allotted our recording sessions. Without the opportunity to be able to comment on Ms. Holmes' agile and commendably faithful picking up of crumbs from composers' tables, I was at first hesitant to question creative omnipotence. Hesse encouraged me to accept the composer's admonitions: "Truth has to be lived, not taught. Prepare for battle!" (The Glass Bead Game) although by that time it had become obvious that once Sitsky had finished composing a work, he rapidly lost all interest in returning to its detail as he moved on to new, creative projects. In *"The Essence of Music"*, Busoni also helped preparations with his remarks about Goethe in the Preface to *Farbenlehre:*

> scarcely half of a good play can be put on paper, and by far the greater
> part of it must be left to the glamour of the stage, the personality of the
> actor, the power of the voice, the characteristics of his movements,
> indeed to the mind and good mood of the audience...

In a composer's pursuit of high-octane performances, it is understandable that many often prefer to call upon the specialized skills of performers (including the skills of performers who may also compose) rather than upon their own neglected skills as would-be performers. Perhaps this explains, at least in part, Sitsky's stream of dedications to performers who specialized in their performer's craft (rather than their compositional one), as opposed to Sitsky, pianist and educator who often found himself with little time to devote to nurturing his own pianistic skills and who prefers to move on straightaway to the next compositional project as soon as he has completed the previous one. After all, *"What artist hasn't longed to get away from the human effort he puts into his work!"* as Feldman remarked in *Give My Regards to Eighth Street.* In this respect, it is fortunate that the result of the first recording of the *Piano Concerto* pleased the composer:

> The final result was staggering and contained that very demonic fire
> which I was after, as well as an other-wordly transcendence. (LS)

When Sitsky had finished composing his (First) *Piano Concerto* I remember reading Andrei Tarkovsky whose inspirational *Diary* had been published almost exactly at the same time. I returned to it at the time of the recording sessions not imagining for a second that Sitsky would dedicate a second Concerto to me twelve years later.

> I want to preserve the level of quality. Like Atlas holding the earth on
> his shoulders. He could, after all, have thrown it off when he got tired.
> But he didn't; for some reason he went on holding it up. That,

incidentally, is the most remarkable point of the legend: not the fact that he held it up for so long, but the fact that he did not become disillusioned and throw it down. (A.T.)

In 1992, Sitsky composed an aleatoric multi-purpose mobile accessible to amateurs, children, students and musicians entitled Foucault's Pendulum as part of an *Anthology of Australian Miniatures*. Its democratic indication, *Molto rubato* offers an inviting *carte-blanche* to create a personalized score complete with a wide range of accents and *fermatas* tailored to individual expression and interpretation. The basic compendium of possibilities notates combinations of chords separated by *fermata* and four linear patterns of varying lengths: 7+15+27+54 between three kinds of clusters involving four-fingers, thumbs, sides of the thumb, hands and palms. Subsections are repeated in a wide variety of ways with indications such as: *include movement from p going to pp, slow, much pedal; p going to mf, secco, presto, scorrevole, nervoso; f going to ff, moderato, maestoso, quavers martellato brillante; quavers not necessarily even, converted to octaves in the louder moments; quarter-notes even in the soft and loud renditions, jagged in the second.*

From October to November, 1992, Sitsky composed *Fantasia No.10* for the Emmanuel Moór double keyboard Bechstein grand piano. Moór (1863-1931) was a Hungarian composer, inventor and student of Liszt, whose works were performed by Ysaÿe and Casals, and whose double-keyboard invention was taken up by firms such as Pleyel, Bechstein, Chickering, Bösendorfer and Steinway. Although Sitsky's work is dedicated to Alistair Noble, homage is paid to Winifred Burston who brought the instrument with her to Australia in the 1930's. She was a great champion of its two-manual possibilities, which included a coupler activated by pedals for the simultaneous sounding of pitches an octave beyond individual sounds. The chords of Sitsky's opening chorale are followed by such octave displacements from earlier *Fantasias*, but with enlarged parameters to encourage one pianist to do the work of two, and to achieve multiple effects by the simple exploitation of Moór's mechanism.

In 1994 Sitsky was promoted to Professor at the Australian National University with a personal chair, and the following year composed two works for solo piano entitled *Lotus*. In 1996, he added three sopranos to the first of the two pieces for the opening incidental music to a production of *Faust* by the Splinters Theatre Co as part of the Australian National University's fiftieth anniversary celebrations. Falling right-hand motifs recall opening and closing sections of the *Piano Concerto*; while undulating left -hand harmonic patterns create textures over three staves. Accessible vertical and horizontal procedures are derived from bitter-sweet major-minor arpeggios from the *Preludio* of the *Sonatina Formalis*, composed forty years earlier after the young composer had read the opening pages of Busoni's *Fantasia Contrappuntistica*. These figures appear in many forms throughout the whole of Sitsky's keyboard music, were redeveloped notably in *Fantasia No.8*, and are evident in *Paths* 3, 6 and 21 of the *Piano*

Concerto. Such delicate patterns exploit the same material to close *Lotus II* (1996) for the ending of the same ANU production.

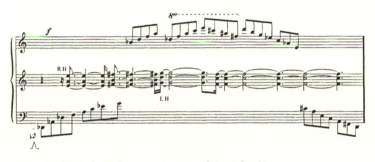

Ex. 20: 4. L. Sitsky. *Lotus (opening of Faust)*. bar 21.

In that same year, Sitsky was commissioned by The Keys Press, W.A. to edit the complete works of the Australian experimental pianist-composer Roy Agnew. His research on Agnew brought this neglected composer-pianist to the attention of the Australian public, and who has since recorded the complete Agnew Piano Sonatas. Agnew, like Grainger, had been alienated by the *arrière-garde* of his time despite the fact that pianists of the caliber of Moiseiwitsch, Gieseking and Cortot were performing his visionary keyboard music. In the early 1930's, Agnew had introduced music to Australia by Berg, Webern, Busoni, Debussy, Skryabin, Stravinsky and Szymanowski among others.

In 1997, Sitsky was awarded a higher Doctorate in Fine Arts by the Australian National University, and in 1998, elected Fellow of the Academy of the Humanities of Australia. In the same year, the Greenwood Press published his research on Anton Rubinstein, and he composed *"E"* and *"E II"* for solo piano followed by an *"E" Fantasia No.11*.

> The Fantasia comprises three movements, the first two of which were written and published, as "E" and "E II" respectively. The first two movements may be played as separate pieces, but the third movement should only be performed as the finale to the complete Fantasia. (LS)

Ex. 21: 4. L. Sitsky. *Fantasia No. 11 "E"*. bars 52-57.

V

Sitsky remained a constant traveller through turbulent historic epochs, living through the Japanese Occupation of China, Mao Tse Dong's Communist Revolution, and the miraculous transformation that took place in the Soviet Union under *Glastnost* and *Perestroika,* which heralded renewal and the rebirth of Russia. Considering the large number of emigrants over the past half century from what has all too frequently been perceived as an intolerant Australian culture, Sitsky's stoic loyalty and steel-like tenacity are remarkable. In the face of hostile opposition, official neglect and the ongoing lack of appreciation shown his international standing by Australians, wide recognition was shown him outside his country. At one stage, this included the offer of a Soviet passport, accompanied by high-level assurances for the continued commissioning and performance of his work. After five decades of building music in Australia, he was eventually appointed a Member of the Order of Australia. However, the administrative breed responsible for Sitsky's music vanishing from the repertoires and recording schedules of State-sponsored radio corporation orchestras and opera companies continue to display even less interest in his music than perhaps their Soviet counterparts from former times toward politically incorrect Soviet composers. Considering the endless humiliation, torments and excesses inflicted by self righteous administrators on major creative artists, and the attempts made to cripple them spiritually, Sitsky's Australian experience was not only unexpected, but remains unjust.

Throughout this long story of cultural dislocation and intolerance, the final piecing together of Sitsky's cultural identity makes it clear that dedication and service meant more to him than matters of recognition withheld by fellow Australians. His phenomenal triumph of self-realization over cultural dislocation was completed with his 1977 visit to the Soviet Union during the *détente* which ultimately led the liberation of Russia from Stalin's ideological excesses and from the perpetrators of cultural repression. Despite the savage attacks against Sitsky in Australia and deliberate repression of his music from the national orchestras and opera, Sitsky's unassailed international standing is confirmed by the many fine performances of his music that constantly take place outside Australia, and by the publication of his music by the SeeSaw Music and Greenwood Press Publishing Houses, New York, both of which are devoted to publishing his prolific compositional output and searching thoughts about music.

Sitsky belongs to that magnificent tradition of composer-pianists in which their keyboard works provided an appropriate engine room for the launching of their grand operatic and symphonic designs. Historically, many such major keyboard-composers offered a wide range of musical aethetics throughout their creative output to conceal subtle stylistic diversity. In that respect, the listener may well be forgiven for sometimes being confused by the aural challenge involved in identifying the composer's characteristic voice. To complicate the issue even further, one needs to be reminded that it was often the case that such keyboard-composers were not necessarily the finest performers of their own keyboard works. Beethoven, Brahms, Schumann, Tchaikovsky, Debussy, Stravinsky, and even Prokofiev spring to mind. In this respect, Sitsky is no exception.

His most recent keyboard works are formidable and include a forty minute Sufist-inspired magnum opus for solo piano entitled *The Way of The Seeker* and a Szymanowskian-Fourth-Symphony-style Concerto for piano and orchestra entitled *Second Symphony*, in which the overriding aesthetic, procedures and textures from earlier keyboard works recall the experimental sound worlds of *Dimensions, Petra, Nocturne Canonique* and *Si Yeoo Ki*. The work's structural and harmonic organization recall Sitsky's post-Silver Age heritage and organization of dynamics (especially in the second part) recall the genius of Efim Golyshev. Sitsky describes the soloist's part as having been written:

> more symphonically than solistically – which is of course not to say
> that the part is any way easier ! After writing my First Symphony, the
> idea of mixing palettes of color and using the orchestra and piano to
> blend in varying ways seemed to become important to me. (LS)

Sitsky's finely-sculpted miniature-art and pedagogical *choses-en-soi* sowed seeds for the evolution of these larger keyboard achievements, beginning with his eight solo piano *Fantasias*. Like fearsome sentinels, this Busoni inheritance guards the hidden gateway to a kingdom where lost forests conceal luxuriant blooms strewn amongst wild, pristine beauty, waiting for the time when they might be seen in all their natural beauty, and nurtured and loved with the same tenderness and care that all such true masterpieces inexorably receive at the hands of the true musician. Such works include the *Concerto for Two Solo Pianos*, many of the kaleidoscopic revolutions in the tiny Universe called *Century,* and a striking series of solo piano works which, together with works by Agnew, Grainger, Hanson, Meale, Butterley, Boyd and few others, represent the most significant body of Australian keyboard music to date.

The dense, mysterious textures of *Petra*, searing ecstasy of the *Nocturne Canonique*, seismic upheavals of *Si Yeoo Ki* and declamatory incantations of the *Twelve Mystical Preludes* cast in a more pragmatic vein remain almost unknown to the Australian public. These rich, inventive keyboard masterpieces happily consummate the marriage of his Russian-Jewish and Faustian-European musical experiences, and are alert, forward-looking achievements.

Sitsky's continuing contribution to the keyboard repertoire and to Australian musical life underlines the need for the restoration of a vital but missing dimension in respect to the need for a reorganization of Australia's national culture. The serious, ongoing lack of tolerance so constantly demonstrated by government-paid arts planners, advisors, and administrators was a valuable lesson that had to be learnt elsewhere as the result of an entire culture permitting itself to foolishly lose its inestimable artistic wealth, including a unique *avant-garde* that could have provided international leadership in its own time, had it not been hacked to pieces by those who were entrusted with the responsibility of nurturing such an inheritance for future generations.

With the benefit of hindsight, arts bureaucrats in Russia have undergone great change throughout the course of the Twentieth Century. As a result, Russia is now forced to try to regain all that it lost as it enters a period in its history in which it finally achieved a meaningful dialogue and unity between creators and bureaucrats to demonstrate how proud it is of its cultural riches and diversity without the accompanying discrimination. One can only hope that current Australian arts bureaucrats might eventually make a similar, genuine effort to try to find a way to come to terms with its own highly-motivated creative talent, more so than demonstrated over the past half-century when Sitsky created the major part of his output. In this respect, Sitsky's internationally recognized research and formidable list of scholarly publications concerning the emergence of early Twentieth Century Soviet and Australian *avants-gardes*, have been extremely revealing.

The great search on which Sitsky embarked early in his creative life has always provided a lofty kind of leadership and clear path forward for art-music at meaningful levels, but his contribution was mostly ignored, as was the case with Agnew, Grainger, Goossens, and countless other talents. At the end of the Twentieth Century it continues to be Australia's loss. Hopefully, Australian arts planners and advisors might be more willing to learn to cultivate a greater tolerance towards the nation's leading composers and creative artists other than the mediocrity to which it seems more comfortable paying allegiance. When the republican dream that was so frequently discussed in the national media provides a real inclusivity for the nation's creative artists, a stronger voice will sing a less discriminatory and more equitable anthem for Australia's sons and daughters to inherit.

In a country that is so proud of equal opportunity, is it going to be the inspirational presence of its creative artists that continues to celebrate the higher part of our existence and to provide the necessary reassurance by which we live in harmony with each other?

Part Three: The Third Generation

The seventies marked a period in Australian music when government support for the arts in general was at its highest point. Organizations directly supporting composers such as the Australian Music Centre and the Australia Council had, for the first time, reasonable funding to encourage the production of new compositions and performances; new music was, moreover, seen as an exportable commodity, and for the first time in Australia's history, publication of art music scores became a reality. It became almost and suddenly fashionable to employ composers in academia and to regard their output as serious personal research. As far as the piano and composers who wrote for it – there was a clear decline of the composer/pianist and pianist–composer; consequently, the volume of new music devoted to the instrument sharply declined. Much has been, and more will no doubt be written concerning the huge cultural shifts that occurred in Australia at this time, to some extent contributed to by the war in Vietnam. Some composers were passionate in their attitudes to the war and to the new sense of multiculturalism that was sweeping the country; others simply used it as a convenient bandwagon.

(i) The Next Wave of Modernism

Pianists

Ann Ghandar (1943)

Ann, who studied with Richard Meale and myself, has lived and taught at the University of New England for many years. A fine pianist, she has performed music such as the Ives *Concord Sonata*, the Schoenberg *Suite for Piano* and the Messiaen *Four Rhythmic Studies* as well as her own compositions. She has studied and performed music from the Middle East, including in her accomplishments mastery of the 'ud and the qanum. This is in stark contrast to other composers who claim non-Western influence without any such substantiation.

The piano music is generally introspective and aphoristic. She has evolved her own language and has stayed within her own sound world. Reading her own programme notes to her piano pieces, one could easily form an impression of a composer who is writing programme music and who is naively reacting to images and events around her. But this would be quite erroneous. That is, although Ann Ghandar has chosen to honestly reveal the initial sources of her inspiration- and many of these sources are reactions to nature- it does not follow that the pieces of music are in any sense imitations of nature or descriptive in an obvious programmatic fashion. Ghandar is very often moved to compose as a result of visual stimulus. In her programme notes to *Photophoresis* she writes that she wanted to translate a series of photographic images into:

> sound images to the extent that was possible...in this photograph small
> flowers like stars shine out of an unfocussed background of stems and
> water. I decided to explore this visual image in sound by
> superimposing clear sonorities over a colourful resonance.

In an earlier era, this type of inspiration would have probably resulted in a music of high kitsch. Just reading the titles and subtitles (see listings) of Ghandar's many miniatures almost irrepressibly suggests the very type of music that has plagued Australia's musical output; so the mere titling is already an act of bravery or even perhaps of defiance. Whichever it might be, Ann's music does not fall into the class of jingoistic naive kitsch.

In fact, Ghandar's personal style is highly sophisticated. Quite often, she writes on three staves, to clearly illustrate the different levels of activity. Here is a typical example from *Paraselene*:

Ex 1:3 A. Ghandar. *Paraselene.* (unbarred).

The music at times looks like an attempt to capture a free improvisation; at the same time there is always room for the performer to move. We find in *The Earth Sings Mi-Fa-Mi* this characteristic passage:

Ex 2:3 A. Ghandar. *The Earth Sings.* (unbarred).

Extreme dynamic changes are not uncommon, as illustrated by this example from *Photophoresis*:

Ex 3:3 A. Ghandar. *Photophoresis.* bars 40-43.

The piano music is very clearly related to Ghandar as a performer. Indications are specific and precise, pedal indications exact where they need to be. In the *Piano Suite* for instance, she tends to use the pedal as a device to deliberately blur and diffuse the polyphony and the harmonic movement; the pedal is sometimes kept down for bars at a time. Ann's pieces tend to brevity, and separate movements of works quite often last no longer than a minute or two. But the haiku-like shortness of the works does not stop eruptions and full textures from happening.

She is fond of using musical monograms and incorporating the pitch equivalents of people's names and initials as thematic materials in her works, thus personalizing the music on one level.

Ex 4:3 A. Ghandar. *Sinai Music*. bar 18.

As a pianist who has played many large-scale works for the piano, it is a sign of Ghandar's integrity and singularity of vision that she has not been tempted to venture into the world of piano music of heroic proportions, preferring to remain in her very personal world. She emerges as a notable figure in the music explored in this book.

Gerald Glynn (1943)

Glynn is a fine pianist who has chosen not to be a professional musician, or to live most of his life in Australia. He is domiciled in Paris and there are the odd visits and residencies to institutions back home. When I taught him, he demonstrated an alert and inquisitive mind, and this has continued to manifest itself in his music.

Of his works for piano the most significant perhaps are the set of four called *Filigrees*.

Filigrees and *Filigree 2* (1981) do exactly what the title suggests. It consists of mostly delicate, lace-like figures, which gradually grow and become embellished from very simple beginnings. The constant elaboration not only gives cohesion - it also creates a hypnotic atmosphere by not-quite-exact repetition. Most of the activity of the piece is in the middle of the piano and this deliberate restriction becomes a real strength as the piece progresses. It is difficult to extract a meaningful quotation from the piece because of its predominantly organic nature:

Ex 5:3 G. Glynn. *Filigrees 2*. bars 30-35.

Filigree 2 is a genuine contribution to Australian piano music- it says something new, and says it with elegance and with understanding of the piano, a rare conjunction of qualities.

Filigrees 3 (1990) is a further exploration of the world described above. There is a wonderfully dramatic moment in the piece, where, after playing in the treble of the piano for a long while, suddenly a low D in the bass is struck.

Filigrees 4 (1997) is a larger work than its predecessors, consisting of: I. *Prelude*; II. *Lulude*; III. *Interlude* and IV. *Conclude*. It is as though the low D in the previous *Filigrees* has opened a door, for here there is more extensive and structural use of the bass register of the piano, especially in the first and last movement. I don't know if the composer envisages the set of *Filigrees* to be played as an extended concert work or not, but, no matter, the works are attractive and will take their place in Australian piano music as an original contribution.

The rest of his output consists of an early work from 1970 called *Mobile-Mosaique*, which uses graphic notation, with gestures fairly sparsely scattered over the page, and a *Toccata-Sonata* (1989), a terse and witty work, repeating a series of phrases in slightly differing contexts.

Graham Hair (1943)

Graham is a distinguished Australian composer, educator, pianist and writer. His strong response to the written word is evident in his large output for voice. The result is that there are only a handful of piano works. Even here, there is a tendency on Graham's part to react to words when writing instrumental music; he calls these his 'fantasy pieces'.

Thus, *Under Aldebaran* (1984) was commissioned for the Sydney International Piano Competition, but the title and driving force for the piece comes from a title of the same name, a book of poetry by the Australian James McAuley, who himself had aspirations to becoming a concert pianist. The volume of poems:

> deals with...intellectual and artistic revolution and counter-revolution of which the changing colour red and blue, of the star Aldebaran is a symbol.

> An opening text fleetingly suggests many different musical gestures, which are then developed into a series of grossly contrasting variations, juxtaposing manic pulsation with liquid rhythmic flow, delicate consonances with start dissonance and so on. (Composer file: Australian Music Centre.)

The variations within *Under Aldebaran* are not numbered, but easy to discern, as the composer has marked the moments with double bars. This idea of building up larger structures by small but connected episodes (be they strict variations, or some less obviously linked) has been translated by Hair into his two other works for piano that I have looked at. Both *Wild Cherries and Honeycomb* and *Five Dances and Devilment and Sunlit Airs* are constructed in a similar fashion. But whereas *Under Aldebaran* has breathing spaces, both in the theme and in the variations, the two other works are dense looking and sounding. There is hardly a rest in either piece and they look positively black thanks to Graham's predilection for small time values. Both are virtuoso piano works. The word 'breathless' springs to mind reading through them. The language since *Aldebaran* has softened and is replete with tonal references as well as added sixth chords, and the episodes are now numbered: so, *Wild Cherries* has nine numbered sections plus a Coda; the *Dances* also consist of nine sections. The writing is linear, like a perpetual motion punctuated with chords and counter lines, so everything is very clean and glittery. The tonal references, when they are made, are very strong, but the music is always restless and shifts away from stability of this kind. It's a little like Debussy and Ravel on speed.

Brief examples will illustrate the change in Graham's piano music between *Under Aldebaran* and *Wild Cherries*:

Ex 6:3   G. Hair. *Under Aldebaran*. opening.

Ex 7:3   G. Hair. *Wild cherries and Honeycomb*. opening.

Roger Smalley (1943)

Smalley is an interesting case in that he was an established composer and well-known in England and Europe when he chose to come to Australia and to settle in Perth. His credentials are impeccable, having studied with composers such as Peter Racine Fricker and Alexander Goehr in the early 1960s and a little later with Stockhausen in Cologne. In the late '60s he was also influenced by the medieval parody and *cantus firmus* techniques as employed by Maxwell-Davies. His early career involved working with live electronics. Just prior to moving to Australia, Roger was composer-in-residence and Research Fellow at King's College, Cambridge and had written critically for the *Musical Times* and *Music and Musicians*.

He had been artist in residence at the University of Western Australia in 1974, moving to Perth permanently in 1976 to assume a position at the University. His compositional approach shifted in the 1970s to a kind of adapted serialism and, according to the composer himself, to shifting from thinking linearly to an approach more closely aligned with chordal thinking. Smalley has said in interview that he was attracted to certain pieces by Webern and to some late Stravinsky not because of the technical sophistication of the music, but initially because he liked the sound; at that early stage "I didn't know how they'd been composed". He first fully understood the mechanics of the music of Maxwell-Davies, attributing this attraction to the "[v]ery telling, economical music language, in which everything seemed to be related to everything else". But soon after that, this was replaced by the new attraction - Stockhausen's 'moment form'. (Ford, Andrew, *Composer to Composer: Conversations about Contemporary Composers*. St.Leonards, NSW: Allen & Unwin, 2001)

His move to Australia forced him to reconsider what and how he was writing. One of the reasons for quitting Europe was to escape the new tyranny of the avant-garde, which had become a kind of new Establishment governing the behaviour of young composers.

> ...And I did increasingly feel that I wanted to communicate. So from 1976, when I finally settled in Australia, I tried all kinds of different approaches. (Ibid.)

One of these new approaches was to "develop modes which concentrated on different intervals so that each part of the piece could have a distinct harmonic character". Smalley says himself that his strength as a composer is not with the invention of material; he thinks that much of his material is fairly basic, but hopes that it is what he does with it that makes it interesting. (Ibid.)

Roger is a distinguished pianist both as soloist and as a chamber musician, and has played and continues to play standard repertoire. In his days in England he gave UK premieres of some of Stockhausen's *Klavierstücke* and Boulez's third sonata.

Among his earliest music is *Piano Pieces* I-V. These still concern themselves with a free sort of serialism affecting both pitch and durations; there are also moments of aleatoric freedom. These works from the 1960s don't have much to do with the mature Smalley or indeed with Australia, but they lay the foundation for his later music and demonstrate Smalley's ability to write for the piano as someone who understands the instrument really well and does not fight against the nature of the keyboard. The clarity of the approach of each of these brief pieces appears in a more developed and dramatic form in the *Missa Parodia I*, still from the late 1960s and inspired by Smalley's detailed study of the music of Maxwell-Davies. The *Missa Parodia* is based on Smalley's own *Missa Brevis* (1966), and is in two parts, only the first of which is for solo piano, whilst the second part is for ensemble. The first part can function as an independent piece, although Smalley has fashioned the two so that they can run into each other. The aleatoric freedom that made only a short appearance in the *Piano Pieces I-V* is here given much more prominence so that a controlled sort of freedom is most evident in this piece.

It was a work for two pianos named *Accord* that, already in Australia, signaled a shift from the typically linear European avant-garde thinking to a more harmonic approach. Smalley considers *Accord* to be a pivotal work in his output.

In an interview from 1994 (Lindsay Vickering, Composer file, Australian Music Centre)), when asked in retrospect how living in Australia might have altered his music, Smalley said:

> I feel the range of my music has been broadened, particularly harmonically. This has led to the use of fragments of Chopin in some of the latest pieces including the Chopin Variations... I could say that my musical language has expanded to an extent where it can accommodate harmonic progressions from Chopin without seeming incongruous.... in Australia I feel completely free to do whatever I choose.

Concerning the *Variations on a Theme of Chopin* (1989), Smalley has written:

> The 'theme' of these variations is the whole of Chopin's *Mazurka in Bb minor Op.24 No.4*, although only the first 6 bars are actually quoted at the beginning of the work- just enough to remind the listener of the original piece. These bars form a series of progressively diminishing intervals from an octave down to a minor second. In each of the twelve short variations elements of the theme are transformed through the prism of one of these intervals- for example the first variation is exclusively in octaves, the second uses major and minor seconds in the right hand rhythmically displaced against the original left-hand part; and the third concentrated on major and minor sixths.

> My variations attempt to mirror the structure of the original *Mazurka*, which changes markedly in character towards the end, introducing new material and slowly winding down in a long coda. The first 8 variations are extremely dynamic, but the 9th variation (an improvisatory melody over a shifting drone bass) is the most extended, drawing ever closer to the original, until the last two bars turn out to be the same as Chopin's.

Ex 8:3 R. Smalley. *Variations on a Theme of Chopin*. opening.

Roger suggests in the score that:

> ... this work be preceded by EITHER my *Barcarolle* OR a group of Chopin mazurkas, ending with *Op.24 No.4.*

The *Chopin Variations* has proved to be an outstanding work for solo piano and certainly one of our very best set of virtuosic variations.

He has written the following notes on the *Barcarolle* (1986):

> *Barcarolle* was written for John White, one of my composition teachers at the Royal College of Music, on the occasion of his 50th birthday. It is a solo piano transcription of an interlude from my music theatre piece *William Derrincourt* (1977-79), originally scored for soprano saxophone, male chorus, two pianos and two percussion. John White introduced me to the works of many late-Romantic composers including Faure, Alkan and Busoni- all of whom wrote Barcarolles- and so it seemed appropriate to allude to their often ambivalent and slightly sinister, melos and characteristic keyboard textures.

Having taught Roger's piece, I know it quite well and can certainly discern the Busoni influence. The Italian's *Berceuse* (there is no *Barcarolle*) is clearly the driving force behind the opening gestures and the long pedal points. The Smalley *Barcarolle* is in fact an excellent demonstration of his shift towards writing music that has elements of tonality and vertical organization about it, for the construction of the work really consists of a series of discrete pedal points, some long and some fleeting, but all clearly discernable to the eye and, more importantly, to the ear. The opening sets the mood for what is to follow:

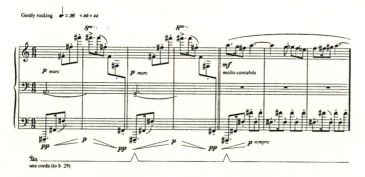

Ex 9:3   R. Smalley. *Barcarolle.* opening.

Roger Smalley is an important figure in Australian music and piano music. His contribution - including the very fine *Piano Concerto* - has enriched the repertoire of Australian music for the piano, in a distinctive refined way.

Non-Pianists

Gillian Whitehead (1941)

Gillian Whitehead is an important Australian/New Zealand composer. However, her piano music is not a significant part of her prolific output. The writing for the instrument appears to be invariably constituted by largely widespread voices, often crossing and in the end not sounding the way they appear on the page, in other words not always fulfilling their musical function on the piano, almost as though they require another medium for their successful realization. The lines seem most uncomfortable under the hands and, whilst possible to play (these days almost anything is possible on the piano!) seem to proclaim that their origin is not from a pianist/composer. The *Bagatelles* are more grateful than other music that I've played through. Gillian describes her style as 'expressionist'; it is certainly strongly atonal and muscular and, given her great successes in the field of theatre music and vocal music, also boldly dramatic. The most important solo work is probably *Tamatea Tutahi*, which weaves two North England folktunes into its texture.

Ian Cugley (1945)

Ian Cugley, a well-known composer who lived in Tasmania, has now, I understand, given up his music career and moved into other spheres of activity. I understand, too, that he no longer lives in Australia. His *Aquarelles*, a set of four short pieces each two pages long, achieved the status of a minor classic, chiefly through the advocacy of the pianist Beryl Sedivka, for whom the work was written in 1972. As far as we know, there is no other music for the piano, except for these short, almost aphoristic and highly sensitive pieces. They are published by Alberts & Son.

Andrew Ford (1957)

I nearly placed Andrew Ford into the chapter dealing with Maximalist composers – partly because the texture and movement of some of the piano music was urging me to do so; but I know some of his other music as well, and it certainly is not of that nature. Andrew is a very well known writer and broadcaster on music, so I will let him describe his own piano pieces in his own words. *Portraits* (1981) is a work in three short movements: *Prestissimo*, *Energico* and *Lento*.

This work employs the same pitch material in each of its three movements, but subjects it to extreme contrasts. The first movement is 'as fast as possible' and ranges across the entire keyboard. But it is also mainly very quiet. The player's hands hurtle about producing hardly any sound. The second movement consists of energetic chord patterns that bounce about in a rather syncopated manner, eventually dissipated in a comparatively lighthearted coda. The final movement presents, firstly, the pitches on which the two previous movements have been built, and then subjects them to a misty, harp-like treatment, pedals down until the end of the piece, which is shattered by a couple of karate chops to the upper part of the keyboard.

The visual impact of this music is important. The pianist must adopt quite different physical poses in each movement, in order to present the full range of pianistic effects. The performer, then, can be seen as the subject of the portraits, painted, as it were by three different artists, in three very different styles.

The second paragraph is somewhat unclear. When the composer, who is not a pianist, says "must adopt", does he issue this as an instruction, or is this a result of the different writing for the keyboard? Some pianists move more than others, and I wonder whether the composer today would concern himself about the visual impact, rather allowing the music to speak for itself. Ford's maximalist tendencies are expressed in the following music:

Ex 10:3 A. Ford. *Portraits*. bars 84-88.

Andrew's only other piece to make it into this boom is *A Kumquat for John Keats* (1987), which has similar frenetic qualities. Here is what the composer says of it:

Tony Harrison's poem, *A Kumquat for John Keats*, describes the bitter-sweet quality of that fruit, comparing it to 'Joy's Grape' in Keat's *Ode on Melancholy*. Harrison views the kumquat as a metaphor for his own life, asking whether the fruit has a bitter skin and sweet flesh, or whether it is the other way around.

A similar dilemma surrounds my piece for solo piano. The music ranges between meditative, musing chords punctuated by long pauses, eventually erupting into a torrent of extremely fast, cascading figures, before returning to the stasis of the opening. However, the vigour of the central episode never completely departs, returning, in the form of short, violent bass trills to disrupt the calm of the ending.

David Worrall (1954)

There are two works known to me by David Worrall who subsequently went on into the electroacoustic sphere and seemed to have abandoned writing for instruments like the piano. While studying with Richard Meale he was obviously influenced by Meale's then infatuation with Boulez and his methods of dealing with pitch by various techniques developed for building up chordal/pitch groups by controlled manipulations of the raw material. The result was a three-movement sonata for the piano dedicated to his teacher- quite difficult and not always pianistic but all possible. It is a finely crafted work with big dramatic gestures. A companion piece is *Scorpion under Glass*, from roughly the same period in Adelaide. The main feature of this piece is the use of the third pedal to create sympathetic vibrations. The language of this work is akin to that of the Sonata, though it is much shorter and not as difficult.

Tim Dargaville (1962-)

I am aware of only four works for piano from this talented composer: two are miniatures: the interesting *Canticles* (1992) included in the Red House Anthology of one-page pieces. Dargaville's solution to this problem was to offer a quiet, multi-layered piece from which the performer could choose the order and combination of layers. There is the atmospheric *Night Song* (1999), originally written as incidental music for the Douglas Stewart play "Ned Kelly". But there is also the substantial piece *Alba* (1994), which demonstrates an impressive control over slowly growing intensity as well as a good understanding of keyboard sonorities. Some of the piano writing is, in one area especially, awkward, but the piece is a fine achievement nonetheless, working like an ever developing set of variations on the initial idea and culminating in a *fff* passage repeated five times.

Ex 11:3   T. Dargaville. *Alba*. ending.

Negra I appeared in 1999. It is a driving ultra-rhythmic piece based on the dance and drumming traditions of West Africa. The composer has also imbedded two folk-songs of the Ga and Ewe people into the score of this thirty four page work. The writing for the instrument is demanding and relentless, although this is alleviated in part by a central more lyrical episode. Complete pianism, including wide leaps, is required to perform this work.

John Polglase (1959)

John Polglase is a serious composer whose main interests lie in the field of chamber music, his output for the piano is therefore relatively slim. He was a pupil of Richard Meale and his music is accordingly marked by intellectual rigour and thematic cohesion – and one can see these qualities clearly demonstrated in the set of *Eight Bagatelles* for piano solo (n.d.) wherein the composer knows when to put a fullstop after raw ideas are stated and briefly explored. His language is both terse and tense and another work of this kind is *Fragments* (1984), a fairly large piece which is made up of mosaic-like 'bits' fashioned together like a jigsaw to create a total picture. There is also a bigger work in three movements: *Quiet this Metal*, with subtitles I. *Sonata* II. *Ballade* and III. *Dances*. This strongly controlled work also uses piano techniques and figurations from the past, and one can just catch fleeting glimpses of nineteenth-century pianistic giants in it. The writing is full and effective, but never impossibly overdone. Everything I tried at the keyboard fitted well under the hands.

More Modernists

Beverley Lea, Michael Barkl, Michael Lonsdale, Andre Oosterbaan (1947), Stephen Benfall (1957), Raffaele Marcellino, Claudio Pompillii (1949), Jim Franklin (1959), Michael Whiticker (1954), Warren Burt (1949), Gordon Kerry (1961), Ross Hazeltine (1961); Julian Yu (1957)

The post-1945 Modernists inevitably got older and in due course there was a second wave. This existed concurrently with the very fashionable and chic minimalism that seemed to grab the attention of emerging composers; but it also ran parallel with the Maximalists, who may be viewed as an even harder line of modernism. The postmodernist ethos of let's mix and match, let's combine hitherto unthinkable elements and styles also came to the fore, and so tendencies which were pure, easily identifiable and perhaps even simple, now became somewhat more obscure.

Hybridity of this type may be observed in works such as:

Beverley Lea's *Embers* (1997) combines tonality "with a twelve-tone serial technique", to quote the composer. The idea had already occurred to Schoenberg in one of his last works, but here is a student of Ann Ghandar trying her hand at it. Michael Barkl's *Drumming* (1983), on the other hand, brings together Indian tabla drumming with jazz pianism, a combination that resulted in an exciting piano piece:

Ex 12:3 M. Barkl. *Drumming.* opening.

It should be said here that this wave of modernism brought to light the new generation of composers for whom the piano was but a working instrument, mostly used in ensemble, often seen as a glorified percussion instrument. Clearly, the nineteenth century inheritance of the composer-pianist is now weakening, and so the repertoire for the instrument by such composers is more incidental rather than all embracing. Many of the composers whose music I played were represented by one or two pieces only.

Witness here Michael Lonsdale's poetic *Mouna* (1986), descending from the upper reaches of the piano, with long silences and in the end, returning where it began, but via a single legato line, instead of the initial fragmentations, or André Oosterbaan's *related contrasts* (1981) with its semi- graphic notations, written for the pianist David Lockett, or the difficult, intricate *Hammers* (1990) written by Stephen Benfall for Roger Smalley.

Raffaele Marcellino's contribution from 1999 is the extravagant set of four pieces called *Daedalus Sequence*, with its melodic and virtuosic flourishes

seeming to come from the past and espousing a new kind of neo-romanticism.
The pieces can be played separately, but it seems to me that they form a set,
more or less like a latter day sonata in four movements:

I: *...like dancing about architecture*
II: *Nuraxi*
III: *The Riddle of the Sicilian Conch*
IV: *The Lesson of Icarus*

There is strong dance element woven into the cycle. A triple pulse dominates the
fourth, whilst the third depends on irregularity for its effect:

Ex 13:3 R. Marcellino. *Dædalus Sequence III: The Riddle of the Sicilian Conch*. bars 8-
11.

A similar luxuriousness may be seen in Claudio Pompili's *Trece* (1981,
rev.1990). The composer also wrote *Three Miniatures for Piano* in the 1980s.

From this same period comes the intriguing, and at times enigmatic, piano music
of Jim Franklin. It is dense, crafted in detail and uncompromising. My personal
response to it is that there is much substance there, which can only be revealed
by persistent exposure and study. It is not easy or glib and has a tough integrity
about it that attracts. Franklin's music is part of the revival, that I speak of
elsewhere in the book, between literature (and other arts) and music, not of the
literal kind, but something more interesting.

Franklin illustrates this tendency in his preface to *Whisperings of Kelian* (1979),
he writes:

> This piece of music is related to (but not pictorial of) an extract from a
> literary work entitles, *The Saga of Gaalran and Kelian*. In my draft
> programme note for this piece (three pages long) I explained many
> details of this work; unfortunately, space prevents the inclusion of this
> note. I feel that one must approach the music either with full
> knowledge of the literary aspects, or with none, so no further
> explanation is offered here.

The work is in five named sections:

1. *Where all approaches; shifting sands*
2. *Ashen flame, smothering*
3. *Grey*
4. *Brutal falling: weeps, the Dreamer.*
5. *A flow of crystal*

Similarly, *Talisman* (1980 rev.1982) hints at a literary connection:

I. *Bright Impulse of the Core*
II. *Years Lament*
III. *Pillars*

Three Glimpses of Aquilon (1980) does not contain sub-headings, but there is a feeling that all three works listed above are somehow connected and possibly form one large whole. The composer is meticulous in his attention to metric details and secondary accentuation; this, too, gives the music an initial layer that needs unveiling. I hope that we will be hearing more of this music.

I had known some of Michael Whiticker's piano music before the writing of this book, having played the little chordal *Hommage to Alban Berg* (1980) and read through *Vibitqi* (1981) a set of four short miniatures as well as *Liexliu* which is really a piece for carillon, but was unaware of his major work for piano, *The Hands, The Dream* (1987) inspired by the surrealist painting of the same name by the Belgian Paul Delvaux. The composer writes about this piece:

> ...the musical 'glue' holding the work together is a series of nine chords which function as a passacaglia. These nine chords realised both vertically and horizontally, are the only pitch material heard throughout the piece and each section of the work is delineated by the completion of a chordal series. As these series can be operating simultaneously on up to three different registral and gestural levels, the sections of the piece do occasionally overlap, and it is difficult for the listener to discern exactly when one ends and another begins. (Composer file, Australian Music Centre)

The Hands, The Dream is a romantically conceived work, with a slow movement in the middle and two clear climactic moments. It demands virtuosic technique and a temperament of the romantic mold to realize the music of this tempestuous dream world.

Ex 14:3 M. Whiticker. *The hands, the dream.* bars 94-97.

It is almost impossible to write briefly about Warren Burt, a larger than life character whom I have known and worked with for many years on and off. Warren has done so many things that it would almost take a chapter just to list them! He is an important presence in the computer world and loves using them to compose and to stimulate composition, but he's also very widely knowledgeable across the whole spectrum of twentieth century music. We sent a questionnaire to composers, asking them the question "Do you think that your works for piano differ to the rest of your output? If so, how? " Here is what Warren wrote back:

> Not particularly, in that no part of my input resembles much any other part. Even among my piano works there are classic mid-20th century 'modernist' works (*Sketches of the Hudson River Valley* (1968); *Aardvarks II* (1971), minimalist works (*Rubber Duck Domination* (1974), *Silver* (1978), tonal works (*Miracles of the Gay Smog Angels* (1979)), non-tonal classic twelve-tone works (*Three Minute Sonata - Quasi Una Fractal - Ernst Krenek stands on the corner of Grand and Snelling, Waiting for the Lights to Change*, 1942 (1999)), and microtonal works (*A Book of Symmetries for Loretta Goldberg* (1994-95)). So that diversity fits in with the greater diversity of my other work, which includes computer graphics, sound poetry, video art, performance art, dance works, and works for live electronics.

Warren Burt forgot to include in this list his *Post-Modern Waltzes* (1985), which are computer generated and which I've played. They are five one-minute waltzes, with no accidentals. On the other hand, we should show the opening of *Aardvarks II: Mr. Natural Encounters Flakey Foont!* (1971, rev. 1973) dedicated to Keith Humble and which Keith actually performed. The whole work is like the opening:

Ex 15:3 W. Burt. *Aardvarks II: Mr. Natural Encounters Flakey Foont!* opening.

Gordon Kerry is a composer active in the theatre and in schools. Although fairly prolific, he has only two solo piano works, *Winter Through Glass* (1980) and *Perpetual Angelus* (1988). Kerry writes for the piano in a dry atonal style akin to twelve-tone of the academic kind. For me, although certainly possible on the piano (the composer has played at least one of these pieces in concert) the music is screaming out to be orchestrated.

Ross Hazeltine, the enterprising publisher of Red House Editions, and the person responsible for a number of compilations of miniatures for the instrument, has written some interesting piano music. On the evidence of the *Landscape Sonata* (1993), written for and performed by my pupil Robert Zocchi, Ross should perhaps be grouped with the Maximalists. This is a twenty-four page long, single movement, very intense work, unrelenting in its purposeful drive for almost a quarter of an hour. The problem with simple characterizing in this case is that his other pieces don't fit into that particular category. I am aware of eight short pieces:

> *Re Member Me-* a two-page work, written on one stave, unbarred.
> *Sequences-* in a similar vein.
> *13th Phrase-* one page, slow chords.
> *Chance X-* a very quick minimalist style piece, with repeated patterns.
> *Stockwell-*
> *Sketch 87-*
> *A Line from Jackson-*
> *Five Colours from a Great Height-* these last five are fully notated on two staves, but still tend to brevity. The pieces can be played separately, or as a cycle. They seem to all date from 1991.
> There is also a piece named *Diminuendo* (1995), which is just that, asking for a controlled diminuendo from the pianist over ca.4 minutes, playing fast semiquavers. Hazeltine's music for piano is somewhat obsessive, but he certainly has a feel for the overview of each piece,

short though it may be, and even allowing for the fact that to him the
piano is really a glorified marimba!

Finally, in this section I would like to mention two works by Julian Yu, whose
manuscripts are a miracle of calligraphic art in themselves. Both works are
written on one stave. *Impromptu* (1981) plays with the notion of contracting and
expanding cells, and because much of the work is written high on the piano and
there are some loud dynamics, this upper portion of the keyboard tends to
dominate the piece.

Ex 16:3 J. Yu. *Impromptu*. opening.

A similar, but more elaborate piece (due to ornamentation) is *Scintillation I*
(1987). The composer says that the original was for piano and percussion and
this piece is actually a reduction of that initial idea.

(ii) Minimalism and Maximalism:

The Minimalists

Robert Lloyd; Robert Davidson; Stephen Lalor; Mark Pollard; Nigel Sabin;
Moya Henderson; Colin Spiers

Because of the geographical size of the country, it is very difficult for an artistic
movement to take root in Australia, even in the larger cities. Composers are
dispersed over a vast country and there are rarely enough of them grouped
together to form a cohesive force, as has happened so often in the European
context. It is perhaps for this reason that -isms of one kind or another are not a
feature of Australian musical life; personally, I regard this as a strength. The
mere whiff of a school of composition makes my blood run cold.

Minimalism was by far the more popular of the two –isms. Unsurprising, really,
considering that it is easy to teach, easy to write and has cosy connections with a
cuddly New Age world. Many of the scores that we looked at were products of
composition factories from some of our tertiary institutions; for a time, and
perhaps even now, minimalism of one kind or another was certainly a very
trendy thing to do; but quite a few of the scores were mindless copies of older
models and had little to add to the idiom. The piano is an ideal vehicle for this

kind of composition, as various triadic patterns fit so comfortably under the hands, and with the sustaining pedal down, one can go on for ever (and some of the scores we looked at, did!)

There are many more examples of minimalism than maximalism. A typical piece would be something like Robert Lloyd's *Perfect Piano*, in which simple patterns using five notes are replicated over and over with little change. Lloyd's *Newborn* and *The Untouched Key* are further instances of the piano used in this manner. Robert Davidson's *Circumference* plays the same texture over and over but seems to have affinities with popular song in the melodic outlines and in the harmonic shifts. Stephen Lalor's *Waltz* and *Antipodie* (1994) might belong here- they exude a cool Satiesque aloofness and are not without charm, avoiding the more irritating traits of minimalism.

A more developed sort of minimalism may be observed in Mark Pollard's *a handful of rain* (1994), with many repetitions of short motives/patterns, but also a propensity for these fragmentary motives to expand in a really organic way. This three movement work "should be performed in single movement form 'attacca' or as three movements spread as single movements throughout a concert program". This 1994 work was a departure for the composer, from my point of view, as the last work I had studied and indeed recorded was his *Krebs*, from 1983. *Krebs* is German for crabs, which is the astrological sign for Cancer. ..."The piece reflects contrasting changes of mood, supposedly characteristic of people born under this sign". *Krebs*, like *a handful of rain*, is in three short movements, each one seizing and concentrating on one simple musical idea; so even though the pieces are a decade apart, there is some consistency of approach. Moreover, in *Krebs* the material is strictly limited, all coming from the first bar, and all used over the three movements. Both works are written with an understanding of keyboard possibilities. Pollard's other work, described as a companion piece to *a handful of rain* is *the prayers of tears* (1989). Neither it, nor *Krebs* can be described as minimalist, pointing up the difficulty of pigeonholing composers, but both pieces are added here for the sake of convenience, having begun to write about Pollard with *a handful of rain*. *The prayers of tears* is in fact a highly emotional piece, a long way away from the often robotic world of minimalism; the pain evident in the *lontano* passages and the repeated chords at times erupts into violent denial:

Ex 17:3 M. Pollard. *The Prayers of Tears*. bars 81-82.

Nigel Sabin belongs to what I perceive as a mainstream style of minimalism, maybe closer to the original American model. I have taught a couple of his pieces written for my pupil Colin Noble and have also looked at a number of pieces such as *A faint qualm, as of green April* (1992) and *Another look at Autumn* (1993). In these, Sabin has moved away from a purely motoric minimalism and interrupts the patterns with more rhetorical material.

Moya Henderson's *Treadmill* (1982) fits here rather neatly, especially given the subject matter and the inevitable repetitive nature of the material. The composer writes: "The treadmill was used in Australian goals last century to keep prisoners gainfully employed and of course, provide a cheap means of threshing the grain. The work was arduous, incredibly boring and the hours were very long." The composer imagines the prisoner trying to escape reality by inserting a dream sequence into the middle of *Treadmill*. The texture is very typical of minimalist writing for the piano:

Ex 18:3 M. Henderson. *Treadmill*. bars 209-212.

Colin Spiers (1957)

Colin Spiers, the Queensland composer and pianist, has written prolifically for the piano. Prominent in his output is his series large-scale sonatas for the instrument.

Sonata No. 1: Deranged Confessions (1990) features a 'frenzied' (the composer's word) kind of minimalism, from which a monolithic theme gradually emerges. This is treated fairly conventionally with left hand arpeggios and the work wends its way back to the opening ideas, all in one movement

Sonata No. 2: Desperate Acts (1992) also contains a number of elements already present in the *First*, mostly featuring repetitive patterns, but now with an element of growth about it, so that the patterns have some organic feel about them. This sonata is also continuous, but has named subsections and gestures such as *Apostrophe, Cadenza, Nocturne, Interlude* and so on. The structure is episodic, though at times thematically linked. The second sonata is a large, sprawling work, with virtuosic demands.

Sonata No. 3: Divine Symmetry (1994) is, like its predecessors, written in memory of a family member. It requires plucking inside the piano and therefore needs dampers of certain notes to be marked, certain notes muted in specified ways, as well as the production of harmonics on certain strings. These effects apart, one is again faced with the aggressive minimalism of earlier works. Spiers by now, it is clear, is attracted to the piano's ability to play *martellato*, and so the sound of a pedaled percussion instrument (which is what the piano actually is!) is ever present. The composer is also fascinated by assymetry within symmetry: a repetitive minimalistic language but one that is not always totally predictable. Many of the patterns come from the instrument's past and are clearly written by someone very familiar with this past and with the possibilities of the keyboard.

Sonata No. 4: Delicate Games (1995) is another large-scale piece of over 800 bars. It features key signatures and once again, begins with an ostinato pattern of a 3/2 bar in semi-quavers, which continues, albeit with some change and development, for over 500 bars! The rest of the sonata is similarly structured, but the sections are rather shorter.

It shouldn't therefore surprise us when we open the score of *Sonata No. 5: Distant Echoes* (1998) to discover that we are faced with another 'In Memory Of' piece. The opening of this latest offering takes us back to the world of the very first *Sonata*; but the fifth delves into the world of poly-rhythms and generally seems less content with long-staying ostinati. As a result, it emerges to my ears as a more interesting rhapsodic and rhetorical piece, somewhat terser in length and expression and with a genuine colouristic sense of the piano. All the *Sonatas*, which form a significant body of work in the last decade of the century, are prefaced by quotations at the head of the scores, perhaps hinting at the meaning of the music.

The *Variations on La Folia* (Michael Dudman in memoriam, 1981, revised 1994) is based on the well-known theme, followed by forty variations, with the last acting as a brilliant *Finale*. The variations follow a rather classical lineage partly forced onto the composer by the theme and partly by the decision to write numbered variations; his minimalistic leanings are well utilised here, as it allows each variation to stay with an established pattern from beginning to end; the theme provides a workable framework for each of the short variations. Halfway through the work (*Variation 19*) the composer chooses to remind us of the original theme. The set, though not easy, is effective and very clear in its structure and grouping of the separate variations into groups of related treatments of the easily remembered theme. There are echoes of Liszt's treatment of this melody in his *Spanish Rhapsody*, but there seem to be other references here from the past, including Rachmaninoff.

A piece from 1987, somewhat related to the above, is Spier's *Fantasy on a Theme of Keith Jarrett*. This, like *Sonata No. 3*, requires the pianist to produce harmonics as well as to play on a piano that has been 'prepared' by placing a sheet of paper over a portion of the strings. Although not formally set out as numbered variations, the *Fantasy* generally functions in such a way. It is considerably shorter than *La Folia*, and the 'fantasy' aspect of the composition doesn't manifest itself until well into the piece. Spiers even writes in the score "If so moved, the performer may improvise a section in keeping with the style at this point". After that, we move again into a more discernable variation form and a grand statement of the theme, although the *Fantasy* finally ends softly.

A smaller work, akin to the above in some ways is *A Small Contrapuntal Fantasy* (1982). In a very clear formal layout, the Fantasy's central and predominant section is a contrapuntal exploration of an austere quasi-Bachian theme, which is thoroughly worked out over approximately six pages of four-part texture; this is flanked at the start and finish by sections which are built on long pedal notes, with an improvised-like arpeggio theme over it. Spiers then gives it the grandiose treatment when it reappears at the end of the piece, as a culmination to the contrapuntal working.

From 1988, an album of twelve pieces: *Tales from Nowhere* (with an obvious play on words in the title). These are essentially miniaturized statements of the composer's ethos, with many of the pieces quite tonal and the whole set fairly easy on the ear. *No.12* recapitulates some of the ideas of *No.1*, so it seems that Spiers intended these to be performed as a cycle. One of the pieces uses the wood of the piano as a percussion study. But the whole set, dedicated to the composer's mother, is amiable, even light-hearted.

Also dedicated to his mother is the *Elegy and Toccata* (1980). Although not quite as large as the Sonatas, this is nevertheless an intense and serious piece with a rich Elegy and a demanding Toccata full of leaps and constant passagework. Playing through all this material by the composer, I kept detecting a Spanish turn of phrase here and there; and certainly in the *Elegy* and in some of the leaps of the Toccata, we sometimes enter the world of Albeniz and other Spanish nationalists. I cannot say whether this is deliberate or not, or even a construct of my own.

The Princess of the Mandala (1981) requires some preparatory marking of dampers and harmonics as well as metal chain of about six inches length. This opus consists of five parts : 1. *The Ice Palace*; 2. *The Unutterable Word*; 3. *The Crystal Rain*; 4. *The Phantom Horseman*; and 5. *The Enchanted Forest*. The technical requirements can be fierce as at times, the repeated patterns become kindred to a jackhammer in demand.

We are left with two medium size pieces: *Anna* (1981) in which a long spun cantilena sounds over a persistently and gently throbbing left hand pattern, and *Flecks* (1991), which, as the title implies, contains sparks of notes and chords only briefly relieved in the middle section by a short legato interlude.

.

The Spiers output is consistent in its style and in its approach to the keyboard. It surely represents one of the more interesting manifestations of the Minimalist movement.

The Maximalists

Chris Dench (1953); Michael Smetanin (1958); Gerald Brophy (1953); Riccardo Formosa (1954)

Maximalism, on the other hand, requires much more effort. The composers who practice maximalism (my term) regard themselves as belonging to The New Complexity movement, but even eloquent advocates for it such as Chris Dench, have failed to gain a mass constituency. Paradoxically, the piano is also an ideal instrument for New Complexity; pianists have long learnt to deal with polyphony and cross-rhythms, so it was just pushing the envelope a little to arrive at New Complexity writing for the instrument. There is one aspect of this music which is fairly constant, and which is probably least effective: it is treating the piano as a vehicle for rhythmically complex polyphony, in the same register and at the same dynamic, played with one hand: what is heard is not separate lines, but one line with some hiccups, no matter how high the skill level of the pianist. If these complex cross-rhythms are really vital and important to the composer, then varying instrumental colour is the obvious way to go, with a conductor laying down the beat.

In an age where the computer reigns supreme, it seems curious to me that such music is not transferred into that realm more and more. Human brains are amazing things and can no doubt, with long hours of practice, achieve some approximation of the amazing demands of some of these scores, but the computer can do them really accurately. If the argument is that the sheer effort of getting it correct is part of the theatre of the piece, I can only say that few pianists would bother, as it is entirely unsatisfying to never get it right or even get close. The exhausting hours of hard slog at the keyboard is something few pianists have at their disposal, and the resultant frustration is more than most would bear. My guess is that most performers open such scores and hastily close them again, as the visual impact alone is enough to frighten even the best-intentioned players. Nevertheless, when it happens, it can be quite exhilarating, like a performance of a piece by Xenakis, or Liszt.

Of the Australian main 'Maximalists' I would single out Chris Dench and Michael Smetanin. Dench writes more complicated polyphonic music, with different layers of activity; Smetanin revels in sheer brutality and although much simpler in many ways than Dench, his piano scores require more physical stamina, as in *Stroke*. I always thought that the title referred to an induced coronary condition, but have been told that it could also mean the action of playing the piano, or even a sexual innuendo. Dench has much more variety and subtlety both in his scores and in his proclaimed antecedents. I have chosen not to reproduce examples of their scores simply because one needs to experience the visual impact of the complete score rather than a mere snippet. For instance, Dench's *Tilt* is only frightening when you see the piece in its entirety- or at least frightening to me. (I have also examined, but cannot claim to have 'played through', Dench's other piano music: *Topologies* from 1980 as well as *Phase Portraits* from 1993, the first of which is dedicated to the memory of Jean Barraqué.

Gerard Brophy's music seems to belong in this section of book - inasmuch as one has to pigeonhole to some extent - but his brand of maximalism is a more refined sort and, in its quieter moments, has elements of minimalism rubbing shoulders with the more frenetic sections. *Spiked Heels* (1992) is a case in point, when the long runs of demisemiquavers give way to the contemplative long notes or, as at the end, repeated phrases. *Angelicon* from the same period (1991) also bridges the gap between the two extremes, gradually building from a beginning consisting of more rests than notes and gradually thickening the texture before retreating again. *Abraco*, in celebration of his teacher Donatoni, is a twenty-two-page long piece of unremitting activity, building in waves and marked 'always exhilarating and exuberant'. It is a kind of maximalist piece in its unrelenting mood, but possesses neither Smetanin's brutality nor Dench's rhythmic complexity; in most of the piece the hands play together in parallel chords and octaves, creating an open, clearly discernable pulsing. The only other piece of Brophy known to me is the much earlier *Ghéranos* from 1980, which contains a tightly controlled aleatoricism as well as elaborate *fioratura* patterns that were common currency in the avant-garde of the day. Riccardo Formosa's *Cinq Variations pour Monsieur T.* (1986) probably belong here as yet another somewhat mannered result of 1980s-style maximalism. In spirit this work is closer to Brophy than the others. So is James Paull's *Fallen Angels* (1983), dedicated to the English maximalist composer Michael Finissy.

Performance of this music is therefore rarely attempted in this country. The composers themselves have not been performers and did not lead by example. I can't help feeling that by the end of the century, this was a spent force. Like most fashionable minimalism, which has little or nothing to say, and therefore repeat the same phrase hundreds of times with sometimes no variation at all, so maximalism, by its dense surface, is also often hiding the vacuum that lurks beneath the glitzy surface.

(iii) Pluralism: Popular Music / Jazz/ Neotonality

The phenomenon of pluralism in Australian piano music has meant that the strict separation of 'art' music from lighter genres has by now been blurred and that many composers have either crossed that imaginary border, or are at least inhabitants of no-man's land. The high fences put up by the law-givers have never been perceived to be real by composers themselves, who have always felt free enough to roam elsewhere.

Pianists

Simplicius Cheong (1942)

Simplicius Cheong is composer who comes to piano music from a non-classical base. I have looked at three works of his: *Three Movements for Piano* (1968), *Three Preludes for Piano* (1973) and the very fine and significant *Jazz Fantasy for Piano* (1984). The composer himself writes:

> As a jazz pianist, I use the piano professionally in my improvisations on stage or in jazz venues. Also, although I compose a lot away from the piano, I use it to test whatever I write. I also play a lot of piano pieces by Ravel, Debussy and other contemporary composers. The piano has been an indispensable musical tool for me, in my capacity as a composer and jazz improviser. I try not to write anything against the piano. Passages, scalic, polyphonic or chordal must be idiomatic for the 2 hands. Textures, voicings, dynamics and formal elements are also important. As a child around 5 or 6, I was encouraged to play written pieces by Bach, Beethoven and other composers. At the same time, I was exposed also to recordings of the jazz piano of Art Tatum, Oscar Peterson, Errol Garner, and Andre Previn. I had to listen repeatedly to these recordings to internalize the various jazz styles, as scores were not available obviously, as they were improvised. You will find that in my *Jazz Fantasy* which I wrote for David Bollard, the influence of not only these jazz masters but also a bit of Ravel and Schoenberg. There is a synthesis of pianistic styles in my piano writing.

Carl Vine (1954)

Carl Vine is a well-known figure in Australian music with wide experience as performer and administrator. His early successes were in the modern dance world and this has permeated his piano writing, as described below.

The earliest Vine music is *Occasional Poetry* (1981-1984). I was actually responsible for eliciting this set of three short pieces from the composer for a projected anthology of Australian music to be published by Breitkopf and Haertel; unfortunately the project came to nought. At that stage Vine hadn't written any music for solo piano, despite being an accomplished pianist; but the piano had certainly featured in his chamber music.

Thus, the Piano Sonata of 1990 was his first big work for the instrument. The performance note on the score tells us much about both the piece and the composer's style:

> Tempo markings throughout this score are not suggestions but indications of absolute speed. Rubato should only be employed when directed, and then only sparingly. Romantic interpretation of melodies, phrases and gestures should be avoided wherever possible.

This note, plus the fact that the composer's earlier work was in the world of dance, sets the tone for Vine's keyboard approach. The First Sonata is strongly tonal, with much of the harmony based on built-up fourths. This, with a constant usage of sequences, gives the work a flavour reminiscent of Paul Hindemith. The balletic aspect is manifest in a collage of rhythms, like a Japanese percussion ensemble moving from one pattern to the next. The second movement is strongly reminiscent of the scherzo from the first sonata by Alberto Ginastera, with its parallel but wide-spaced semi-quavers.

The *Bagatelles* of 1994 are sometimes a little more 'orchestral' in texture but more often than not this is again the kind of use of the piano as a set of pitched drums. This whole assemblage has links to synthetic computer music and even drum machines, but it is more sophisticated involving sequencers in the making of it.

The *Second Sonata* (1999) may be a little warmer than No.1, perhaps a little more eclectic in its sources, whether they be simple octave displacements, or more clichéd figurations from the past. These include many arpeggio patterns from the nineteenth century, but also there are more echoes from the early twentieth century that bring the music of figures like Copland and Hindemith to mind. The world is the early rise of modernity, with its ambiguous major/minor mixtures and sometimes rough parallel harmonies. Once again, we have the piled-up fourths and the collages of drum patterns. Overall, *Sonata No. 2* is even more conservative than the first.

Vine's music is always skillfully put together and aims for maximum effect, and consequently has appealed to many pianists and student pianists. It is always pianistic in a dry glittery sort of way, and the collages have a timing that comes from exposure to the theatre. The surface sheen of a mild modernity barely masks a simplistic melodic approach. The overall picture of Vine's piano music is a flirtation with commercialism, a result that is showy but not profound, with plastic surface but not emotional depth.

Elena Kats-Chernin (1957)

Elena Kats-Chernin was trained as a pianist and composer in Moscow, arriving in Australia as a teenager. She has gradually turned away from professional and public piano playing, even though her graduation exercise was, like Prokofiev's, to perform her own *Piano Concerto*. Thus, although part of the composer-pianist tradition, with a Russian background to reinforce this birthright, one would have expectations of this composer going for the jugular, as it were, in the realms of piano music. However, Elena is that curious exception in that she had chosen to write for the piano essentially in a lighter vein, often a dance vein, with emphasis on rag-music.

A good starting point is the *Purple Prelude* a wash of Eb minor sonority, gradually thickening and become busier, but preserving the opening idea of hands an octave apart, playing a plaintive, Russian folk-song like melodic motive. Elena writes at the keyboard, which means that the piano music is very pianistic and an extra bonus is the feeling of a spontaneous improvisation occurring as one plays – or hears – the music. The *Schubert Blues* reinforces such an initial impression. Everything is melodically driven, and there is an underlying motoric restlessness to the music, which sometimes also gives it the air of a mild flirtation with minimalism. The *Charleston Noir* on the other hand (a quite extended essay into the rhythm) to my ears had that somewhat excited sound of early Hindemith venturing into the daring zone of popular music. Kats-Chernin likes the sound of the sustaining pedal left down for long periods of time, and many of the works ask for long stretches of colour thus created.

The rags have a strong affinity with the melodic shapes and harmonic shifts of popular Russian music of a particular type, one especially linked with the rather sentimental *romans* genre. This is most evident in one of Kats-Chernin's best known pieces, the *Russian Rag* (there are in fact two rags with this title), where, unsurprisingly, these elements are allowed full play. Such characteristics ally Elena's rags not so much with flash display pieces, but rather with the more elegant and even sometimes sombre world of the Joplin rags, as the Kats-Chernin counterparts tend to proceed at a rather controlled pace and even remind one occasionally of the music of Satie, not only in its pensive simplicity but as well in the unexpected shifts of tonal centre. Little chromatic grace figures, like trombone slides, are added reminders of how close this music is to cafe and cabaret.

In the midst of all this, the composer's classical training also rears its head, as some of the more decorative piano passages, used when rag melodies are reprised and elaborated, could have come from a work of Chopin, a composer much beloved by the Russians (it is should be noted here that the *Zee Rag*, for the most part is a close companion to the Chopin final *Prelude*, complete with wide left hand arpeggiation, the double third chromatic run in the right hand, and in the overall passionate mood). Polyphony is virtually non-existent in these pieces, as the more complex moments are put together by adding flourishes to the tunes.

Kats-Chernin's classical training is touched upon in a curious little piece called *Stur in Dur* for piano and pianist's voice, in which the pianist is obviously practising or composing at the keyboard rattling through exercise-like broken octaves, arpeggios and Alberti bass patterns, whilst voicing a desire to move to major keys. The original text was in German, but an English translation is added below.

There is a larger scale work, *Sonata Lost and Found*, consisting of four movements:
> 1. *Sunglare on the roof of the house opposite my window.*
> 2. *Unfinished Lullaby.*
> 3. *Give Back that Smile*
> 4. *Chorale*

The opening movement is an unbroken chain of semiquaver patterns in both hands, somewhat in the manner of *Stur in Dur*, set out as a controlled tremolo, with certain notes accenting, creating a clearly perceived melodic line, with strong tonal arrival points. Most of the semiquavers are broken octaves – a favourite pianistic figuration of the composer. The sense of an opening toccata then leads to the *Lullaby* movement. Initially a simple quasi-popular melody begins high on the piano, unaccompanied but with the sustain pedal down creating a wash of sound. An interesting and somewhat disturbing effect occurs when a second voice enters out of phase and out of key:

Ex 19:3 E. Kats-Chernin. *Sonata Lost and Found*. bars 18-22 of II.

This bitonal passage eventually leads to a much thicker version still high on the keyboard, creating a Messiaen-like clangour of bells. The third movement, for me, was by far the most dramatic and structurally persuasive of the work. The foundation of popular melody is still there, but increasingly getting swamped, or angrily reiterated in a context that destroys the original idea. This generally loud and percussive movement is also the most extensive and demands some difficult leaps from the pianist covering the whole keyboard. The ending *Chorale* is a tiny one-page, possibly necessary to act as a gentle coda to what preceded it.

There remain only two works that seem to lie outside the reference point of popular Russian song. *Shestizvuchiya* (which means six-sound sonority in Russian) is a relatively early work and quite short. It is a dry excursion using postwar European avant-garde techniques revealing perhaps the influence of her teacher Helmut Lachenmann. The much later *Tast-en* is also more extended and explores to a great extent the effect of the third pedal and the overtones of the piano. It is not easy, and at its height makes the sort of demands already encountered in the third movement of the Sonata. At this stage it is not representative of the composer's output for the piano, but this might well change in the twenty-first century. At the moment Elena Kats-Chernin holds a personal niche in the genre of Australian piano music.

Mark Isaacs (1958)

Mark Isaacs, like Simplicius Cheong, is another example of a jazz pianist who has worked successfully across the divide and has composed in his own style embracing both aspects. He has a collection of twelve notated pieces, which I have played through and one of which I have edited for publication. The pieces are: I. *Visitation*, II. *What I see in You*; III. *Have One More*; IV. *Shards*; V. *Unrecognizable*; VI. *Grace City;* VII. *Bunyip Friend*; VIII. *Voidless*; IX. *Convenient Penguins*; X. *Tender Earth*; XI. *Only Winds Change*; and XII. *Venture On.*

Non-Pianists:

Bruce Cale (1939)

Coalesce Op.74. Nancy Salas in Memoriam: This is a fairly major work, dedicated to the memory of on outstanding Australian pianist and teacher Nancy Salas, founder of the Bartok Society when Bartók was considered extremely daring and new. A sonata-like composition in three movements, Cale's " in memoriam" piece is meticulously notated (a little ironic given Cale's strong jazz background) giving the work a 'New Complexity' –like appearance when in fact it is not that at all. Despite some notational curiosities mostly in the realms of grammar, the composition vacillates between single note or two voiced strands alternating with chorale like chords which give the texture its particular flavour. The manuscript is dated 16/8/1992 and the composer's timing of this work is eighteen minutes.

Martin Wesley-Smith (1945)

Another Adelaide born composer, Martin Wesley-Smith, is not primarily a composer for the piano, making his real mark in theatre and computer music. Nevertheless, there are three *Waltzes* for the piano: *Olya's Waltz and Waltz for Aunt Irina* (both 1992) followed by the *White Knight Waltz* (1996). There is also a full-scale solo piano piece called *On A. I. Petrof* (1993), from which the first two waltzes are derived. This last piece charts the short life of a mythical Russian student. Since this student was very fond of Chopin, the opening and closing sections of the work are in a very tonal A major and A minor, with extremely florid right hand writing over a quasi waltz left hand; these are the basis for the two aforementioned waltzes with Russian names.

Ex 20:3 M. Wesley-Smith. *On A. I. Petrof.* opening.

The middle section of the work is more in the nature of a turbulent *Toccata*, with many repeated notes and octaves, no doubt picturing the short and unhealthy life of the imaginary Aleksandr Ilych.

The *White Knight Waltz* pushes the idea of elaborate waltz writing a step further. The composer says:

> This, like several other pieces of mine, is based on the nursery rhyme 'Pat-a -Cake, Pat-a-Cake, Baker's Man', which might have been one of Lewis Carroll's favourites: "Baker's Man"- Carroll portrayed himself in his epic nonsense poem The Hunting of the Snark as the Baker; "mark it with B'": the name of every character in the poem starts with a 'B'; and the fifth bar of the melody is the first bar backwards, which would surely have pleased Carroll if he'd been a musician, which he wasn't.
>
> In my full-length choral nonsense piece *Boojum!* which is about the life, work and ideas of Carroll, I used "Pat-a-Cake", or variations of it, as the theme for Carroll's real-life self the Reverend Charles Lutwidge Dodgson. Here it appears in several forms: upside-down; upside-down and backwards - the way a music box would play if its cylinder were put in the wrong way round; and in a minor key.

The White Knight of the title refers to Carroll's representation of himself in *Through the Looking-Glass - and What Alice Found There.*

Ex 21:3 M. Wesley-Smith. *White Knight Waltz*. bars 9-15.

The two quotes are quite good representations of Martin's style in that they show his connection to both tonal and popular music, his very individual take on compositional craft, and the inherent music-theatre lurking in all of his pieces.

Nigel Westlake (1958)

Nigel Westlake is probably best known in Australia for his film music, but there was certainly nothing stopping him writing his exuberant *Piano Sonata* in 1997. Its too early yet to say whether this Sonata will become a classic in our repertoire, but it seems to me to be an important piece, full of an energy rivaling that of Villa-Lobos, with a similar earthy approach and a similar piling up of cumulative ostinati. The Westlake *Sonata* treats the piano like a giant percussion ensemble; the writing is lean and muscular and devoid of any intricacies of counterpoint, that is, it tends to be either sinewy lines or else the two hands in massive chordal effects.

Ex 22:3 N. Westlake. *Piano Sonata*. bars 77-79.

Margaret Brandman (1951)

Whereas the Westlake excursion into piano repertoire is more an exception than the rule, Margaret Brandman has actually made a career out of writing pragmatic educational music for piano in which the jazz background of her upbringing and training and her own fundamental orientatation at the piano are clearly utilized. Brandman's out put for the instrument is large, but concert pieces are less in number and some which are representative of her style include *Winter Piece* for left hand alone (1992), *Churinga* (Sacred Amulet of the Australian Aboriginals) (1992) and *Six Contemporary Piano Pieces* (1982), consisting of *Badinerie* Nos.1 and 2, *Invention, Tango Tranquille, Sunshowers on the River (Variations in a Modern Style)* and *Mini-Suite*. Even here, the music is 'useful' in the sense that three of the works are also designated as suitable for the classical accordion.

Graeme Koehne (1956)

Graeme Koehne wrote for the piano very early in his career: there is a short *Sonata* (1976) as well as *Harmonies of Silver and Blue* (1977) and *Twilight Rain* (1977), all probably written whilst under the influence of Richard Meale, who himself had a strong interest in French music. Since then, Koehne has repudiated any tendencies of post-war modernism and has therefore actively preached a return to a populist way of thinking, so these works do not represent his mature thought.

David Joseph

David Joseph, another Meale product, has a lengthy *Rhapsody for Piano Solo* (1997), sprawling over almost sixty pages and perhaps - if Liszt was the model, as seems likely - not learning enough from the model about structural brevity and directness. Joseph certainly knows what he is about, and understands the piano very well; there are probably too many ideas in this one piece for ultimate survival.

Wendy Hiscocks (1963)

Wendy Hiscocks represents composers who have chosen to work with exotic scales and modes as well as Indian ragas, exemplified by her exciting *Toccata* (1983), which first brought her into prominence:

Ex 23:3 W. Hiscocks. *Toccata.* opening.

The piece has Bb as its reference point and it keeps returning to this pitch, distributed all over the piano. Her subsequent music is more modally inclineed and rhythmically more regular, and includes a concert or ballet suite, with programmatic notes, entitled *The Piper at the Gates of Dawn*.

I don't know whether post-modernism is also resulting in a return to programmatic or semi-programmatic considerations; but another piece with similar inclination is Stuart Greenbaum's *Ice Man* (1992); there is a type of musical symbolism as well is his other works such as *Homage to Professor Peter Dennison* (1989), *New Roads, Old Destinations* (1996), *First Light* (1997) and *But I want the Harmonica* (1996)

(iv) "Australian" Composers: The Next Generation

Non-Pianists

Moya Henderson (1941)

Moya Henderson is often described as a composer whose concerns with the Australian environment and Aboriginal spirituality have had a profound influence on her music. She is also often depicted as a strong feminist. I am far too timid to venture into discussion of such interactions, preferring to deal directly with the sound.

I have already touched upon Moya's piece *Treadmill* in the section on minimalism, and will add to those comments here. *Cross Hatching* (1984, rev.1998) refers to a common bark painting technique used by the Aborigines. This is an attempt by the composer to apply a similar idea to the piano, with lines in the two hands crossing or interacting with each other. This piece, too, uses minimalist techniques, but the tempo is constantly fluctuating and the work emerges more as a series of tiny mosaic fragments, put together to make up the whole. A lot of the cross-hatching is achieved by one hand playing off the beat; but overall there is still a strong motoric element. Moya Henderson also has two short Preludes to her credit, as well as *Nolle Prosequi* (1973); they all use unbarred and graphic notations.

Ross Edwards (1943)

Ross Edwards is an example of a composer, who, like Colin Brumby, began his career as a modernist and then veered away from this path and settled into a less confronting, even comfortable, conventionalism.

Edwards' early piece for the piano, *Monos II*, dedicated to Roger Woodward (not the first composer to be inspired by this pianist) shows all the characteristics of a young composer fired up and ready to go: it is full of energy and a restless questing. One could also of course point out that it is music very much of its time (the 1970s) with some of the attendant mannerisms and notational quirks of the then avant-garde. Nevertheless, it is an impressive debut piece for the instrument. But it may also have brought about a crisis of style for the composer.

Edwards did not write for the piano for ten years. In 1980 and 1984, two new pieces appeared: *Kumari* and *Etymalong*. I group these together, because they have many characteristics in common. Both are slow, with many repetitions and spaces between the repeated gestures. Little grace notes or figures are sometimes used to minimally decorate the chord progressions. But the exuberance of *Monos II* is gone and has now given way to a low-charge poor-man's Messiaen, with navel gazing mantras without the French composer's shouts of ecstasy, or his fevered excitement. Gone, too, is any suggestion of pianistic challenge. The problem with this kind of writing (and it applies to Messiaen as much as to Edwards) is that the attempt to hypnotize and to entrance can easily rebound and cause good old-fashioned boredom!

The more recent piano music such as *Five Little Piano Pieces*, *Three Children's Pieces* or *Three Little Piano Pieces for the Right Hand Alone* all show a strong tendency towards extreme miniaturization. Similar to these are the nine bagatelles entitled *Mantras and Night Flowers*, with subtitles which include such Australianisms as *Snail Bay Mantra*, *Frangipani* and *Pipyarnyum Mantra*. All of these pieces are now not only miniature but the passion of *Monos II* and the inward meditation of *Kumari* has now been replaced by sentimentalism coupled with prettiness and occasionally laced with a quasi-Japanese melodic line.

The last pieces I looked at are the *Three Australian Waltzes* (1997-1998), again with Australian titles such as *Sassafras Gully Waltz* and *Annandale Waltz*. These pieces sound like salon music of a long time ago and whereas they might have been natural to composers like Hutchens or Evans, one does wonder what their relevance is now. In the first of these waltzes, Edwards' introduction talks about connections with nineteenth-century Romantic piano music; as someone who has played much of such repertoire, all I can say is that I didn't find points of contact.

Ross Edwards' piano music is a curious case of a promising beginning leading to a world of arch cuteness.

Robert Allworth (1943)

Robert Allworth has done Australian music a great service by running his own CD company (JADE) and issuing dozens of recordings of Australian music. His own piano music may be best described as aphoristic, as even the longer pieces are put together by a string of very short ideas. Many of the pieces are no longer than one or two pages. Thus, *Prelude* (1972) is one page. *Past Horizons* (n.d.) is in three movements, but takes up six minutes in all. *Nocturne for a Pensive Evening* (n.d.) is two pages. So is *Yesteryears* (1986) as well as *Purple Noon's Transparent Night* (no date on ms). Two larger pieces that I have come across are *Morning by an Ocean* (composer's duration is 14') and *Sonata-Fantasy (Last Look at Bronte - William Parsons In Memoriam)* (1983) (duration 22', unusually long for this composer). The writing for piano is very open in texture, and difficult passages are rare. Allworth is fond of dreamy and clean sounds, and he consistently shifts from one idea to another. The style is eclectic and can include twelve-tone sounding passages rubbing shoulders with strongly tonal material.

Anne Boyd (1946)

There was a time in the seventies when Sydney composers felt that they had to prove their Australian identity by writing music inspired by Asia. Some of them had evidently looked at a map and discovered the startling fact that Europe was further away than Bali. I'm not certain why this was revelatory, but some composers treated it as such.

Anne Boyd's *Angklung* (1974) is one such piece, *Angklung* being one of two similar works dedicated to Roger Woodward. The score has an instruction on it: "This Fb may be retuned to a 'true' (i.e. untempered) Fb". Since this is the totality of the instruction, it is almost impossible to work out what it means, since no context for the tuning is given. There is no such thing as a true Fb, and one would have to specify the actual vibration rate. I suspect that what the composer wants is a slightly flattened F, but she doesn't say so, nor is the amount of micro-deflection made clear. The only other comment I would make is that tuners hate doing this kind of thing and that it is not good for concert grands to be subjected to it: its hard enough keeping them stable. Having said all that, the music is predictably Balinese, using only four pitches, with a reiterated crotchet pulse. Once again, 'Lento possibile' could mean a lot of things, but I suppose it can be a measure of the nerve of the player. The cultural derivation apart, the music can be thus described as belonging to the minimalist school, consisting as it does, a few flourishes apart, of crotchets in the same register of the piano. There is some play of tension with the sounding of the active pitches over and over, altering the spacing of the chord a little. The piece works perfectly well without worrying about the Fb, and the instruction does use the word 'may be retuned'.

A somewhat more adventurous piece is *Book of the Bells* (1980). Like *Angklung*, it concerns itself with repeated chimes, but now there are levels of activity and dynamics, written on different staves, which contribute to the work's effect. It is a little like having different collections of wind chimes sounding at different times and metrically often uncoordinated with each other. The score is graphic in terms of occurrences, and the pianist is asked to think in quavers. This apart, like *Angklung* this is a delicate atmospheric piece, although it grows more than its predecessor, and has a more explicit multi-layering cumulative sound.

Boyd is not a pianist and the writing of both works was more an inspiration by Woodward rather than her own attraction to the instrument. The technical demands in these two pieces are relatively modest.

Colin Bright (1949)

In a different, more minimalist way, Colin Bright's piano pieces, with hints of Aboriginal influences, may be added to this list - works such as *Tango Dreaming* (1984), *The Dreaming II*, *Earth-flowering Time* (1987). Bright's minimalism is characterized by shifting bar lengths. His *In the Pacific* (1999) has three movements: *The Tsunami, Voices from the Desert Ocean*, and *Golden Beasts come from the Sea*.

Andrew Schulz (1960)

Andrew Schultz is another composer often linked in the public's mind with notions of 'Australian'. There are only two piano works. *Sea Change* (1987) and *Sonata* (1982). The Sonata is an obviously early work and gets stuck in a minimalistic groove, the first movement tending to be very soft and heavily pedalled, the second more strongly measured and driven. *Sea Change* is more colouristic and impressionistic in its approach to the keyboard, but once again, the range of ideas and passagework is severely limited by design.

(v) The Youngest Composers

Non-Pianists

Matthew Bienick (1976), Stephen Adams (minimalist), Stephen Leek, Andrew Harrison (jazz), Elliott Gyger (1968), Robert Davidson (1965)

Dealing with music of the most recent generation is particularly difficult: the margin for error is, naturally, huge, and the amount of evidence, as it were, is very small. One can be completely off the beam, unless the composer has already produced a sizable amount of work. The reader will see from the database that a sizable quantity of music by such composers has been looked at. As with all composers, omission in the body of the book does not necessarily imply anything at all. Can one, for one small example, divine the potential and ethos of a composer like John Peterson, represented in our files by one piece *Walking on Glass* (1992) composed for my ex-pupil Robert Zocchi? Obviously one cannot, apart from making some comment on the one piece. In due time, such composers will make their way; indeed, some of them might already have made their way in a sphere other than piano music. We cannot pretend to have a handle on every composer in the country! Or, if I only have Matthew Bieniek's *Succession and Style, a poetic essay* (1997) to look at, do I assume that the words are inextricably linked to the music and that this is the composer's trait; or else that a form of diluted maximalism is still out there? That minimalism is still alive and well, we know, so its not a surprise to see pieces like Stephen Adams' *Obsession I and II* (1985), but since nothing else by him has surfaced in our search for music, do I (perhaps wrongly) come to the conclusion that the obsession has spent itself? Composition requires more than talent and opportunity - it requires indomitable will over a great span of time. Unless one is a Chopin, or a Mozart, forty is a young age for a composer.

Stephen Leek is a composer with a ready reputation, although it is in choral writing for young voices, not in piano music. However, he has produced a series of elegant and well-crafted short pieces that are always interesting and directed at youngish players without the technical baggage often imposed on new piano music. There are three sets of seven pieces each, one named *Seven Windows*, *Seven Days*, (n.d.) and the other *Seven Places* (1988). The second set has subtitles as well. There is also a piece for prepared piano called *Hammered-* outside the scope of this book really, but I couldn't help wondering whether the shortness of the piece would justify the preparation that needs to be made? Some of these pieces would do good duty as encores.

Like Stephen Leek, Andrew Harrison worked with me for a time. His *Piano Fantasia No.1* (1997) is a big work, using a fully developed technique and incorporating some improvisational elements within tightly controlled parameters. I am unaware of a second one, but on the basis of just the first *Fantasia* one can cautiously say that there are possibilities for this composer (I only do so because I also know something of his other music). Andrew doesn't seem to subscribe to any 'ism', although he studied in the jazz department of the School of Music here at the Australian National University.

On the basis of two works, one short and one major, I think that Elliott Gyger could well be a composer who will contribute to the piano repertoire. I have played through *Threshhold* (1994), a lyrical little two-minute piece and the big *Compass Variations* (1993). He is currently Associate Professor in Composition at Harvard and has not as yet written anything else for piano. *Compass Variations* is an impressive first major work for the piano, consisting of eleven sections, each dedicated to a different mood and a different way of playing the piano. It requires a pianist with a complete technique to get through the set of variations

I have already mentioned one score by Robert Davidson in the chapter on minimalism, and might be appropriate here to add one more. *Zĕmar* from 1987 is a largish – still minimalist – piece, with strong tonal centres and medium difficulty.

Pianist

Alistair Noble (1968)

One of the most interesting young composers working today lives in relative obscurity in the little town of Glen Innes, New South Wales, and has produced some strikingly individual works for piano.

Fantasia Pange Lingua (Sonata No.2) is dedicated to his brother Colin, with whom Alistair has given numerous two piano recitals. The score contains a quotation from Peter Ackroyd's *Hawksmoor*:

> And then in my dream I looked down at myself and saw in what rags I
> stood; and I am a child again, begging on the threshold of eternity.

Alistair has issued a CD recording of the Busoni *Sonatinas* and this *Sonata* seems to me to be spiritually related to them, especially to the "Christmas 1917" *Sonatina*. Alistair's work, in one movement, has the same 'white' sound, and like the Busoni is interspersed with a quasi-chorale interlude. The opening suggests a timelessness but is a long way from the arty New Age wind chimes that have become such a cliché:

Ex 24:3 A. Noble. *Fantasia "Panga Lingua" (Sonata No. 2)*. opening.

These opening sounds generate the whole organic growth of the movement. The quasi-chorale, always written in breves, appears like a mantra throughout the sonata, never quite the same. Here is one appearance:

Ex 25:3 A. Noble. *Fantasia "Panga Lingua" (Sonata No. 2)*. page 4 (unbarred).

The Sonata is a contemplative piece, which owes nothing to current fashion.

The Sonata No.3, like its predecessor, utilizes a bell-like sound, but this time it is low on the keyboard and, like the quasi-chorale of its predecessor in Sonata No.2, is widely spaced and pervasive. This Sonata is interrupted by two *Interludes* in its unfolding and it seems likely that Noble will next move to a multi-movement form for his next major piano work. The Sonata No.3 is dated 1999. Like in the second, poetry is quoted in the score.

As well as these larger works, Noble has a few shorter works to his credit. These, too, seem to have a poetic springboard. *Manteena*, for example, comprises three short, contemplative pieces. *Thamanya*, somewhat more active, has two movements. Some other works that I saw were still in rough manuscript form, but complete: *Sun Mountain Cloud Forest* as well as *Night Rain (Three Reflections of a Chinese Poem)*. Since Noble is an accomplished pianist, there are open vistas in existence as far as his compositional development on the piano is concerned.

Perhaps his interest in Busoni will result in an expansion of technical means, a move towards a more challenging transcendental approach to the keyboard. He has, with his brother, performed the Messiaen *Visions of Amen* and the French mystical master could well be an added influence on his compositional development.

Part 4: The Australian Piano Concerto

In stark contrast to the musical scene in Europe, and to some extent in America, Australia did not establish a virtuoso concerto tradition in the nineteenth century. This was due to the ad hoc nature of the orchestral scene and the paucity of homegrown virtuosi and composers. In the opening years of the twentieth century, the music-loving public would have been informed about the concerto repertoire only through the public performances of imported artists and then, in the early days of recorded music, via the availability of gramophone recordings.

The number of surviving concerto scores from the earlier part of the twentieth century is, therefore, small. It was only with the advent of more permanent state orchestra run by the Australian Broadcasting Corporation, modeled on the BBC, that home-grown concerti had a chance of performance and some sense of survival and historical placement.

One of these early survivors, albeit only in the form of a two-piano reduction, is *A Northern Ballad- The Saga of King Orry* (c.1907) by Mona McBurney (1862 – 1932). McBurney was the first woman Bmus graduate from the University of Melbourne, and later taught Margaret Sutherland piano at this very university. The concerto was performed at the Exhibtion of Women's Works in 1907 and by the Marshall-Hall orchestra in the following year.It is a one-movement work, with the atmosphere and difficulty of a romantic concerto. The composer was obviously imbued with a particular legend; at one point in the score, a folk song is identified as "Til fjelds over Bygden staar min Hue". The Ballade commences with a cadenza and generally the soloist has a prominent and showy role.

Another curiosity is the concerto written in 1929 by Roy Maling. I was made aware of it just as the book was going to press. The composer is almost completely forgotten now and this find is miraculous in itself. Maling went on from a 'classical' beginning to work in the jazz field, and this one-movement work seems to have survived only in its two-piano format. It would be a fairly straightforward task to orchestrate the second piano part, if there were a performance planned, or else one could possibly air the work just on two pianos. The researcher Clive Cooper is working on Roy Maling's story and at this writing there is even a website on the subject. In the classical world, no one seems to know the name, let alone any of the music, so perhaps there are discoveries to be made here. I have only come across Maling's name in listing of piano music from Australian publishers. The Concerto is in a late-romantic idiom.

Australia's first international success in the concerto form was George Boyle's *Concerto in D Minor* (1912), published by the prestigious firm of G. Schirmer in New York. It is now of course out of print, but the parts must exist somewhere and I would suggest that it is long overdue for a revival. It could well be our very first fully-fledged concerto. Boyle was a virtuoso pianist and so the solo part is written with himself in mind. It requires good octaves, a big stretch especially in the left hand, as well as double notes. The orchestra is largely written to support the flamboyant solo part, which enjoys many unaccompanied passages. In an act that perhaps has never been followed this concerto was performed by the New York Philharmonic with the composer at the piano, and his good friend and fellow Australian, the then President of Juillard, Ernest Hutcheson conducting.

Mirrie Hill's *Rhapsody* was first performed in 1913 or 1914 by Laurence Godfrey-Smith. The manuscript (here is another unpublished work worth resurrecting) is interesting in that Mirrie rubbed out her maiden name 'Solomon' from the title page and wrote 'Hill' over it. The first page of the score is in Alfred Hill's handwriting, as he was showing her how to set out the score, but the rest is in her own hand. Someone has written '21' minutes on the title page, probably from a later performance. The style is late romantic and there are many octave passages in the solo part. The music works well in its own context and evokes a now lost age.

Edgar Bainton's *Concerto-Fantasia for Pianoforte and Orchestra* was written in 1921, before the composer came to Australia. It is actually an effective work in a somewhat unusual form, which is now completely forgotten. The movements are: I. A mostly unaccompanied movement in which the solo part is marked 'quasi cadenza', and which makes abrupt shifts of tempo with the solo part providing a showy opening and closing material. II: Scherzo, III: Improvisation, which once again focusses on the solo part; IV. Finale, an energetic allegro and ending with, surprisingly, an Epilogue, winding up the work in a hushed introspective Adagio.

There are four extant concerti in manuscript in Hooper Brewster-Jones' archive at Adelaide University. They present, as so much of his output does, great editorial problems. In the case of Brewster-Jones' Concerto No.3 (1925) these verge on the extreme. The composer says on the score 'completed' and gives the date. But what might have been complete to him, presents, to us, a jumble of pages with hasty scribbles and shorthand notations, sometimes very difficult indeed to decipher. He is an important composer and eventually work will have to be done on these scores in an attempt to salvage them for posterity. There is a good copy of the reduction of the Brewster-Jones Concerto No.2 in Ab major (1922) so this one should be less problematic to reconstruct. Brewster-Jones and Nadra Penalurik performed the two piano version on ABC radio sometime in the 1930s, and one can still see the pencil markings on this manuscript, for the second piano, which Nadra Penalurik played. In three movements, this is much more conventional than some of his solo piano pieces. The orchestra is for double wind and brass, timpani and strings, and the full score has a timing of twenty-nine minutes on it.

It appears that Brewster-Jones and his student Edith Piper performed the second and third movements of what was called *A Pastoral Concerto*. Once again, we have an ink score of these movements. There are some written annotations. Firstly (at the head of the second movement):

> II: By the Waterfall (An Impression) . III: Outback, a mood. The vigorous sweeping opening theme of this movement suggests the rich colours of Australian life, a contrasting section in quieter tones depicts the star-crown'd solitute of night. Later we hear the galloping hooves of wild scrub cattle as they wheel into the station yard. Bird Song and the fullness of Spring enrich the mood. (This may have been a text for a radio introduction).

Later, on another page, the composer has typed:

> Annotations to Pastoral Concerto. The following quotations form the key to the Pastoral Concerto:
> ...O father of the stately peaks...
> ...Year by year
> The great sublime cantata of thy storms,
> Strikes through my spirit.   (Henry Kendall)
>
> a. The teams bogged down to the axle trees
> Or ploughing the sodden loam.   (Henry Lawson)

b. I love you, wind o' the Autumn, that came
From I know not where,...

(Will. H. Ogilvie)

c. ...Where the river runs those giant hills between;
I have seen full many horsemen since I first
commenced to roam...

(A.B.Paterson)

Whether this is another orchestral concerto or a genuine two piano piece is at this writing unclear. And there is also the question of the first movement. The date on the manuscript is 1922.

Concerto No.4 (192?) has some parts copied neatly and some not – there is clearly work to be done on this and other scores by this composer.

The Concerto by Alfred Hill (1936) is something of a Kapellmeister piece; it is revived now and then, principally to show a historic face, rather than for its own intrinsic worth. I have taught it to a few students and found that although well-made it is hardly memorable. The piano part is of medium difficulty, written by someone who could play the instrument but hardly at professional level. Alfred Hill is an important composer in Australia's early twentieth century history, but this is hardly a piece that would lift an audience today.

Miriam Hyde's two concerti are remarkable achievements for a young composer making a beginning in pre-World War II London; even more remarkable was the fact that she accomplished performances of the works in England with major orchestras and conductors with herself as the soloist. The works, written between 1932 and 1935, are, in retrospect, conventionally Rachmaninovian in most respects. Miriam even performed a very nineteenth century operation on the slow movements of both concerti: she made transcriptions of these movements for solo piano, inviting pianists to play these as separate pieces. They are effectively nostalgic and work well within solo concert programmes. Both the *Eb Minor Concerto* (No.1) and the *C# Minor Concerto* (No.2) were written close together in prewar London. The difficulties are those one would expect in a romantic concerto, although less taxing than the Rachmaninov model. Conventional though they might be, nevertheless the writing is most effective and the scoring serves to heighten the solo part. Both concerti are in the usual three movement form. There is also a shorter *Fantasy-Romantic* (1939) in a similar vein.

Eugene Goossens' *Phantasy Concerto Op.60* (1942) was written before he came to Australia, but it seems wrong not to write a few words about his huge influence on music in Australia by his dual appointment as Director of the State Conservatorium of Music and as conductor of the Sydney Symphony Orchestra.

As far as piano music in general in concerned, once again, all his piano music predates his arrival in this country. Some of the solo music crept into the repertoire, especially the easier pieces from *Kaleidoscope*, Op.18 (1918), a collection of 12 pieces. Most of his other solo music is far from easy and requires full pianism to present. I have in mind the *Concert Study* Op.10 (1915), *Two Studies* Op.39 (1923) and the slightly less difficult *4 Conceits* Op.20 (1917) and *Nature Poems* Op.25 (1919) as well as the short *Hommage a Debussy* Op.28 (1920). Whether one can claim it as in any sense 'Australian' is dubious, but it would be nice to feel that we at least have part-ownership of this great musician.

It is thanks to Goossens that the Arthur Benjamin *Concerto quasi una Fantasia* (1949) was written. The composer describes the work as:

> a piece d'occasion, the occasion being when I was invited to Australia in 1950 by the Australian Broadcasting Commission to celebrate my fiftieth year of public appearances as pianist, having started in Brisbane at a ridiculously young age. I played it under Sir Eugene Goossens eight times in the different big Australian cities... Incidentally, my Australian appearances were my swansong as a pianist. (Composer files, Australian Music Centre).

The work, in keeping with its title, fluctuates in mood even within its three movement format. Thus, the first movement progression is *Con fuoco - Molto Meno Mosso - Andante tranquillo - Adagio – Largamente.* The second is a scherzo *Fantastico e presto ma non troppo,* whilst the Finale is a Passacaglia, *Allegro Moderato – Andante appassionato – Largamente – Allegro.*

Benjamin also wrote (1927) a Concertino. Whereas the longer and ostensibl;y more serious Concerto is˙ in the nature of an unashamed showpiece for the soloist, the Concertino may well turn out to be a more interesting and valuable work. It was composed at a time when composers were exploring the possible relationship with jazz and popular music, and it resulted in such works as the Ravel Concerto and the Lambert *The Rio Grande.* Benjamin, in his Concertino made an attempt to explore the world of rhythmic counterpoint.

Moneta Eagles composed two works for piano and orchestra. The shorter of the two, *Autumn Rhapsody*, with a slightly reduced orchestra, is in one movement and in a quasi popular vein, the genre of concerti that used to appear in films, and which gave birth to works like the *Warsaw Concerto* and the *Cornish Rhapsody.* It only lasts about five minutes. There is no date on the ms, but my guess is that it was written for the composer herself to play. The larger work is *Diversions On a Hungarian Folksong* (1951), from her days at the Sydney Conservatorium and working with Eugene Goossens, a role model and inspiration for many an Australian composer. Moneta Eagles writes on the score:

A set of variations on a Hungarian folksong, beginning with an introduction based upon a fragment of the main theme, which is announced shortly afterwards and is then followed by three clearly defined groups of variations, different in character, corresponding to the three movements of the classical concerto, ending with a short cadenza for the soloist, followed by a final statement of the theme as a coda.

We know that Moneta played the piece herself in 1954. The scoring is for double wind and the normal complement of orchestral forces. The work lasts for seventeen minutes. The writing is very similar to the *Passacaglia* for solo piano. In the score, the variations are not numbered. The work, like so much from that period, is still in manuscript. The composer prepared a reduction for two pianos.

A student work from the distinguished composer David Lumsdaine, a Concerto written in 1950 should be noted here. It is a long way from the composer's mature style, but does show an early command of orchestration and a clear sense of structure. It contains a double fugue. This piece, now in the Symphony Australia Collection at the National Library, has only survived because the Sydney Symphony Orchestra, despite repeated entreaties from the young composer, never bothered returning his score.

Just as David Lumsdaine is an Australian expatriate, so Peggy Glanville-Hicks is often described in reference books as American. The Glanville-Hicks *Etruscan Concerto* is a short, quarter hour work with a lean chamber orchestra behind the soloist. She wrote it for the Florentine pianist Carlo Bussotti, who premiered it with Carlos Surinach at the Metropolitan Museum of Art (New York) in 1956. The work was inspired by the Etruscan tombs of Tarquinia, and so each of the movements is inscribed with a quotation from D.H.Lawrence's *Etruscan Places*. Glanville-Hicks always did have a penchant for the exotic and the ancient, and so much of her music, whilst perhaps exhibiting some of the outward traits of neoclassicism, has retained a freshness and directness stemming more from that other aspect of her art. She in fact says, in an article called "Music: How it Works" (Vogue, March 1,1966) that the last phase of modernism in the twentieth century "will be concerned with bringing together the assets of East and West" and declares that there is much future discovery to be made in the ancient and pure scales. This fascination with the archaic is present in the *Etruscan Concerto* and is also manifest in assymetric rhythms, which were a favourite of Peggy's. Incidentally, Glanville-Hicks only wrote one work for solo piano, a *Pastoral* and we mention it here in passing. The manuscript says Vienna, October 1936. This is an ingratiating little piece in A minor, with hardly a black note in sight. Lasting a mere two pages, this moderate difficulty little piece is awaiting inclusion in some anthology.

A work with some connections to the Glanville Hicks by reason of inspiration from Greek mythology, literary allusion and cleanliness of writing must be the

Mary Mageau concerto *The Furies* (1995). The movement names have some kind of hidden programme: Alecto, Tisiphone, Megaera. The subject matter must be very tempting for a woman composer! Mageau wrotes:

> The Furies (Erinnyes). In Greek legend the furies were the three daughters of Mother Eartth who lived in the underworld. They personified humanity's developing conscience and were powerful divinities who ruthlessly pursued all evildoers.

There are two works by Frank Hutchens: the *Concerto for Piano and Strings* (1950) and the *Concerto* (n.d.) (sometimes listed as *Concerto Symphonique*). I have sometimes used the 1950 work as a first concerto for students: it is relatively easy to perform and the ensemble is not too strenuos. Both works are in that late-romantic, laid back atmosphere so typical of Frank's music. There is no *Sturm und Drang* about these pieces, or if there is, it is wearing a velvet dressing gown! The Concerto is especially grateful to play and immediately likeable. Both works are still in manuscript and in need of typesetting.

James Penberthy wrote four piano concerti, which occupy a special place in his wide-ranging output for orchestra, spanning his entire career. The third Concerto – written for me in 1974 – could be Australia's first score using the computer as a compositional tool. James was very proud of the fact, especially as the computer was also allowed to make decisions about scoring; I found this last a little difficult to understand, as the computer sometimes pitted the solo piano against massed brass and the pianist has to struggle to be heard. I broke a number of strings during the recording! The score of this work had originally a subtitle "Beyond the Universe No.2"- this was subsequently crossed out. Jim's fourth and final concerto was written for Beryl Sedivka in 1982 and so far I believe she is the only pianist to have played it. The work is still in manuscript but has been recorded by Beryl. I don't think he used a computer for scoring this time! There were no balance problems in preparation. The craggy piano part has many tonal references and lies well under the hands, although the tonality is not always of the obvious kind. Jim was always rather secretive about his first two concerti, saying they were 'no good' and 'music for sissies'. The first concerto was composed in 1949. I wouldn't know about 'sissies'; it is certainly an advance over the Alfred Hill concerto which preceded it, moving from a Kapellmeister to a professional level, from something sometimes smacking of amateurism to assuredness. Penberthy might have used the first movement in one of his balletic productions. At the end of the first movement, there is a scribble in the score which says 'lights out'. The second movement is heartfelt, with a reiterated F for much of the movement. *Concerto No.2* (1954) has a subtitle "Aboriginal" on the score. The chant-like thematic ideas of the first movement might explain the reason for the subtitle, or perhaps the trombones asked to sing 'oo-yah oo-yah" into their instruments; but both early concertos now need reviving and reappraising.

Raymond Hanson's Concerto (1972) is full of merit and hasn't received the recognition it deserves. Ray was unlucky in that he produced this work at the height of the avant-garde movement in Australia and so it was seen as backward looking. Now, it doesn't seem to matter very much at all which school of theory he was an adherent to. It is a no-nonsense, strong concerto which needs publishing and disseminating.

Explorations (1970) by Nigel Butterley is not a concerto at all, just a piece in which the piano filigree is more prominent than that of other instruments. There is a long solo passage near the start but it is not all soloistic and is a very long inverted pedal on C#-Db after which the piece really gets going. *Explorations* reminded me somewhat of the Stephen Cronin Concerto (1989). Cronin also uses the piano as an important, but integrated member of the orchestra. The passage work in this piece tends to be unvarying, however, and the overdone arpeggios with fourths and fifths, in patterns of threes, is overused; but Cronin is an expert orchestrator and milks the combination of piano and other instruments for all he's worth.

The concerto by Donald Hollier was a casualty of rules and regulations. I was with him during the gestation of this work and during his preparation of the solo part. The concerto written in the 1970s, in a very theatrical manner, divides the orchestra into various groups seated in clumps on the platform, with the piano acting as a kind of arbitrator between these groups. As well, Hollier had conceived the idea of players having small percussion instruments attached to their music stands, and occasionally they would activate these small bells with bows or by hand, thus allowing a massed sound of percussion. All this came adrift as soon as the first rehearsal commenced. The players – or their union representative- demanded 'doubling money' for playing an extra instrument, which meant effectively that the cost of mounting the *Concerto* instantly also doubled, making it prohibitively expensive. The performance and recording were cancelled on the spot and the work was never done.

The prolific Felix Werder has of course produced more than one piano concerto. I have before me the score of the second (1975), dedicated to Keith Humble and which I have heard Keith play. Like all of Werder's music, this is aggressively post-Schoenbergian in sound, with the solo part bristling with *fioratura* and partially written out gestures, often frantically working around a beat, not on it. The piano part is rarely on its own and is integrated into a colourful orchestra. In the right hands and with a sympathetic conductor, this piece can create a powerful impression. It is in one movement.

Malcolm Williamson, contrariwise, never had a problem writing piano concerti. There are four of them, plus one for piano and strings. Today, their bustling, busy exterior seems to have dated them badly, and the kind of industrial neo-classicism that drives them sounds tired and jaded, even if occasionally, the composer inserts a 3/8 bar into a 2/4, or something similar, to break up the jaunty rhythms. Many Australian composers don't even regard these pieces as part of the Australian continuum – that may be harsh, but does reflect Malcolm's relationship with his native country.

Philip Bracanin's *Concerto* from 1980 is for a chamber sized orchestra and is, not unexpectedly, a neo-classic piece with the piano used in clean, linear fashion, with neat, clear-cut rhythms driving the piece. The technical demands are moderate.

For the sake of completeness, I list here the Michael Smetanin concerto *Zyerkala* (1981), which is for amplified piano and also requires amplification for other instruments. I am not certain that this fits with the general tenor of the works here, so will not comment on the piece. There is no date on the score.

Elsewhere, I have already commented on the dense and serious style of Jim Franklin, so it was doubly interesting to discover a concerto (1982) by the same composer, with the same detailed craft exhibited in the solo music. The composer has supplied the following note with his score:

> The title of this work, *Across the Swan's Riding*, is a translation of the first two feet of line 200 of the old English epic poem *Beowulf: ofer swan-rade*. It was selected as a title not because of any programmatic significance, but because the image it suggests, of a swan in flight over a landscape, encapsulates the relationship within the work between piano and orchestra. The piano is, of necessity, a dynamic instrument: because of its inherent pattern of attack and decay, movement must be maintained in its part in order that its sound not die away completely. The orchestra, on the other hand, is capable of infinite sustaining of notes without audible new attacks, and thus can produce static textures impossible to realize on piano. These contrasting natures are juxtaposed in the work; as a result the piano part, in its largely continuous motion, assumes the role of the swan, flying over the comparatively static orchestral background or landscape.

> The two movements of the work embody two processes derived from this juxtaposition. In the first, the piano and pianistic writing emerge from, and gradually pervade, the orchestra and orchestral writing; in the second, the piano is reabsorbed into the orchestra, becoming unified with it at the close of the piece. These processes take place within a structure based on internal symmetries: a continuous chain of subdivision into halves and pairs occurs at all levels of the work, from the large-scale division into two equal movements to the divisions within single subsections. These symmetries are articulated by the disposition of the various musical ideas. In this respect, the opening texture of the work is of particular note: it recurs, in varied form, at the

end of each movement, thus creating a large scale mirror symmetry around a central axis.

Such a structure could easily be made totally static, bound by its internal relationships. In this work, however, an attempt has been made to avoid such staticism, despite the nature of the orchestral writing: all relationships and divisions are subservient to the fundamental processes of emergence and re-absorption of the piano part. These processes are strongly directional, and serve to give the symmetrical architecture a continuous sense of movement and progression.

Roger Smalley's concerto is a perfect example of what can occur when a virtuoso pianist and an outstanding composer are the one person. The *Concerto* (1985) has won international acclaim and there has been much written about it, which I do not propose to recapitulate here. With absolutely no concession to originality or individuality, Roger has produced a work that is at the same brilliantly idiomatic and original, with powerful orchestration requiring much divisi in the strings, but no extravagant orchestral demands. The craft of the piece does not demand huge rehearsal investment either, so the work scores highly on all fronts. Undoubtedly a landmark!

Eric Gross' *Concerto* Op. 135 (1983) is on a large scale and an unashamedly romantic work. The composer, always a pragmatist, believes that audiences have a certain expectation of a 'concerto' and he tried to satisfy rather than challenge that expectation, so the piece is big on melody and Gross strives to make his materials memorable. Also, for similar reasons, pyrotechnics are justifiable. This Concerto therefore does not perhaps typify Australian music of the period, but on the other hand may be symptomatic of a return to romanticism, perhaps of a new kind. Eric has been a pianist all his life and easily identifies with the solo part.

The *Piano Concerto No.1* by Colin Brumby was written in 1984. I found it rather conventional and not as interesting as his earlier music, but it is a full-blooded quasi-romantic concerto.

In the same year, Dulcie Holland composed her *Concertino for Piano and Strings*. The composer herself writes of it:

> A light-weight piece to give pleasure to players and listeners, it poses no real problems in its three movements, the first of which is outgoing, the second meditative, the third bouncy.

The work lasts about twenty minutes, but does not approach some of the issues addressed in the composer's fine *Sonata*.

There is another Australian concertino of similar length, this one for piano and full orchestra, by Felix Gethen (1957). This one, though musically light, is more difficult than Dulcie Holland's; the piano part more ruggedly aggressive, requiring good double octaves and double thirds. Probably a better companion piece for the Dulcie Holland is the Margaret Brandman *Lyric Fantasy* (1991), a modally inclined work, with a mood complementary to that of Dulcie's *Concertino*.

Sculthorpe 's concerto (1982) sounds like travelogue for a Japanese tourist promotion. There is lack of drama and little sense of the role of the soloist. The piano acts as a surrogate koto, tinkling away on the quasi-Japanese tunes. The writing tends to be of one particular type (alternating hands, mainly single notes) and the piece is all over quickly.

The concerto by Ross Edwards (1984) received terrible press and reading through the score one can see why. The piano part seems to consist of unceasing and repetitive arpeggios for the most part, of the tonic/dominant variety. If composers such as Edwards and Sculthorpe shy away from addressing the inherent drama of placing a large instrument in front of the orchestra, then the piano needs to be somewhere within the orchestra, and the word 'concerto' should be used with some caution, otherwise disappointments all-round are bound to happen.

The concerto by Brenton Broadstock (1987) is to a large extent based on an earlier piano piece. Why? Was the composer stuck with writer's block? I gave the premiere performance of the work and some of my fellow-pianists confirmed my feeling that it was a short piece still awaiting development, like a Prelude to a Concerto that never happened in the end. Perhaps the whole idea of a piece for piano and orchestra sat uncomfortably with the composer?

Moya Henderson's work called *Celebration 40,000* (1987), meant to mark the long years that Aboriginals have lived in this land is not perhaps even meant to be a concerto. The piano writing is quite tame and the raw materials not really memorable. The critics had a field day with it. Given the amount of percussion in Moya's orchestra, I was expecting something quite spectacular, but this did not eventuate; the rhythmic elements of the work are, too, quite static.

Graeme Koehne's *Capriccio for piano and string orchestra* (1987) is written in a light rhythmic style. Like most of Graeme's work, it presents few problems for the listener and is invariably highly coloured and effective. The model for this work was, to my ears, early twentieth century French music by people such as Poulenc and possibly Milhaud.

An even earlier model is used in David Morgan's *Norwegian Fantasy* (1997); Morgan used his considerable technical skills to complete a work after sketches made by Edvard Grieg in 1883 for a second piano concerto.

Another light piece is the Michael Easton *Concerto on Australian Themes* (1996), with chamber orchestra, which uses very well-known folk-songs as the basis for each of the three movements; the role of the piano is not just to play the tunes, but also to embellish and play dazzling figurations around the melodies. The orchestral writing is very straightforward and the whole work is in the nature of a divertimento.

In total contrast, Gerard Brophy's *Le Réveil de L'ange* (1987) is not going to get many performances as few pianists will have the time and energy to learn a piano part written often on four staves, with the most complex rhythmic layering occuring, asking for combinations of things such as sevens with sixes (when there are four layers, these kind of combinations may well occur in one hand), but with the parts themselves containing involved internal problems. It's classic maximalism, putting the performer off as soon as the page is opened.

The David Joseph *Chamber Concerto for Piano and Strings* (1991) lies somewhere in between, that is, it is not a light piece, but neither is it prohibitively difficult. Rather, the composer has produced a serious work for the combination. The strings are treated very fully and they and the piano work together to define the many time changes and give point to them. As a consequence, much of the piano writing is detached or staccato; even the phrases are short and *ritmico*. Not until the second movement (*Poem of Love*) does the composer allow himself some relaxation from the nervous tension of the first. Here the piano comments and decorates, with arabesques, what is happening in the strings. The conclusion is not what one would normally expect at all, but a *Meditation* in which the piano plays almost exclusively slow crotchet chords against the strings' more elaborate material. His *Concerto* (1996) is a larger piece with full orchestra running for about twenty-five minutes and asking for four percussion players. The full orchestra is now treated like the strings were before, that is, the scoring is very full and colourful, with the piano adding to the effect with passage work. The keyboard part, though busy and ever-present, lies beautifully under the hands. Somewhere about page 100 of the full score, the piano finally breaks free of the orchestra and plays a cadenza, but it still more or less continues the perpetual cascade of semi-quavers. The thick writing and doubling reminded me of Messiaen. As to whether this concerto is overscored or not and whether the piano writing is too much of one kind or not will eventually be resolved by more hearings.

Mark Isaacs, a fine jazz pianist, has written two works for piano and orchestra, both of which require the soloist to improvise to a greater or lesser extent. *Moving Pictures* (1982) and *Litany* (1994) are both accomplished works, with the earlier piece indulging in more time changes than the latter. The solo parts are not easy, especially in the earlier piece, and the pianist needs to feel comfortable with improvisation and following jazz chart notation.

Ann Carr-Boyd's *Concerto* (1991) is, like most of her music, fairly traditional in character and idiom, but is unusual in that the composer has here attempted integration into a Western genre of Aboriginal material. The listener is reminded of the origin of much of the thematic material by using clap-sticks and imitating the didgeridu calls on the bass clarinet, as well as on the bassoon and cello. She writes:

> The work is in three movements. The first movement contains three separate themes which are eventually brought together in triple counterpoint. There is a second subject which is more lyrical in style. The second, slow movement, is based on one of the Aboriginal themes in the third movement... The third movement echoes some of the opening material and commences with a march which then gives way to a tutti final section. The two Aboriginal themes heard here were given to Carr-Boyd's father, composer Norbert Wentzel, by a fellow musician who returned from Darwin after World War II. Their Westernized character suggests some of the imported music which the Aboriginal people may have heard at this time. The score contains a part for a second, orchestral, piano. The tone of this piano has been altered by use of different tuning, and masking tape on the strings.

The Andrew Ford Concerto *Imaginings* (1991) has suffered a similar fate to Hollier, except that he didn't even make it as far as a rehearsal. Having sent the score in, and despite various attempts to elicit a response, he was simply ignored and so in the end, as one does, he gave up. This is a great pity; I have studied the score and found it to be an intricate and structurally fascinating work. Andrew has incorporated a second piano into the orchestral texture which acts as a kind of commentary on the solo line. There is an electronic organ amongst the big line-up, and a large percussion section. The work would require a good allocation of rehearsal time, something which our orchestras don't seem to believe in any more.

Don Kay's *Concerto for Piano and Orchestra* (1992) was written for Beryl Sedivka. It is in three movements, titled *Con Fierezza, Con Desiderio* and *Vivace* and is for double wind and brass. Like all of Don's music, it is lyrical rather than barnstorming, linear rather than chordal, meditative rather than neurotic.

Carl Vine has provided a traditional concerto working with established forms and gestures (1997). He is an expert orchestrator and the *Concerto* is full of colour and rhythmic drive. The writing might not be very original, but it is aimed at maximum immediate effect. Much of it has a drum-machine beat feel about it, redolent of disco and flashing lights. Carl Vine is a fine pianist himself, so he knows very well what works and what does not, and has drawn on his knowledge of the traditional repertoire to put this piece in three movements together.

There are three works by Elena Kats-Chernin. The first of these was a graduation work, for which she performed the solo part; unfortunately due to the physical enormity of the score we were unable to look at it! The second, *Lamento the Gestures for piano and full orchestra* has been withdrawn by the composer as a performance piece. It is a score not representative of her current work and directions but looks fascinating and one hopes can be revived, but of course not as long as the composer is actively prohibiting this from occuring!. The piano part is essentially colouristic and the large orchestra treated with great panache. The third and most recent is *Displaced Dances, Concerto for piano and orchestra* (2000). The work is a set of dances and is in reality a suite, like the Milhaud *Carnaval d'Aix*. The titles of the Dances:

1. Spin the Wheel
2. Dance of the Moral Finger
3. Dance of the Reduced Material
4. Dance of the Missing Links
5. Dance of the Skyscrapers
6. Dance of Naive Thoughts
7. Dance of Smoothing the Edges (piano solo)
8. Gigue (Counntry Dance)
9. Dance in Seven-Four
10. Chthonic Melody
11. Dance of the Intervals
12. Dance of the Octaves

The piano is not necessarily dominant and tends to come forward and then retreat; the movements are all almost balletic but there is usually a twist, like something familiar but seen in a different light, or somehow warped, giving an air of burlesque to this strongly tonal music.

There is, by all accounts, an exciting *Concerto* by Nigel Westlake (2000), but unfortunately, I didn't get to see or hear the score. The composer describes the piece as very much a soloist's work, with plenty of opportunity for display.

It is unfortunate that composer/pianists such as Humble, Meale and Banks did not produce music for piano and orchestra – no doubt something interesting would have occured. Meale certainly had the beginnings of a Concerto down on paper but it did not go beyond that. Roy Agnew, as mentioned before, spoke in interviews about a Piano Concerto, but there was nothing among his manuscripts; perhaps it was lost together with some other missing pieces; or else, it existed in his mind only and did not make the transition to paper.

So, this is the bird's-eye-view of the Australian Piano Concerto.

In summary, the ABC has a lot to answer for in this context. There were, earlier in the century, at least some brief forays into performances of Australian concerti so that some works, albeit briefly, were at least heard. I now have in mind works such as the Alfred Hill and the Moneta Eagles. Ghettoised they may have been, presented almost apologetically they may have been, but at least they were performed. From the ultra-conservative period which lasted until approximately 1960, there was a rapid transition to a situation where new Australian music suddenly became fashionable for a time, and so there was a brief period when new concerti were commissioned and performed with many subsequently recorded. Alas, this did not last for any historically significant period. The old conservatism was still there lurking and biding its time. Financial imperatives began to creep into concert giving, with concerns about filling seats in the concert halls. And so, a slow but probably inevitable decline in adventurous programme-making, and less and less Australian content. By the time the century drew to a close, young composers were told that ten-minute works that did not require much rehearsal were the go. Easy pieces: easy to rehearse, easy on the ear, easy on the budget. Hardly a blueprint for evolution and brave ventures into unknown territory. Any idealistic or cultural initiatives were sacrificed on the altar of populism, and so we returned to an almost anachronistic 19th Century model of concert giving, with the old war-horses of concerti and symphonies, and sometimes the token short piece by an Australian composer. These orchestras are still drawing government monies, but increasingly they seem to be relying on corporate sponsorship. In this country, sponsoring new music is hardly an every-day activity; if it were sport – that would be another matter! Current policy of playing only short pieces represents the worst kind of tokenism and lipservice.

So the century and the genre of the piano concerto mirror the changes that occurred during the hundred years and in a very real way reflect the changing government funding policies. This accounts for the overall dearth of fine works as well as the shift towards soft-edged, almost commercial music. The picture also reveals that the concerti by non-performing composers are the least interesting of what is there, something that surely is not a surprise to anybody. There isn't room to do little more than list the works, with a few asides. Perhaps the subject matter deserves a separate study.

In the context of music everywhere, are we finally witnessing the demise of the piano virtuoso/composer and therefore the dying embers of the Piano Concerto, at least as an exciting dramatic and innovative vehicle? Personally, I hope not, but the evidence is there for all to see. Sometimes there is a glimmer of light. For instance recently I examined a student folio by a young composer named Ian Cresswell, which included a structurally innovative as well as keyboard challenging Concerto. Perhaps it is not quite scrap-heap time.

Conclusion

The Anti-composer in Australian Society:
Kitsch Is Alive and Well.

Art is not a pastime, but a priesthood. (Jean Cocteau)

Over twenty years ago, in the July issue of 24 HOURS, I contributed an article entitled "The composer and the anti-composer". The piece was designed to expose some of the then current charlatanistic practices in fashionable compositional enclaves. As such, the article caused widespread comment and reaction, some of it furious, in many musical circles. I remembered the article when commencing work on this book, and decided to revisit the topic and view it from the perspective of the whole of the twentieth century, particularly as it now appears obvious, that the phenomenon of the anti-composer is still with us and indeed has always been present in Australian society. I intend to quote from the original article and follow it with pertinent comment. The philosophical premise for the notion of the presence of the anti-composer is quite obvious.

> With the rise of increased opportunities for the Australian composer in the 1960s, two types emerged: the real composer, fulfilling the classical definition of the word, i.e. 'one who composes music'; and the anti-composer: this specimen I will gradually define as we proceed.

These dualistically opposed types were ever-present, and it is now clear that even early in the twentieth century they were already present, even though the opportunities were minimal and one had to be a true idealist as a composer to continue to produce. The so-called 'opportunities' that emerged in the 1960s were, historically, of a relatively short duration and were effectively whittled away towards the end of the century. A paradoxical situation now exists: the battles that were fought in the 60s to establish the Australian composer as a viable presence on the concert stage are now taken for granted and Australian music appears cheek to cheek with mainstream repertoire; however, much of the financial support necessary for this to occur has been eroded by philistine governments and conservative organizations. The size of the cake has shrunk and the surviving support is poured more and more towards conservative, artistically safe or politically correct endeavours.

> The great weakness of organizations assisting composers is that firstly, the make-up of its constituent committees includes a large proportion of non-professionals. These can be well-intentioned amateurs, not so well intentioned social climbers, dilettantes, people on the committee as a penalty for being a "prominent citizen", and of course, the political appointee. Secondly, the committees operate on the curious principle that democracy and the arts are compatible. In the arts, people are demonstrably not equal! Thirdly, the committees avoid putting themselves into any sort of censorious situation, whether artistic or even just of policing return of results in exchange for grants.

How little has changed! There was almost no assistance of any kind to composers in the first part of the twentieth century; towards the end, we have in some ways reverted back to the bad old days.

> On the surface, such policies seem perfectly fair, if questionable. In practice it allows the anti-composer not just an in, but a positive advantage. Firstly, the element of the non-professional is perfect for the anti-composer: he knows just who these people are, where to meet them, how to get them on side. Secondly, the established anti-composer gradually puts himself in the position of being able to push through assistance for other anti-composers and hangers-on, by dint of knowing the correct people, and being able to abuse the democratic principle. A real old-boys' network is by now established. Thirdly, and most importantly, the anti-composer can now not only receive fat grants and three-year holidays, but also do no work and deliver no goods in return; for once the initial application is approved and the moneys paid out, the Boards and committees do not involve themselves any further.

Some of these comments are no longer relevant, although there was certainly abuse of the kind described for a period. There was and, curiously, still is, some perceived glamour is being described as a composer. Where such an idea comes from, who knows: it is totally erroneous. One anti-composer once said to me rather pompously that "one doesn't have to write a note of music to be called a composer". Another pointed out to me that sitting under a tree and thinking about a piece was enough to justify a grant. I'm glad that my plumber doesn't operate on the same principle. Some things have improved – there is probably more safeguard in place now against unprofessional behavior; but then, there is precious little commissioning going on in comparison to the 70s.

> The anti-composer realizes early in his career that, in the absence of real compositional talent, he must concentrate on pleasing. And so please he does. Whereas the composer is a lone wolf, working desperately to catch and cage that elusive vision inside his head, the anti-composer socializes like mad; he makes sure that he is seen at all the right events, not a mean feat; and with the right people. In time, the socializing attracts a group of pretentious people round him: other anti-composers, who feel safe in his company, and lend him support; trendies of one kind or another, including trendy composers, a step down in the ladder of charlatanry, since trendy composers don't even possess a modicum of technique, although they may have the same potentialities of talent that the anti-composer has; various other camp-followers; art-loving socialites, a very important part of the entourage, since these same socialites are often sitting on vital committees that will be awarding the anti-composer grants and recognitions.

I suppose I should have pointed out that politicians and ex-politicians are a very handy kind of person to cultivate, as they often combine the characteristics of financial power, socialite status and dilettante rolled in to one. As for the business of pleasing – that has accelerated of late and become an art-form in itself. Thanks to the rise and rise of minimalism as well as the admission of popular music into art-music, the possibility of pleasing has risen hugely and the possibility of writing non-confrontational, anti-intellectual, non-threatening 'art music' has increased exponentially thereby.

> The desire to please helps the anti-composer's career even among so-called professionals. Performers, having to pay lip-service to the local composer, prefer a simple score with no problems; so do audiences with lazy ears, particularly if they have been correctly buttered up, for they then suffer under the illusion that they have just heard a modern piece, and emerged unscathed. Conductors who are told to play some Australian content, and therefore do so under sufferance, also love the anti-composer: he takes away so little rehearsal time, leaving more for that sadly under-rehearsed Brahms symphony. Some critics, too, fall for the anti-composer's charm and lack of challenge, the rationale

being that the composers are being difficult and obscure whilst the anti-composer is lucid and direct. Critics have even been known to write long essays and even books about anti-composers.

There always were a tiny group of professional performers who played new Australian music, now and a hundred years ago. However, it is very clear, surveying the music and history of the past century, that the above comment holds sway and performers perfectly willing to spend hundreds of hours to perfect a Liszt Rhapsody might still prefer an Australian work that they can sight-read. Rehearsal time is even more expensive today and so the instant coffee fix of a score (just add a cup of tepid time) that can be assembled quickly is too seductive to ignore.

> The composer is caught in his own trap: it is not in his nature to be pleasing. On the contrary, he is only too often challenging, exploratory, prickly and just plain difficult to all counts. His pieces cause dreadful problems: the conductors have to do their homework, the audiences have to concentrate. It's too bad.

The whole past century of Australian music is now clear in that, over the whole hundred years, there have been at least three clear streams: true art-music-inquisitive, exploratory, challenging, embodying what used to be called modernism; then there was always light music, parlor-music, dance music, unashamedly populist; and finally there was always what I now call the soft under-belly of Australian music, that lies somewhere in between, and allows the anti-composer an entry. This is not to say that all music of this sort is anti-music written by anti-composers; but some of it certainly is, and I will have more to say about it at the end of this chapter.

> Yet another characteristic of the anti-composer is his inability to sustain compositional structures beyond a certain miniaturistic limit, due to limitations both intellectual and compositional. The few examples that we have of attempts by the anti-composer to produce large scale works are proof of this: the works not only constitute failures, but are further proof, if such were needed, of how the pieces are composed of tiny bits glued together - a procedure that one can almost get away with in a smaller piece, if the bits in themselves are attractive enough, but which, in a large scale work, spell disaster.

This is not only patently true (and there are plenty of examples), but also highlights the possibility of writing small pieces and giving them grandiose titles to achieve an illusion of monumentality. In itself, mosaic structure is an interesting notion, and some of what I said above was perhaps a little fascistic; neither do I have any entrenched bias against miniatures, in themselves an important art-form.

> The anti-composer is thus reduced to a number of alternatives, all, in the short view, viable: (i) make a catalogue of pretty sounds, making certain that they are also contemporary in use; (ii) pinch a rhythm or a melody from the folk culture of another country, making sure it is musically, trendily and politically correct; (iii) give the piece a title that will appeal to the lowest level of parochial, nationalistic element of his future audience. Scramble well. Serve up. Again. And again.

The range of pretty sounds has increased lately thanks to the New Age mentality; prior to 1950 it constituted a soft-edged excursion into impressionism with lots of added-sixth chords and the like, much pedal, pentatonic and modal melodies. Much of this has now returned in the post-modern age and is adding to the available mush of the vocabulary. What was old-fashioned is now new-fashioned. The business of other cultures is an on-going issue. Earlier in the century, most 'other culture' came from Maori and Aboriginal sources, apart from the use of folk material from the British Isles. The Aboriginal material was harmonized in a Western way for a long time, and forced into Western bar-lengths. Title references to Aboriginals were at first racist, then patronizing. Later they became trendy to use, although in recent times there has been a question as to whether even the use of place-names and personal names is offensive to Aboriginal culture. As for other countries, with the constant shifting of political currents, what was trendy/correct at one time suddenly becomes an embarrassment at another time. Particularly, the extraordinarily revelatory discovery that we are close to Asia is fraught with danger for the anti-composer how is one to know which are the good guys and likely to remain so?

> The anti-composer, too, because of his aural and compositional defects, tends to write slow music, since he can't cope with the technical demands of music more complex or faster moving. Besides, it's a whole lot simpler, takes less time to write, and best of all, more time to perform. Since large structures are beyond him, the anti-composer by instinct will attempt to stretch his flimsy music as far as it will go by slowing down the unfolding process.

Slow, minimalist, feel-good New Age music is certainly still in; the slow tempo is also presented as deeply meditative and therefore profound in content; earlier in the century, a vast proliferation of soupy Nocturnes, Lullabies, Berceuses etc etc; dreamy pieces with some reference to water, islands, the sea almost engulfed us.

> One of the more impressive aspects of the anti-composer's activities is his highly geared public relations machinery: he spends considerable time, energy and money in keeping the machine well-oiled, the contacts well-greased, the right people supplied with constant data. The photographic detail of this machinery is also worth a mention in that the photos of the anti-composer are most specifically orchestrated;

> the anti-composer can never wear clothes like anyone else: the gear is always trendy.

PR has become even bigger business than ever and use of the www.anti-composer sites ubiquitous. Photographs are exploited by the anti-composer as a vehicle for carefully-posed propaganda as always. This whole field was in its infancy in earlier years as far as composers were concerned.

> The anti-composer is acutely aware of current political thought, and acts accordingly. This malleability allows him to write a work in one political climate, and dress it up with a programme referring to 'the yellow peril'; and then, some years later, to produce a new philosophy for the work, and declare it as 'Asian inspired'. The composer on the other hand, knows that disparate cultures cannot be mated under hot-house conditions, and certainly not by any phoney-baloney consisting of borrowing tunes, rhythms and pretty sounds. He knows that music is international; the time for nationalism, particularly opportunistic nationalism, is long past, and we should be suspicious of it. Eventually East will meet West; the composer in Australia knows his cultural heritage, and recognizes that it comes from the West, but his ears are open to the East, and in time some sort of synthesis will be achieved. But not by trendies, and not overnight.

Twenty years on, this is still an issue, since Australia is declared as a multi-cultural society and the idea of co-existence, if not direct mixing, is the official line. When Samuel Johnson declared that 'nationalism is the last refuge of a scoundrel' he was voicing an obvious truth even all that time ago. Heart-on-sleeve Nationalism was, in the good doctor's view, a smoke screen for something shady going on. In the case of the anti-composer it represents some kind of compensation for truly musical effort. After all, one can't go far wrong by declaring love for one's country, can one? Then it doesn't matter which party is in power, does it?

> The great and prominent composers of the past have nearly all been great and prominent performers: there were very, very few exceptions to this general rule, and the rule still applies, for very good and obvious reasons. And so, the composers of this country are real performers. The anti-composer is not; it's one of his really fatal flaws, he simply cannot do it, and has to therefore work all the harder in his non-musical areas. The actual doing of music is foreign to him, and during rehearsals of his works one can catch him at his very weakest; he not only does not know how to do it, but, by implication, is not too sure how his own score should sound; and so that studied casualness that serves him so well in his other activities is now turned on for the rehearsals. But hopefully, there is little or no problem in rehearsal, since his scores are basically simple. Then, in the end, everybody is

> happy, the players for a thankfully simple score, the anti-composer, for
> no controversy, and the audience, for no aural problems posed.

It has become very clear, in this study of Australia's piano music, how close the
above correlation is and how almost all the successful piano music was written
by performing pianists. The corollary is not necessarily true, naturally enough!

> The real composer is anything but casual about rehearsals: for him this
> is the absolute moment of truth; so he often antagonizes the players
> with his pesty insistence on accuracy, exhausts and worries himself in
> the process, and quite often poses very real problems for the listener.
> No one is happy.

This problem has lately been exacerbated by the real inroads into rehearsal time,
so there is a sense of pieces being thrown together in defiance of the clock,
quickly and not always accurately.

> Finally, there is that quality in music called 'content'; no amount of
> verbal paraphernalia, programmatic description, evocative titles, pretty
> sounds, exotic instruments and folktunes, can in the end fill the awful
> void left by the anti-composer. Do not be deceived: music which is
> digestible at one hearing, is often the kind that should have no other;
> the anti-composer is dangerously close to producing the glitter of pop
> music, which is both instant and disposable. As for the slow tempi, the
> long silences, supposedly derived from some exotic source: they are
> there because the anti-composer has little to say.

Ironically, that surface glitter of pop and rock alluded to above is now trendy
and kosher for the so-called art composer. My continued contention is that fine
works of art have layers of meaning not unlike onion skins; and no sooner is one
layer peeled back, when there is yet another one underneath; and so each
generation hears the works in a new way. Superficial works only have the one or
two layers: the rest is hot air.

> The real composers in Australia, and there are very few of them,
> know. They know and respect one another, they know who they are,
> and they know the anti-composer. With the real composer and real
> musician, the anti-composer carries no weight. In terms of history, in
> the long term, there is absolutely no question as to the outcome of the
> struggle between the two. But remember that in human terms, this
> could be costly. Some composers cannot fight indefinitely: they are
> killed by neglect, they suffocate in a vacuum, they are depressed into
> silence by the spectacle of a society incapable of telling truth from
> lies, willing to take the easy way out to salve their conscience.

The exposed panorama of the twentieth century reveals the truth of this statement. The real composers, after a period of time, are now recognized and closely studied and admired. The anti-composers and other purveyors of soft-edged material, are recognized for what they are, rather than what they were in their heyday.

Peter Warlock, fighting the good fight in 1918, wrote in a letter:

> It is not the mere neglect or negation of art that is art's worst enemy: it is as Blake said ' a pretence of art' that destroys art. This is the monster we are out to slay – the perversion of the very function of art...It is when this true purpose is forgotten, when such things as these are done in the name of art, in the name of a spiritual principle of which they are themselves the embodied refutation that the supreme blasphemy takes place, that – relatively speaking – evil arises...

I suppose that ultimately, the comforting lesson learnt from the work carried out in the preparation of this book, is that there has always been and continues to be a serious and worthwhile thread of serious art music in this country; though quite often thin and frayed, it has nevertheless been continuous. The parallel threads of music impelled by trends and political correctness and cheap expediency have also always been there and continue. The difference is that in the harsh light of retrospectivity, the two become easily separable and the productions of the anticomposer begin to fade with time as they are exposed for what they truly represent; the music of the true composers, on the contrary come from the darkness of neglect into an ever more brilliant light.

Select Bibliography

The bibliography is not meant to be exhaustive. Composer files held at the Australian Music Centre have provided a major source of information. They contain newspaper clippings, programs, program notes and journal articles for all composers represented at the Centre. Similar biographical files held at the Newspaper Room at the National Library of Australia have been accessed. The Australian Music Centre website www.amcoz.com.au also provides short biographies for all represented composers and in many instances provides links to individual composers' websites. Space is not available to list all citations individually.

Books

Bainton, Helen. *Remembered on waking: Edgar L. Bainton.* Sydney : Currawong, 1960.

Bebbington, Warren. *The Oxford Companion to Australian Music.* Melbourne: Oxford University Press, 1997.

Broadstock, Brenton (ed.) *Aflame with Music: 100 years of music at the University of Melbourne.* Parkville, Vic.: Centre for Studies in Australian Music, University of Melbourne, 1996.

Broadstock, Brenton (ed.) *Sound ideas: Australian composers born since 1950, a guide to their music and ideas.* Sydney: Australian Music Centre, 1995.

Brown, Nicholas, Peter Campbell, Robin Holmes and Larry Sitksy (eds.). *One Hand on the Manuscript: Music in Australian Cultural History 1930-1960.* Canberra: Humanities Research Centre, Australian National University, 1994.

Bull, Inez.*The Immortal Ernest Hutcheson.* Elmira, N.Y.: Elmira Quality Printers, c1993.

Callaway, Frank and David Tunley (eds.). *Australian Composition in the Twentieth Century.* Melbourne: Oxford University Press, 1978.

Collins, Diane. *Sounds From the Stables.* Sydney: Allen & Unwin, 2001.

Covell, Roger. *Australia's Music: Themes of a New Society.* Melbourne: Sun Books, 1967.

Ford, Andrew. *Composer to Composer: Conversations about Contemporary Composers.* St. Leonards, NSW: Allen & Unwin, 1993.

Glennon, James. *Australian Music and Musicians.* Adelaide: Rigby, 1968.

Hyde, Miriam. *Complete Accord.* Sydney: Currency Press, 1991.

Jobson, Sandra. *Frank Hutchens: notes on an Australian musician.* Sydney: Wentworth Books, c1971.

McCredie, Andrew D. *Catalogue of 46 Australian composers and selected works.* Canberra: Canberra Advisory Board, Commonwealth Assistance to Australian Composers, 1969.

McCredie, Andrew D. *The composers and their work.* Canberra: Canberra Advisory Board, Commonwealth Assistance to Australian Composers, 1969.

McCredie, Andrew D. Musical Composition in Australia (including select bibliography and discography). Canberra : Canberra Advisory Board, Commonwealth Assistance to Australian Composers, 1969.

McCredie, Andrew D. (ed.) *From Colonel Light into the Footlights: the performing arts in South Australia from 1836 to the present.* Norwood, S. A: Pagel Books, 1988.

Macarthur, Sally (ed.). *The Composer Speaks 3: Proceedings of the New Music Australia Conference 1992.* Sydney: Sounds Australian, (1998)

Moreley, Isobel. *Australia Makes Music.* Melbourne: Longmans, Green and Co., 1948.

Murdoch, James. *Australia's contemporary composers*. South Melbourne [Vic.]: Macmillan Co. of Australia, 1972.

Orchard, W. Arundel. *Music in Australia*. Melbourne: Georgian House, 1952.

Orchard, W. Arundel. *The Distant View*. Sydney: Currawong Pub. Co., 1943.

Report of the Australian UNESCO Seminar For Composers. Adelaide: 1960.

Symons, David. *The Music of Margaret Sutherland*. Sydney: Currency Press, 1997.

Tate, Henry. *Australian Musical Resources*. Melbourne: Edward A. Vidler, 1924.

Tate, Henry. *Australian Musical Possibilities*. Melbourne: Edward A. Vidler, 1924.

Thomson, John Mansfield. *A Distant Music : the Life and Times of Alfred Hill, 1870-1960*. Auckland, New Zealand: Oxford University Press, c1980.

Thönell, Judy. *Poles Apart: The Music of Roger Smalley*. Nedlands, W.A.: CIRCME, School of Music, University of Western Australia in conjunction with Evos Music Ltd., 1994.

Waters, Thorold. *Much Besides Music: Memoirs of Thorold Waters*. Melbourne: Georgian House, 1951.

Werder, Felix. *More or Less Music*. Melbourne: Council of Adult Education, 1994.

Werder, Felix. *More than Music*. Melbourne: Council of Adult Education, 1991.

Wunderlich, Ernest. *All my yesterdays: a mosaic of music and manufacturing*. Sydney: Amgus & Robertson, 1945.

Articles

"Australia and Its Composers: The Modernism of Roy Agnew." *Australian Musical News* October (1931): 14-15.

"Australian Composers and Their Influences" *Sounds Australian*, No. 26 1990.

"Boyle's Concerto for Piano, a Work of High Value. A Sydney Boy's Success. Some extracts from 'Musical America'." *Australian Musical News*, December (1912): 149.

"Elena Kats Chernin: The Next Wave from Australia." *Boosey & Hawkes Newsletter* xxix no.3 October (2000).

"Festival of Perth: Australian Music to be Featured." *Canon* February (1957): 242.

"Lindley Evans," *Canon* 10/5 December (1956): 179.

"Men Who Write the Music: Australian Arthur Benjamin in Forefront," *Australian Musical News* June (1938): 17.

"Mirrie Hill." *APRA Journal* July (1971): 24.

"Only the Creation of Music can make us a Musical Nation say Arthur Benjamin," *Australian Musical News* October (1950): 34.

'Roy Agnew Makes "Opuses": Fantasie-Sonata and Others' *Australian Musical News* August (1927): 13.

"Roy Agnew Returns: A Twelve Months' Visit." *Australian Musical News* July (1928): 25-26.

"Three Australian Women Composers in Profile." *Sounds Australian* 21 Autumn (1988/1989): 18-20.

"Who Knows Our Music? A Perth Experiment." *Canon* 10/3 (1956): 79-80.

Alomes, Stephen. "Home and Away: The Expatriation of Australian Creators and Performers to Britain (1945-1990)." *Sounds Australian*, Spring 1990.

Biddy Allen, "Louis Lavater," *Meanjin* XII, (1953): 319-321.

Boyle, George. "Pianists Page: Piano –Playing Faults: The Most Common Kinds, Hints by Famous Australian." *Australian Musical News*, June (1927): 18-19.

Bradley, Jim. "The Mirrie Hill Story," *APRA Journal* (1979): 15-20.

Brophy, Gerard, "The Music of Gerard Brophy," *AMC News: Australian Music Centre Newletter* 5. September (1984): 5.

Covell, Roger. "Richard Meale: Intuitions of a Solitary Modernist." *Sounds Australian* 20 Summer (1988/89): 5 – 9.

Burke, Kelly. "Profile: Elena Kats-Chernin/Composer: Notable Success." *Sydney Morning Herald Spectrum* Saturday, December 19 (1998).

Elm, Wych. "Airing Our Views: Australian Compositions on the Air." *Canon* 2/2 (1948): 70-72.

Fogg, Anthony. "Keith Humble: a 60th birthday celebration." *2MBS-FM Programme Guide* September (1987): 18-19.

Ford, Andrew. "Gerard Brophy: Forbidden Colours, but Muted Tones," *ABC Radio 24 Hours* April (1993): 74-76.

Ford, Andrew. "Making an Impact: Roger Smalley," In *Composer to Composer: Conversations about Contemporary Composers*. St. Leonards, NSW: Allen & Unwin, 1993: 216-222.

Ford, Andrew. "Meale in Mullumbimby: Richard Meale: 30 – 36." In *Composer to Composer: Conversations about Contemporary Composers*. St. Leonards, NSW: Allen & Unwin, 1993.

Gifford, Helen. "'An Interview with Keith Humble." *Music Now* March (1970): 11.

Gifford, Helen.. "Raison d'etre." In *The Half-open door : sixteen modern Australian women look at professional life and achievement.* Edited by Patricia Grimshaw and Lynne Strahan. Sydney: Hale & Iremonger, c1982: 174-193.

Hall, Michael. "The Country Of My Childhood: Reflections on David Lumsdaine's Music," *Musical Times* July (1992): 329-331.

Hardie, Graham. "Raymond Hanson (1913-1976): Notes towards a Biography." In *Aflame With Music: 100 Years of Music at the Melbourne University.* Melbourne: Centre For Studies in Australian Music, University of Melbourne: 1996: 305-310.

Hince, Kenneth. "Musical Australia: A Retort." *Meanjin* XIII (1954): 300-303.

Holford, Franz. "Obituary - "Mirrie Hill (1889-1986)." *2MBS-FM Programme Guide* July (1986): 7

Hordern, Sam. "Richard Meale." *APRA Journal* December (1986): 6-8.

Hutchens, Frank. "Eagle's Eye View on Newer Music: Composers and Conductors in London." *Australian Musical News* August (1938).

Keogh, Max. "Raymond Hanson – Ten Years On." *2MBS FM Programme Guide* December (1986):14-16.

Keogh, Max. "Suffering the 'Sinding Syndrome': A Diagnosis of Arthur Benjamin (1893-1960)," *2MBS-FM Program Guide* September 1993: 10-12.

Lawson, Olive. "At 90 – a Hill alive with the sound of music." *ABC FM 24 Hours*, December (1982).

Lawson, Olive. "Mirrie Hill, OBE." *Stereo FM Radio* December 1982: 28-9.

McCallum, Peter. "David Lumsdaine: The Quiet Achiever" *ABC FM 24 Hours*, Vol. 1 No. 4 May (1989): 14.

McCredie, Andrew D. "Hooper Brewster-Jones: A Post-Centennial Tribute." *Miscellanea Musicologica*. Adelaide Studies in Musicology, vol. 16 (1989): 19-34.
Meale, Richard. "Composers Overseas: Richard Meale writes from America." *Fellowship of Australian Composers – Composers' Newsletter* June (1961): 9.

P.F. "Australian Composers Advance." *Brolga Review* June (1965): 6-8.

Peart, Donald. "The Australian Avant-Garde." *Proceedings of the Royal Music Association* (1967): 1-11.

Philips, Linda. "Creative Music in Australia." *Meanjin* 5/4 (1946): 312-315.

Prior, James. 'This was Australia: Composer's Art Was Poetic Fancy" *The Sun* (Sydney) March 2 (1988):34.

Sanders, Noel. "Gillian Whitehead in Discussion with Noel Sanders," *NMA* 4 (1985): 10-12.

Sculthorpe, Peter. "Musician of the Month: Mirrie Hill: a personal note," *Stereo FM Radio* March (1977): 7.

Shanahan, Ian and Chris Dench (eds.). "An Emotional Geography of Australian Composition." *Sounds Australian*, 1992.

Shineberg, Susan. "Elena Kats-Chernin," *ABC FM 24 Hours* November (1997): 28-31.

Sitsky, Larry. "Contemporary Composers in Australia." In *The Australian Contemporary Composers Series*. Canberra: Canberra School of Music, 1982.

Stevens, Lynne, "Helen Gifford: an Interview," *NMA* 4 (1983): 35-37.

Thorn, Benjamin. "How to Write Real Australian Music." *Sounds Australian* 38 (1993).

Walsh, Stephen. "Roger Smalley," *Music and Musicians*, June (1969): 37-44.

Whitehead, Gillian. "A student of Peter Maxwell Davies." *Canzona* 3/11 May (1982): 15-18.

Whiteoak, John. "Obituary Keith Humble." *Sounds Australian* June (1995).

Unpublished Theses and Essays

Crew, Rita. *An Analytical Study of the Piano Works of Roy Agnew, Margaret Sutherland and Dulcie Holland, including biographical material.* PhD diss., University of New England, Armidale, 1994.

Ghandar Ann. Words Written in Water: The Language of Music Composition. (sent by the composer, 2003).

Ward, Lisa-Jane. *The Piano Music of Hooper Brewster-Jones: with special reference to the sonatas and suites.* Honours thesis. Adelaide: Department of Music Studies, Faculty of Performing Arts, University of Adelaide, 1992.

Peery, I.W. *George F. Boyle: Pianist, Teacher, Composer.* PhD diss., Peabody Conservatory of Music, 1986.

Richard W. Stanton, *The Life and Piano Music of George F. Boyle* PhD diss., Butler University, 1968.

Archives

Banks, Don. *Papers of Don Banks.* [MS 6830] Manuscript Collection, National Library of Australia.

Beutler, Adolphe. *Papers of Adolphe G. Beutler.* [MS 2589) Manuscript Collection, National Library of Australia.

Brewster-Jones, Hooper. *Hooper Brewster-Jones Archive.* [uncatalogued] Special Collections, Barr Smith Library, University of Adelaide.

Burnard, Alex. *Papers of Alex Burnard.* [A8276 – A8284] Archives, Rare Books and Special Collections, University of Newcastle.

Glanville-Hicks, Peggy. *Papers of Peggy Glanville-Hicks.* [MS 9083] Manuscript Collection, online catalogue guide: http://www.nla.gov.au/ms/findaids/9083.html, National Library of Australia.

Glanville-Hicks, Peggy. *Peggy Glanville Hicks Papers.* [MLMSS 6394] Manuscript Collection, Mitchell Library, State Library of New South Wales.

Hanson, Raymond. *Raymond Hanson Manuscripts.* [961144, 961064, 961157] Rare Music Collection, Sydney Conservatorium of Music.

Hart, Fritz Bennicke. *Fritz Bennicke Hart Papers*. [LaTL 9528] Manuscript Collection, State Library of Victoria.
Hill, Alfred. *Hill Family Papers*. [MLMSS 6357] Manuscript Collection, Mitchell Library, State Library of New South Wales.

Hill, Mirrie. *Hill Family Papers*. [MLMSS 6357] Manuscript Collection, Mitchell Library, State Library of New South Wales.

Hince, Kenneth. *Papers of Kenneth Hince*. [MS 6566] Manuscript Collection, online catalogue guide: http://www.nla.gov.au/ms/findaids/6566.html, National Library of Australia.

Holland, Dulcie. *Papers of Dulcie Holland*. [MS 6853] Manuscript Collection, National Library of Australia.

Humble, Keith. *Papers of Keith Humble*. [MS 9402] Manuscript Collection, National Library of Australia.

Hutchens, Frank. *Papers of Frank Hutchens* [MS 2066] Manuscript Collection, National Library of Australia.

Hutchens, Frank. *Frank Hutchens Manuscripts*. [931520] Rare Music Collection, Sydney Conservatorium of Music.

Hutcheson, Ernest. *Ernest Hutcheson Manuscripts*. [970693] Rare Music Collection, Sydney Conservatorium of Music.

Hyde Miriam. *Papers of Miriam Hyde*. [MS 526] Manuscript Collection, National Library of Australia.

Hyde Miriam. *Miriam Hyde Manuscripts*. [8903064 and 942277] Rare Music Collection, Sydney Conservatorium of Music.

Kelly, Frederick Septimus. *Papers of Frederick Septimus Kelly*. [MS 3095 and MS 6050] Manuscript Collection, National Library of Australia.

Le Gallienne, Dorian. *Dorian La Gallienne Papers*. [MS 7655] Manuscript Collection, State Library of Victoria.

Orchard, William Arundel. *Papers of William Arundel Orchard*. [MS 5782] Manuscript Collection, National Library of Australia.

Penberthy, James. *Papers of James Penberthy*. [uncatalogued] Manuscript Collection, National Library of Australia.

Select Bibliography 291

Perkins, Horace. *Horace Perkins Archive*. [MSS 0027] Special Collections, Barr Smith Library, University of Adelaide.

Platt, Peter. *Peter Platt Papers*. [uncatalogued] Manuscript Collection, Mitchell Library, State Library of New South Wales.

Sitsky, Larry. *Papers of Larry Sitsky*. [MS5630], Manuscript Collection, National Library of Australia.

Interview Transcripts from the Oral History Department at the National Library of Australia

Banks, Don. *Conversation with Donald Banks*. Interviewer: Hazel de Berg. Aug 12 1972. ORAL DeB 626, NLA.

Butterley, Nigel. *Conversation with Nigel Butterley*. Interviewer: Hazel de Berg. Oct 24 1967. ORAL DeB 303, 305.,NLA.

Eagles, Moneta. *Interview with Moneta Eagles, composer*. Interviewer: Catherine Bowan. 2001. ORAL TRC 3969/4, NLA.

Evans, Lindley. *Conversation with Lindley Evans*. Interviewer: Hazel de Berg. Mar 23 1972. ORAL DeB 587-588, NLA.

Gifford, Helen. *Conversation with Helen Gifford*. Interviewer: Ruth Lee Martin. Jan 31 2000. ORAL TRC 3969/2. NLA.

Glanville-Hicks, Peggy. *Interview with Peggy Glanville-Hicks, composer and musician*. Interviewer: Diana Ritch. 1983. ORAL TRC 1548, NLA.

Hanson, Raymond. *Conversation with Raymond Hanson*. Interviewer Hazel de Berg. Aug 31 1973. ORAL DeB 700/1, NLA.

Hill Mirrie. *Conversation with Mirrie Hill*. Interviewer: Hazel de Berg. June 10 1975. ORAL DeB 840, NLA.

Holland, Dulcie. *Conversation with Dulcie Holland*. Interviewer: Hazel de Berg. April 18 1975. ORAL DeB 824, NLA.

Humble, Keith. *Conversation with Keith Humble*. Interviewer: Hazel de Berg. Nov. 20 1969. ORAL DeB 417-419.,NLA.

Hyde, Miriam. *Conversation with Miriam Hyde*. Interviewer: Hazel de Berg. Aug 13 1975. ORAL DeB 847 – 848, NLA.

Hyde, Miriam. *Interview with Miriam Hyde, musician and composer.* Interviewer: Larry Sitsky. 1990. ORAL TRC 2559, NLA.

Penberthy, James. *Conversation with James Penberthy.* Interviewer: Hazel de Berg. May 30 1965. ORAL DeB 989.99, NLA.

Penberthy, James. *Interview with James Penberthy.* Interviewer: Lane Langridge. Dec 29 – 30, 1988. ORAL TRC 2377, NLA.

Sitsky, Larry. *Interview with Larry Sitsky, composer, musicologist, pianist and teacher.* Interviewer: Ruth Lee Martin. May 4 – June 18, 2001. ORAL TRC 2442, NLA.

Sutherland, Margaret. *Interview with Dr. Margaret Sutherland.* Interviewer: Mel Pratt. Apr 5 1972. ORAL TRC 121/131, NLA.

Werder, Felix. *Interview with Felix Werder, composer.* Interviewer: Ruth Lee Martin. April 24, 2001. ORAL TRC 3969/6, NLA.

Appendix: Database of Piano Works Considered

Composer	Title	Details	Source
	Australian Pno. Miniatures	Red House (c1998)	AMC
	Australian Pno. Music vol. 1	Currency (1990)	AMC
	Australian Pno. Music vol. 2	Currency (1994)	AMC
	Australian Pno. Music vol. 3	Currency (1996)	AMC
	Australian Pno. Music vol. 4	Currency (2000)	AMC
	Bicentennial Pno. Album	Allans (1988)	AMC
	Contemporary Australian Pno.	Melb.: La Trobe Uni. Press (1985)	AMC
	Contemporary British Pno. Music	Schott (c1956)	AMC
	Four Australian Tone Poems	Nicholson's (1947)	AMC
	First Light: a selection of solo Pno. pieces vols. 1-3	Keys (1998 - 1999)	AMC
Abbott, Clifford	Musical Impressions of Greece	FS (no date)	AMC
Adams, Ernest Harry	The Singing Brook	Allans (1950)	Mitchell
Adams, Stephen	Obsession I & II	FS (1985)	AMC
Agnew, Roy	Collected Edition of Roy Agnew's Pno. Works. vols. 1 - 11	Keys (1997 - 2000)	NLA
	Album Leaf	Augener (1949)	Sitsky
	Australian Forest Pieces	Nicholson's (1913)	Sitsky
	Contrasts: A Pno. Cycle in Five Pieces	NY: Schmidt (1929)	Sitsky
	Sonata Legend: "Capricornia"	Augener (1949)	Sitsky
	Symphonic Poem (La Belle Dame Sans Merci - Keats)	FS (no date)	Sitsky
	Three Poems for Pno.	Augener (1927)	Sitsky

	Three Preludes	OUP (1925)	Sitsky
	Three Preludes	Augener (1927)	Sitsky
	The Windy Hill	Augener (1928)	Sitsky
Ahearn, Michael	Cloudmaker	FS (1989)	AMC
Albery, Dorothy	Prelude in D-flat major	Sydney: Musical Association of NSW (no date)	Mitchell
Allen, Geoffrey	After the Rapture: four pieces for Pno.	Keys (2001)	Sitsky
	Child's Play: Suite for Pno.	Keys (1991)	Sitsky
	In the Dark: Seven Nocturnes	Keys (2000)	Sitsky
	Lullaby for a favourite doll	Keys (1991)	Sitsky
	Pno. Sonata no. 1	Keys (1995)	Sitsky
	Sonata Espanola: Pno. Sonata no. 2	Keys (1996)	Sitsky
	Pno. Sonata no. 3	Keys (1996)	Sitsky
	Pno. Sonata no. 4	Keys (1997)	Sitsky
	Pno. Sonata no. 5	Keys (1998)	Sitsky
	Six Preludes for Pno. op. 19	Keys (2001)	Sitsky
	Serenatella	Keys (1997)	Sitsky
	Three Impromptus op. 31	Keys (1997)	Sitsky
	Three Nordic Pieces	Keys (1969)	Sitsky
	Three Pno. Pieces op. 23	Keys (1994)	Sitsky
	Well Wishing	Keys (19--)	sbc
Allen, Harold	Eight Episodes for Pno.	FS (no date)	Symphony Australia
Allworth, Robert	Moonbeams	FS (19--)	Sitsky
	Morning by an Ocean	FS (1999)	AMC
	Nocturne no. 7	FS (19--)	Sitsky
	Nocturne for a Pensive Evening	FS (1998)	AMC
	Past Horizons	FS (1999)	Sitsky
	Prelude	FS (19--)	Sitsky
	Prelude 'Indian Summer'	FS (19--)	Sitsky
	Purple Noon	Grevillea (c1996)	Sitsky
	Sonata-fantasy (last look at Bronte)	FS (no date)	AMC
	Yesteryears	FS (1986)	AMC
&erson, Olive	Mosquitoes	FS (1991)	AMC
	Spectrum: Three Shades	Alberts (1974)	AMC
	Where the Brigalow Grows	FS (1975)	AMC
Arlen, Albert	Requiem for a Siamese Cat	Southern (c1965)	Mitchell
	Spinnakers: A Sketch of Sydney Harbour	Southern (1970)	Mitchell
Arlom, Wilfred	Prelude in A minor	Allans (1922)	Mitchell
	Prelude in D minor	Allans (1922)	NLA
Austin, Richard	Meditations	FS (1999)	AMC
Baer, Werner	Five Mini Preludes	Allans (1975)	NLA
	Happy Harvesters	Boosey & Hawkes (c1952)	NLA
Bainton, Edgar	Capriccio in G minor	London: Ascherberg Hopwood & Crew (c1920)	Sydney Con.
	Humoresque	Augener (c1915)	NLA
	Shadowy Woodl&s	Augener (1915)	NLA
	Visions	Allans (1941)	NLA
	White Hyacinth	OUP (19--)	Symphony Australia
Banks, Don	Commentary	Schott (c1971)	Sitsky
	Pezzo Dramatico	Schott (1956)	Sitsky
	Sonatina in C# minor	MS (no date)	Sitsky
Barkl, Michael	Drumming	FS (1983)	sbc

	Jazz Music I	FS (1979)	AMC
	Five Pieces	FS (1995)	AMC
Basden, David	Spin	FS (1998)	AMC
Batterham, &rew	Blackstone	FS (1999)	AMC
Beath, Betty	Asmaradana	FS (1988)	AMC
	Black on White	FS (1998)	AMC
	Contrasts	FS (1990)	AMC
	Dreams & Visions: 1. Prelude to dreams; 2. Birds the colour of the moon; 3. The she-wolf; 4. Earth spirit ; 5. Toward dawn; 6. Day dream	Keys (1999)	AMC
	Golden Hours	MS (c1995)	sbc
	Lament For Kosovo	FS (1999)	sbc
	Prelude	FS (2001)	sbc
	Prelude 2	FS (2001)	sbc
	Woman's Song 1	FS (1997)	AMC
	Woman's Song 2	FS (1998)	AMC
	Woman's Song 3	FS (1998)	AMC
Beilharz, Kirsty	floriforous rage (jarman's dungeness)	FS (1999)	AMC
Belcher, Florence	In the Garden: A Cycle for the Pno.	Palings (no date)	Mitchell
Bell, Josephine	In a Thoughtful Mood	Palings (1937)	Mitchell
	Murmuring Trees	Palings (1937)	Mitchell
	Waltz in D	Palings (1937)	NLA
Benfall, Stephen	Hammers for Pno.	FS (1990)	AMC
Benjamin, Arthur	Chinoiserie	Boosey & Hawkes (1936)	Sydney Con.
	Fantasies for Pno. solo. Bk. One	Sydney : Hawkes & Son, (c1933)	Sitsky
	Fantasies for solo Pno.. Bk. Two	Sydney : Hawkes & Son, (c1933)	Sitsky
	Forest Peace	Boosey & Hawkes (19- -)	Sitsky
	A Gay Study	Allans (c1933)	NLA
	Jamaicalypso	Boosey & Hawkes (19- -)	Sitsky
	Two Jamaican Street Songs	Boosey & Hawkes (19- -)	Sitsky
	Odds & Ends Bk. Two. Legend; 2. A negro sings a sad song; 3. The Hobgoblins	London: Stainer & Bell Ltd. (1925)	NLA
	Pastorale, Arioso & Finale	Boosey & Hawkes (1948)	Mitchell
	Romance - Impromptu	London: Ascherberg, Hopwood & Crew (1913)	Sitsky
	Scherzino	Boosey & Hawkes (1938)	Sydney Con.
	Siciliana	Boosey & Hawkes (1936)	NLA
	Suite for Pno.	OUP (1927)	Mitchell
	Three Little Pieces: The Tired Dancer, White Note Tune, Buffoon's March	OUP (1929)	Mitchell
	Three New Fantasies: Dance at Dawn; March; Driftin	Boosey & Hawkes (1938)	CSM ABC
Berndt, Amy	Evening Star Schottische	C. G. Roder, Leipzig (no date)	Sitsky
Berry, Rhonda	Trivet June	FS (1996)	AMC
Bertram, Michael	Fantaisie-Sonate	FS (1999)	NLA

	Five Pieces for Pno. op.9 (1984)	Keys (1998)	AMC
	Sonatina for Pno. op.2 (1977)	Keys (1998)	AMC
Beutler, Adolphe	Arabian Scenes: The Passions of the Caravan, Nocturnes, Dance	MS (1914) copyright F. Beutler 2003	uncatalogued archive, NLA
	Hyperion: Tone Poem for Pno. after the poem by J. Keats	MS (1926) copyright F. Beutler 2003	uncatalogued archive, NLA
	Praeludium	MS (1914) copyright F. Beutler 2003	uncatalogued archive, NLA
	Rhapsodie Hongroise	MS (1911) copyright F. Beutler 2003	uncatalogued archive, NLA
	Variationen ueber einem Choral von Sebastian Bach	MS (1914) copyright F. Beutler 2003	uncatalogued archive, NLA
	Variations & Fugue "Gilderoy"	MS (1914) copyright F. Beutler 2003	uncatalogued archive, NLA
Bieniek, Matthew	Succession & Style: Poetic Essay	FS (1997)	AMC
Bird, Alfred H.	A Dance on the Green	Allans (1937)	Mitchell
Black, Edward	Danse Fantastique	Allans (1943)	NLA
Bostock, John	Enneagram' for Pno.	FS (1997)	AMC
Bourne, Una	By Sunny Streamlet	Palings (1922)	Mitchell
	Cradle Song	Allans (19--)	Sitsky
	Gavotte	Allans 19--)	Grainger
	Humoresque	Palings (1922)	Sitsky
	In Mother's Garden Suite of Six Small Pieces for Pno.	Palings (19--)	Sitsky
	Marche Grotesque	Palings (c1922)	Sitsky
	Petite Valse Caprice	Allans (19--)	Grainger
	Two Impressions	London: J.B. Cramer (1927)	NLA
Bowden, Mary	Badinage op. 17	Melb.: Atlas Press (19--)	NLA
	Ballade in D minor op. 36	C.G. Roeder, GMBH Leipzig (no date)	NLA
	"Balletto" op.12	Allans (1922)	NLA
	Barcarolle op.15	Atlas Press (1922)	NLA
	Chanson d'Amour	Allans (1922)	NLA
	Oana: Valse Impromtu op.9	Allans (1921)	NLA
	Reverie op.10	Allans (1921)	NLA
Boyd, Anne	Angklung	Faber (1976)	AMC
	Book of the Bells	FS (1981)	AMC
Boyle, George F.	Ballade	NY: Composers' Music Corp. (1921)	Sitsky
	Five Pno. Pieces	NY: Composers' Music Corp. (1922)	Sitsky
	Gavotte & Musette	NY: Carl Fischer (1919)	Grainger
	Habanera	NY: Carl Fischer (1919)	Grainger
	Marionette Suite	NY: Composers' Music Corp. (1921)	Sitsky
	Sonata no. 1 for Pno. (To Ernest Hutcheson)	NY: Carl Fischer (1925)	Boston Conservatory
	Three Sketches for Pno.: The White Rose, A Spring Breeze, Evening	Baltimore, G. Fred Kranz Music Co. 1915)	Grainger
Bračanin, Philip K.	al ma' luma: Three Pieces for Pno.	FS (1976)	AMC
	Sonata Mescolanza	FS (1978)	Sitsky
Brahe, May	Gay Pastorale	Boosey & Hawkes	Mitchell

		(1950)	
	Marita	Boosey & Hawkes (1950)	NLA
	Minuet for Ninion	Boosey & Hawkes (1950)	NLA
	Toy Town Patrol	Boosey & Hawkes (1950)	Mitchell
Br&man, Margaret	Churinga	Sydney: Jazzem Music, 1992	AMC
	Six Contemporary Pno. Pieces	Sydney: Castle Music (1982)	AMC
	Reflections	Sydney: Modern Music Craft (1990)	AMC
	Sonorities	Sydney: Castle Music (c1986)	Sitsky
	Three Sketches	Canada: Waterloo Music (1973)	AMC
	Winter Piece for Left H& Alone	Glenbrook, NSW: Margaret S. Br&man (1992)	AMC
Brash, James	Carillon from Four Original Australian Tone Poems	Nicholson's (1947)	AMC
	Cobweb's Valsette	Chappells (1936)	Mitchell
	The Dance of Columbine	Chappells (1928)	Mitchell
	The Dance of Harlequin	Chappells (1934)	Mitchell
	Graceful Minuet	Palings (1949)	Mitchell
	Miniature Prelude	Palings (1949)	Mitchell
	My Dance, I think?	Chappells (1941)	Mitchell
	The Shy One	Chappells (1935)	Mitchell
	Stately Dance	Palings (1949)	Mitchell
	Zephyrs	Nicholson's (1947)	Mitchell
Brentnall, Geo. H.	Nocturne	Allans (1927)	Mitchell
Brewster-Jones, Hooper	Ballet Preludes (approximately 40)	MS (1924-1926)	uncatalogued archive, Barr Smith
	Bird Call Impressions Bk 1	MS (9/8/23 - 23/9/23)	uncatalogued archive, Barr Smith
	Bird Call Impressions Bk. 2	MS (13/8/23 - 24/8/23)	uncatalogued archive, Barr Smith
	Bird Call Impressions Bk. 3	MS (21/9/23 - 12/10/23)	uncatalogued archive, Barr Smith
	Bird Call Impressions Bk. 4	MS (23/9/23 - 16/10/24)	uncatalogued archive, Barr Smith
	Bird Call Impressions Bk. 5	MS (1924)	uncatalogued archive, Barr Smith
	Bird Call Impressions Bk. 6	MS (1924)	uncatalogued archive, Barr Smith
	Church Air	MS (no date)	uncatalogued archive, Barr Smith
	Country Sketches: 1. Le Ruisseau, 2.The Rain, 3. The Murmuring Stream Below, 4. The Gallop, 5. By the Stream	MS (no date)	uncatalogued archive, Barr Smith
	Danse Negre	MS (no date)	uncatalogued archive, Barr Smith
	Eight Preludes	MS (1921)	uncatalogued archive, Barr Smith
	Five Impressions: Russian Impression, Dirge, The Bird By the Brook, The Waves Lap Idly byt	MS-1921	uncatalogued archive, Barr Smith

the Moonlit Shore, Will-o-the-Wisp

Formula Series: Six Preludes	MS (1924)	uncatalogued archive, Barr Smith
Fugue	MS (no date)	uncatalogued archive, Barr Smith
Gavotte	MS (no date)	uncatalogued archive, Barr Smith
Intermezzo no. 1 in E flat major	MS (1917)	uncatalogued archive, Barr Smith
Intermezzo no. 2 in E flat major	MS (1918)	uncatalogued archive, Barr Smith
Intermezzo no. 5	MS (no date)	uncatalogued archive, Barr Smith
Legende (found at back of Sonata no. 4	MS (1921)	uncatalogued archive, Barr Smith
Moorl& Suite: Au Pres de Petit Ruisseay de Brizere, Across the Moor, Valse Insouciance, Song of the Night, Shadow Dance	MS (1926)	uncatalogued archive, Barr Smith
Nature Series 1or 3 Nature Preludes: The Passing Storm, Mist, Sunshine	MS date?	uncatalogued archive, Barr Smith
Nature Series 2 or 3 Nature Preludes: The Rain Ceases, The Song of the Rustling Leaves, Frost	MS (1924)	uncatalogued archive, Barr Smith
Nursery Rhymes: Nelly Bly, Three Blind Mice, Little Bo Peep Has Lost Her Sheep, Baa Baa Black Sheep, Yankee Doodle, Twinkle Twinkle Little Star	MS (1925)	uncatalogued archive, Barr Smith
Pastoral Concerto for Pno. & orchestra (two Pno. version)	MS (1922)	uncatalogued archive, Barr Smith
Portrait Waltzes (about 20)	MS (1922 - 1925)	uncatalogued archive, Barr Smith
Prelude: Australian Aboriginal Scene in "Heritage"	MS (1936)	uncatalogued archive, Barr Smith
Prelude in D major	MS (date?)	uncatalogued archive, Barr Smith
Prelude: Loves Pleading (1	MS (1926)	uncatalogued archive, Barr Smith
Prelude: No Man's L&	MS (192?)	uncatalogued archive, Barr Smith
Reedwarbler	MS (19--)	uncatalogued archive, Barr Smith
Rhapsodie in B minor: 'Elusion' for Pno.	MS (1913?)	uncatalogued archive, Barr Smith
Rosella's Wooing	MS (no date)	uncatalogued archive, Barr Smith
Seven Preludes 1924 (includes "Poingnoi")	MS (1924)	uncatalogued archive, Barr Smith
Seven Preludes: Extase, Meditation, Desolation, 29th March, 1945, Le Soir, Valse Romantique, 4 November, 1945	MS (1944-1945)	uncatalogued archive, Barr Smith
Shrike Thrush	MS (no date)	uncatalogued archive, Barr Smith
Six Nature Preludes: Song of Autumn, Song of the Dawn, Song of the Dusk, Song of the Night, Song of Pleading "Sous Bois", Song of the Waves	MS (c.1924)	uncatalogued archive, Barr Smith
Six Rustic Pieces: The Distant Magpie, The Clucking Hens, Dripping Water, Willy Wagtail,	MS (1921)	uncatalogued archive, Barr Smith

	The Cow Bells, The Brooklet		
	Six Short Pieces Bk 2: nos. 2 & 6 missing	FS (no date)	uncatalogued archive, Barr Smith
	Sonata no. 1	MS (no date)	Sitsky
	Sonata in F minor no. 2	FS (no date)	Sitsky
	Sonata no. 2 (second Finale found at back of Sonata)	FS (no date)	uncatalogued archive, Barr Smith
	Sonata no. 3 (incomplete)	MS (1921)	uncatalogued archive, Barr Smith
	Sonata no. 4 in E flat	MS (1922)	uncatalogued archive, Barr Smith
	Sonata no. 5 (first movt. only)	MS (1908)	uncatalogued archive, Barr Smith
	Sonata no. 6	MS (1924)	uncatalogued archive, Barr Smith
	Sonata no. 7 (incomplete)	MS (1928)	uncatalogued archive, Barr Smith
	Sonata no. 8	FS (192?)	Sitsky
	Sonata no. 9 (same as Sonata no. 8 provenance of this numbering unknown)	MS (1927)	uncatalogued archive, Barr Smith
	Sonatina no. 1	MS (1924)	uncatalogued archive, Barr Smith
	Sonatina no. 3	MS (no date)	uncatalogued archive, Barr Smith
	Song of the Moonbeam	MS (1924)	uncatalogued archive, Barr Smith
	Song of the Yellowed Breasted Shrike Tit at Bridgewater	FS (no date)	Sitsky
	Suite no. 1	MS (1922)	uncatalogued archive, Barr Smith
	Suite no. 2	MS (1922)	uncatalogued archive, Barr Smith
	Suite no. 3	MS (1921-1922)	uncatalogued archive, Barr Smith
	Suite no. 4	MS (1925)	uncatalogued archive, Barr Smith
	Ten Etudes	MS (1925)	uncatalogued archive, Barr Smith
	"Tes cheveux descendent vers moi"	MS (no date)	uncatalogued archive, Barr Smith
	Three Impressions: By the Tanunda Fountain, Under the Pine, no title	MS (1922)	uncatalogued archive, Barr Smith
	Three Preludes	MS (1923)	uncatalogued archive, Barr Smith
	Train Journey I & II	MS (no date)	uncatalogued archive, Barr Smith
	Twelve Preludes	MS (1923-1924)	uncatalogued archive, Barr Smith
	Twenty Studies	MS (1925)	uncatalogued archive, Barr Smith
	Twenty-two Horse Rhythms	MS (1923-1926	uncatalogued archive, Barr Smith
Brier, Percy	Intermezzo giocoso	Palings (1950)	Mitchell
Bright, Colin	Earth-flowering Time	FS (1987)	AMC
	Tango Dreaming	FS (1984)	AMC
	The Dreaming II	FS (no date)	AMC
Broadstock, Brenton	Aureole 2	MS	Sitsky

	Aureole 4	FS (1984)	AMC
	The Dying of the Light	FS (1996)	AMC
	Giants in the L&	FS (1990)	AMC
	In the Silence of the Night	FS (1989)	AMC
Brophy, Gerard	Abraco	FS (2000)	AMC
	Angelicon	FS (1991)	AMC
	Gheranos	FS (1980)	AMC
	Spiked Heels: a Carmen Fantasy	FS (1992)	AMC
Brown, Charis	Country Fair: Fiesta Campestre	Allans (1932)	Mitchell
Brumby, Colin	Antistrophe	FS (1976)	Sitsky
	Demotica	FS (1980)	Sitsky
	Doubles	FS (1972)	AMC
	Four Little Pno. Pieces	FS (1963)	AMC
	Harlequinade	Corby, Engl&: Fentone Music (c1987)	AMC
	Intermezzo	FS (1995)	AMC
	Romance	FS (19--)	Sitsky
	Scherzo	Allans (1988)	AMC
	Theme & Variations	FS (19--)	Sitsky
	Twilight Pastoral	FS (1994)	AMC
Buck, Vera	Marche Orientale	Allans (1928)	Mitchell
	Piper's Dance	Allans (1931)	Mitchell
Burke, Brigid	A Mode in a Valley	FS (2000)	AMC
Burnard, Alex	Chorale Prelude on "Wachet Auf"	MS (no date)	Burnard Papers [A8282 - A8284] UNA
	Faschingschwank op. 42	MS (1962)	Burnard Papers [A8282 - A8284] UNA
	Further Scenes from Childhood op. 43	MS (1966)	Burnard Papers [A8282 - A8284] UNA
	March Op. 40 no. 8	MS (no date)	Burnard Papers [A8282 - A8284] UNA
	Mixed Emotions-& Styles-& Periods - perhaps a Suite for Pno. op.40 (two versions)	MS (1961)	Burnard Papers [A8282 - A8284] UNA
	Prelude & Fugue on "Aus tiefer Not" op. 42	MS (1962)	Burnard Papers [A8282 - A8284] UNA
	Puffing to Penrith - with James the Red Engine	MS (1957)	Burnard Papers [A8282 - A8284] UNA
	Seven Pno. Preludes op. 28 (two versions)	MS (1942-46)	Burnard Papers [A8282 - A8284] UNA
	Six Chorale Preludes op. 46	MS (1968)	Burnard Papers [A8282 - A8284] UNA
	Three Experimental Preludes Op.7: Voices From the Past	MS (1928)	Burnard Papers [A8282 - A8284] UNA
	Three Preludes & Fugues op. 48	MS (1970)	Burnard Papers [A8282 - A8284] UNA
	Twelve Folksong Settings op. 47 (two versions)	MS (1968)	Burnard Papers [A8282 - A8284]

			UNA
	Two Canons op. 45 - to my D.O.M.	MS (1967)	Burnard Papers [A8282 - A8284]
			UNA
	Two Fugues (incomplete) no. 1 D major	MS (no date)	Burnard Papers [A8282 - A8284]
			UNA
	Two Preludes & Fugues op. 31	MS (1949-51)	Burnard Papers [A8282 - A8284]
			UNA
	Two Preludes on "Wie Schoen leuchtet der Morgenstern" (two versions)	MS (1949)	Burnard Papers [A8282 - A8284]
			UNA
	Variations on a Somerset Folk Tune	FS (1927)	NLA
Burt, Warren	Aardvarks II: Mr Natural Encounters Flakey Foont!	FS (1973	AMC
	For Lisa	FS (1984)	AMC
	Love Songs (After Mancini et al)	FS (1989)	AMC
	Miniatures	FS (1985)	AMC
	Post-modern Waltzes	FS (1985)	AMC
Butterley, Nigel	Arioso	Alberts (c1965)	AMC
	Comment On A Popular Song	Alberts (1960)	AMC
	Grevillea	FS (1985)	Sitsky
	Il Gubbo (in the Bicentennial Pno. Album)	Allans (1988)	AMC
	Laurence Hargrave Flying Alone	FS (1981)	AMC
	Letter from Hardy's Bay	Alberts (1972)	Sitsky
	Toccata	FS (1960)	AMC
	Uttering Joyous Leaves (In Contemporary Australian Pno.)	Latrobe (1985)	Sitsky
Cale, Bruce	Coalesce	FS (1992)	Sitsky
Campbell, Steven	Incantation	FS (1992)	AMC
Carleson, Rosalyn	Three Australian L&scapes	Dural, NSW: Flexi-Fingers (1995)	sbc
Carmichael, John	From the Dark Side: Four Gothic Tales	S.L.: J. Carmichael (c1995)	AMC
Carr-Boyd, Ann	Blues in Orange	Grevillea (1996)	AMC
	Grasstree Hill	Grevillea (1996)	AMC
	Look at the Stars	Alberts (1978)	AMC
	The Millenium Rag	FS (2000)	AMC
	Northbridge Blues	FS (1995)	AMC
	Perpetual motion	FS (1992)	AMC
	Prelude (in the Bicentennial Pno. Album)	Allans (1988)	AMC
	The Shoalhaven Suite	FS (1999)	AMC
Cary, Tristram	Polly Fillers	FS (1989)	Sitsky
	Strange Places, an Exploration for Pno.	FS (1992)	Sitsky
	T&oori Blues (in First Light vol. 2)	Keys (1998)	AMC
Chatpo Koo, Brian	The Picture of Li-Po Reciting Poetry Op. 33	FS (no date)	AMC
Cheong, Simplicius	Jazz Fantasy for Pno.	FS (1984)	Bollard
	Three Movements for Pno.	FS (1968)	AMC
	Three Preludes for Pno.	FS (1973)	AMC
Chu Wang - Hua	Five Preludes	FS (1961)	AMC
Chua, Sonny	Genesis: Five Transcendental Studies Bk 1	S.L.: Midnight Editions (1993)	AMC
	Red Hot Rhapsodies	S.L.: Midnight Editions	AMC

		(1997)	
Clarke-Jones, Catherine	Conversations	Keys (1997)	Sitsky
Clifton, Neil	Fantasy: a Pno. piece for the left h&	FS (no date)	AMC
Clutsam, George	Aubade	London: Stanley Lucas, Weber Pitt & Hatzfield (c1897)	NLA
	Berceuse	London: Ascherberg, Hopwood & Crew (1919)	NLA
	Fileuse	MS Musica Australis Collection	Symphony Australia
	Metzler's Original Cinema Music vol. 5	London: Metzler & Co. (1920)	NLA
	Metzler's Original Cinema Music vol. 7	London: Metzler & Co. (1926)	NLA
	Pastoral Pictures	London: Alfred Lengnick & Co. (c1918)	NLA
	Romanesque no. 5 of Six Etudes Pittoresques	London: Enoch & Sons (c1904)	NLA
Colbert, Brendan	Akkord 1	FS (1997)	AMC
Colley, Constance	Bring Down the Sky	FS (2000)	AMC
Conyngham, Barry	ppp 1979	Universal (1970)	AMC
	Snowflake	Universal (1973)	AMC
Cosgrove, Herbert	Night Thoughts (Nocturne)	Nicholson's (1948)	Mitchell
Cowie, Edward	Kelly Variations	Schott (c1983)	Sitsky
Crawford, Laurence	Arcadian Pictures Five Pno. Solos	Palings (1935)	Sitsky
	Carnival Time : Six Pno. Solos	Palings (1935)	Mitchell
	A Nautical Suite	Palings (1936)	Sitsky
Cronin, Stephen	Fragments for solo Pno.	FS (1983)	AMC
	The Perihelion Rag	FS (1989)	AMC
Crossman, Bruce	...Back to the Centre	FS (1997)	sbc
Cuckson, Robert	Amoretti	FS (1974)	Sitsky
	Ballade	FS (1982)	Bollard
	Capriccio	FS (1994)	Bollard
	Carillon	Alberts (c1977)	Sitsky
	Sonata no. 1	FS (1967)	Bollard
	Sonata no. 2	FS (1977)	Bollard
Cuddigan, Nellie M.	Meditation	Allans (1937)	Mitchell
Cugley, Ian	Aquarelles for Pno.	Alberts (1974)	Mitchell
Dargaville, Tim	Alba	FS (1994)	sbc
	Canticles (in Australian Pno. Miniatures)	Footscray, Victoria: Red House Editions (1992)	sbc
	Night Song	Keys (1999)	CSM
Davidson, Robert	Circumference	FS (1997)	AMC
	Variations & Episodes	FS (1990)	AMC
	Zemar	FS (1987)	AMC
Davies-Slate, Stuart	Four Pno. Pieces	FS (19--)	Bollard
Davis, Charles	Lullaby	Nicholson's (no date)	Sitsky

	Pno. Solos: Spring, In the Meadow	MS photocopy (1927)	Rare Music Coll. Sydney Con.
	Nocturne in F major	Palings (19--)	NLA
De Beaupuis, Emanuel	Bolero	unknown	Sitsky
	Chant de la Nuit	Glasgow: James S. Kerr (188?)	Sitsky
	Deuxieme Mazurka	Allans (19--)	Sitsky
	Dors, mon Enfant	Palings (1897)	Sitsky
	"Hygeia" Valse	Sydney: W.H. Glen & Co. (1891-1900)	NLA
	Irish Airs, Wearin' o' the Green, Oft in the stilly Night, Dear Little Shamrock	Palings (19--)	Sitsky
	Irresistible Gavotte	Sydney: J.W. Hammond (189?)	NLA
	Le Chant du Berger	J.W. Hammond (189?)	Sitsky
	Marche Hongroise	Glasgow: James S Kerr (19--)	NLA
	Minuet	Glasgow: James S. Kerr Music (1880-1900)	Sitsky
	The Merry Peasant	Glasgow: James S Kerr (189?)	NLA
	The Mocking Bird	Palings (19--)	NLA
	Prelude op.34	Palings (19--)	Sitsky
	Premiere Mazurka	Ricordi (19--)	Sitsky
	The Queen's Reign March	Palings (c1897)	Sitsky
	Sur la Mer	Ricordi (19--)	NLA
	Troiseme Valse	W. H. Glen & Co. (1889 - 1899)	Sitsky
	Valse-Impromptu op. 15	Glasgow: James S Kerr (1880 - 1900)	NLA
De Cairos-Rego, George	Inamorata: melodie nuptiale for Pno.	Nicholson's (1913)	NLA
	La Cascade Caprice for Pno.	Nicholson's (c1913)	Sitsky
	Moment Musicale	London: A. Hammond & Co. (191?)	Sitsky
De Cairos-Rego, Iris	A Frolic	Chappell (c1928)	Sitsky
	Albatross	Augener (1933)	Sydney Con.
	Arabesque in A minor	London: Joseph Williams Ltd. (1941)	Sitsky
	Canzonetta	Chappell (c1924)	Sitsky
	English June	Chappell (c1941)	Sitsky
	Firelight	Augener (1933)	Sitsky
	Folk Dance	Chappell (1949)	Mitchell
	Four Sketches	Chappell (1935)	Sitsky
	Graneen Vale	Allans (1949)	NLA
	"Tarrel" (a Highl& Song)	Chappell (1935)	Sitsky
	Toccata	Chappell (c1936)	Sitsky
	Waltz in A	Augener (1933)	Sitsky
	Waltz Caprice	Chappel (c1941)	Sitsky
	White Cloud	Chappell (c1935)	Sitsky
De Cairos-Rego, Rex	Intermezzo in C no. 1op. 3	G. Shrimpton & Sons (1913)	NLA
	Intermezzo no. 2 in D minor op. 3	S.L.: Rex De Cairos Rego (1913)	NLA

	Nocturne in E flat major	London: G. Shrimpton & Sons (c1912)	Sitsky
De Groen, Milly Gordon	A Spring Morn	Palings (1928)	Mitchell
De Jong, Sarah	Three Waltzes	FS (no date)	AMC
De Oleveira, Bernard	Waltz	Allans (1966)	Mitchell
De Pinna, Herbert	Eight Interesting Pno. Pieces	Palings (no date)	Mitchell
Della Bosca, Roxanne	Five Miniatures	FS (1998)	AMC
Dench, Chris	Crur	FS (19--)	Sitsky
	Phase Portraits 1-3	FS (1993)	AMC
	Phase Portraid no. 5: Into the Wormworks	FS (1995)	AMC
	Tilt	London: United Music (1985)	AMC
	Topologies	London: United Music (1985)	AMC
Devene, Claude	Chant D'Amour	Allans (1928)	Sitsky
Dollarhide, Ted	The Night Life	FS (1988)	AMC
	Punk (1980)	NY: American Composers' Alliance (198-)	AMC
	Ragings of a One-pot Screamer (in Contemporary Australian Pno. Music)	Latrobe (1985)	Sitsky
Dowling, Bernadette	Little Transformations	FS (2000)	AMC
Dutton, Phillip	Pno. Sonata	Alberts (1975)	AMC
Dreyfus, George	Outbreak of Love	FS (1980)	sbc
Eagles, Moneta	Aquarelles: A Miniature Suite for Pno. (Quasi Minuet, Nocturne, Toccatina)	FS (no date)	sbc
	Arabeske	FS (no date)	sbc
	Impromptu in G	FS (no date)	sbc
	Sailor's Dance	Southern Music (1956)	AMC
	Theme & Variations (Passacaglia)	FS (no date)	sbc
	Two Impressions for Pno.: Mirage, Whirlwind	FS (1950)	sbc
Easton, Michael	Conversations	Sydney: Castle Music (1989)	AMC
	Moods	Sydney: Castle Music (1987)	AMC
Edwards, Ross	Emily's Song	FS (19--)	Sitsky
	Etymalong	Universal (c1990)	AMC
	Five Little Pno. Pieces	Faber (1977)	Bollard
	Kumari	Universal (c1982)	AMC
	Mantras & Night Flowers: Nine Bagatelles for Solo Pno.	Ricordi (2001)	sbc
	Monos II	Alberts (1971)	AMC
	Three Australian Waltzes	Ricordi (1997-98)	AMC
	Three Children's Pieces	FS (1980)	Bollard
	Three Little Pno. Pieces for the Right H& Alone	FS (1983)	AMC
Evans, Lindley	Berceuse (in Four Original Australian Tone Poems)	Nicholsons (1947)	Sitsky
	Fragrance	Palings (c1936)	AMC
	Lavender Time	Allans (1949)	NLA
	Merrythought	Allans (c1940)	Sitsky
	Rhapsody	Palings (1927)	AMC
	Tally Ho	Palings (1932)	Sitsky

	Vignette	Palings (1949)	Sitsky
Ewing, Montague	Four Vignettes: In Cupid's Bower, Stardust, Meditation In C, To A Portrait	Allans (1927)	unknown
Exton, John	Give or Take a Few dB	FS (19--)	Bollard
Farr, Ian	the girl with the dancing air	FS (1991)	AMC
Featherstone, Gary	Barcarolle	S.L.: G. Featherstone (1995)	AMC
	Berceuse	S.L.: G. Featherstone (1996)	sbc
	Dance Song	S.L.: G. Featherstone (1995)	sbc
	Etude in Bb Major	S.L.: G. Featherstone (1995)	sbc
	Four Nocturnes	S.L.: G. Featherstone (1995)	sbc
	Improvisation no. 2	S.L.: G. Featherstone (1995)	sbc
	Preludes Bks. 1 & 2	Keys (1995)	sbc
	Scherzo	FS (1995)	sbc
Fetter, Marjorie	Berceuse	Allans (1969)	Mitchell
	Namouna	Allans (1953)	Mitchell
	Scherzo	Allans (1949)	Mitchell
Fiddes, Ross	Four Ceremonies	S.L.: R. Fiddes (1982-84)	AMC
Ford, &rew	A Kumquat for John Keats	FS (1986-1987)	AMC
	Portraits	FS (1981)	AMC
Ford, C. Edgar	Ballerina	Allans (1940)	NLA
	Lady Betty	Allans (1942)	Mitchell
	Playfellows	Allans (1945)	Mitchell
	Toccatina	Allans (c1942)	NLA
Formosa, Riccardo	Cinq Variations pur Monsieur T.	FS (1986)	AMC
Foster, Ivor R.	Arietta	Allans (19--)	Mitchell
Fowler, Jennifer	Music for Pno. - Acending & Descending	Universal (1980)	AMC
	Piece for an Opera Theatre	Universal (1973)	AMC
	Piece for E. L.	Universal (1981)	Sitsky
Franklin, Jim	Talisman	FS (1982)	AMC
	Three Glimpses of Aquilon	FS (1980)	AMC
	Whisperings of Kelian	FS (1979)	AMC
Friedman, Ignaz	A La Mazourka op. 96 no. 1	Allans (1940)	Sydney Con.
	Dance & Double op. 96 no. 2	Allans (1940)	NLA
	Prelude op.96 no. 3	Allan (1940)	NLA
Gh&ar, Ann	Atomies	FS (undated)	AMC
	Autumn Chimes	Grevillea (1995)	AMC
	The earth sings mi-fa-mi	FS (19--)	Sitsky
	Eshelgharam in Contemporary Australian Pno. Music	Latrobe (1985)	Sitsky
	Estuary	FS (1990)	AMC
	For Adam	FS (no date)	Sitsky
	Four Bagateiles	Grevillea (1996)	Sitsky
	Four Pieces for Pno.	FS (no date)	AMC
	Fragments of a Song	Keys (1998)	AMC
	Major/Minor	FS (1972)	AMC
	Night Pictures	Keys (1997)	AMC
	Paraselene	FS (no date)	Sitsky
	Photophoresis	Grevillea (1996)	Sitsky
	Pno. Suite	FS (no date)	Sitsky

	Shadows	FS (1990)	AMC
	Sinai Music: Ras Mohammed, Synapsis, Scillitin, Dehab, For Mostafa	FS (1993)	Sitsky
	Six Simple Pieces	Grevillea (1995)	Sitsky
	Toushka	photocopy (1998)	AMC
	...Uncertain Comets, Chance Drifting	FS (1973)	AMC
Gheysens, Camille	A Gem	Sydney: Van Dyke Productions (1966)	Sydney Con.
	A Poeme op. 102	Van Dyke Productions (19--)	Sydney Con.
	Ballade no. 35 op. 288	Van Dyke Productions (19--)	Sydney Con.
Gifford, Helen	as foretold to Khayyam	FS (1999)	AMC
	The Gifford Collection, Pno. Music 1960 - 1994: Pno. Sonata (1960, Catalysis (1963), Three Pieces: Cantillation(1966); The Spell (1966); Waltz (1966), Toccata attaco (1990), A Plaint For Lost Worlds (1994).	Footscray, Victoria: Red House Editions (1996)	AMC
Glanville-Hicks, Peggy	Pastorale for Pno.	MS (1936)	Glanville-Hicks Papers [MLMSS 6394] Mitchell
Glynn, Gerald	Filigrees	FS (1981)	AMC
	Filigrees 2	FS (1987)	AMC
	Filigrees 3	FS (1991)	AMC
	Filigrees 4	FS (1997)	AMC
	Mobile-Mosaique	FS (1970)	AMC
	Toccata-Sonata	FS (1989)	AMC
Goodman, Isador	Hidin' Away (samba)	Chappell (1955)	NLA
Goosens, Eugene	Capriccio (on the "Hurdy Gurdy Man" from Kaleidoscope)	London: J & W Chester (1960)	Sydney Con.
	Concert Study	London: J & W Chester (1916)	Sydney Con.
	Four Conceits: The Gargoyle; Dance Memories; A Walking Tune; The Marionette Show	London: J & W Chester (1918)	Sydney Con.
	Kaleidoscope: twelve short pieces	London: J & W Chester (1918)	Sydney Con.
	Nature Poems op. 25	London: J & W Chester (c1920)	NLA
	Three Preludes	London: J & W Chester (19--)	Sitsky
	Two Studies	London: J & W Chester (c1924)	Sitsky
Graham, Peter	Moments pour Pno.	FS (1984)	AMC
Grainger, Percy	Arrival Platform Humlet	Schott (1916)	AMC
	Beautiful Fresh Flower (Chinese melody)	Aylesbury, Engl&: Bardic Edition (c1991)	AMC
	Blithe Bells – concert & easy versions	Schott (c1931)	AMC
	Children's March "Over the Hills & Far Away"	Schirmer (1918)	NLA
	Country Gardens	Allans (1919)	Sitsky
	Eastern Intermezzo (in Percy Grainger: Music for solo Pno. vol. 4)	Schott (1999)	Sydney Con.
	Gay But Wistful (in Percy Grainger: Music for solo Pno. vol. 3)	Schott (1998)	Sydney Con.
	Harvest Hymn (Pno. solo) (in Percy Grainger: Music for solo Pno. vol. 2)	Schott (1997)	Sydney Con.
	The Hunter In His Career (in Percy Grainger: Music for solo Pno. vol. 2)	Schott (1997)	Sydney Con.

The Immovable Do (in Percy Grainger: Music for solo Pno. vol. 4)	Schott (1999)	Sydney Con.
In Dahomey: Cakewalk Smasher	NY: Henmer Press (1987)	NLA
"In a Nutshell": Suite for Pno. Solo: Arrival Platform Humlet; Gay but Wistful; Pastoral; The "Gum-Suckers" March	Schirmer (c1916)	NLA
Irish Tune from County Derry	Allans (1911)	Sitsky
Jutish Medley (in Percy Grainger: Music for solo Pno. vol. 4)	Schott (1999)	Sydney Con.
Knight & Shepherd's Daughter (in Percy Grainger: Music for solo Pno. vol. 2)	Schott (1997)	Sydney Con.
Let's Dance in Green Meadow; 'Neath the Mould Shall Never Dancer's Tread Go	Faber (c1967)	Sitsky
Lullaby from 'Tribute to Foster' (in Percy Grainger: Music for solo Pno. vol. 4)	Schott (1999)	Sydney Con.
The Merry King (in Percy Grainger: Music for solo Pno. vol. 2)	Schott (1997)	Sydney Con.
'Molly on the Shore' Irish Reel	Schott (1918)	NLA
'My Robin is to the Greenwood Gone' Settings of Songs & Tunes from William Chappell's 'Old English Popular Music' (in Percy Grainger: Music for solo Pno. vol. 1)	Schott (1997)	NLA
Near Woodstock Town (no. 1 Mock Morris)	Bardic Edition (c1990)	AMC
Near Woodstock Town (Old English Song) British folk-music settings	Bardic Edition (1951)	AMC
'One more day, my John' Sea Shanty Settings no. 1 (in Percy Grainger: Music for solo Pno. vol. 4)	Schott (1999)	Sydney Con.
Pastoral (in Percy Grainger: Music for solo Pno. vol. 3)	Schott (1998)	Sydney Con.
The "Rag"-Time Girl (American popular song)	Bardic Edition (c1990)	AMC
The Rival Brothers	Bardic Edition (c1990)	AMC
Room Music Tit-Bits: H&el in the Str&	Schott (1930)	AMC
Room-music Tit-bits - no. 1 Mock Morris	Schott (1930)	NLA
Scotch Strathspey & Reel (in Percy Grainger: Music for solo Pno. vol. 4)	Schott (1999)	Sydney Con.
Sentimentals, no. 1 Colonial Song	Allans (1921)	Sitsky
Shepherd's Hey	Allans (1911)	Sitsky
Spoon River (American Folk Dance) (in Percy Grainger: Music for solo Pno. vol. 2)	Schott (1997)	Sydney Con.
Three Scotch Folksongs	NY: Henmer Press (1983)	AMC
To a Nordic Princess (in Percy Grainger: Music for solo Pno. vol. 4)	Schott (1999)	Sydney Con.
Walking Tune (in Percy Grainger: Music for solo Pno. vol. 4)	Schott (1999)	Sydney Con.
Grant, Quentin	Seven Mysteries	FS (1997)	AMC
	Meditations & Essays	FS (1993)	AMC
Greenbaum, Stuart	But I Want the Harmonica...	FS (1996)	AMC
	First Light	Wellington, N.Z.: Promethean Editions (1999)	AMC
	Homage to Professor Peter Dennison	S.L.: S. Greenbaum (1995)	AMC
	Ice Man	Wellington, N.Z.: Promethean Editions	AMC

		(1997)	
	Innocence & Experience	North Fitzroy, Vic.: GRT Press (1996)	AMC
	New Roads, Old Destinations	North Fitzroy, Vic.: GRT Press (1995)	AMC
Gross, Eric	An Idyll for Idil op. 244	FS (2000)	AMC
	"Brian David Hess" op. 131/3	FS (no date)	AMC
	Five Simple Pieces for Pno. op. 169: 1. Lonely Desert; 3. Me&ering In Series; 5.Little Jazzeroo (nos. 2 & 4 missing?)	FS (1989)	AMC
	Glebe Isl& Minuet	S.L.: E. Gross (c1995)	AMC
	Habanera - Serenade op. 31/2	FS (1960)	AMC
	Klavierstuck I op. 120	Darlinghurst, N.S.W.: MCA Music Australia (c1983)	AMC
	Klavierstuck III op. 127	Darlinghurst, N.S.W>: MCA Music Australia (c1983)	AMC
	Klavierstuck III op. 150	FS (1986)	AMC
	Klavierstuck IV op. 225	Sydney: E. Gross (c1998)	AMC
	Miniature for Ray op. 195	FS (1994)	AMC
	Minuetto Capriccioso op. 238 A	FS (1999)	AMC
	Moon Interlude	Leeds (1972)	AMC
	Nostalgic Interlude	S.L.: E. Gross (1996)	AMC
	"Pensive Prelude" op. 208	S.L.: E. Gross (1996)	AMC
	Rondino Tranquillo op. 34/1	FS (1962)	AMC
	Sallee in the Mallee (Interlude for Pno.) op. 250	FS (2001)	AMC
	Sonata Piccola op. 188	FS (1992)	AMC
	Thanksgiving op. 149	FS (1986)	AMC
	Toccata op. 184/2A	FS (1996)	AMC
	Toccata: "No Pno. at Three" op. 226 A	FS (1998)	AMC
Gyger, Elliott	Compass Variations	FS (1993)	AMC
	Threshold	FS (1994)	AMC
Hadwen Ch&ler, H.	Album of Miniatures for the Pno.	Allans (19--)	Sitsky
Hair, Graham	Dances & Devilment & Sunlit Airs (no. 4 from Twelve Transcendental Concert Studies on Themes from the Australian Poets)	Sydney: Southern Cross Publishing (199?)	sbc
	Seven Fleeting Glimpses (in the Bicentennial Pno. Album)	Allans (1988)	AMC
	Under Alderbaran	Sydney: Sydney International Pno. Competition (1985)	AMC
	Wild Cherries & Honeycomb	Sydney: Southern Cross Publishing (1998)	sbc
Hall, Frederick	Chanson D'automne	Allans (1928)	NLA
	Conchita: Spanish Schottische	Allans (19--)	NLA
	Consolation	Allans (1928)	NLA
	Egyptian Tone Poems	Allans (1922)	NLA
	English Country Dance: 1. Fogs & Fens; 2. A day at the Fair; 3. The Minstrel; 4. Donegal Air; 5. The Farewell; 6. Village Dance; 7. Irish Croons; 8. Lullaby	Allans (1922)	NLA
	The Evening Prayer	Allans (1925)	Sitsky
	Gates of Bagdad	Allans (1929)	NLA
	Graceful Dance	Allans (1923)	NLA

	Intermezzo Brillante (a study in octaves)	Allans (1927)	NLA
	In The Garden of Our Dreams	Allans (19--)	NLA
	Lavender & Lace	Allans (1919)	NLA
	Omar: An Eastern Fox-Trot	Allans (c1923)	NLA
	Poppies: Intermezzo	Allans (1926)	Mitchell
	Prelude in F for left h&	Allans (1926)	NLA
	Japonette: Japanese Tone Poem	Allans (1919)	NLA
	Romance Parisienne	Allans (1926)	NLA
	Valse Caprice	Allans (1931)	Mitchell
	A Venetian Reverie	Allans (1923)	NLA
	Viennese Serenade	Allans (1929)	NLA
	White Cargo: African Tone Poems	Allans (1926)	NLA
H&el, Am&a	Blue Bay	FS (1987)	AMC
	Sun Shower	FS (1987)	AMC
	Tiny Flower	FS (1998)	AMC
Hannan, Michael	Beethoven Deranged	FS (no date)	sbc
	Homage to Chopin	FS (19--)	sbc
	Fortune Pieces	FS (1978-80)	sbc
	Mood Variations	FS (1991)	sbc
	Mysterious Flowers	FS (1998)	sbc
	Modal Melodies for Single H&s (in Pno. Music for One H& by Australian Composers)	Allans (1978)	sbc
	Resonances (1 - 4)	FS (1987 - 1997)	sbc
	Riff Madness	FS (1981)	sbc
	Seven Studies for Single H&s	FS (1981)	sbc
	Star Cycle	FS (no date)	AMC
	Three Improvisatory Mobiles	FS (1981)	sbc
	Three Meditations for Dane Rudhyar	FS (1984)	sbc
	Voices in the Sky	FS (1987)	sbc
	Zen Variations	FS (1982)	sbc
Hanson, Raymond	Episode on an English Flk Tune: 'Tarry Trowsers' op.24	FS (1948)	Sitsky
	Five Portraits op. 23: 1. Daddy Back; 2. King Arthur; 3. Hans &erson; 4. Scrooge; 5. Ginger Megs	Southern Music (1954)	NLA
	Idylle in D major	Nicholson's (c1943)	Sitsky
	On Holidays	Allans (c1948)	Sitsky
	Pno. Sonata op. 12	Alberts (1976)	Sitsky
	Preludes op. 11	Alberts (1941)	Sitsky
	Procrastination	FS (1939)	Sydney Con.
	Quizzic	FS (1940)	Sitsky
	Sonatina op. 24	FS (1949)	Sitsky
Harrhy, Edith	Maori Sketches	Allans (1939)	Mitchell
Harrison, &rew	Pno. Fantasia no. 1	FS (1997)	Bollard
Hart, Fritz Bennicke	Cold Blows the Wind To-night, True Love: Folk-Song Fantasy On the Somerset Folk-Song	Allans (1923)	Grainger
	English Folk-Songs Books 1 & 2	London: Stainer & Bell Ltd. (1920)	Grainger
	Strawberry Fair: Folk-Song Fantasy On the West Country Folk-Song	Allans (1922)	Grainger
	Four Episodes for Pno.	MS (1906)	Hart Papers [LaTL 9528/11+12] Victoria
	Four Pno. Pieces op.147	MS (1941)	Hart Papers [LaTL 9528/11+12] Victoria
	Fourteen Experiments for Pno.	MS (1941)	Hart Papers [LaTL

			9528/11+12] Victoria
Hart, Lionel	Pour Toi J'ai Chante Valse Intermezzo	Chappell (19--)	Sitsky
	Valse Mysterieuse	Allans (1927)	Mitchell
Hazeldine, Ross	diminuendo	FS (1995)	AMC
	Elastic Fog (in Ausralian Pno. Miniatures)	Red House (c1998)	AMC
	L&scape Sonata	FS (1993)	AMC
	Re member Me	FS (1992)	AMC
	Seven 80s Pieces	FS (1990)	AMC
Heim, Christian	Journey	FS (1983)	AMC
Hellemann, Christian	Air de Ballet op. 15	Palings (c1923)	NLA
	Humorette	Palings (1923)	NLA
	Marche Mignon	Palings (c1923)	Sitsky
	Puck Pictures: Suite for Pno.	Palings (1935)	NLA
	Valse Caprice	Palings (19--)	Mitchell
Hill, Frederick	Allegro Furioso	FS (1970)	AMC
	Non Troppo	FS (1988)	AMC
Henderson, Moya	4 Treadmill	FS (19--)	Sitsky
	Cross Hatching or Rarrk	FS (1984)	AMC
	Nolle Prosequi	FS (1973)	AMC
	Prelude I	FS (1969)	AMC
	Prelude 11	FS (1972)	AMC
Hesse Marjorie A.	All Suddenly The Wind Comes Soft	Augener (1939)	Sitsky
	"At Play" A Pno. Suite for Young People	Nicholson's (1938)	Sitsky
	The Ballerina	Leeds (1961)	NLA
	Growing Up: Three Impressions for Pno.	Palings (1936)	Sitsky
	La Pastourelle	Leeds (1961)	Sydney Con.
	The Piper	Augener (1939)	Sydney Con.
	Romance (in Four Original Australian Tone Poems)	Nicholsons (1947)	Sitsky
	The Skipping Suite for Pno.	Palings (1937)	Sitsky
	Twilight	Palings (1937)	Sitsky
	Valse Gracieuse	Allans (1950)	NLA
Hill, Alfred	Adagio	MS (1959) Alfred Hill Listing, Item 403	SAC NLA
	After Glow	MS (1941) Alfred Hill Listing, Item 385	SAC NLA
	Air for Pno.	MS (no date) Alfred Hill Listing, Item 429	SAC NLA
	Air for Pno.	microfilm (no date)	Hill Family Papers [MLMSS 6357] Mitchell
	An un-named piece (also known as Prelude in E minor or In Search of Peace)	MS (no date) Alfred Hill Listing, Item 423	SAC NLA
	As Night Falls	Palings (1952)	Sitsky
	"The Beating Heart"	microfilm (no date)	Hill Family Papers [MLMSS 6357] Mitchell
	Berceuse	Nicholson's (c. 1920)	Sitsky
	A Bird At My Window	MS (1947) Alfred Hill Listing, Item 388	SAC NLA
	A Birthday Greeting	MS (no date) Alfred Hill Listing, Item 415	SAC NLA
	A Bit O' Scotch	microfilm (no date)	Hill Family Papers

		[MLMSS 6357] Mitchell
Black Baby	Chappell (1950)	Sitsky
The Broken Ring, an Old German Melody	Allans	Sitsky
Come Again Summer	Chappell (1947)	NLA
Concert Waltz	microfilm (no date)	Hill Family Papers [MLMSS 6357] Mitchell
Concerto in A for Pno. & Orchestra	FS (no date)	AMC
Country Dances	microfilm (no date)	Hill Family Papers [MLMSS 6357] Mitchell
The Cross of Inverness	microfilm (no date)	Hill Family Papers [MLMSS 6357] Mitchell
The Dance	microfilm (no date)	Hill Family Papers [MLMSS 6357] Mitchell
Dance of the Wooden Shoes	MS (1942) Alfred Hill Listing, Item 390	SAC NLA
Dancing Faun	Boosey & Hawkes (1942)	Mitchell
The Dawn of a New Year with Revelry, Gaiety, & Dancing ing the Streets	MS (1960) Alfred Hill Listing, Item 440	SAC NLA
A Day Dream	microfilm (no date)	Hill Family Papers [MLMSS 6357] Mitchell
The Days of Romance	MS (1941)Alfred Hill Listing, Item 420	SAC NLA
Doves	Chappell (1932)	Sitsky
Down sunlit glades	microfilm (no date)	Hill Family Papers [MLMSS 6357] Mitchell
"A Drowsy Afternoon"	microfilm (no date)	Hill Family Papers [MLMSS 6357] Mitchell
Early One Morning	MS (1936) Alfred Hill Listing, Item 432	SAC NLA
A Folksong	microfilm (no date)	Hill Family Papers [MLMSS 6357] Mitchell
For those who weep	microfilm (no date)	Hill Family Papers [MLMSS 6357] Mitchell
Four Pieces for Pno.: Goodbye Summer, Rendezvous, A tale that is told, There is crying in the night	MS (1942) Alfred Hill Listing, Items 387 a-d	SAC NLA
Fugue in 3 parts	microfilm (no date)	Hill Family Papers [MLMSS 6357] Mitchell
Fugue in G no. 4	MS (no date) Alfred Hill Listing, Item 439	SAC NLA
Fugitive Thoughts	microfilm (no date)	Hill Family Papers [MLMSS 6357] Mitchell
Gavotte	MS (1959) Alfred Hill Listing, Item 381	SAC NLA
Goodbye Summer	microfilm (no date)	Hill Family Papers

		[MLMSS 6357] Mitchell
Happy Hearts	MS (1959) Alfred Hill Listing, Item 391	SAC NLA
Her Passing	MS (1932) Alfred Hill Listing, Item 405	SAC NLA
Hesitation	MS (1947) Alfred Hill Listing, Item 400	SAC NLA
Highl& Air: Air collected by Captain S Fraser	Chappell (1946)	NLA
Highl& Airs	microfilm (no date)	Hill Family Papers [MLMSS 6357] Mitchell
I heard you singing	MS (1959) Alfred Hill Listing, Item 401	SAC NLA
Joyous Rain	Boosey & Hawkes (c1942)	NLA
"Linthorpe": Prelude, Fugue & Chorale	microfilm (no date)	Hill Family Papers [MLMSS 6357] Mitchell
"The lonely glen"	microfilm (no date)	Hill Family Papers [MLMSS 6357] Mitchell
Loose Leaves	Allans (1935)	Mitchell
Menuet	microfilm (no date)	Hill Family Papers [MLMSS 6357] Mitchell
Minuetto	Boosey & Hawkes (1942)	NLA
"The Moon's Gold Horn"	microfilm (no date)	Hill Family Papers [MLMSS 6357] Mitchell
Morning Song	MS (1959) Alfred Hill Listing, Item 398	SAC NLA
Moto Perpetuo	MS (1959) Alfred Hill Listing, Item 407	SAC NLA
My Lady Dances	Boosey & Hawkes (1942)	NLA
Old Man Kangaroo	Boosey & Hawkes (1942)	Mitchell
Old Time Menuet	MS (1941) Alfred Hill Listing, Item 410	SAC NLA
The Old Year Ends (a soliloquy)	microfilm (no date)	Hill Family Papers [MLMSS 6357] Mitchell
One Came Fluting	Chappell (1949)	NLA
Prelude	MS (no date) Alfred Hill Listing, Item 402b	SAC NLA
Prelude (12.10.1944)	MS (1944) Alfred Hill Listing, Item 438	SAC NLA
Prelude in A	microfilm (no date) Alfred Hill Listing, Item 437	Hill Family Papers [MLMSS 6357] Mitchell
Prelude in D	MS photocopy (1942) Alfred Hill Listing, Item 434	SAC NLA
Three Preludes for Pno.	MS (no date) Alfred Hill Listing, Item 409	SAC NLA
Prelude no. 4 (Through a Veil of Mist)	MS (1924) Alfred Hill	SAC NLA

	Listing, Item 436	
Prelude & Fugue in E flat	MS (1936) Alfred Hill Listing, Item 422	SAC NLA
Prelude & Fugue in three parts	MS (1947) Alfred Hill Listing, Item 404	SAC NLA
The Question	microfilm (no date)	Hill Family Papers [MLMSS 6357] Mitchell
Quiet is the Night (In Quietness)	microfilm (no date) MLMSS 6357	Hill Family Papers [MLMSS 6357] Mitchell
Quiet River	Boosey & Hawkes (1942)	Sitsky
Rendezvous	microfilm (no date)	Hill Family Papers [MLMSS 6357] Mitchell
Retrospect	Nicholson's (1920)	Sitsky
Reverie	MS (1930) Alfred Hill Listing, Item 435	SAC NLA
Reverie	MS (1959) Alfred Hill Listing, Item 379	SAC NLA
She Walks in Beauty	microfilm (no date)	Hill Family Papers [MLMSS 6357] Mitchell
Short Pieces for Pno.	microfilm (no date)	Hill Family Papers [MLMSS 6357] Mitchell
Sing on, O bird! (Thoughts of Home/ Home Thoughts)	MS (1941) Alfred Hill Listing, Item 406	SAC NLA
A Slumber Song	MS (1959) Alfred Hill Listing, Item 396	SAC NLA
Sonatina in C	MS (no date) Alfred Hill Listing, Item 430	SAC NLA
A Song of Hope	MS (1942) Alfred Hill Listing, Item 417	SAC NLA
Song Without Words	MS (1959) Alfred Hill Listing, Item 399	SAC NLA
Summer is Waning	MS (1934) Alfred Hill Listing, Item 426	SAC NLA
A Summer's Day On the Mountains	MS (1948) Alfred Hill Listing, Item 418	SAC NLA
A Tale of the Sea	MS (1947) Alfred Hill Listing, Item 425	SAC NLA
A Tale That Is Told	MS (1928) Alfred Hill Listing, Items 387c/402a,	SAC NLA
Theme Song from 'The Broken Melody'	microfilm (no date)	Hill Family Papers [MLMSS 6357] Mitchell
There was a crying in the night	microfilm (no date)	Hill Family Papers [MLMSS 6357] Mitchell
Thoughts	FS (1933) Alfred Hill Listing, Item 421	SAC NLA
A Troubled Mind	microfilm (no date)	Hill Family Papers [MLMSS 6357] Mitchell
Two-part fugue	microfilm (no date)	Hill Family Papers

			[MLMSS 6357] Mitchell
	Un-named (5.1.1947)	MS (1947) Alfred Hill Listing, Item 380	SAC NLA
	Un-named (18.5.1959)	MS (1959) Alfred Hill Listing, Item 411	SAC NLA
	Un-named (25.5.1959)	MS (1959) Alfred Hill Listing, Item 397	SAC NLA
	Valse	MS (1923) Alfred Hill Listing, Item 431	SAC NLA
	Valse Triste	Nicholson's (1920)	Sitsky
	Victory March: The Return	MS (no date) Alfred Hill Listing, Item 419	SAC NLA
	Waiata Poi	Chappell (1949)	NLA
	Waltz Caprice	MS (1942) Alfred Hill Listing, Item 384	SAC NLA
	When Fields Were Green	microfilm (no date)	Hill Family Papers [MLMSS 6357] Mitchell
	Willier auld news	microfilm (no date)	Hill Family Papers [MLMSS 6357] Mitchell
	Winged Melodies	Allans (1935)	Sitsky
	A Woodl& Serenade	MS (no date) Alfred Hill Listing, Item 408	SAC NLA
	The Woodpecker	MS (1959) Alfred Hill Listing, Item 395	SAC NLA
Hill, Fred	Non Troppo	FS (no date)	Bollard
Hill, Mirrie	A Maori Rhapsody	Allans (1934)	NLA
	A Moonlight Dance	Allans (1953)	Sydney Con.
	Aboriginal Rhythms	MS (no date)	Hill Family Papers [MLMSS 6357] Mitchell
	Aboriginal Song (two versions)	MS (no date)	Hill Family Papers [MLMSS 6357] Mitchell
	Arnhem L&	MS (no date)	Hill Family Papers [MLMSS 6357] Mitchell
	At the End of the Little Dream	MS (no date)	Hill Family Papers [MLMSS 6357] Mitchell
	Boat Song	MS (no date)	Hill Family Papers [MLMSS 6357] Mitchell
	Brolga (the Dancer) with cymbal part (from the Aboriginal Dances)	MS (no date)	Hill Family Papers [MLMSS 6357] Mitchell
	Bush Sunset	MS (no date)	Hill Family Papers [MLMSS 6357] Mitchell
	Butterflies	MS (no date)	Hill Family Papers [MLMSS 6357] Mitchell
	By A Quiet Stream	MS (no date)	Hill Family Papers [MLMSS 6357] Mitchell
	Child Fancies	Allans (1935)	AMC

Dreams	Boosey & Hawkes (1942)	Sitsky
The Dream-Time	MS (no date)	Hill Family Papers [MLMSS 6357] Mitchell
"Do you remember an inn, Mir&a!"	MS (no date)	Hill Family Papers [MLMSS 6357] Mitchell
Garden Sketches	Allans (1934)	Sydney Con.
Haste Away	MS (no date)	Hill Family Papers [MLMSS 6357] Mitchell
Improvisation	MS (no date)	Hill Family Papers [MLMSS 6357] Mitchell
In Reflective Mood (Many versions)	MS (no date)	Hill Family Papers [MLMSS 6357] Mitchell
Lament (two versions)	MS (no date)	Hill Family Papers [MLMSS 6357] Mitchell
Leafy Lanes of Kent	Palings (1950)	Sitsky
Longing (two versions)	MS (no date)	Hill Family Papers [MLMSS 6357] Mitchell
Machinery	MS (no date)	Hill Family Papers [MLMSS 6357] Mitchell
Maori Folk Tune	MS (no date)	Hill Family Papers [MLMSS 6357] Mitchell
Marche	MS (no date)	Hill Family Papers [MLMSS 6357] Mitchell
Meditation	Southern Music (1954)	Mitchell
Merry Imp	Alberts (1976)	Sitsky
Minuet	Boosey & Hawkes (1942)	NLA
Odnyamatana Rhythm (Song to the Whirlwind) (many versions)	MS (no date)	Hill Family Papers [MLMSS 6357] Mitchell
Old Gaelic Dance & Song	MS (no date)	Hill Family Papers [MLMSS 6357] Mitchell
The Old Unquiet Ocean	MS (no date)	Hill Family Papers [MLMSS 6357] Mitchell
Rhapsody for Pno.	MS (no date)	Hill Family Papers [MLMSS 6357] Mitchell
Rotha's Lament	FS (no date) A/C HIL-M 07	SAC NLA
The Sea	MS (no date)	Hill Family Papers [MLMSS 6357] Mitchell
Sea Study	MS (no date)	Hill Family Papers [MLMSS 6357] Mitchell
She Dances (two versions)	MS (no date)	Hill Family Papers

			[MLMSS 6357] Mitchell
	Sonatina	MS (no date)	Hill Family Papers [MLMSS 6357] Mitchell
	Study	MS (no date)	Hill Family Papers [MLMSS 6357] Mitchell
	Summer Rain	MS (no date)	Hill Family Papers [MLMSS 6357] Mitchell
	Three Aboriginal Dances: Brolga (the Dancer),The Kunkarunka Women, Nalda of the Echo	Southern Music (1950)	Sitsky
	Three Highl& Tunes	Sydney: Castle Music (1971)	AMC
	Three Miniature Pieces for the Pno.: Will O' the Wisp, Prelude, Fun	Nicholson's (c1911)	NLA
	Waltz	Boosey & Hawkes (1942)	Sitsky
	Waltzing Matilda	Allans (1950)	NLA
	Willow Wind	Alberts (1973)	Sitsky
	The Wonder of Night	MS (no date)	Hill Family Papers [MLMSS 6357] Mitchell
Hille, Stuart	Five Little Pno. Pieces (in memoriam Benjamin Britten)	FS (19--)	Bollard
Hind, John	Four Preludes (plus two additions by h&)	Southern (1973)	Bollard
Hiscocks, Wendy	Cordelia: for whom the Angesl dance	Morden, Surrey: Creativity & Music (c1996)	AMC
	The Piper at the Gates of Dawn - Prelude, Nocturne, Caprice, Finale.	S.L.: W. Hiscocks (1995)	AMC
	Rainforest Toccata	Morden, Surrey: Creativity & Music (c1988)	AMC
	Toccata	Claremont, W.A.: Hovea Music Press (1998)	AMC
Hoey, Denis	Five Moods in Five Modes	Allans (1976)	NLA
Holgate, Stephen	Prelude for a Psalm	FS (1982)	AMC
Holl&, Dulcie	A Scattering of Leaves: a collection of six Pno. solos 1. The Scattering of Leaves; 2. Toccatina; 3. Unaswered Question; 4. Bagatelle for Selma; 5. The dry west; 6. Valse ironic	Allans (1986)	AMC
	A Song Remembered	MS (1937)	Holl& Papers [MS 6853] NLA
	Asterisk	FS (1950)	AMC
	At the Fountain	FS (1995)	AMC
	Autumn Gold	MS (1993)	Holl& Papers [MS 6853] NLA
	Autumn Pastorale	S.L.: D. Holl& (1995)	AMC
	Autumn Piece	MS (1947)	Holl& Papers [MS 6853] NLA
	Bird at the Window	FS (1995)	AMC
	Cat-walk	FS (1985)	AMC
	Composer Falling Asleep	FS (1993)	AMC

	Concert Study no. 2 in A minor	MS (1920)	Sydney Con.
Holl&, Dulcie	Concertino for Pno. & Strings	FS (1983)	AMC
	Christmas Greeting	MS (1956)	Holl& Papers [MS 6853] NLA
	Dreamy John	MS (1957)	Holl& Papers [MS 6853] NLA
	The End Of Summer	MS (1946?)	Holl& Papers [MS 6853] NLA
	Fairy Penguins	MS (1994)	Holl& Papers [MS 6853] NLA
	Farewell My Friend	FS (1994)	AMC
	Four Aspects for Pno.	FS (1996)	AMC
	Green Lizards	MS (1936)	Holl& Papers [MS 6853] NLA
	Hornpipe	Palings (1955)	Sitsky
	The Lake	FS (1940)	AMC
	Lyric Piece	MS (1937)	Holl& Papers [MS 6853] NLA
	Nocturne	FS (1947)	AMC
	Northbridge Sketches: 1. Twin Towers; 2. Valley Below; 3. Weekend	FS (1995)	AMC
	Old Tunes in New Garments	Palings (1937)	Sitsky
	Pno. Rag	FS (1996)	AMC
	Pno. Sonata	FS (1952)	AMC
	Prelude I	MS (1950)	Holl& Papers [MS 6853] NLA
	Prelude III	MS (1950)	Holl& Papers [MS 6853] NLA
	Quiet Procession: Pno. solo for one h&, right or left	FS (1992)	Sitsky
	Retrospect	FS (1991)	AMC
	Shade of Summer	FS (1992)	AMC
	Sonatina	FS (1993)	AMC
	The S&man Comes	MS (1944)	Holl& Papers [MS 6853] NLA
	Three Dances for a New Doll	S.L.: D. Holl& (1994)	AMC
	Tribute To Clem Hosking	MS (1965)	Holl& Papers [MS 6853] NLA
	Winter Lament	S.L.: D. Holl& (1996)	AMC
Holl&, William	Festival of Sydney	FS (1994/2001)	AMC
	Reflection (consideration of the past)	FS (2001)	AMC
Hollier, Donald	Sonatina for Pno.	FS (1971)	AMC
	Twelve Sonnets for Pno.	FS (1975-77)	School of Music Library, Australian National University
Hooke, John	Tessellations for Pno.	Alberts (c1975)	Sitsky
House, Daniel	Inserts	FS (1996)	Sitsky
Horsphol, Michael	Toccatta or the Sun (composer's own spelling)	FS (2000)	AMC
Howlett, May	Kryptiques, six miniatures for Pno.	Grevillea (1995)	NLA
	Stimmungen: five pieces for Pno.	Keys (1999)	NLA
Hughes, William	The Pno. Sampler - Selections from Premier Ordre Pour Pno., & Deuxieme Ordre Pur Pno.	FS (19--)	sbc
Humble, Keith	Arcade II	Universal (c1975)	Sitsky
	Children's Tunes: Teddy Bear, The Wind , A Dream Bewilderment	MS (1947)	Humble Papers [MS 9402] NLA
	Eight Bagatelles	Melb. Astra Pub.	AMC

		(1999)	
	Essay for Pno.	MS (1949)	Humble Papers [MS 9402] NLA
	Sonata no. 1	MS (1959)	Sitsky
	Sonata no. 2 in Contemporary Australian Pno. Music	Latrobe (1985)	AMC
	Sonata no. 3	FS (1983)	AMC
	Sonata no. 4	FS (1990)	Sitsky
	Pno. Pieces - Miniatures (in progress)	MS (1994)	Humble Papers [MS 9402] NLA
	Three Pno. Pieces: Intermezzo, Waltz, Final	FS (1967)	Sitsky
	Three Statements for Pno.	MS (1959)	Humble Papers [MS 9402] NLA
	To Jill - the first day of spring, Paris 1954	MS (1954)	Humble Papers [MS 9402] NLA
	Two Preludes (F minor & F major)	MS (1948)	Humble Papers [MS 9402] NLA
Hush, David	Sonata for Pno.	Sydney: Hush Editions (1999)	AMC
Hutchens, Frank	At the Bathing Pool	Palings (c1932)	NLA
	Ballade	FS (1939) A/C HUT 25g	SAC NLA
	By the River (in Four Original Australian Tone Poems)	Nicholson's (1947)	NLA
	Concert Prelude	FS (no date) A/C HUT 16b	SAC NLA
	Dance of the Hours	FS (no date) A/C HUT 14c	SAC NLA
	The Enchanted Isle	Palings (1956)	NLA
	Evening	Allans (1954)	NLA
	Fairy Ships	Allans (1956)	NLA
	Gavotte Brilliante	Allans (c1938)	NLA
	Gnomes	Palings (1939)	Mitchell
	Goblins	Allans (1936)	NLA
	In a Boat	Allans (c1949)	Sitsky
	The Isl&	Chappell (c1934)	NLA
	Lord Howe Isl&	FS (no date) A/C HUT 25d	SAC NLA
	Lullaby in F	FS (no date)	AMC
	Lullaby on a Hidden Theme	FS (no date) A/C HUT 25c	SAC NLA
	Minuet	Palings (19--)	NLA
	Paganini	FS (no date) A/C HUT 25h	SAC NLA
	Pno. Works of Frank Hutchens: 15 facsimile scores	FS (no date)	AMC
	Prelude in B Major	Palings (c1937)	NLA
	Prelude Romantique	Allans (c1952)	NLA
	Sea Fantasy	FS (no date)	SAC NLA
	Sea Music	Palings (c1934)	Sitsky
	Serenade	FS (no date) AC/HUT 25e	SAC NLA
	Ship Ahoy	Allans (1949)	NLA
	Smuggler's Cave	Allans (1969)	Mitchell
	Song of the Cello	FS (no date) A/C HUT 24c	SAC NLA
	The Surfer	FS (1954 - 1955) A/C	SAC NLA

		HUT 24e	
	Toccata	FS (no date) A/C HUT 24d	SAC NLA
	The Voyage	Boosey & Co. Ltd. (19- -)	Sitsky
	Waltz	FS (no date) AC/HUT 25e	SAC NLA
	Vienna Interlude	Allans (1954)	NLA
	Weeping Mist	Palings (19--)	NLA
Hutcheson, Ernest	E Flat Major Sonata	MS (1887)	Rare Music Coll. [970693] Sydney Con.
	Sarab&e (no.3 from Four Pieces for Pno. op. 10)	Schirmer (1904)	Grainger
	Three Pieces for Pno. Op. 12 (nos. 1 & 3)	NY: Composer's Music Corp. (1923)	Grainger
	Prelude in F# minor (no. 1 fromTwo Pieces for Pno. Op. 11)	NY: Composer's Music Corp. (1921)	Grainger
Hyde, Miriam	A River Idyll	FS (1931)	AMC
	Ballerina	FS (1987)	AMC
	Birds in Sunlight	FS (no date)	Hyde Papers [MS 526] NLA
	Bridal Study	FS (1973)	NLA
	Brown Hill Creek in Spring	FS (1942 rev. 1984)	AMC
	Burlesque	FS (1933)	Hyde Papers [MS 526] NLA
	Caprice in G minor	MS (1933)	Hyde Papers [MS 526] NLA
	Christmas Card Fantasy	Allans (1961)	AMC
	Concert Study in F# Minor no. 1	FS (1934)	AMC
	Concert Study in F# no. 2	FS (1967)	AMC
	Three Concert Studies for Pno.	Keys (2001)	Sitsky
	Divertimento	FS (19--)	Sitsky
	Dragonflies	Alberts (1973)	Mitchell
	Drought-stricken Grasses	FS (1964)	AMC
	Ear-rings from Spain	Southern (1971)	AMC
	Evening in Cordoba	Keys (2000)	CSM
	Fantasia on Waltzing Matilda	FS (1936)	AMC
	Firewheel	Keys (1999)	NLA
	The Forest Stream	Chappell (1943)	AMC
	Forest Echoes op. 12 no. 1	Allans (1936)	Mitchell
	The Fountain	Allans (1955)	AMC
	Grey Foreshore	Allans (c1961)	Sitsky
	Humoresque	Allans (1974)	Mitchell
	Ivy Leaves	FS (1969)	Hyde Papers [MS 526] NLA
	Lamp With A Fringe	Allans (1974)	Mitchell
	Lengthening Shadows	FS (1974)	AMC
	Lonely Trees Op. 12 no. 2	Allans (1936)	Mitchell
	Lullaby for Christine	Chappell (1952)	AMC
	Magpies at Sunrise	Chappell (1952)	AMC
	Memories of a Happy Day	FS (1939 rev. 1975)	AMC
	The Nest in the Rosebush	Southern Music (1966)	Mitchell
	On the Hillside op. 12 no. 3	Allans (1936)	Mitchell
	Pastorale Study	FS (1973)	Hyde Papers [MS 526] NLA
	Pauline	FS (193?)	AMC

	Pigeons in the Studio	FS (1984)	AMC
	The Poplar Avenue	Allans (1974)	AMC
	The Quiet Meadow op.12 no. 4	Allans (1936)	Mitchell
	Reflected Reeds	Allans (1974)	AMC
	Returning Tide at Sunset	FS (1987)	AMC
	Reverie	Allans (c1943)	Sitsky
	Rhapsodic Study (for left h&)	FS (1976)	AMC
	Rhapsody no. 2 in A minor	FS (1954)	AMC
	Scherzo in G	FS (1937)	AMC
	Scherzo in G	FS (1965)	Hyde Papers [MS 526] NLA
	Scherzo Fantastico (in the Bicentennial Pno. Album)	Allans (1988)	AMC
	Sonata in G minor	Keys (2000)	AMC
	Sonatina (First Movement)	FS (1973)	Hyde Papers [MS 526] NLA
	Spring	Allans (1974)	Mitchell
	The Spring of Joy	FS (1946)	Sitsky
	Study in A flat	FS (1970)	AMC
	Study in A minor	FS (1973)	Hyde Papers [MS 526] NLA
	Study in Left H& Tenths	FS (1982)	AMC
	Study for Right H& Tenths	FS (no date)	AMC
	To a Skylark	FS (1957)	AMC
	Study in A minor	FS (1973)	Hyde Papers [MS 526] NLA
	Study in Blue, White & Gold	Allans (1974)	AMC
	Tap Tune	Schirmer (1952)	Sitsky
	Valley of Rocks	Alberts (1976)	Sitsky
	Variations in C Minor on a theme by M.G. Hyde	FS (1931)	AMC
	The Vine Trellis	FS (1988)	AMC
	The Vision of Mary McKillop	FS (1992)	AMC
	Water Nymph	Allans (1986)	AMC
	Wet Night on the Highway	Chappell (c1959)	Sitsky
	Wind in the Wood op. 12 no. 5	Allans (1936)	Mitchell
Isaacs, Mark	Preludes for Pno.	FS (1986)	AMC
James, William, G.	Four Dances for Young Pianists	Ricordi (1958)	Sydney Con.
	Happy Moments Entr'acte	Ricordi (c1959)	NLA
	Priscilla	Allans (1970)	AMC
	Sea Sketches	Allans (1935)	Sydney Con.
Jenkins, Cyril	Chatterbox	Allans (1935)	Mitchell
	Hawkesbury River	Palings (1937)	Mitchell
	The Passion Flower	Palings (1935)	Mitchell
	The Song of the Sea	Allans (1935)	Mitchell
	The Song of Youth	Palings (1937)	Mitchell
	The Whirligig	Palings (1931)	Mitchell
Jones, Percy	Fairy Dance	Allans (19--)	NLA
Joseph, David	Rhapsody	FS (1997)	AMC
Kats-Chernin, Elena	Alex&er Rag	FS (1998)	AMC
	Backstage Rag	Boosey & Hawkes (1999)	AMC
	Charleston Noir	FS (1996)	AMC
	Combination Rag	Boosey & Hawkes (1999)	AMC
	Four Rags for Ian Monro	FS (1996)	AMC

	Get Well Rag	FS (1998)	AMC
Kats-Chernin, Elena	Lamento the Gestures for Pno. & orchestra	FS (no date)	AMC
	Purple Prelude	Boosey & Hawkes (1996, rev. 1998)	AMC
	Russian Rag	FS (1996)	AMC
	Schubert Blues	FS (1996)	AMC
	Shestizvuchiya	FS (1977)	AMC
	Sonata Lost & Found	FS (1998-1999)	AMC
	Stur In Dur	FS (1998)	AMC
	Suburban Rag	FS (1998)	AMC
	Sunday Rag	FS (1997)	AMC
	Tast-en	FS (1991)	AMC
	Variations in a Serious Black Dress	FS (1995)	AMC
	Zee Rag	FS (1998)	AMC
Kay, Don	Bird Chants	FS (19--)	sbc
	Blue Sky through Still Trees	FS (199?)	sbc
	Dance Rituals	FS (19--)	sbc
	Different Worlds	FS (19--)	sbc
	Legend	FS (19--)	Bollard
	Looking North from Tier Hill	FS (19--)	sbc
	Sonatina	FS (1965)	AMC
	Sonata	FS (19--)	sbc
Keats, Horace arr. By Brendan Keats	Echo	Culburra Beach, N.S.W.: Wirripang Pub. (1999?)	NLA
Keats, Horace	Three Spanish Dances op. 27	Palings (c1922)	NLA
Kelly, Frederick	Allegro de Concert (1907 – 1911) Opus III	Schott (1913)	Sydney Con.
	A Cycle of Lyric Pieces for the Pno.	FS (no date)	Kelly Papers MS 3095 & MS 6050 NLA
	Allegretto Grazioso	FS (no date)	Kelly Papers MS 3095 & MS 6050 NLA
	&ante & Variations	FS (no date)	Kelly Papers MS 3095 & MS 6050 NLA
	Fugue	FS (no date)	Kelly Papers MS 3095 & MS 6050 NLA
	Irish Air with Variations	FS (1898)	Kelly Papers MS 3095 & MS 6050 NLA
	Pastorale	FS (no date)	Kelly Papers MS 3095 & MS 6050 NLA
	Scherzo - Etude	FS (1904)	Kelly Papers MS 3095 & MS 6050 NLA
	Sonata in F minor (incomplete)	FS (no date)	Kelly Papers MS 3095 & MS 6050 NLA
	Twelve Studies for the Pno. op.9 (different version)	FS (1913)	Kelly Papers MS 3095 & MS 6050 NLA
	Twelve Studies for the Pno.	FS (1912)	Kelly Papers MS 3095 & MS 6050 NLA

	Twenty-Four Monographs op. 11	FS (1916)	Kelly Papers MS 3095 & MS 6050 NLA
	Study no. 12 in D Minor	FS (1913)	Kelly Papers MS 3095 & MS 6050 NLA
	Waltz Pageant (1905-1912) op. IIB	Schott (1913)	Sydney Con.
Kelly, Neil	Absinthia Taetra	FS (no date)	AMC
	Pno. Pieces	FS (1986)	AMC
Kerry, Gordon	Perpetual Angelus	FS (1988)	Bollard
	Winter Through Glass	FS (1980)	Bollard
Koehne, Graeme	Capriccio for Pno. & orchestra	FS (1987)	AMC
	Harmonies of Silver & Blue	FS (1999)	AMC
	Sonata	FS (1976)	AMC
	Twilight Rain	FS (1977)	AMC
Koo, Brian Chatpo	The Picture of Drunken Zhong Kui	FS (1988)	AMC
Kos, Bozidar	Kolo	Sydney: Bosidar Kos (c1984)	AMC
	Pno. Sonata	FS (1981)	AMC
	Reflections	FS (1976)	AMC
Kouvaras, Linda	Bundanoon Suite for Pno.	FS (1999)	sbc
	The Ormond Collection	FS (1998-1999)	sbc
	Three St Kilda Sketches	FS (1994-1997)	sbc
Krips, Heinrich	Gruss Gott, schoene Muellerin	FS (no date) Item A/C KRI 04	SAC NLA
	Habanera	FS (no date) Item A/C KRI 04	SAC NLA
Lalor, Stephen	Antipodie	S.L.: S. Lalor (c1995)	AMC
	The Rollercoaster	FS (1992)	AMC
	Three Pieces for Pno.: Prelude,Waltz, Postlude	FS (1989)	AMC
Lavater, Louis	A Passing Fancy (A Humoreske for Pno.)	Allans (1935)	Mitchell
	Dance of the Saplings	Allans (1922)	Mitchell
	Hornpipe in G	Allans (c1923)	NLA
	A Passing Fancy	Allans (1935)	NLA
	Queen Mab Waltz	Melb.: W.H. Glen (1880-85)	NLA
	The Rose-Burner: (Orientale)	Allans (1944)	NLA
	Sonata in A for Pno.	FS (194?)	NLA
	Three Waltz Impressions: Valse Eleganté, Valse Orientale, Valse Romantique	Chappell (c1940)	NLA
	Three Waltz Moods: Valse Capricieuse, Valse Triste, Valse Joyeuse	Chappell (c1940)	NLA
	Twelve Preludes	Allans (1937)	Sitsky
Lavers, Gordon V.	Blue Mountains: Three Impressions for Pno. Solo	Palings (1934)	NLA
	Scenes from Fairyl&	Palings (19--)	Mitchell
	A Summer Holiday	Palings (1939)	Mitchell
Lavin, Sr Duchesne	Papua New Guinea: Suite for Pno.	Alberts (1976)	Mitchell
	Pentatonic Miniatures	FS (no date)	AMC
	Three Poetic Tone Rows: Caprice, Valse Elegante, Pastorale	FS (no date)	AMC
Le Gallienne, Dorian	Incidental Music to Macbeth	FS (1947)	AMC
	Jinker Ride	Allans (c1965)	AMC
	Nocturne	Allans (1964)	Sitsky

	Sonata for Pno. (1951)	Keys (2001)	Sitsky
	Sonatina for Pno.	MS (no date)	Symphony Australia
	Symphonic Study	Keys (2002)	Sitsky
	Symphonic Study	FS (c1940) Item Y/P 3 GAL.NE 01	SAC NLA
	Three Pno. Pieces	FS (1946) Item Y/P-AL 1 GAL.NE 01	SAC NLA
Lea, Beverley	Embers	Grevillea (199?)	sbc
Leek, Stephen	Hammered	FS (1989)	AMC
	Seven Days	FS (1987)	AMC
	Seven Places	FS (1988)	AMC
	Seven Windows	FS (1989)	AMC
Lemmoné, John	Dainty Dance	Palings (192?)	Mitchell
	Fascination (Graceful Dance no. 2)	Palings (19--)	CSM AMC
	Graceful Dance	Palings (1912)	Mitchell
	Minuet (Caprice)	Palings (19--)	Mitchell
	Spring Time	Palings (192?)	Mitchell
	Valse Bluette	Palings (19--)	AMC
Libaek, Sven	Etude no. 4 for Pno.,"Double Stops" op. 33	Sydney: Sven Libaek Music (1997)	AMC
	Machine Dreams op. 26	Sydney: Sven Libaek Music (1996)	AMC
	Nature Pieces for Pno. op. 23	Sydney: Sven Libaek Music (1996)	AMC
	Nature Pieces for Pno. op.24 (nos. 7 - 9)	Sydney: Sven Libaek Music (1996)	AMC
	Nocturne op. 25	Sydney: Sven Libaek Music (1996)	AMC
	Toccata in D Minor op. 4	Sydney: Sven Libaek Music (1996)	AMC
	Three Etudes for Pno. op. 16, no. 1, "Spring Shower"	Sydney: Sven Libaek Music (1996)	AMC
	Three Small Waltzes op. 18	Sydney: Sven Libaek Music (1996)	AMC
	Two Baroque Preludes for Pno., op. 30	Sydney: Sven Libaek Music (1996)	AMC
Lisle, Vernon	Sonata no. 1 in A minor	FS (no date)	AMC
Lloyd, Robert	Newborn	FS (1997)	AMC
	The Perfect Pno.	FS (1981)	AMC
	The Untouched Key	FS (1997)	AMC
Loam, Arthur	Along the Shore	Allans (c1957)	Sitsky
	Butterfly Chase	Allans (c1964)	Sitsky
	By a Wayside Shrine	Palings (c1942)	NLA
	Caprice	Allans (c1967)	NLA
	Four Australian Sketches: Aboriginal Suite	MS (no date)	Mitchell
	Green Sleeves: Old English Air arranged for Pno.	Allans (1956)	Sitsky
	Londonderry Air : Irish Air arranged for Pno.	Allans (1938)	Sitsky
	Maranoa Fantasy for Pno. on an Australian Aboriginal Theme	Allans (c1938)	Sitsky
	The Snowy Breasted Pearl : Old Irish Air Transcribed for Pno.	Allans (1941)	Sitsky
Longas, Frederico	Catalana	Allans (1938)	NLA
	Two Words Waltz	Chicago: Forster Music Pub. (c1929)	NLA

Lonsdale, Michael	Mouna	FS (1986)	AMC
Loughlin, George	Three Short Pno. Pieces	Allans (1978)	NLA
	Toccata	Allans (c1964)	NLA
Lovelock, William	Aquarelles	Chappell (1973)	Mitchell
	By the Lakeside	Southern (1958)	Mitchell
	On the Run	Southern (1958)	Mitchell
	Scherzo	Allans (1968)	Mitchell
	Siciliano	Southern (1970)	Mitchell
Lumsdaine, David	Cambewarra	FS (1980)	AMC
	Kelly Ground	Universal (1966)	AMC
	Ruhe Sanfte Ruh	FS (1974)	AMC
Maclean, Hector	Rondo in A major: Sketch for Pno. Solo	Palings (1929)	Mitchell
	Sun Music.Five Pieces for Pno.: Sunrise, Sunshine, Sunbeams, Sunday, Sunset	Palings (1913)	Mitchell
McBurney, Mona	A Northern Ballad: The Saga of King Orry Fantasie for Pno. & Orchestra (two Pno. version)	London: Novello (19--)	Uni. of Melb. Library
McCaughey, John	Five Small Pieces	FS (1983)	Sitsky
McCombe, Chris	divergence	FS (1998)	AMC
	Song of Truth & Loneliness	FS (1995)	AMC
Maddox, Peter	City Pictures	FS (1978)	sbc
	Four Fugues for Pno.	FS (19--)	sbc
	Pno. Sonata no. 1	FS (19--)	sbc
	Suite for two Pno.s	FS (19--)	sbc
	Toccata for Pno. Solo	FS (19--)	sbc
	Tyringham Mailboxes	FS (19--)	sbc
Mageau, Mary	Cityscapes	FS (1978)	AMC
	Cycles & Series: Three Pieces for Pno. Alone	NY: Lyric Press (2000)	AMC
	Etude	FS (1970)	AMC
	Elite Syncopations (in Contemporary Australian Miniatures)	LaTrobe (c1985)	Sitsky
	Ragtime	FS (1977)	Sitsky
	Ragtime Remembered	FS (2000)	AMC
	Soliloquy	FS (1984)	AMC
Mahler, Hellgart	Photons	Devonport, Tas.: Quamby Books (1992)	AMC
	Scherzo & Quatro	Devonport, Tas.: Quamby Books (1989)	Sitsky
	Three Galactic Fragments	Devonport, Tas.: Quamby Books (1991)	AMC
Marcellino, Raffaele	Daedulus sequences 1 - 4	FS (2000)	AMC
Marks, Glenn	Pno.phonics	Southern (c1953)	NLA
Marsh, Olive	Three Pieces: 1. A Song of June; 2. A Song of Roses; 3. A Valse Song	Allans (1926)	NLA
Marshall-Hall, G.W.H.	Jubilum Amoris	MS (no date)	Musica Australis Collection, Symphony Australia
Mather, Martin	Chorale Partitas	FS (2000)	AMC
Meale, Richard	Coruscations	Universal (1971)	Sitsky
	Four Bagatelles	FS (19--)	Sitsky
	Sonatina Patetica	FS (1957)	Sitsky
Melvaine,	* NB -Numerous short pieces written for his	FS (19--)	sbc

Maurice	cats		
	Solenarda in C major Opus 1. nos. 1 & 2	Sydney: Van Dyke (1974)	Mitchell
Mexis, Themos	Byzantine Melody	FS (1982)	AMC
Middenway, Ralph	Sonata Capricciosa	FS (1989)	AMC
	Toyokawa: East River Pno. Sonata	FS (1994)	AMC
Milford, Robert	Preludio in C# minor	Palings (1922)	Mitchell
Monk, Varney	Serena	Chappell (c1962)	NLA
Morgan, David	Divers Paces: Suite for Pno. "Time travels in divers paces . . ." (Shakespeare)	FS (1999)	AMC
	Norwegian Fantasy	FS (1997)	AMC
	Pno. Sonata no. 1 in D major [composed at the age of sixteen]	FS (1948, rev. 1998)	AMC
	Pno. Sonata no. 4: The Heart of the Matter	FS (19--)	Sitsky
Morgan, Rees	Bagatelle	Boosey & Hawkes (c1943)	NLA
Nagorcka, Ron	Fugilism	FS (1977)	AMC
	Pentaphase 11	FS (1974)	AMC
	Prelude	FS (1995)	AMC
	Requiem	FS (1976)	AMC
	Zygodactyl Dance	FS (1999)	AMC
Needham, Pascal	The Gr& Processional March	unknown	Sitsky
Newmann, Ray	The Dice Were Loaded	FS (19--)	Sitsky
Nickson, Noel	Sonatina	Allans (1956)	NLA
Nicolet, Robert	Moto Perpetuo	unknown	NLA
Noble, Alistair	Fantasia Pange Lingua (Sonata no. 2)	FS (1995)	Sitsky
	Manteena	FS (1998)	Sitsky
	Night Rain: Three Reflections on a Chinese Poem	FS (1998)	Sitsky
	Sonata no. 3	FS (1999)	Sitsky
	Sonata no. 4	FS (2000)	sbc
	Sun, Mountain, Cloud, Forest	FS (199?)	Sitsky
	Thamarya	FS (1997)	Sitsky
Oldaker, Max	A Bird Market in Peking A Chinese Episode for Pno.	Allans (c1941)	Sitsky
Olive, Vivienne	The Dream Gardens	Kassel, Germany: Furore Edition (1989)	AMC
	Five Australian L&scapes	Kassel, Germany: Furore Edition (1998)	AMC
	Perpetuum Mobile	FS (no date)	AMC
	Text III	Kassel, Germany: Furore Edition (1993)	
Oosterbaan, &re	related conrasts	photocopy computer notated (1981)	AMC
Orlovich, Matthew	Sea Spirits & Watercolours	FS (199?)	sbc
Orchard, W. Arundel	Ariel	Allans (c1943)	NLA
	Rhapsody in A minor	Augener (1939)	NLA
	Scherzo	MS (no date)	Orchard Papers [MS 5782] NLA
	A Spring Morning	Allans (1956)	NLA
	Toccata	Chappell (1943)	NLA
Overman, Meta	Sonata 1	FS (1939)	AMC
	Sonata 11	FS (1953)	AMC

	Sonatina	FS (1940)	AMC
	Three Dances for Pno.	FS (1955)	AMC
	Three Impressions for Pno. Solo	FS (1942)	AMC
Palmer, Alma	A Fairy Pool	Allans (1953)	Mitchell
	Sweet Meadow	Allans (1929)	Mitchell
Panvino, Calogero	Anodyne Rustle op. 1a	FS (19--)	sbc
	Anodyne Rustle op. 1b	FS (19--)	sbc
	Lethargy 1-11	FS (19--)	sbc
	Toccata Kaleidoscopique op. 2	FS (19--)	sbc
Parker, Kitty (Katharine)	Arc-en-ciel: Valse Ballet for Pno.	Augener (1936)	Grainger
	Four Musical Sketches for Pno.: A Patchwork of Shadows, Down Longford Way, One Summer Day, The Red Admiral	London:Winthrop Rogers (1928)	NLA
	Nocturne	Augener (1925)	Grainger
Paull, James	Fallen Angels	FS (1983)	AMC
Paviour, Paul	Alice In Pno. L&	London: Mills Music Ltd. (1967)	Sydney Con.
	Let's Go Walkabout	Keys (1996)	AMC
	The Rondo Rag	Keys (1994)	AMC
	Pno. Sonata no. 2	Engl&: Barry Brunton Music Publisher (c1991)	AMC
	The High Paddock (from Seven Pieces for Pno. no. 3 op.110)	FS (1993)	AMC
	Sketches From Dickens	Sydney: Castle Music (c1972)	AMC
	They Went to Golgotha	Keys (1999)	Sitsky
	A Wedding Piece	Goulburn, N.S.W. Aurora Pub. (1994)	AMC
Peachey, &rew	Contrasting Scenes for Pno.	S.L.: A. Peachey (c1996)	AMC
	Suite For Pno.	S.L.: A. Peachey (1997)	AMC
Penberthy, James	Clocks	Sydney: James Penberthy (c1983)	AMC
	Concerto for Pno. & Orchestra no. 3 (Beyond the Universe) (solo Pno. part)	FS (1974)	Sitsky
	Earth Mother Fantasy	FS (1990)	AMC
	For Pno.	MS (1985)	AMC
	Prelude 2	MS (1978)	uncatalogued archive, NLA
	Preludes nos. 4 & 5	MS (no date)	uncatalogued archive, NLA
	Sad Music For Thursday	MS (1985)	uncatalogued archive, NLA
	Simple Study	MS (1985)	uncatalogued archive, NLA
	Three Happenings for Pno.	MS (1970)	uncatalogued archive, NLA
	Three Pieces for Pno. op. 53: Danza, Brolga, Allegro	MS (1952)	uncatalogued archive, NLA
	Trivial Pursuit	MS (1985)	uncatalogued archive, NLA
Penicka, Miroslav	Kookaburra's Friends	FS (1990)	CSM AM
	Musings	FS (1996)	AMC

	Sonatina	FS (1989)	AMC
	Second Sonata for Pno.	FS (1979)	AMC
Perkins, Horace	Agitato (illegible title)	MS (no date)	Perkins Archive [MSS 0027] Barr Smith
	Allegretto	MS (no date)	Perkins Archive [MSS 0027] Barr Smith
	Allegro Maestoso	MS (1924)	Perkins Archive [MSS 0027] Barr Smith
	Allegro Maestoso (different version)	MS (1924)	Perkins Archive [MSS 0027] Barr Smith
	&antino (unfinished)	MS (no date)	Perkins Archive [MSS 0027] Barr Smith
	Bagatelle	MS (no date)	Perkins Archive [MSS 0027] Barr Smith
	Ballad & Ballad IIa	MS (no date)	Perkins Archive [MSS 0027] Barr Smith
	Cantabile non troppo lento	MS (1926)	Perkins Archive [MSS 0027] Barr Smith
	Con molto maesta, Tranquillo, Cant&o, &ante, Largo, Scherzo & Presto, Allegretto, Molto Allegro e scherz&o	MS (no date)	Perkins Archive [MSS 0027] Barr Smith
	Elves	MS (no date)	Perkins Archive [MSS 0027] Barr Smith
	Intermezzo	MS (1927)	Perkins Archive [MSS 0027] Barr Smith
	Intermezzo I	MS (no date)	Perkins Archive [MSS 0027] Barr Smith
	Legend	MS (no date)	Perkins Archive [MSS 0027] Barr Smith
	Legend	MS (no date)	Perkins Archive [MSS 0027] Barr Smith
	Legends from a Far Country	MS (1931)	Perkins Archive [MSS 0027] Barr Smith
	Lowl& Song	MS (no date)	Perkins Archive [MSS 0027] Barr Smith
	The Pipes of Pan (A Romance in Miniature) 2 copies	MS (no date)	Perkins Archive [MSS 0027] Barr Smith
	The Poet, A Lover's Tale, Interlude, con violenza, &ante	MS (no date)	Perkins Archive [MSS 0027] Barr Smith
	Prelude	MS (no date)	Perkins Archive [MSS 0027] Barr Smith

	Prelude on a Bach Chorale	MS (no date)	Perkins Archive [MSS 0027] Barr Smith
	The Prince's Song	MS (no date)	Perkins Archive [MSS 0027] Barr Smith
	Romance in F sharp minor	MS (1925)	Perkins Archive [MSS 0027] Barr Smith
	Romance in G	MS (no date)	Perkins Archive [MSS 0027] Barr Smith
	Romance in B minor	MS (1925)	Perkins Archive [MSS 0027] Barr Smith
	Rondo	MS (1925)	Perkins Archive [MSS 0027] Barr Smith
	Scherzo	MS (1921)	Perkins Archive [MSS 0027] Barr Smith
	"We're all bound to go": Fantas on a Sea Chanty	MS (c1921)	Perkins Archive [MSS 0027] Barr Smith
	"Wistaria"	MS (no date)	Perkins Archive [MSS 0027] Barr Smith
Peterson, John	Walking On Glass	MS (1992)	AMC
Phillip, Laurance	Romantic Sketches	Palings (no date)	Mitchell
Phillips, Linda	Sea Impressions: Mermaid & Harp, The Dancing Sunlight, Waves	FS (no date)	AMC
Phillips, Rohan	Pno. Piece	FS (1994)	AMC
Platt, Peter	A Thoughtful Piece for Eric	MS (July, 1991)	uncatalogued archive, Mitchell
	&ante lirico for the left h&	MS (July, 1997)	uncatalogued archive, Mitchell
	Boulez Notations (incomplete)	MS (no date)	uncatalogued archive, Mitchell
	Cantilena	MS (1998)	uncatalogued archive, Mitchell
	Largo	MS (no date)	uncatalogued archive, Mitchell
	Two Views of Eternity	FS (19--)	Sitsky
Plush, Vincent	Franz Liszt Sleeps Alone	FS (1985)	Sitsky
Polglase, John	Eight Bagatelles	FS (no date)	AMC
	Fragments	FS (1984)	AMC
	Quiet This Metal	FS (1995)	AMC
Pollard, Mark	A H&ful of Rain	FS (1994)	AMC
	The Prayers of Tears	FS (1989)	AMC
	Carillon for Sacha (in Australian Pno. Miniatures)	Red House (1998)	AMC
	Krebs	FS (1983)	Sitsky
Pompili, Claudio	Three Miniatures for Pno.	FS (no date)	AMC
	Trece	FS (1981)	AMC
Raine, Kathleen	Crux	FS (1972)	Sitsky
Reeder, Haydn	Cantus: three pieces for Pno.	FS (c1997)	AMC
	Masks (in Contemporary Australian Pno. Music)	LaTrobe (c1985)	Sitsky

	Re-creation: music for a New Year Festival	FS (1998)	AMC
	Tolling Bell Song	FS (1998)	AMC
Reiner, Thomas	Baby Orang Utan (in Australian Pno. Miniatures)	Red House (1998)	AMC
	Fragment	FS (1994)	AMC
	Kalorama Prelude	FS (1989)	AMC
Rofe, Esther	Pno. Music: Pro-tem Suite: little suite for the left h& (1937), The Isl& (1938 re. 1993), Jester (1962), Fuer Else (1989)	FS (no date)	AMC
Rota, Nino	Legend of the Glass Mountain	Palings (c1949)	Sitsky
Sabin, Nigel	Another Look At Autumn	FS (1993)	AMC
	A Faint Qualm As Of Green April	Fs (1993)	AMC
Sauer, Carl	The Fountain & the Wind	Palings (1931)	Mitchell
	La Babillarde (The Chatterbox)	Palings (1929)	Mitchell
	Song of Venice	Palings (1929)	Mitchell
	Three Aquarelles	Palings (c1922)	Mitchell
Scammell, Annette	Humoresque	London, Murdoch, Murdoch & Co. (19--)	Sitsky
	In Summer Fields	London, Murdoch, Murdoch & Co. (19--)	Sitsky
Schiemer, Greg	Iconophony	S.L.: Greg Schiemer (1973)	AMC
Shlomowitz, Matthew	Thinking, Remembering	FS (1997)	AMC
Schulz, &rew	Sea Change	FS (1987)	AMC
	Sonata	FS (1982)	AMC
Schultz, Chester	The Magpies of Aldinga Scrub	FS (2001)	CSM - sbc
Sculthorpe, Peter	A Little Book Of Hours	Faber (1998)	AMC
	Mountains	Faber (1982)	AMC
	Night	Allans (1972)	AMC
	Night Pieces	Faber (1973)	AMC
	Nocturnal	Faber (1987?)	AMC
	The Rose Bay Quadrilles	Faber (c1989)	AMC
	Siesta	FS (1946)	AMC
	Snow, Moon & Flowers	Allans (1972)	AMC
	Sonatina	Leeds (1964)	Sitsky
	Three Pieces for Pno.: Djilile, Callabonna, Simori	Faber (1997)	AMC
	Two Easy Pieces: Sea Chant, Left Bank Waltz	FS (no date)	AMC
Seeto, Melissa	Miniatures for Pno.	FS (19--)	sbc
Sheppard, Doris	Romanza	Nicholson's (1954)	NLA
Sitsky, Larry	E: for solo Pno.	Keys (1997)	AMC
	EII: for solo Pno.	Keys (c1998)	Sitsky
	Fantasia no. 1 in Memory of Egon Petri	Ricordi (1972)	AMC
	Fantasia no. 2, in Memory of Winifred Burston	NY: Seesaw Music (1980)	Sitsky
	Fantasia no. 4: Arch in Contemporary Australian Pno. Music	LaTrobe (c1985)	AMC
	Fantasia no. 5: Sharagan	NY: Seesaw Music (1984)	AMC
	Fantasia no. 7 on a theme of Liszt	Canada: Sikesdi Press (1985)	AMC
	Fantasia no. 8, on D-B-A-S	Keys (1996)	AMC
	Fantasia no. 10: for the Moore double keyboard Pno.	FS (1992)	AMC
	Fantasia no. 11: "E"	Keys (1998)	Sitsky
	Foucalt's Pendulum (in Australian Pno.	Red House (1998)	AMC

	Miniatures)		
	Four Pno. Pieces	Allans (1969)	AMC
	Little Suite for Pno. (in five movements)	Allans (c1969)	Sitsky
	Lotus	NY: Seesaw Music (1995)	Sitsky
	Lotus II	MS (1996)	Sitsky
	Nocturne Canonique	MS (1974)	Sitsky
	Perele's Song (in the Bicentennial Pno. Album)	Allans (1988)	AMC
	Petra	FS (1971)	AMC
	Seven Statements for Pno.	FS (1964)	AMC
	Si Yeoo Ki (The Great Search)	MS (1985)	Sitsky
	Sonatina formalis	Allans (1969)	AMC
	Twelve Mystical Preludes	FS (1973)	AMC
Smalley, Roger	Barcarolle	Claremont, W.A.: Hovea Music Press (1999)	AMC
	Chopin Variations	Claremont, W.A.: Hovea Music Press (1999)	AMC
	Missa Parodia 1	Faber (c1967)	AMC
	Monody	Faber (1975)	AMC
	Pno. Concerto	FS (1985)	AMC
	Pno. Pieces I-V	Faber (c1969)	AMC
Smetanin, Michael	Something's Missing Here...a postcard from Holl&	FS (1988)	AMC
	Stroke	FS (1988)	AMC
Spiers, Colin	Anna	FS (1981)	AMC
	Elegy & Tocccata	S.L.: Colin Spiers (1998)	AMC
	Fantasy on a Theme by Keith Jarrett	FS (1987)	AMC
	Flecks	FS (1991)	AMC
	Pno. Sonata no. 1: the quiet geometry of madness	FS (1990)	AMC
	Pno. Sonata no. 2: desperate acts	Fs (1992)	AMC
	Pno. Sonata no. 3: divine symmetry	FS (1994)	AMC
	Pno. Sonata no. 4: (delicate games)	FS (1995)	AMC
	Pno. Sonata no. 5	FS (1998)	AMC
	The Princess of the M&ala	FS (1981)	AMC
	A Small Contrapuntal Fantasy	FS (1982)	AMC
	Tales From Nowhere	FS (1988)	AMC
	Variations on La Folia	FS (1981)	AMC
Stanley, Jane	Three Pieces for Pno.: 1. Nefas 2. Fas 3. Nefarious Dance	FS (2000-2001)	sbc
St&ring, Helen	The Dancers	FS (1984)	AMC
Stanhope, Paul	Three Little Pieces for Pno.	FS (2000)	AMC
Stankiewicz, Marian	Chamber Music for Pno.	FS (no date)	AMC
Stewart, D. Henry	Musette (Rhapsodie)	Palings (no date)	Mitchell
Strahan, Derek	Atlantis Variations	FS (1993)	AMC
Sutherl&, Margaret	Chiaroscuro I & II	FS (1968)	Sitsky
	Extension	FS (1967)	Sitsky
	First Suite: The Adventurer, The Dreamer, The Bustler, The Humorist	Allans (1937)	Sitsky
	Holiday Tunes	Palings (c1937)	Sitsky
	Miniature Sonata	Allans (1940)	Sitsky

	The Pno. Works of Margaret Sutherl&	Allans (c2000)	AMC
	Second Suite: Chorale Prelude, Mirage, Lavender Girl, The Quest	Allans (1937)	Sitsky
	Six Profiles	Augener (1953)	NLA
	Sonatina	Melb.: Australian Music Fund (1956)	Sitsky
	Two Chorale Preludes	Allans (1936)	Sitsky
	Valse Descant	Allans (c1968)	Sitsky
	Voices 1 & 2	FS (1968)	Sitsky
Szeto, Caroline	Moon on Night's Water	FS (1990)	Bollard
	Yunny's Treat	FS (1991)	Bollard
Tahourdin, Peter	Cappriccio	FS (1963)	AMC
	Expose	S.L.: P. Tahourdin (1995)	Sitsky
Tait, John	Three Little Sketches	Allans (1937)	Mitchell
Tate, Henry	Morning in the Gully	FS (192?)	Sitsky
Thompson, Lesleigh	Sphygmus	FS (1992)	AMC
Thorn, Benjamin	A' Pierre	FS (no date)	AMC
	The Colours of Paradise	FS (no date)	AMC
	Froggy Feet	FS (no date)	AMC
	Three Pno. Interludes from Dante's Inferno for Pno.	FS (no date)	AMC
Thwaites, Penelope	Dancing Pieces: Spanish Dance 2. Dreamy Waltz 3. Hop	Aylesbury, Engl&: Bardic Edition (1990)	AMC
Tibbits, George	Stasis	FS (19--)	Sitsky
Tiutiunnik, Katia	Aggressi Sunt Mare Tenebrarum Quid In Eo Esset Exploraturi	FS 1996)	sbc
	Bhairawa	FS (1995)	sbc
Tobin, Clare Sr	L'Encens se Leve	Alberts (1976)	Sitsky
	Reflection	Alberts (1974)	Mitchell
Truman, Ernest	Gr& Prelude & Fugue op. 44	Sydney: Sydney College of Music (1909)	NLA
Tunley, David	Two Preludes for Pno.	FS (1961-1962 revised 1968)	CSM sbc
Vella, Richard	Memory Pieces	FS (1985)	AMC
	Four Pno. Pieces	FS (1977)	AMC
Vick, Lloyd	Adagio & Fugue	FS (19--)	Sitsky
	Café piece	FS (19--)	Sitsky
	Dream Circles no. 1	FS (2000)	AMC
	Dream Circles no. 2	FS (2000)	AMC
	Dream Circles no. 3	FS (2000)	AMC
	Dream Circles no. 4	FS (2001)	AMC
	Fantasia (For the Wayne Stuart gr& Pno.)	FS (1999)	AMC
	Group of Three	FS (no date)	AMC
	Modal Suite for Harpsichord	FS (c1954)	AMC
	"A Noise That Annoys"	FS (2002)	AMC
	Short, Sharp & Shiny no. 2	FS (2001)	AMC
	Short, Sharp & Shiny no. 4	FS (2002)	AMC
	Sound Shapes no. 2	FS (1998-99)	AMC
Vine, Carl	Five Bagatelles	Faber (1995)	AMC
	Occasional Poetry: Three Excerpts for Solo Pno.	FS (1984)	AMC
	Pno. Sonata	London: Chester (1990)	AMC
	Pno. Sonata no. 2	Faber (c1997)	Sitsky

Vines, Nicholas	Terraformation: Sonata no. 1	FS (19--)	sbc
Vois, Paul	Sonate in D minor	Boosey & Hawkes, (1940)	Mitchell
	Three Little Pieces	Boosey & Hawkes (1939)	Mitchell
Wade, Simon	Four Incidental Keyboard Pieces	FS (1979 -85)	AMC
Walker, Allan	Two Small Pieces	FS (1980)	AMC
Webb, Peter	Variations	FS (1990)	AMC
Werder, Felix	Board Music	FS (196?)	Sitsky
	Daktulophy	FS (1968)	Sitsky
	A Little Pno. Music	Centraton Musikverlag (19--)	Sitsky
	Monograph	Keys (2000)	Sitsky
	Pno. Concert 2	FS (1975)	AMC
	Pno. Music op. 97	FS (1968)	NLA
	Sonata IV	Allans (1973)	CSM
	Sonata V	FS (19--)	Sitsky
	Three Blake's Songs of Innocence (1985)	Keys (2001)	AMC
Wesley-Smith, Martin	Beta-Globin DNA for performer/s & tape	FS (1987)	AMC
	Two Waltzes from On A.I. Petrof : 1. Olya's Waltz; 2. Waltz for Aunt Irina	Sydney: Purple Ink (1992)	Bollard
	On A.I. Petrof	Sydney: Purple Ink (1993)	Bollard
	Oom Pah Pah Oom Pah	FS (1989)	AMC
	Three Little Pno. Pieces: 1. Red Rag; 2. Grey Beach; 3. Griff's Riffs	Sydney: Purple Ink (1991)	AMC
	White Night Waltz	FS (1996)	Bollard
Westlake, Nigel	Pno. Sonata	FS (1997)	AMC
Wheeler, Eve	Budi's Journey	FS (199?)	Sitsky
Wheeler, Tony	Pno. Variations	FS (1982)	AMC
Whiffin, Lawrence	The Garfield Suite	FS (1985)	AMC
	Poly Waltz	FS (1985)	AMC
	Prelude for Pno.	FS (1983)	AMC
	Sonata: Mechanical Mirrors	FS (1999)	AMC
	Sonatina	FS (1985)	AMC
Whitehead, Gillian	Fantasia on Three Notes	Wellington, N.Z.: Wai-te-ata Press (1969)	AMC
	Five Bagatelles	FS (1986)	Bollard
	Four Short Pieces (in the Bicentennial Pno. Album)	Allans (1988)	AMC
	Lullaby for Matthew	FS (1981)	AMC
	Tamtea Tutahi	FS (1980)	AMC
Whiticker, Michael	The H&s, the Dream	FS (1987)	AMC
	Pno. Pieces: Hommage to Alban Berg, Liexliu, Vibitqi	FS (1979-81)	AMC
	A Song Without Words	FS (1991)	AMC
Wilcher, Phillip	Arabesque	FS (1997)	AMC
	Chiaroscuro: Suite for Solo Pno.: Picasso, Degas, Monet	FS (1993)	AMC
	Cobwebs	FS (1995)	AMC
	Daybreak	Alberts (1974)	NLA
	Etude Rorem	FS (1993)	AMC
	Kumoi Prelude	FS (1997)	AMC
	Rhapsody Sonata	FS (1994)	AMC

	Seachange	FS (1998)	AMC
Williamson, Malcolm	Five Preludes	London: Josef Weinberger Ltd. (1966)	AMC
	Haifa Watercolors	Edward B. Marks Music Co. (1975)	AMC
	Pno. Sonata	Boosey & Hawkes (1956)	Sitsky
	Pno. Sonata no. 2	London: Josef Weinberger Ltd. (1972)	Sitsky
	Travel Diaries Impressions of Famous Cities for Pno. (London, Naples, Sydney, New York, Paris)	Chappell (c1962)	Sitsky
Wood, Steve	The Wind Whispers in the Trees; Einstein Fugue	FS (no date)	AMC
	To whom it may concern	FS (no date)	AMC
Worrall, David	Scorpion Under Glass	FS (19--)	Sitsky
	Sketch Portrait	FS (19--)	Sitsky
	Sonata	FS (19--)	Sitsky
Wunderlich, Ernest	Eight Pno. Pieces in Fugal Style	Privately printed by Breitkopf & Härtel (19--)	Sydney Con.
	Six Pieces for Pno.	Privately printed by Breitkopf & Härtel (19--)	NLA
	Twelve Small Pno. Pieces	Palings (19--)	Sitsky
	Theme & Variations (3rd series)	Privately printed by Breitkopf & Härtel (19--)	Sitsky
	Theme & Variations	Privately printed by Breitkopf & Härtel (19--)	Sitsky
Yardley, Judith	Fantasie	Nicholson's (1953)	Mitchell
Yee, Adam	Lot	FS (1995)	AMC
Yu, Julian	Impromptu	Universal (1989)	AMC
	Scintillation I	Universal (1989)	AMC
Zadro, Mark	Sculpture	FS (1997)	AMC
Zoch, Katerina	Sonatina	Hindmarsh, S.A.: Kelly Sebastian (1992)	NLA

Complete list of piano concerti

Composer	Title	Details	Source
Bainton, Edgar	Concerto - Fantasia	Stainer & Bell (1921)	Sitsky
Benjamin, Arthur	Concertino	Schott (1927)	Sitsky
	Concerto quasi una Fantasia	Boosey & Hawkes (1949)	Sitsky
Boyle, George f.	Concerto in D minor for Pno. & Orch.	Schirmer (1912)	NLA
Bračanin, Philip K.	Concerto for Pno. & Orch.	FS (1980)	AMC
Brandman, Margaret	Lyric Fantasy: Concerto for Pno. & String Orch.	FS (1991)	AMC
Brewster-Jones, Hooper	Concerto no. 2 in A flat major for Pno. & Orch. (full score)	MS (1922)	uncat. archive, Barr Smith

	Concerto no. 3 (two Pno. version)	MS (1925)	uncat. archive, Barr Smith
	Concerto no. 4 (second Movement)(full score)	MS (no date)	uncat. archive, Barr Smith
Broadstock, Brenton	Pno. Concerto	FS (19--)	Sitsky
Brumby, Colin	Pno. Concerto	FS (1984)	AMC
Butterley, Nigel	Explorations for Pno. & Orch.	FS (c1970)	AMC
Carr-Boyd, Ann	Concerto for Pno. & Orch.	FS (1991)	AMC
Cronin, Stephen	Concerto for Pno. & Orch.	FS (1989)	AMC
Eagles, Moneta	Autumn Rhapsody for Pno. & Orch.	FS (no date)	sbc
Eagles, Moneta	Diversions for Pno. & Orch. (full score & Pno. reduction)	FS (no date)	sbc
Easton, Michael	Concerto on Australian Themes for Pno., Strings & Percussion	FS (1996)	AMC
Edwards, Ross	Pno. Concerto	Universal (1984)	AMC
Featherstone, Gary	Pno. Concerto no. 1	FS (1992)	AMC
Ford, &rew	Imaginings: for Pno. & Orch.	FS (1998)	sbc
Franklin, Jim	Across the Swan's Riding for Pno. & Orch.	FS (1998)	AMC
Gethen, Felix	Concertino for Pno. & Strings	FS (1955)	AMC
Glanville-Hicks, Peggy	Etruscan Concerto	FS (1954)	AMC
Gross, Eric	Pno. Concerto op. 135	FS (1983)	AMC
Hanson, Raymond	Concerto for Pno. & Orch.	FS (1972) A/C HAN 01	SAC NLA
Henderson, Moya	Celebration 40 000 for Pno. & Orch.	FS (1987)	AMC
Hill, Mirrie	Rhapsody in A major for Pno. & Orch.	FS (c.1913) A/C HIL-M 06d	SAC NLA
Holl&, Dulcie	Concertino for Pno. & Strings	FS (1983)	AMC
Hutchens, Frank	Concerto for Pno. & Strings	FS (c1950) A/C HUT 02	SAC NLA
	Pno. Concerto	FS (no date) A/C HUT 01	SAC NLA
Hyde, Mirrie	Fantasy Romantic for Pno. & Orch.	FS (1938, scored 1940) A/C HYD 36	SAC NLA
	Pno. Concerto no. 1 in E flat minor	FS (193?)	AMC
	Pno. Concerto in C# minor no. 2	FS (193?) A/C HYD 45	SAC NLA
Isaacs, Mark	Litany for Pno. & Orch.	FS (1991 rev. 1994)	AMC
	Moving Pictures for Pno. & Orch.	FS (1982)	AMC
Joseph, David	Chamber Concerto for Pno. & Strings	FS (1991)	AMC
	Concerto for Solo Pno. & Orch.	FS (1996)	AMC
Kats-Chernin, Elena	Lamento the Gestures for Pno. & Orch.	FS (no date)	AMC
Kay, Don	Concerto for Pno. & Orch.	FS (1992)	AMC
Lovelock, William	Concerto for Pno. & Orch.	FS (1963) A/C LOV 14	SAC NLA
Lumsdaine, David	Pno. Concerto	FS (c1950) A/C LUM 01	SAC NLA
Mageau, Mary	The Furies: a concerto for Pno. & Orch.	FS (1994-95)	AMC
Mahler, Hellgart	Pno. Concerto	FS (19--)	Sitsky
Maling, Roy	Pno. Concerto	MS (1929)	Sitsky
Penberthy, James	Concerto no. 1 (full score)	FS (1948-1949)	uncat. archive, NLA
	Concerto no. 2 (Aboriginal) (full score)	MS (1954)	uncat. archive, NLA
	Concerto for Pno. & Orch. no. 3 (Beyond the Universe) (full score)	FS (1974)	uncat. archive, NLA
	Pno. Concerto no. 4 (full score)	FS (1982)	uncat. archive, NLA
Sculthorpe, Peter	Pno. Concerto	Faber (1982)	AMC
Sitsky, Larry	Concerto for Pno. & Orch.: The 22 Paths of the Tarot	NY: Seesaw Music (1991)	Sitsky
Smetanin, Michael	Zyerkala for amplified Pno. & Orch.	FS (1981)	AMC

Vine, Carl	Pno. Concerto	Faber (1997)	AMC
Williamson, Malcolm	Concerto	Chappel (c1961)	NLA
	Concerto no. 3 for Pno. & Orch.	London: Josef Weinberger (1964)	AMC

ABOUT THE AUTHOR

LARRY SITSKY is Head of the Composition Department, School of Music, Australian National University. He is also the author of *Music of the Twentieth-Century Avant-Garde* (Greenwood Press, 2002).